FUNDAMENTAL ANALYSIS

A Back-to-the-Basics Investment Guide to Selecting Quality Stocks

Revised Edition

John C. Ritchie, Jr.

IRWIN
Professional Publishing®
Chicago • London • Singapore

© John C. Ritchie, Jr., 1993 and 1996

This publication is designed to provide accurate and authoritative information in regard to the subject matter covered. It is sold with the understanding that neither the author or the publisher is engaged in rendering legal, accounting, or other professional service. If legal advice or other expert assistance is required, the services of a competent professional person should be sought.

From a Declaration of Principles jointly adopted by a Committee of the American Bar Association and a Committee of Publishers.

Irwin Professional Book Team

Publisher: *Wayne McGuirt*
Executive editor*: Kevin Commins*
Developmental editor*: Patrick Muller*
Senior marketing manager: *Tiffany Chenevert Dykes*
Managing editor: *Kevin Thornton*
Project editor: *Amy E. Lund*
Production supervisors: *Pat Frederickson/Carol Klein*
Assistant manager, desktop services: *Jon Christopher*
Jacket designer: *Palmer Design Associates*
Compositor: *Judy Brown*
Typeface: *11/13 Times Roman*
Printer: *Buxton Skinner Printing Company*

Times Mirror
Higher Education Group

Library of Congress Cataloging-in-Publication Data

Ritchie, John C. 1996
    Fundamental analysis : a back-to-the-basics investment guide to selecting quality stocks / John C. Ritchie, Jr. — Rev. ed.
      p.   cm.
    Includes bibliographical references and index.
    ISBN 1-55738-866-0
    1. Stocks.   2. Investments.   I. Title.
    HG4661.R48   1996
    332.63'22—dc20   95–39277

Printed in the United States of America
1 2 3 4 5 6 7 8 9 BS 2 1 0 9 8 7 6 5

To my wife Shirley with gratitude for her encouragement and total support throughout the writing of this book.

Contents

Preface

This book is for the individual investor, professional analyst, or portfolio manager who desires to select common stocks in an intelligent manner. It offers a thorough and rigorous approach to the selection of common stocks and the management of a common stock portfolio.

Many people are achieving the financial affluence that requires a sophisticated approach to investment decisions. Common stocks have long been an important component of the investment portfolios of successful individuals recognizing their growth potential and the possibility they offer of offsetting the adverse effects of inflation.

Ibbotson and Sinquefield have carefully studied historical rates of return for five major classes of financial assets in the United States: (1) common stocks, (2) small capitalization stocks (3) long-term U.S. government bonds, (4) long-term corporate bonds, and (5) U.S. Treasury bills. Common stocks, on average, more than doubled the returns recorded by the other financial instruments over the period 1926–1986, offering further support to the attractiveness of including well-selected common stocks in a portfolio.

Success in investments in common stocks depends on a knowledge and application of sound principles of investment analysis in a consistent manner. The emphasis should be on long-run growth of capital committed. We do not advocate rapid in-and-out trading, which has not typically produced good results. This book will help you learn to avoid investment pitfalls and mistakes that have plagued an army of unsuccessful investors.

Successful investors need reasonable intelligence, a knowledge of market history, a value-oriented and fundamentally sound analytic approach, patience, the courage of their convictions, and the ability to ignore crowd psychology. The background information and analytic techniques presented in the book supply the reader with the tools and approach needed for successful investment. Selectivity, based on long-run fundamental considerations and consistency, is the key to success.

Part I of the book carefully develops useful background information and a value oriented fundamental analysis approach used by many successful investors. The book recommends coupling the fundamental analysis approach with a low price–earnings ratio approach which is supported by several studies, including one completed by the author, with financial support from Provident Capital Management, a Philadelphia fund manager. Mr. Paul Lesutis, a senior vice-president of that organization has been generous with his time and help in developing my appreciation of this approach.

John C. Ritchie, Jr.

Acknowledgments

I wish to express gratitude to Mr. Oommen Thomas, a Ph.D. student at Temple University, and to Mrs. Lynell Burke, secretary of the finance department at Temple University. Mr. Thomas gathered much of the data used in preparing many of the tables in this book and also provided useful analytical comments. Mrs. Burke typed the entire manuscript and offered useful style and organizational observations.

P A R T

I

INVESTMENT: ANALYTICAL FOUNDATIONS AND BACKGROUND

Chapter One

Investments: An Introduction

This book provides the background information and an analytical framework needed for wise investment decision making. The sophisticated analytical framework is designed to assess important economic, political, and social dynamics as well as company data, and suggest their potential impact on the capital markets and security values. We will concentrate on analyzing common stocks, though the framework also can be used to analyze bonds and other investments.

Serious application of the suggested approach will enable you to structure an investment program with both security and capital appreciation over a lifetime. The book does not provide guidelines for traders—those who expect to build capital by attempting to forecast the short-term (less than one year) action of the market. The record of short-term, in-and-out traders generally has been poor, though it is difficult to gain objective information on the performance of such individuals. Sidney Weinberg, a highly respected member of the investment community and successful investor, emphasized that he did not believe that one builds capital by short-term trading. Bernard Baruch agreed with this conclusion. Moreover, the longer-term approach advocated in this book has been well tested by investors such as Benjamin Graham and David Dodd, Douglass Bellemore, Warren Buffett, Walter Schloos, Charles Munger and William Ruane.[1]

Short-run speculation can be profitable, and it can be carried out in an intelligent manner. An intelligent speculation differs, however, from the

---

[1] See "Can You Beat the Stock Market?," *Fortune,* December 26, 1983, p. 83.

long-term investment viewpoint advocated in this book. Speculators who stress short-term, as opposed to long-term capital appreciation operate on more limited information and assume a higher degree of risk than the average investor is willing or able to assume. Moreover, a speculator tends to trade on the basis of information that he or she believes is not yet known or fully understood, while an investor makes no such assumption.

For a great many speculative situations, careful appraisal is almost impossible, for there are insufficient facts and the information that is available is of questionable reliability. The purchase of stocks on "market tips," a glamorous name, or other rather casual approaches is more akin to gambling than investment. It is interesting to note that many individuals believe that while their chosen vocation requires a long period of training, experience, or ability, successful investing can be accomplished with little training, experience, ability, or hard work. Successful investment or intelligent speculation requires a relatively high degree of technical knowledge, good judgment, and diligence in seeking facts and information.

RISK AND RETURN

Investment decisions are based on the expectation of receiving a positive return in the future. Investors sacrifice the opportunity for current consumption when making an investment, and require reward for making this sacrifice. They need large expected returns to compensate for deferring consumption and for undertaking the risks associated with holding financial assets.

Investors logically aim at maximizing the expected return for the degree of risk accepted. Webster's dictionary defines risk as "the chance of injury, damage, or loss." Risk is a significant constraint for all investors. A key determinant is the degree of risk an investor is willing to accept for a given rate of return or the probability of realizing a given rate of return.

Financial Investment Risk

Risk is a part of any financial investment decision and must be analyzed along with other facets of a potential investment. Various types of risk can affect an investment decision. Thus, a comprehensive analysis of risk for investment decisions is one that attacks the problem simultaneously from various points of view.

Expectations: Concept of risk. Decisions made under conditions of certainty will turn out to be correct. When these conditions apply, there is no variation of outcomes relative to one's expectations and there is no risk. In a reasonably efficient capital market, the reward for investing in a riskless asset should approach a limit that we refer to as the *riskless rate of return*. For example, the purchaser of a short-term treasury bill is certain of realizing the calculated rate of return based on the purchase price. The purchase of treasury bills, however, is not truly a riskless investment when one considers opportunity costs, changing yield patterns over time, and inflation.

Because the outcome of an investment decision is determined by chance events, the environment of investment decision is deemed *uncertain*. A financial asset purchased on the basis of imperfect knowledge about future events is called a *risky asset*. The degree of risk differs for different financial assets, but all financial assets, in the opportunity sense, are risky assets. For example, uncertainty exists over whether the issuer of a bond will make all promised payments, what the price will be at various times prior to maturity if liquidity is desired, and what the impact of inflation will be over a relatively long investment horizon. Predicting the future cash flow to be generated through investment in a common stock and the impact of inflation on the return from such an investment could be considered even more uncertain, since no contractual promises have been made.

Traditional risk concepts. Traditional analysis discusses specific types of risk that could lead to an investor not realizing the anticipated return from a specific investment decision.

Purchasing power risk. Table 1–1 shows the Consumer Price Index (CPI) for the years 1967 through 1985. The value of a dollar relative to the base year 1967 also is shown. The effect of inflation on the purchasing power of payments received under a fixed-income contract, such as a bond or a nonparticipating, nonconvertible preferred stock, is obvious. If the market correctly anticipates inflation it will be built into required returns that are an important determinant of security valuation, as we will see in Chapter 3. It is unanticipated inflation, therefore, that brings the purchasing power risk.

To illustrate the impact that purchasing power risk can have, assume that a savings account was opened on January 1, 1967, with a deposit of $1,000, and that a 5 percent interest rate, compounded annually, was paid from then until the end of 1985. By December 31, 1985, the dollar value of the account

TABLE 1–1
Consumer Price Index (CPI), 1967–1985

Year	CPI	Price Relative	Year	CPI	Price Relative
1967	100.0	1.00	1977	181.5	.55
1968	104.2	.96	1978	195.4	.51
1969	109.8	.91	1979	217.4	.46
1970	116.3	.86	1980	246.8	.41
1971	121.3	.82	1981	272.4	.37
1972	125.3	.80	1982	289.1	.35
1973	133.1	.75	1983	298.4	.34
1974	147.7	.68	1984	311.1	.22
1975	161.2	.62	1985	322.2	.31
1976	170.5	.59			

would have grown to $1,000 $(1.05)^{19}$ = $2,526.95. By year-end 1985, however, the value of a dollar would have shrunk to just $.31 in terms of 1967 purchasing power. Therefore, $2,526.95 spent at year-end 1985 would not purchase as much as $1,000 spent in 1967:

1967 Purchasing Power   = $2,526.95 (.31)

                                         = $ 783.35

The holder of the savings account lost $216.65 in terms of 1967 purchasing power because of inflation. The compound interest payments on commercial bank passbook savings accounts (typically paying a 5 percent interest rate) were not sufficient to maintain the purchasing power of the funds originally deposited over the period 1967–1985.

Interest rate risk. Interest rate risk comes about as a result of unanticipated changes in interest rates. To the extent that *future changes in the interest rate are anticipated,* such changes will be reflected in the current period prices of fixed-income securities. The double-digit inflation of 1973 and 1974 was not anticipated by the market, and thus its impact was not reflected properly in the prices of fixed-income securities before the fact. For example, investors who purchased investment-quality corporate bonds late in 1973 would (in horror) have seen market prices drop by as much as

20 percent from 1973 highs to 1974 lows, reflecting rising interest rates.[2] With the tapering off of the rate of inflation in 1975 and an easing of monetary policy by the Federal Reserve, the average price of investment quality corporate bonds came back up to a point approaching the 1973 high. Many bondholders were forced to take substantial losses during the period. Interest rates reached historic highs in August 1981, again causing serious losses for many earlier purchasers of bonds. Such outcomes are evidence that substantial interest rate risk is taken by participants in the securities market and that efficient markets are able to predict the future only imperfectly.

Further evidence of the high degree of interest rate risk present in bond markets is offered in Table 1–2. Interest rates over the period rose strongly through 1981, and, as a result, bond prices generally were falling until 1981. Bond prices then recovered sharply by 1986 as interest rates fell to early 1970s levels. An individual who had to sell bonds acquired toward the beginning of the 1960–1981 period could have suffered substantial losses because of the interest rate price risk. If the individual held the bonds to maturity, he would have avoided at least some of the loss due to falling prices, but he would have realized lower interest payments relative to those available later in the period. Interest rate expectations are important when investing in securities.

Business risk and financial risk. When purchasing a fixed-income security, an investor enters into a contract that provides for a promised and legally obligatory periodic cash flow over the life of the contract and the return of the principal amount at maturity of the instrument. A common or preferred stock offers no certain future cash flows but is bought on the expectation of realizing some minimum in terms of future cash flow. In the event of default or temporary disruptions in the cash flow received by a business, the promised or expected future cash flow may not be received (or only received in part) by an investor.

Business risk is intrinsic in the firm's operations. This type of risk is defined in terms of the ratio of fixed to variable costs and the resultant implications for the variability of the firm's net cash flow under changing business conditions and sales levels. *Financial risk* stems from the firm's capital structure decisions. The higher the proportion of capital raised

---

[2] The inverse relationship between change in interest rates and security prices is carefully developed in Chapter 3.

Table 1–2
Bond Yields and Prices

Year	U.S. Government Long-Term (%)	Corporate AAA (%)	Municipal High Grade (%)	U.S. Government Long-Term	Corporate AAA	Municipal High Grade
	Yield			*Related Bond Price Index*		
1946	2.19	2.44	1.64	110.40	123.40	140.10
1960	3.99	4.26	3.73	88.94	94.64	103.90
1967	4.90	5.47	3.98	80.04	81.75	102.50
1970	6.75	7.76	6.51	65.00	61.55	72.34
1975	8.21	8.43	6.89	55.52	56.23	68.94
1980	11.22	11.56	8.51	41.17	41.38	57.43
1981	13.20	13.72	11.23	34.18	33.74	43.25
1982	12.51	13.03	11.57	36.68	35.79	41.92
1983	11.09	11.50	9.47	41.56	41.15	51.36
1984	12.34	12.43	10.15	36.97	*	47.96
1985	10.74	10.94	9.18	43.06	*	53.02
1986	7.68	8.53	6.93	58.70	*	68.58

* No longer reported by Standard & Poor's.

Source: *Security Price Index Record*, 1986 ed., Standard & Poor's Statistical Service.

through the issuance of fixed-income contracts (debts and preferred stocks), the greater the variability of the firm's net cash flow under changing business conditions and sales levels.

Calculations of the degree of operating and the degree of financial leverage are discussed as leverage measures in most business finance texts,[3] and is further developed in this book in a later chapter. Much controversy surrounds the use of various accounting data in making such calculations, and these approaches make assumptions that can limit their usefulness. But the concepts have been found to be useful by investment analysts and practicing financial analysts, in spite of the limitations.

---

3 For example, see Eugene F. Brigham and Louis C. Gapenski, *Financial Management: Theory and Practice*, 7th ed. (New York: The Dryden Press, 1994), Chapter 12, especially pages 520–531.

RISK AND RETURN—AN HISTORICAL OVERVIEW

History may not repeat itself, but it is reasonable to utilize past performance as a basis for forming realistic investment goals.

Figure 1–1 shows the year-by-year results obtained from investing in a portfolio represented by a specifically identified type of financial security, such as common stocks, as calculated by Ibbotson Associates over the period 1926–1993. The rate of return is calculated as the percentage change in a hypothetical investor's wealth from the beginning to the end of each year. The investor is assumed to have purchased one unit of the given security at the beginning of the period.

Table 1–3 shows the yearly results over the 68-year period (1926–1993) for each type of security in terms of annual total returns (dividends or interest, plus or minus capital gains or losses). Returns for common stock have ranged from an exciting 53.99 percent in 1933 to a dismal loss of 43.34 percent in 1931. Interestingly, though losses on the Dow Jones Index were at historically high levels for a particular day (October 12, 1987), common stocks actually showed a return of 5.23 percent over the period January 1, 1987, through December 31, 1987.

Stocks clearly were the best performers over the study period, but risk (in terms of variability of return) also was higher for stocks. The substantially higher returns earned on average over the period 1926–1993 by the stock series seems to compensate well for the added risk associated with stock investment. The key is to maintain broad diversification and adequate liquid funds (invested in Treasury Bills or money market funds) to meet emergencies and avoid forced sales of common stocks. One could also become more liquid when fundamental analysis suggested sales of many stocks, accumulating cash for a more favorable buying opportunity. In general, however, it is better to invest consistently and gain the advantages of dollar averaging. The long-term averages of returns in Table 1–3 would assume continuous investment in the given instrument.

The high degree of common stock returns from year to year certainly suggest relatively high-market risk for these securities. While the standard deviations of the average return earned on common stocks is quite high (20.44 percent), Table 1–3 suggests it would be reasonable to anticipate an average return of about 12 percent over long periods of time (the average return for the period 1926–1993 was 12.34 percent) for an investment in a well diversified portfolio of common stocks. The 12 percent return is before consideration of taxes or transaction costs, and is not adjusted for inflation or for the effects of compounding. Several studies have estimated that the

FIGURE 1–1
Annual Returns, 1926–1993

TABLE 1–3

Annual Returns: Stocks, Bonds, Treasury Bills, and Changes in the Consumer Price Index

Year	Treasury Bills	Long-Term Government Bonds	Long-Term Corporate Bonds	Common Stocks	Change in CPI
1926	3.27%	7.77%	7.37%	11.62%	−1.49%
1927	3.12	8.93	7.44	37.49	−2.08
1928	3.56	.10	2.84	43.61	−.97
1929	4.75	3.42	3.27	−8.42	.20
1930	2.41	4.66	7.98	−24.90	−6.03
1931	1.07	−5.31	−1.75	−43.34	−9.52
1932	.96	16.84	10.82	−8.19	−10.30
1933	.30	.07	10.38	53.99	.51
1934	.16	10.03	13.84	−1.44	2.03
1935	.17	4.98	9.61	47.67	2.99
1936	.18	7.52	6.74	33.92	1.21
1937	.31	.23	2.75	−35.03	3.10
1938	−.02	5.53	6.13	31.12	−2.78
1939	.02	5.94	3.97	−.41	−.48
1940	.00	6.09	3.39	−9.78	.96
1941	.06	.93	2.73	−11.59	9.72
1942	.27	3.22	2.60	20.34	9.29
1943	.35	2.08	2.83	25.90	3.16
1944	.33	2.81	4.73	19.75	2.11
1945	.33	10.73	4.08	36.44	2.25
1946	.35	−.10	1.72	−8.07	18.16
1947	.50	−2.62	−2.34	5.71	9.01
1948	.81	3.40	4.14	5.50	2.71
1949	1.10	6.45	3.31	18.79	−1.80
1950	1.20	.06	2.12	31.71	5.79
1951	1.49	−3.93	−2.69	24.02	5.87
1952	1.66	1.16	3.52	18.37	.88
1953	1.82	3.64	3.41	−.99	.62
1954	.86	7.19	5.39	52.62	.50
1955	1.57	−1.29	.48	31.56	.37
1956	2.46	−5.59	−6.81	6.56	2.86
1957	3.14	7.46	8.71	−10.78	3.02
1958	1.54	−6.09	−2.22	43.36	1.76
1959	2.95	−2.26	−.97	11.96	1.50
1960	2.66	13.78	9.07	.47	1.48
1961	2.13	.97	4.82	26.89	.67
1962	2.73	6.89	7.95	−8.73	1.22

(continued)

TABLE 1–3 *(concluded)*

Year	Treasury Bills	Long-Term Government Bonds	Long-Term Corporate Bonds	Common Stocks	Change in CPI
1963	3.12%	1.21%	2.19%	22.80%	1.65%
1964	3.54	3.51	4.77	16.48	1.19
1965	3.93	.71	−.46	12.45	1.92
1966	4.76	3.65	.20	−10.06	3.35
1967	4.21	−9.18	−4.85	23.98	3.04
1968	5.21	−.26	2.57	11.06	4.72
1969	6.58	−5.07	−8.09	−7.50	6.11
1970	6.52	12.11	18.37	4.01	5.49
1971	4.39	13.23	11.01	14.31	3.36
1972	3.84	5.69	7.26	18.98	3.41
1973	6.93	−1.11	1.14	−14.66	8.80
1974	8.00	4.35	−3.06	−26.47	12.20
1975	5.80	9.20	14.64	37.20	7.01
1976	5.08	16.75	18.65	23.84	4.81
1977	5.12	−.69	1.71	−7.18	6.77
1978	7.18	−1.18	−.07	6.56	9.03
1979	10.38	−1.23	−4.18	18.44	13.31
1980	11.24	−3.85	−2.62	32.42	12.40
1981	14.71	1.86	−.96	−4.91	8.94
1982	10.54	40.36	43.79	21.41	3.87
1983	8.80	.65	4.70	22.51	3.80
1984	9.85	15.48	16.39	6.27	3.95
1985	7.72	30.97	30.90	32.16	3.77
1986	6.16	24.53	19.85	18.47	1.33
1987	5.47	−2.71	−.27	5.23	4.41
1988	6.35	9.67	10.70	16.81	4.42
1989	8.37	18.11	16.23	31.49	4.65
1990	7.81	6.18	6.78	−3.17	6.11
1991	5.60	19.30	19.89	30.55	3.06
1992	3.51	8.05	9.39	7.67	2.90
1993	2.90	18.24	13.19	9.99	2.75
Average return	3.74%	5.36%	5.90%	12.34%	3.25%
Standard deviation	3.32%	8.67%	8.46%	20.44%	4.63%

real national income of the U.S. economy has grown at about a 3 percent compound rate over long periods of time.[4] If we allow for inflation at a rate of 5 percent (based on experience since 1970), it would suggest that it was reasonable to assume an average compound annual return on a long-term investment of common stocks of about 8 to 9 percent. While average returns on common stocks have been higher, one might argue that the expected return should be lower to allow for compounding over the time period of measurement.

Compound returns do assume that all interim cash flows (such as dividends or interest) are reinvested over the time period considered for the calculation. We advise adhering to this assumption. A consistent and systematic savings and investment program incorporates the advantages of dollar averaging and increases the return earned when returns are rising from year to year. To illustrate the potential from compounding when a systematic program is put in place, consider a 30-year-old individual who saves $500 a month until retirement at age 70. This individual would accumulate a total of $2,358,214.60 by the end of the 40-year period, if a return of 9 percent compounded annually were realized and all interim cash flows were reinvested. Compounding is a powerful force, and recognition of this allows setting reasonable goals. We would aim at doubling the value of an investment portfolio of common stocks in seven to eight years, in accordance with compound growth calculations.

Professor Sharpe has noted that Table 1–3 supports the conclusion that the "past pattern of stock returns provides little help in predicting next year's return."[5] You can observe this by uncovering the value for 1941 and preceding years and then trying to guess the return for 1942. If you continue in this manner year-by-year, we are confident you will agree with the above conclusion. You cannot accurately estimate short-term market movements based on past history of returns.

Returns and Shorter Holding Periods

Mr. Robert J. Doyle, in an interesting study, extends the Ibbotson Associates data already reviewed by studying varied holding periods, adding a small-

---

[4] For example, see E. F. Denison, *The Sources of Economic Growth in the United States,* Supplemental Paper No. 13 (New York: Committee for Economic Development, 1960), and Table 6–1 in this book.

[5] William F. Sharpe, G. Alexander, and J. Bailey, *Investments,* 5th ed. (Englewood Cliffs, NJ, Prentice Hall, Inc., 1995), p. 8.

TABLE 1–4
1926–1990 Nominal Returns (Unadjusted for Inflation)

Series	Compound Return	Simple Return	Standard Deviation
Small stocks	11.632%	17.070%	35.41
Common Stocks	10.091	12.148	20.17
Long-term corporate bonds	5.212	5.515	8.41
Long-term government bonds	4.545	4.862	8.54
Intermediate government bonds	4.992	5.126	5.50
U.S. Treasury bills	3.673	3.726	3.38
Inflation	3.141	3.248	4.75

TABLE 1–5
1926–1990 Real Returns (Inflation Adjusted)

Series	Compound Return	Simple Return	Standard Deviation
Small stocks	8.233%	13.516%	34.74
Common Stocks	6.739	8.833	20.95
Long-term corporate bonds	2.009	2.462	9.87
Long-term government bonds	1.363	1.831	10.07
Intermediate government bonds	1.788	2.016	6.96
U.S. Treasury bills	0.516	0.610	4.35
Inflation	0	0	0

Source: Used with permission of Mr. Robert J. Doyle, Jr., the author of the study referred to in footnote 6.

stock category, and calculating both nominal and inflation-adjusted returns.[6] He also calculated total annual compound and simple nominal returns, assuming reinvestment of cash flow. The returns for common stocks were based upon the S&P composite index, and, for small-capitalization stocks, the bottom 20 percent of the stocks listed on the New York Stock Exchange ranked by capitalization. Table 1–4 reports the nominal returns for each security group over the period 1926–1990, while Table 1–5 reports real returns (inflation-adjusted). The nominal simple returns and

---

6 Robert J. Doyle, Jr., "Risk, Return, and the Investment Planning Horizon: The Financial Planner's Guide to Asset Selection," *Course Guide for HS328* (Bryn Mawr, PA: American College of Life Underwriters, 1991) p.p. 12.24–12.43.

their standard deviations for the period 1926–1990 are consistent with the Ibbotson Associates data. The inflation-adjusted returns are significantly lower, allowing for the reduced buying power of the dollar over the study period. As does the Ibbotson data, these tables show that common stocks have substantially outperformed the other investment instruments studied, but are more risky in terms of variability over the entire study period. The potential return does appear to increase as the risk increases. Moreover, Table 1–5 offers evidence that common stocks have been successful infla-tion hedges over the study period. The compound real return for common stocks was 6.739 percent, after allowing for inflation, over the study period. Note that investment in Treasury Bills hardly offset inflation over the study period, so that an investor earned a real compound annual return (adjusted for inflation) of only about ½ of 1 percent by investing in these securities over the period 1926–1990.

Investors may well hold stocks for shorter periods than the 65 years covered by the period 1926–1990, and would be interested in performance over shorter periods. Doyle found that nominal annualized compound returns were positive in about two-thirds of the years 1926–1990 (44 out of 65). Accordingly, Doyle reviewed performance over all possible 5-year, 10-year, and 20-year holding periods during the years 1926–1990, as summarized in Table 1–6 and Figure 1-2.

Returns for 5-year, 10-year and 20-year holding periods

5-Year Holding Periods. Nominal annualized compound returns were positive in about 85 percent of the 5-year periods over 1926–1990 (52 of 61), ranging from a high of 45.9 percent (1941–45) to a low of –27.5 percent (1928–1932). Investors over these 5-year periods would have experienced negative returns in only 9 of the 61 5-year periods. Real compound annualized returns were positive in 47 of the 61 5-year holding periods, suggesting a complete inflation hedge about 77 percent of the time.

10-Year holding periods. Nominal annualized compound re-turns were positive in 54 of the 56 10-year periods over 1926–1990 (96 percent of the time), ranging from a high of 20.1 percent (1948–1958) to a low of –0.9 percent (1928–38). Real annualized compound returns were positive in 49 of the 56 10-year holding periods.

20-Year holding periods. Nominal annualized compound re-turns were positive for all 46 of the 20-year holding periods, ranging from a high of 16.9 percent (1942–1961) to a low of 3.1 percent (1928–1948).

TABLE 1-6
Summary: Holding Period Returns

Asset	Years in Holding Period	Simple Average	Nominal High	Nominal Low	Nominal Range	Real Simple Average	Real High	Real Low	Real Range
S&P Stocks	5	10.0	23.9	-12.5	36.4	6.5	23.5	-9.3	32.9
	10	10.3	20.1	-0.9	21.0	6.5	17.9	-3.8	21.7
	20	10.5	16.9	3.1	13.8	6.6	13.0	0.8	12.2
Small Cap Stocks	5	13.5	45.9	-27.5	73.4	9.8	47.1	-23.4	70.4
	10	14.4	30.4	-5.7	36.1	10.4	21.5	-3.8	25.3
	20	14.4	21.1	5.7	15.4	10.4	17.2	4.0	13.2
L-T Corp Bonds	5	5.1	22.4	-2.2	24.6	1.9	18.5	-10.3	28.8
	10	4.6	14.1	1.0	13.1	1.1	9.9	-5.2	15.1
	20	3.9	9.6	1.3	8.2	0.3	5.4	-2.7	8.1
L-T U.S. Gov't Bonds	5	4.4	21.6	-2.1	23.8	1.2	17.7	-10.1	27.8
	10	4.0	13.8	-0.1	13.8	0.4	8.9	-5.4	14.2
	20	3.4	9.0	0.7	8.3	-0.3	4.5	-3.1	7.6
U.S. T-Bills	5	3.6	11.1	0.1	11.0	0.4	8.4	-6.1	14.5
	10	3.5	9.2	0.1	9.0	-0.1	4.7	-5.1	9.7
	20	3.2	7.7	0.4	7.3	-0.4	1.3	-3.0	4.4
Consumer Price Index	5	3.3	10.1	-5.4	15.5	NA	NA	NA	NA
	10	3.6	8.7	-2.6	11.1	NA	NA	NA	NA
	20	3.7	6.4	0.1	6.3	NA	NA	NA	NA

Annualized Compound Rates of Return %

Used with permission of Robert Doyle, the author of the study.

FIGURE 1–2
Minimum/Maximum Holding Period Performance
Historical Real Returns

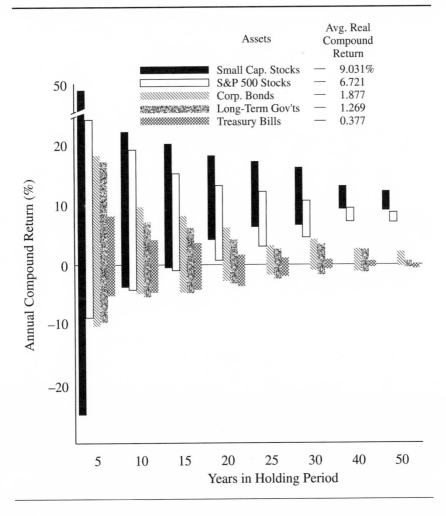

Assets		Avg. Real Compound Return
▬▬▬	Small Cap. Stocks	— 9.031%
☐	S&P 500 Stocks	— 6.721
░░░	Corp. Bonds	— 1.877
▒▒▒	Long-Term Gov'ts	— 1.269
▓▓▓	Treasury Bills	— 0.377

Notes:

1. Data for these analyses come from the *SBBI/PC* Software package, Ibbotson Associates, Inc., 8 South Michigan Avenue, Chicago, Illinois 60603 (1991).

2. For more information regarding risk, return, and investment holding periods and other aspects of investment and financial planning refer to *The Tools and Techniques of Financial Planning,* 3d ed., Stephan R. Leimberg, et al. The National Underwriter Company, 420 East 4th Street, Cincinnati, OH 45202.

Used with permission of Robert Doyle, the author of the study.

Real annualized returns were positive in all 46 of the 20-year holding periods, ranging from a high of 13.0 percent (1942–1961) to a low of 0.8 percent (1965–1984).

Summary of results. The above results suggest that investors can generally expect returns on a well-diversified portfolio of common stocks to deviate less from the long-term average return for common stocks the longer the holding period. Accordingly, common stocks appear to be less risky the longer an investor plans to hold them. Common stocks do appear to be a desirable investment instrument for building long-run capital growth, even for those investors who would be unwilling to bear the risk for short-term objectives.

A Realistic Approach

Successful investing for the average investor should:

1. Aim at realistic rather than spectacular results; we suggest an average compound annual return of 9 percent over long periods of time.
2. Remain immune to changing moods and emotions of the marketplace while concentrating on long-run value and fundamental considerations;
3. Purchase only securities that represent reasonable values based on rigorous analysis as developed in this book;
4. Sell securities purchased only when targets set for these securities have been realized and/or more attractive alternative investment opportunities exist; and
5. Keep an efficiently diversified portfolio.

The culmination of fundamental security analysis for a common stock is an estimate of "intrinsic" value based upon the expected cash flow that an investment will generate, the return required by the investor, and the relative risk associated with that stock. These estimated values offer a consistent framework for purposes of comparing alternative investment opportunities, and providing a mechanism for testing the reasonableness of the assumptions that seem to make a particular stock an attractive purchase candidate. Professor Graham (a successful investor) once said,

> To establish the right price for a stock, the market must have adequate information, but it by no means follows that if the market has this information it will thereupon establish the right price. The market's evaluation of the same data can

vary over a wide range, dependent upon bullish enthusiasm, concentrated speculative interest and similar influences, or bearish disillusionment. Knowledge is only one ingredient in arriving at a stock's proper price. The other ingredient, fully as important as information, is sound judgment.[7]

This book provides the background material and analytic approaches needed to render sound judgment.

ORGANIZATION OF THE BOOK

As noted, the objective of this book is to present a sound, comprehensive framework for analyzing investment in stocks and bonds. The book is divided into three parts. Part I develops the investment environment that underlies an investor's perspectives. A perspective for analysis is offered in Chapter 2.

In Part II of the book, the logic and analytical structure of fundamental security analysis begins with an in-depth study of the economy and its implications for industries and companies. It continues with a valuation of a security based on its future earning power and dividend-paying expectations utilizing the valuation approaches developed in Chapter 3. Both qualitative and quantitative information and analyses are used in developing valuation estimates. The stock's intrinsic (present) value is then compared with market value for purposes of determining whether or not a desirable investment candidate has been found.

Statistical evidence supporting the *efficient market* hypothesis questions the ability of analysts to produce superior returns through fundamental analysis. Proponents of the efficient market hypothesis argue that the impact of all information publicly available concerning a company's future prospects already is reflected in the price of that company's common stock. Moreover, new information enters the market on a random basis. Therefore, stocks are appropriately valued by market price and an investor using fundamental analysis cannot "beat the market."

Impressive evidence does exist supporting the idea that the market is efficient. The evidence of market inefficiencies has been accumulating rapidly, however, especially when longer time horizons underlie the investment decision. One can, at a minimum, avoid bad situations by careful

---

7 Benjamin Graham, "The Decade 1965–74: Its Significance for Financial Analysts," *The Renaissance of Value* (Charlottesville, VA: The Financial Analysts Research Foundation, 1974), p. 10.

analysis. Sound analysis can estimate return expectations, the riskiness of investment in different securities, and the impact of changing market conditions. We believe that fundamental analysis can help recognize temporarily undervalued situations and develop strategies for improving returns by investing in such situations, especially when longer-run considerations are present.

Part III of the book develops a framework for analyzing special classes of securities. There are differences between industrial securities and those of companies in regulated industries that should be recognized.

Chapter Two

Security Analysis: Approach and Basic Issues

The objective of security analysis is to screen and classify financial assets in terms of investment quality and expected return. A security analyst utilizes expectations for the economy and for industry groupings (product line analysis) to forecast earnings, dividends, and intrinsic values for particular companies. Estimates of expected return and relative risk rankings serve as a basis for appraising relative attractiveness of the particular securities under consideration. This approach to security selection is called *fundamental analysis*.

Fundamental analysis is concerned with the historical performance of the economy, industry, and firms for the insight into future firm performance that these data may offer. Financial analysis explores not only the financial relationships that exist for a given firm at a moment in time, but, more importantly, trends in those relationships over time. The composition and liquidity of corporate resources, the company's capital structure and leverage, the competitive position, and company earnings are all studied for the clues they provide as to future performance. Share prices reflect expected future profitability, risk (as reflected in the financial condition of the firm, the competitiveness of its markets, and leverage considerations), dividend policy, and supply and demand conditions for the given financial asset.

PUBLISHED RATINGS AND QUALITY GRADING

Several reporting services compile and publish financial data useful for evaluating companies, and also rate bonds and some common stocks.

Bond Ratings

The major emphasis when grading bonds is on the ability of the firm to meet all obligations in years of poor as well as good economic conditions. The highest bond ratings suggest coverage for obligations by earnings and cash flow such that the probability a firm will not be able to meet its obligations, even in a recession, is close to nonexistent. Bonds are rated in terms of probability of default. Moreover, such quality ratings are based on analysis of one type of risk—the financial risk—and ignore other aspects of risk. The ratings of the two most widely used agencies and a brief summary of their meanings are shown in Table 2–1. An old study concluded that "The record of the agencies over the period studied (1900–1943) was remarkably good insofar as their ratings pertain to default."[1] Defaults and losses were larger during the period studied for issues rated low-grade (below BBB) than for higher-rated issues as indicated below:

Rating Category	Default Rate (% of Par Value)
I (AAA)	5.9
II (AA)	6.0
III (A)	13.4
IV (BBB)	19.1
V–IX (BB and below)	42.4

Hickman concluded that the high default risk associated with bonds rated below BBB make them unsuited for individual long-term investors who are not in a position to diversify away default risk.

The information above is not meant to imply that agency ratings are an infallible guide. For example, the agencies failed to predict (i.e., by lowering ratings) the difficulties experienced by holders of New York City obligations during the early 1970s. Moreover, there are hundreds of issues that attain an investment-quality rating. An independent analysis still is necessary to help spot the most desirable bonds within a given rating category and to possibly reveal fundamental changes that have not yet been reflected in the ratings.

Stock Ratings

Quality ratings for common stocks also emphasize the risk that a series of expected cash receipts for a given security will not be realized. The less the

---

[1] W. Braddock Hickman, *Corporate Bond Quality and Investor Experience*, National Bureau of Economic Research (Princeton, NJ: Princeton University Press, 1958).

TABLE 2–1
Description of Agency Ratings

Moody's	Standard & Poor's	Quality Indication
Aaa	AAA	Highest quality
Aaa	AA	High quality
A	A	Upper medium grade
Baa	BBB	Medium grade
Ba	BB	Contains speculative elements
B	B	Outright speculative
Caa	CCC & CC	Default definitely possible
Ca	C	Default, only partial recovery likely
C	DDD to –D	Default, little recovery likely

uncertainty foreseen in realizing expected dividends and earnings growth, and the stronger the underlying financial condition of the company, the higher the rating. Standard & Poor's, for example, explains that their common stock ratings are designed to indicate . . . the relative stability and growth of earnings and dividends of the most recent years while also making adjustments for corporate size and "special considerations such as natural disasters, massive strikes and nonrecurring accounting adjustments."[2] Standard & Poor's point out that "a ranking is not a forecast of future market performance, but is basically an appraisal of past performance of earnings and dividends. . ."[3]

Published quality ratings for common stocks are less widely used and quoted than those for bonds, possibly because bonds typically have been purchased as a defensive investment, emphasizing the yield to maturity and relative certainty of receiving that yield rather than growth.

VALUATION: A CORNERSTONE OF FUNDAMENTAL ANALYSIS

Valuation of common stocks rests on the ability of the analyst to anticipate future performance of the firm and the market in which the financial asset

---

[2] *Stock Guide* (New York: Standard & Poor's Corporation, November 1981) p. 7.

[3] Ibid.

trades. Valuation would be easy in a world of certainty, but once uncertainty about future earnings, dividends, and stock prices is recognized, one realizes that fundamental analysis can offer only a range of values based on assumed conditions.

Such an analysis does provide a basis for varying assumptions concerning the factors underlying valuation—the analyst can ask "what if" questions. Moreover, one could assign probabilities to key assumptions and develop estimates with given probabilities.

Portfolio Selection and Fundamental Analysis

The fundamental approach suggests selecting that stock whose intrinsic value, as determined in the valuation process, is highest relative to current market price. Risk is taken into account by varying the discount rate or capitalization factors used in calculating intrinsic value. This does not imply a one-stock portfolio, as suggested by Markowitz.[4] If all investors calculated the same highest intrinsic value relative to market price for a given security, the resultant demand for that security quickly would push up its price until the margin of intrinsic value over current market price would be greater for other securities. A given security would be most attractive only at a given moment in time. Since investors commit funds over time, have different expectations, and change their expectations over time, they would acquire more than one security.

It is correct to say that valuation analysis incorporates a different and less-complete concept of risk than that developed in the literature of modern portfolio theory. By concentrating on individual securities, it overlooks the importance of covariation of returns and the logically related idea that risk for an individual security and risk for that security as part of a portfolio of securities are two different things. Risk reduction through diversification can be attained only when the covariance relationships are taken into account. Modern portfolio theory has added a new and important dimension to the problem of security selection that is not considered in the fundamental analysis approach to selecting securities. An integration of the two approaches is needed, though not really available in the current literature.

Basic changes occur in a firm's characteristics over time—changes in product mix, technology, new products, capital structure, and merger. It is

---

4 Harry Markowitz, "Portfolio Selection," *Journal of Finance,* 7, no. 1 (March 1952), pp. 77–78.

important to assess the implications of these changes for the cash flow of a firm and the value of its stock. Fundamental analysis provides a framework for analyzing such changes.

Capital Market Theory and Fundamental Analysis

In an efficient capital market, stock prices always reflect all publicly and privately available information concerning the securities traded. Security prices would adjust instantaneously and in an unbiased manner to new information as it enters the market. Furthermore, price changes in such efficient markets would perform a random walk—that is, behave in a patternless manner reflecting the random introduction of new information.

It is true that, in a perfectly efficient market, no technique or analytical tool can be expected to yield systematically above-average returns. However, security analysis is essential to market efficiency; only if investors make conscientious and competent efforts to learn about and apply relevant information promptly and perceptively can efficient markets exist. In a real world, users of available information do not necessarily agree on the implications that information has for future corporate performance and stock prices. Furthermore, information is not costless to market participants. Finally, transactions costs do exist. Existing capital markets probably are efficient, but disequilibrium situations are likely to exist in the short run. Such disequilibrium situations, which come about because of varying and changing interpretations by the various participants in the market, are likely to be short-lived.

The analyst must recognize that acceptance of the two ideas—that capital markets are efficient and that stock prices perform a random walk—does not imply that security analysis is useless. Fundamental analysis, unlike technical approaches and charting, is not based on historical price data. The analyst is attempting to uncover information that is not known generally. It is consistent with the concept of relatively efficient capital markets to recognize that proper use of such information could result in above-average gains.

The major contributions of security analysis in relatively efficient markets will be the understanding it brings of the effects of company- and economywide events on security prices, and alertness in directing attention to new developments. Opportunities for gains that may result from effective analysis may well be short-lived in our capital markets, and originality in analysis and alertness in applying the results are necessary conditions for successful security analysis.

THE INGREDIENTS OF SECURITY ANALYSIS

In making an analysis of securities, both qualitative and quantitative factors are considered. *Qualitative factors* refer to subjective information, such as the quality of management or research and development efforts, and to projections of quantitative data such as earnings and dividends. *Quantitative factors* are historical numerical data concerning the economy and financial markets or the company as reported in financial statements or other sources. Quantitative data appear to be objective, but the determination of the figures reported often depends on numerous subjective judgments. Expressing qualitative factors in quantitative terms does not change the fact that such data are subjective in nature. The data that analysts utilize in their decision-making process often are thought of as probability distributions rather than point estimates, as they are typically presented. The job of the analyst is to develop the probability distributions. The fact that projections and other data are qualitative and subjective in nature does not mean that such data are not useful or even essential—the data merely emphasize the uncertainties and the need for an analysis capable of dealing with uncertain situations.

Ratio Analysis: A Basic Tool of Security Analysis

Investors have long used ratio analysis as a major tool for evaluating and interpreting the financial statements of companies. The object of ratio analysis is to reduce the large number of items contained in the statements to a relatively small number of meaningful relationships.

Mere examination of the absolute figures included in financial statements cannot be expected to lead to definite conclusions in regard to the financial status of a business. Assume, for example, that Company A reports earnings after taxes of $100,000, while Company B reports earnings after taxes of $1,000,000. To assume that Company B is ten times as profitable as Company A, and therefore worth ten times as much, would be incorrect. Suppose the balance sheet of Company A showed total investment capital of $200,000, while that of Company B showed total investment capital of $10,000,000. Company A is earning 50 percent on invested capital, while Company B is earning only 10 percent. The overall objective of a business is to earn a satisfactory return on the funds invested in it, consistent with maintaining a sound financial position. An acceptable return on invested capital ratio is a logical test of the success experienced in achieving this objective.

Interpretation requires comparison of meaningful components. Appropriate relationships (ratios) will depend on the purpose of the ratios selected and should relate components in which a logical decision-making relationship exists between the two variables, as was shown for profits and invested capital. The numerator and denominator chosen should be based on commonly calculated values. For example, cost of sales (not net sales) should be used as the numerator in an inventory turnover ratio, since the denominator (inventory) is valued at cost and the purpose is to assess the adequacy of the physical turnover of that inventory.

Screening Procedures

Screening processes are used by analysts to select, from the thousands of stocks and bonds offered in the market, a limited number worthy of extensive analysis. The screening process should be based on the objectives and risk tolerance of the investor. Provident Capital Management, for example, follows a low price-earnings (P/E) ratio philosophy in selecting stocks, based on historical studies indicating that low P/E stocks have consistently outperformed high P/E stocks over most of the time periods considered. They, therefore, concentrate their analytical efforts on those stocks whose P/E ratios fall among the lowest 40 percent of all firms at a given moment in time.

Computers are a valuable aid for purposes of screening stocks. Obviously, the computer can screen only on the basis of data already gathered and stored in the system. The Compustat tapes, prepared by Standard & Poor's Investors Management Sciences, Inc., provide detailed financial data on thousands of firms that could be helpful in a screening effort.

Stock screens could be set up to reflect any of the following criteria:

A. Growth Criteria

1. A minimum compound annual growth rate for a specified time period for sales and/or earnings could be required.

2. Risk could be limited by specifying a minimum standard deviation of sales or earnings data around the above-mentioned growth rate. Steady growth usually is preferred to growth that comes in fits and starts.

3. A minimum growth rate, and possibly standard deviation, could be required for dividend payments. A minimum dividend payout

ratio and/or dividend yield could be set by an investor to whom current cash flow is highly important.

B. Profitability Screens

A minimum return on total assets and/or owners' equity could be required. The efficiency with which the firm utilizes assets or owners' capital is a significant indicator of performance. A study by Faulkner, Dawkins, and Sullivan, Inc., indicated that high rates of return on owners' equity were well related to investment performance.[5]

C. Price-Related Screens

1. A screen could be based on the P/E ratio, either in relation to past history, to other firms in the industry, or to all firms. Provident Capital Management ranks P/E ratios relative to all firms.

2. One could build a market-price-to-book-value component into a screen.

3. The P/E ratio could be related to risk or other characteristics in a screen.

D. Risk Characteristics

1. Beta, as calculated in modern portfolio theory, could be entered as a risk constraint in a screen. Beta could also, of course, be related interactively with other characteristics of the firm in preparing a screen.

2. A liquidity standard could be entered as a requirement. Liquidity might be defined in terms of the current ratio, the acid-test, turnover ratios, or the interest coverage or fixed charges coverage ratios. A cash flow variable could also be built into a screen.

3. A minimum debt-to-equity requirement could also be part of a screen. Again, firm differences in terms of revenue stability would make it unlikely that a single standard would be useful.

E. Marketability Tests

An investor could be interested in assuring reasonable marketability for a commitment. A minimum number of shares outstanding and/or a minimum daily or weekly trading volume requirement for the stock of a firm could be included in the screen.

---

[5] Robert P. Colin and Howard E. Willie, *Interrelationship of Stockholder and Company Return on Investment* (New York: Faulkner, Dawkins & Sullivan, Inc., November, 1972).

The computer also could be used to test the efficiency of screens that have been developed and improve them. Returns performance of securities selected by the screen could be checked over time, and other characteristics could be tested to see if inclusion could improve the screen. Such tests only can be based on historical performance, and the future may not mirror the past. The tests are not conclusive; on-going evaluation is necessary.

THE FINANCIAL REPORTING PROBLEM

The dissatisfaction of investors and other financial analysts with corporate financial reports is evident from the following selected remarks:

> If accountants want to continue to enjoy a role in the investment management process, they should prepare to focus their energies on supplying whatever data a workable theory of security valuation requires, rather than defending the present ritual.[6]
>
> Congress has become increasingly alert to the lack of uniformity in accounting rules and to the deleterious effects this situation can have on the legislature's attempts to write laws.[7]
>
> It is going to be difficult to detect from 1973 financial reports whether a company's fundamentals are deteriorating since there are many accounting, operating, and financial gimmicks that management can use in the short-run to hide the effect on profits of a deterioration in fundamentals.[8]

The federal securities acts have gone a long way toward eliminating fraudulent or purposely misleading financial statements. However, the Equity Funding case proves that fraudulent financial reports have not been entirely eliminated, and it must be remembered that some small and intrastate firms are exempt from federal reporting requirements. Investors do have to depend on the certification of corporate reports by outside accountants as protection from inadequate reporting and fraudulent practice.

---

6 J. L. Treynor, "The Trouble with Earnings," *Financial Analysts Journal*, no. 28 (September–October 1972), p. 43.

7 "Who Will Set CPA Rules?" *Dun's Review* (September 1976), p. 62. Reprinted with the special permission of *Dun's Review*, September 1976. Copyright 1976. Dun & Bradstreet Publications Corporation.

8 David F. Hawkins, "Accounting Dodos and Red Flags—A Guide to Reading 1973 Annual Reports," *Financial Executive* (May 1974), p. 84.

Inadequate Disclosure versus Lack of Uniformity

For some years a battle has raged over whether the information problem is largely one of "inadequate disclosure" or one of "lack of uniformity" in corporate reporting.

Disclosure problems certainly exist, but the Securities & Exchange Commission (SEC) is exerting considerable effort to assure full, accurate, and adequate disclosure of material corporate financial information. Sufficient information should be given, either in the body of the report or in footnotes, to facilitate comparisons among firms using alternative accounting techniques. Admittedly, the cost of gathering and reporting this additional information would have to be weighed against its usefulness in performing a sound analysis.

Where adjustments are relatively easy and necessary for useful comparison, sufficient information should be given for adjustment from the method used to other acceptable methods. Footnotes, explanations, and qualifications to the annual reports taken by the accountants for preceding years should be repeated in current annual reports and in comparative statements to the extent that they continue to be of significance. Differences between net income reported to stockholders and that reported to the Internal Revenue Service should be explained. The analyst should not be required to spend time and effort searching SEC filings and old reports to gather the information necessary to interpret the data currently reported. Unfortunately, these suggestions have not been uniformly adapted by accountants.

Accountants should prepare statements that are useful to the user. Users desire statements that are reliable and informative for the purpose of appraising the financial strength and profitability of the firm and for making interfirm comparisons. Users are not so much interested in a past accounting of stewardship as in developing a base useful for projecting earnings, dividends, and financial strength. What is needed is disclosure of *material* information necessary for proper evaluation of a corporation's securities, not greater disclosure per se. Under SEC regulations, S-X-Rule 1-02 states, "The term 'material,' when used to qualify a requirement for the furnishing of information as to any subject, limits the information required to those matters on which an average prudent investor ought reasonably be informed." Rule 3-06 goes beyond this to say, "The information required with respect to any statement shall be furnished as a minimum requirement to which shall be added such further material information as is necessary to make the required statements, in the light of the circumstances under which they are made, not misleading."[9] A mere proliferation of details may only make sifting out the really significant information more difficult. As G. K. Chesterton pointed out, "The best place to hide a leaf is in a forest."

Absolute uniformity in accounting data should not be expected or sought. The complex and varied nature of business operations and a rapidly changing economy suggest a need for flexibility in reporting. Firms should be allowed to continue choosing among generally accepted accounting principles, but they should also be required to disclose, in dollar amounts, the impact on net income and balance sheet values of the accounting alternative chosen.

The analyst has the responsibility to interpret the information and recognize economic reality, assuming the facts are fully and accurately disclosed. The accountant and management should seek to present the information in the form most useful to users. Reports should not be so prepared that only a very experienced professional analyst can dig out, rearrange, and adjust published figures by interpreting the notes to financial statements and other supplementary information in order to make them useful.

SUMMARY

The function of security analysis is to determine the best relative values and portfolio composition at any point in time. This requires the investor to screen and classify financial assets on the basis of quality (financial risk), and then in terms of intrinsic values. The necessary screening process has become more practical since the introduction of computers and data banks of corporate financial information.

The investor must understand the differing concepts of risk underlying fundamental analysis as compared to the portfolio selection models, and must understand that modern portfolio theory has added a new and important dimension to the problem of security selection. Historically, this has not been considered in the fundamental analysis approach to security selection. Therefore, the material in this chapter recommends an integration of the two approaches.

Security analysis deals with both qualitative and quantitative data. Qualitative factors are subjective. All projections are qualitative, for they strictly are subjective, although expressed in quantitative terms. It is important to

---

9 William Holmes, "Materiality—Through the Looking Glass," *Journal of Accountancy* (February 1972), p. 45.

remember that the future always is uncertain and that projections only can be stated in terms of probabilities.

In analyzing quantitative accounting data, investors will use ratio analysis, which facilities comparison of meaningful components of financial statements. Once ratios are calculated, they must be interpreted in absolute terms and in terms of trends, which involves certain subjective judgments. In any case, the underlying factors that have resulted in the ratios and their trends are most important as a basis for assessing the future prospects of the firm.

In spite of the great improvement in financial reporting, there still exist problems of inadequate disclosure and lack of uniformity in reporting financial data. The SEC, the Financial Analysts Federation, and the American Institute of Certified Public Accountants, as well as committees of the stock exchanges and the National Association of Security Dealers, are working cooperatively for continuing improvement in the area of financial reporting.

Chapter Three

Security Valuation: The Cornerstone of Fundamental Analysis

The objective of fundamental analysis is to screen and classify financial assets in terms of investment quality (an assessment of risk) and expected return. Security analysts utilize expectations for the economy in the aggregate and for industry groupings (product line analysis) as a basis for forecasting profits, dividends, and possibly a future stock price for an individual security. This forecast allows calculation of an intrinsic value and expected return, which are important factors used by knowledgeable investors in deciding whether to buy, hold, or sell a particular security.

Intrinsic value of an asset reflects investors' expectations about future cash flow that will be generated by means of acquisition of that asset. It is a forecasted value that is likely to be quite different than current market price. Moreover, intrinsic value estimates for a given security could differ among individuals since the personal projection of future cash flow and risk could differ.

An important point to recognize is that, under conditions of uncertainty, intrinsic value estimates can never be precise. They merely provide a yardstick against which to measure current prices on the basis of expectations for future economic and other events. Such estimates are no more accurate than the expectations underlying them. Still, a standard is necessary and useful, even if it is only a loose one, to serve as a check on the reasonableness of estimations that underlie the selection of securities.

EXPECTATION, UNCERTAINTY, AND VALUATION THEORY

Investors, acting individually or with others through institutions, invest in order to increase wealth. An investor should seek the highest level of expected return for any given level of risk. However, expectations about future events can be based only in part on known facts, and in part on forecasts that are subject to uncertainty. The interest payments which are supposed to be made on a corporate or municipal bond, for example, may be counted among the known facts; but, whether or not such future commitments will be met will be determined, at least in part, by chance factors.

Forecasts which underlie financial decisions are continually reassessed, whether implicitly or explicitly, and securities that trade in organized markets are "revalued" accordingly. According to Keynes, "Our knowledge of the factors which govern the yield of an investment some years hence is usually very slight and often negligible."[1] It is important, therefore, not to make the assumption of perfect certainty when creating valuation estimates.

THE TIME VALUE OF MONEY

The time value of money is a phenomenon common to all valuation approaches. This concept will therefore be developed at the outset. An investor commits a given sum of money, foregoing present consumption, in exchange for the promise of a future stream of benefits. A dollar to be received today, however, is worth more than one to be received at some future date because:

1. The risk that a dollar due to be received at a future date may not be received would be avoided were it forthcoming immediately.

2. A dollar in hand could earn a return in each period it is available, leading to an increase in investor wealth.

The timing of cash flows, therefore, is highly important in determining the expected return from an investment.

---

[1] John M. Keynes, *The General Theory of Employment, Interest Money* (New York: Harcourt Brace, 1936).

TABLE 3–1
The Annual Effect of Compounding at 8 Percent Over a Five-Year Period

Year	Initial Balance	Interest on Principal	Interest Earned on Reinvested Interest	Total Interest Earned	Year-End Balance
1	$1,000.00	$80.00	0	$ 80.00	$1,080.00
2	1,080.00	80.00	$ 6.40	86.40	1,166.40
3	1,160.40	80.00	13.31	93.31	1,259.71
4	1,259.71	80.00	20.78	100.78	1,360.49
5	1,360.49	80.00	28.84	108.84	1,469.93

Future Values and Compound Interest

The process by which interest earns interest upon itself is called *compounding*. Table 3–1 shows the effect of interest compounding at an annual rate of 8 percent on an initial balance of $1,000 over a five-year period. Note the growing importance of interest earned through reinvestment. For long-term bonds, for example, the interest-on-interest component may amount to over half the total return received by an investor, depending on the reinvestment assumptions that are made.[2]

The process of interest compounding may be represented compactly in equation form as follows:

$$TV_t = A_0(1 + r)^t, \tag{3.1}$$

where

TV_t = the terminal value of the investment at time t,
A_0 = the cash flow at time $t = 0$, or the invested principal,
r = the periodic interest rate,
t = the number of interest periods for which compounding takes place.

Thus, were $1,000 placed in an 8 percent interest-bearing account compounded annually, assuming no withdrawals were made during the period,

2 Sidney Homer and Martin L. Leibowitz, *Inside the Yield Book* (Englewood Cliffs, NJ: New York Institute of Finance, 1972), pp. 21–22.

balances for the first and second years corresponding with those shown in Table 3–1 may be calculated as follows:

$$TV_1 = \$1,000(1 + .08)^1 = \$1,080.00$$

$$TV_2 = \$1,000(1 + .08)^2 = \$1,166.40$$

Compound return is a more potent growth force than investors sometimes realize. At a compound growth rate of 8 percent, for example, a $1,000 principal would double approximately every nine years. Thus, $1,000 would grow to $8,000 in about 27 years, $50,540 in about 50 years, and $2,550,749 in 100 years. As one wit has said, "Thrift is a marvelous virtue in one's ancestors." The annual rate available on high-quality bonds generally exceeded 8 percent during the 1970s, surpassing 15 percent in 1981 and then falling back toward 6 percent by the early 1990s. Rates then began to rise again. Long-term Treasury bonds were yielding about 7½ percent by May 1995.

Present Value

Suppose that a security whose par value is $1,000 is retired at the end of one year with a single lump-sum payment of $1,080, and that there are no payments on the security in the interim. Also assume that the actual per annum yield on an ordinary passbook account in a bank is 8 percent. Let us disregard the tax implications for the moment. If the market price of the security were $1,000 or more, the investor would be at least as well off putting the money in the bank at 8 percent. The present value of a single payment to be received at some future point in time, t, may be obtained as follows:

$$PV_t = A_t \times \left[\frac{1}{(1+r)^t} \right], \tag{3.2}$$

where

A_t = cash flow at time t,
r = the discount rate or opportunity cost.

Present value, in the sense of Equation (3.2), is an amount of money, A_0, which, if it were on hand today and invested at a compound rate (r), would grow to equal the future payment (A_t) by the end of time period t. For example, substituting into Equation (3.2):

$$PV_t = A_t \left[\frac{1}{(1+r)^t} \right]$$

$$= \frac{\$1,080}{(1+.08)^1}$$

$$= \$1,000.$$

Given the alternative provided by an ordinary passbook account whose effective yield is 8 percent, one should not pay more than $1,000 for this security.

Present value tables are presented at the end of this chapter. In Equation (3.2), the present value of any cash flow A_t is obtained by multiplying that cash flow by the quantity:

$$PV_\$ = \frac{1}{(1+r)^t} \tag{3.3}$$

This quantity is the present value of *one dollar* forthcoming at time t. The present value of a one-dollar cash flow, $PV_\$$, will vary, depending on the discount rate r and the timing of that cash flow t. The present value table shows the present value of $1 for various combinations of the discount rate and the timing of cash flow. For example, assume that a financial instrument promised to pay you $1,360.00 four years from now, and you believe you could earn 10 percent in alternative uses of the money with equivalent risk. What is the maximum price you should be willing to pay for this instrument today? Using Table 3–A in the Appendix [or Equation (3.3)], we find that the present value of $1 received four years from now is .683 (68.3 cents). The maximum price one should pay, therefore, is $928.88 (.683 × $1,360). This will assume that the required 10 percent compounded annual return is earned over the four years, and assume that the payment of $1,360.00 is actually received.

Contracts and annuities. Suppose that a contract involved a stream of cash flows At, where t = 1, 2, . . . T represents payments of various amounts for T periods beginning at time $t = 1$. The present value of a series of cash flows is simply the sum of the present values associated with each cash flow:

$$PV = \sum_{t=1}^{T} A_t \left[\frac{1}{1+r)^t} \right], \tag{3.4}$$

An *annuity* is a special form of contract whose payment stream, A_t, where $t = 1, 2, \ldots T$, consists of payments, A_c, which are the same from one period to the next. If we substitute the constant A_c for the variable A_t in Equation (3.4), the constant factors out, and the result simplifies as follows:

$$PV = A_c \left[\sum_{t=1}^{T} \frac{1}{(1+r)^t} \right], \tag{3.5}$$

Equation (3.5) defines the present value of an annuity which offers a constant payment, A_c, where the appropriate discount rate is r. In the special case where the constant payment is $A_c = \$1.00$, the constant A_c drops out of Equation (3.5) and we obtain:

$$PV_\$ = \left[\sum_{t=1}^{T} \frac{1}{(1+r)^t} \right], \tag{3.6}$$

Equation (3.6) defines the present value of a one-dollar amount to be received for T periods, beginning at the end of period $t = 1$, where the discount rate is r. The present value of *any* annuity, of course, will vary, depending on the variables A, T, and r.

Table 3-B presented in the chapter Appendix is an annuity table which sets out the present value of a one-dollar annuity for various combinations of the discount rate r and time periods T. For example, suppose an investor wished to know the present value of $1 to be received one year from today, assuming 8 percent interest compounded annually could be earned in alternative uses of the money. Using Equation (3.3), the present value is:

$$PV_\$ = \frac{1}{(1+r)^t} = \frac{1}{(1+.08)} = .92593.$$

The present value of $1 to be received each year for the next three years, assuming 8 percent can be earned in alternative uses of the funds, is determined by adding the present values of each individual receipt, as determined from Table 3-A in the chapter Appendix:

$$
\begin{array}{rcl}
PV_1 & = & .926 \\
PV_2 & = & .857 \\
PV_3 & = & \underline{.794} \\
\text{Present value of series} & = & \$2.577
\end{array}
$$

If $850 is expected each year for three years rather than $1, the present value of such a series can be calculated by multiplying 850×2.577; the present value is $2,190.45. We could, therefore, say we would not be willing to pay more than $2,190.45 for a security that offered a cash flow of $850 a year for three years, if we believed we could earn 8 percent compounded annually in investments of equivalent risk.

Perpetuities.   While all bonds in the United States have a maturity date, British consuls are perpetual bonds. A consul pays interest to perpetuity to whoever happens to own it, but the principal is never repaid.

The present value of a consul at any moment in time is equal to the net present value of all interest payments due into perpetuity, and may be expressed as follows:

$$PV = A_c \left[\sum_{t=1}^{\infty} \frac{1}{(1+r)^t} \right], \qquad (3.7)$$

where A_c is the constant interest payment and r is the discount rate.

The calculation of this present value is simplified by exploiting the fact that the summation in Equation (3.7) has a limit:

$$PV = \frac{A_c}{r} \qquad (3.7a)$$

Equation (3.7a) may be used in actual computations. For example, the maximum price an investor, who could earn 9 percent on alternative investments of equivalent risk, would pay for a 6 percent, $1,000 par consul would be $666.67 ($60/.09).

BOND VALUATION

The basic idea underlying all valuation approaches is the present value concept. Let us first consider the valuation of a bond, since it is somewhat easier than valuing common stock. The value of a bond can be defined as the total present value of all interest payments plus the present value of the return of principal upon maturity. The amount of each interest payment, the time pattern in which they will be paid, and the face value of the bond are specified in a bond contract.

It is important to understand that, when purchasing bonds, investors seek a yield that is commensurate with alternative possible uses of funds. The yields desired by investors change over time as the supply of and the demand

TABLE 3–2

Determination of Present Value of a 4 Percent Coupon, $1,000 Par, Five-Year Bond When 6 Percent Yield to Maturity is Desired

Period	Cash Flow	Present Value Factor at Three Percent	Present Value of Cash Flow
1	$ 20	.970874	$ 19.418
2	20	.942596	18.852
3	20	.915142	18.303
4	20	.888487	17.770
5	20	.862609	17.252
6	20	.837484	16.750
7	20	.813092	16.262
8	20	.789409	15.788
9	20	.766417	15.328
10	$1,020	.744094	758.976
Sum of present values			$914.699

Note: Three-place present value tables, both for the present value of $1 received at the end of year and for $1 received annually at the end of each year for *n* years, are presented in an Appendix at the end of this chapter. Six-place accuracy for discount factors was used in the example to minimize rounding error.

for loanable funds change. Bond prices also change over time, reflecting changing desired yields and other market phenomena.

Yield to Maturity

The yield to maturity on a bond is that discount rate which equates the purchase price to the present value of the cash inflows. This is merely the internal rate of return, r^*, which is defined in the following identity:

$$\sum_{t=0}^{T} \frac{A_t}{(1 = r*)^t} = 0 , \tag{3.8}$$

where A_t is the cash flow for period t, whether it be a net cash outflow or inflow, and T is the last period in which a cash flow is expected.

To illustrate, suppose that a $1,000 par bond has five years remaining to maturity, a 4 percent coupon rate, and interest that is payable semiannually. If market conditions are such as to require a 6 percent yield to maturity, we see from Table 3-2 that the bond would sell for $914.70 (which is the present value of the future cash inflows). Since cash flows are received semiannually, they are not discounted at the 6 percent annual rate, but at one-half the annual rate.

Bond yield tables eliminate the necessity of performing laborious calculations such as that illustrated in Table 3-2. Table 3-3 shows the various prices required to offer given yields to maturity for a 4 percent coupon bond maturing in five years. The number in the body of the table represents a percentage of par value. For example, a five-year, 4 percent coupon bond should sell at 91.47 percent of par value to yield 6 percent to maturity, or at a price of $914.70 for a $1,000 par bond.

Computer programs are also available that will make the illustrated calculations, and some hand-held calculators are programmed to make these calculations.

The reinvestment assumption.   Yield-to-maturity calculations assume that all interim cash flows are reinvested at the yield-to-maturity rate. This can be illustrated by noting that if $914.70 were invested at a 6 percent rate compounded semiannually for five years, it would grow to $1,229.28. Alternatively, a receipt of $20 every six months for five years, assuming receipts are reinvested at 6 percent compounded semiannually over the five-year period, plus $1,000 at the end of the fifth year, would also result in a wealth position of $1,229.28 at the end of the period, as shown in Table 3-4.

The realized yield on a bond held to maturity will, in most instances, be quite different from the yield to maturity calculated at purchase due to changing money market conditions and reinvestment rates over the life of the bond. If the $20 semi-annual interest payments in the previous illustration were reinvested at less than the assumed 6 percent annualized rate, the realized yield would be less than 6 percent upon maturity. Of course, if interest payments were reinvested at a rate higher than 6 percent, realized yield would exceed 6 percent upon maturity. If a bond is not held to maturity, the realized yield may again be quite different since the reinvestment period has changed and the price at which the bond was sold could be quite different from face value.

Rising interest rates after purchase of a bond would allow reinvestment at higher rates than assumed by the yield-to-maturity calculation, but would cause the price of the bond to fall, resulting in a lower terminal value if sold before maturity. A decline in quality (as perceived in the market) after purchase would also result in a fall in price, other things being equal.

TABLE 3–3
Coupon Yield Tables, 4 Percent Coupon

				Years and Months				
Yield	4–9	4–10	4–11	5–0	5–3	5–6	5–9	6–0
2.00	109.02	109.17	109.32	109.47	109.92	110.37	110.81	111.26
2.20	108.07	108.21	108.34	108.48	108.88	109.28	109.67	110.07
2.40	107.14	107.26	107.38	107.50	107.85	108.20	108.54	108.89
2.60	106.21	106.32	106.42	106.52	106.83	107.13	107.43	107.73
2.80	105.30	105.39	105.47	105.56	105.82	106.08	106.33	106.59
3.00	104.39	104.46	104.54	104.61	104.82	105.04	105.24	105.45
3.20	103.50	103.55	103.61	103.67	103.83	104.01	104.17	104.34
3.40	102.61	102.65	102.69	102.74	102.86	102.99	103.11	103.23
3.60	101.73	101.76	101.79	101.82	101.89	101.98	102.06	102.14
3.80	100.86	100.87	100.89	100.90	100.94	100.98	101.02	101.06
4.00	100.00	100.00	100.00	100.00	100.00	100.00	100.00	100.00
4.20	99.14	99.13	99.12	99.11	99.06	99.03	98.98	98.95
4.40	98.30	98.27	98.25	98.22	98.14	98.06	97.98	97.91
4.60	97.46	97.42	97.38	97.35	97.22	97.11	96.99	96.89
4.80	96.63	96.58	96.53	96.48	96.32	96.17	96.02	95.87
5.00	95.81	95.75	95.68	95.62	95.43	95.24	95.05	94.87
5.10	95.40	95.33	95.27	95.20	94.98	94.78	94.57	94.38
5.20	95.00	94.92	94.85	94.78	94.54	94.32	94.10	93.88
5.30	94.60	94.51	94.43	94.36	94.10	93.87	93.62	93.39
5.40	94.20	94.11	94.02	93.94	93.67	93.41	93.15	92.91
5.50	93.80	93.70	93.61	93.52	93.23	92.96	92.68	92.42
5.60	93.40	93.30	93.20	93.11	92.80	92.52	92.22	91.94
5.70	93.01	92.90	92.80	92.69	92.37	92.07	91.76	91.46
5.80	92.61	92.50	92.39	92.28	91.95	91.63	91.30	90.99
5.90	92.22	92.10	91.99	91.88	91.52	91.19	90.84	90.52
6.00	91.83	91.71	91.59	91.47	91.10	90.75	90.39	90.05
6.10	91.44	91.32	91.19	91.07	90.68	90.31	89.94	89.58
6.20	91.06	90.93	90.79	90.66	90.26	89.88	89.49	89.12
6.30	90.68	90.54	90.40	90.26	89.85	89.45	89.04	88.65
6.40	90.29	90.15	90.01	89.87	89.43	89.02	88.60	88.20
6.50	89.91	89.76	89.62	89.47	89.02	88.59	88.16	87.74
6.60	89.54	89.38	89.23	89.08	88.61	88.17	87.72	87.29
6.70	89.16	89.00	88.84	88.69	88.21	87.75	87.28	86.84
6.80	88.79	88.62	88.46	88.30	87.80	87.33	86.85	86.39
6.90	88.41	88.24	88.08	87.91	87.40	86.91	86.42	85.95
7.00	88.04	87.87	87.70	87.53	87.00	86.50	85.99	85.50
7.10	87.67	87.49	87.32	87.14	86.60	86.09	85.56	85.07
7.20	87.31	87.12	86.94	86.76	86.20	85.68	85.14	84.63
7.30	86.94	86.75	86.57	86.38	85.81	85.27	84.72	84.20
7.40	86.58	86.38	86.19	86.00	85.42	84.86	84.30	83.76
7.50	86.22	86.02	85.82	85.63	85.03	84.46	83.88	83.34

TABLE 3–3 *(concluded)*

| Yield | \multicolumn{8}{c}{Years and Months} |
	4–9	4–10	4–11	5–0	5–3	5–6	5–9	6–0
7.60	85.86	85.65	85.45	85.25	84.64	84.06	83.47	82.91
7.70	85.50	85.29	85.08	84.88	84.26	83.66	83.06	82.49
7.80	85.14	84.93	84.72	84.51	83.87	83.26	82.65	82.06
7.90	84.79	84.57	84.36	84.14	83.49	82.87	82.24	81.65
8.00	84.44	84.21	83.99	83.78	83.11	82.48	81.84	81.23
8.10	84.09	83.86	83.63	83.41	82.74	82.09	81.44	80.82
8.20	83.74	83.50	83.28	83.05	82.36	81.70	81.04	80.41
8.30	83.39	83.15	82.69	82.69	81.99	81.32	80.64	80.00
8.40	83.04	82.80	82.57	82.33	81.62	80.93	80.24	79.59
8.50	82.70	82.45	82.21	81.98	81.25	80.55	79.85	79.19
8.60	82.36	82.11	81.86	81.62	80.88	80.17	79.46	78.79
8.70	82.02	81.76	81.51	81.27	80.51	79.80	79.07	78.39
8.80	81.68	81.42	81.17	80.92	80.15	79.42	78.69	77.99
8.90	81.34	81.08	80.82	80.57	79.79	79.05	78.30	77.60
9.00	81.00	80.74	80.48	80.22	79.43	78.68	77.92	77.20
9.20	80.34	80.06	79.79	79.53	78.71	77.94	77.16	76.43
9.40	79.68	79.39	79.12	78.84	78.01	77.22	76.42	75.66
9.60	79.02	78.73	78.45	78.17	77.31	76.50	75.68	74.90
9.80	78.37	78.08	77.78	77.50	76.62	75.78	74.95	74.15
10.00	77.73	77.43	77.13	76.83	75.93	75.08	74.22	73.41

Source: Reproduced from *Expanded Bond Values Table,* Publication #83, p. 299. Copyright 1970, Financial Publishing Company, Boston Massachusetts.

Therefore, an investor is subject to "price risk" when interest rates rise after purchase or when quality of the bond declines. If interest rates fell after purchase or quality improved, of course, the result would be precisely the opposite.

The reinvestment assumption has other important implications, as when selecting among discount, par, and premium bonds. When rising interest rates are anticipated, an investor should prefer premium or par bonds, since their coupon rates will be higher than those on discount bonds of equivalent quality. Under these conditions, an investor seeks to maximize the current interest receipts so as to obtain more to reinvest at rising rates. On the other hand, when interest rates are expected to decline, deep discount bonds would be attractive. A large part of the total yield for a deep discount bond is represented by the accumulation (excess of face value over purchase price) received upon maturity, which will not have to be reinvested at falling rates.

TABLE 3–4
An Illustration of the Reinvestment Assumption

Period	Cash Received and Reinvested	Terminal Value of $1 Invested for T Years	Terminal Value
1	$ 20	$(1.03)^9$	$ 26.097
2	20	$(1.03)^8$	25.337
3	20	$(1.03)^7$	24.599
4	20	$(1.03)^6$	23.882
5	20	$(1.03)^5$	23.186
6	20	$(1.03)^4$	22.511
7	20	$(1.03)^3$	21.855
8	20	$(1.03)^2$	21.218
9	20	$(1.03)^1$	20.600
10	1,020	1	1,020.000
Total			$1,229.285

Yield to call. A call clause gives the issuing corporation the right, at its discretion, to require that the bonds be submitted for payment prior to maturity at a designated price. Corporations will only exercise the call privilege when they can refinance at lower interest cost, which can adversely affect the bondholder's economic interest since reinvestment of the funds received will have to be at the lower prevailing rates.

Accordingly, a sophisticated investor will consider both the yield to maturity and the yield assuming the bond is called when evaluating callable bonds. Actually, neither the yield to maturity nor the yield to call can be considered accurate measures of the yield that will be realized from holding a bond for two reasons. First, both measures assume reinvestment of cash flows to the terminal date used at the calculated yield rate, which is not likely to match actual experiences (the reinvestment assumption previously discussed). Second, the yield to call does not recognize what will happen to the proceeds after the bond is called and prior to maturity. Thus, it cannot be directly compared to calculated yields to maturity for other bonds. Still, both measures offer reasonable estimates of potential realized yield for comparative purposes, and can be calculated on a "what if" basis to consider future reinvestment rates and the date of call, which are uncertain.

A yield to call is defined as that discount rate that equates the present value of the promised cash flow until the assumed date of call (coupon payments plus call price) to the market price. To illustrate, assume that 10 percent bonds issued by corporation X are callable after five years at $1,050 per bond. The bonds currently sell at par and thus yield 10 percent to maturity. If the bonds are called at the earliest call date, they would pay $50 semiannually for the five years and $1,050 at the end of the fifth year. A trial-and-error approach and a hand-held computer can be used to determine the yield to call through an interactive process. The calculated yield to call for the above bond is about 10.2 percent.

Approximating net yield to maturity. When bond yield tables and calculators equipped for present value calculations are not readily available, an approximation of the net yield to maturity is provided by

$$YTM = \frac{C + \dfrac{F - P}{T}}{\dfrac{F + P}{2}} , \qquad\qquad (3.9)$$

where

YTM = net yield at maturity,
  C = annual dollars paid in interest,
  F = face or par value of the bond,
  P = selling price of the bond,
  T = number of years to maturity.

For a 4 percent, $1,000 bond purchased at $914.70, with five years remaining to maturity, we obtain

$$YTM = \frac{40 + \dfrac{1000 - 914.70}{5}}{\dfrac{100 + 914.70}{2}} = \frac{57.06}{957.35} = 0.59602 ,$$

according to this approximation. This approximation could serve as a beginning point for a trial-and-error approach when calculating a yield to maturity or a yield to call.

Conclusions Concerning Bond Yields and Prices

Under conditions of perfect certainty, the value of a bond (or any other investment asset) is the present value of all anticipated cash flows. Bond prices change from time to time, reflecting changing market conditions and quality ratings for individual bonds. Bond prices vary inversely, moreover, with each change in minimum required yield.

Yield-to-maturity calculations assume reinvestment of all cash flows at the yield-to-maturity rate. This explains the advantage of discount over par or premium bonds for an investor who expects interest rates to decline over the time a bond will be held, since a part of the return on a discount bond is fixed and thus would not be subject to reinvestment at a lower interest rate. If interest rates are expected to increase over time, by contrast, premium bonds would have an advantage. One's expectation concerning future interest rates, therefore, is an important consideration when purchasing bonds (or any security), and the accuracy of interest rate assumptions is crucial when valuing bonds.

STOCK VALUATION

Under conditions of certainty, a stock's intrinsic value, as with a bond, would be the discounted present value of all future cash flows. Stocks (preferred or common), however, offer no legal commitment to pay dividends or return principal as bonds do, and thus the valuation of future cash flows is more complicated. The stream of income that will flow to stockholders is highly uncertain and depends on corporate success and the outcome of other chance events. As noted earlier, an intrinsic value can never be precisely determined. The systematic use of valuation theory, however, should serve an important purpose as a check on the reasonableness of current market price when considering the purchase or sale of a stock.

Historical Background

The stock market crash in 1929, which by 1932 culminated in a 90 percent decline in the Dow Jones Index, stimulated efforts to develop a theory of stock valuation. The development of formal stock valuation approaches seems to have begun in 1930, when Robert F. Weiss stated that "the proper price of any security, whether a stock or a bond, is the sum of all the future income payments discounted at the current rate of interest in order to arrive at present value."[3]

Samuel Elliot Guild[4] was the first to present a series of tables based on the present value approach for the purpose of measuring intrinsic value. Guild's approach was an ad hoc approach that assumed the following:

1. The average rate at which company earnings would grow over the time period in question.
2. The dividend–earnings ratio that would prevail for the stock at the end of the holding period selected.
3. The price–earnings ratio that would prevail for the stock at the end of the holding period selected.
4. The internal rate of return or yield required by the investor.

Guild's objective was to provide an investor with a simple procedure for calculating the maximum price, given a set of known parameters, that would be commensurate with a specified rate of return.[5]

John Burr Williams[6] was the first to provide a comprehensive and rigorous foundation on which the intrinsic value of a stock could be defined. While Williams's contribution was singularly important to the development of a modern theory of security valuation, it suffered from at least one serious shortcoming: No account was taken by Williams of uncertainty regarding either future cash flows, one's knowledge about these flows, or the likelihood that the appropriate discount rate would not remain constant over the holding period assumed for the stock.[7]

These shortcomings must always be kept in mind when using intrinsic value calculations. Multiple intrinsic values can be calculated to allow for

3 R. F. Weiss, "Investing for True Value," *Barron's* (September 8, 1930).

4 S. E. Guild, *Stock Growth and Discount Tables* (Boston: Financial Publishing Co., 1931).

5 For expansions of the Guild tables utilizing a present value approach and incorporating more sophisticated assumptions, see R. M. Soldofsky and J. T. Murphy, *Growth Yields on Common Stocks: Theories and Tables,* Rev. ed. (Iowa City: Bureau of Business and Economic Research, State University of Iowa, 1964); W. Scott Bauman, *Estimating the Present Value of Common Stocks by the Variable Rate Method,* Monograph (Ann Arbor: Bureau of Business Research, The University of Michigan, 1963); and N. Molodovsky, C. May, and S. Chottiner, "Common Stock Valuation: Theory and Tables," *Financial Analysts Journal* (March–April 1965), pp. 104–112.

6 J. B. Williams, *The Theory of Investment Value,* reprint ed. (Amsterdam, The Netherlands: North Holland Publishing Co., 1964).

7 See F. H. Knight, *Risk, Uncertainty and Profit* (London School of Economics and Political Science, Series of Reprints of Scarce Tracts, no. 16, 1933).

a range of assumptions, and these calculations will serve to usefully test the reasonableness of current market prices.

Present Value Approaches

Asset values, as recorded on a balance sheet, are not utilized in stock valuation theory. Accounting values (original cost less accumulated depreciation) tell us little about the current worth of a company. The liquidation value of a firm's assets is also of little significance since liquidation will usually occur only when serious financial difficulties have been encountered.

An investment asset has *value* because an owner anticipates receiving future cash flows from it. The value of an asset, therefore, depends on the size of the future cash flows generated, the time patterns over which they are to be received, the risk involved, and the rate that could be earned in alternative uses of the funds. What is important, therefore, is current expectation concerning the cash flows, and not what was paid to acquire an asset at some time in the past.

Dividend–capitalization models. A corporation is granted a charter into perpetuity, and the presumption is made that it will be in existence for an infinite period. Therefore, the current value of a stock should represent the discounted present value of the dividend payments that would be forthcoming over that infinite time horizon. This relationship is expressed by the equation:

$$PV = \sum_{t=1}^{\infty} D_t \left[\frac{1}{(1+k)^t} \right],$$ **(3.10)**

where

    D_t = the dividend per share in period t,
    k = the market return appropriate to a pure equity stream, or the discount rate.

Where the dividend payment is to be made into perpetuity at a constant rate (the no-growth case), Equation (3.10) simplifies to

$$PV = \frac{D_c}{k},$$ **(3.10a)**

which defines the present value of a perpetuity.

Book value versus intrinsic value.   The no-growth assumption would apply to a firm whose capital (C) and the rate of return earned on that capital (r) remained constant, further assuming that the firm paid all profits as dividends in the year earned. Total profits of the firm could be defined as (rC). The value of the firm's stock would then equal

$$V_0 = \frac{rC0}{(1+k)} + \frac{rC0}{(1+k)^2} + \ldots + \frac{rC0}{(1+k)^\infty}$$

$$V_0 = \frac{rC0}{k}$$

Although this model is unrealistic, it does provide interesting insight into the relation between book value of the firm (C_0) and intrinsic value (V_0). If $r = k$, then book value (C_0) equals intrinsic value (V_0). If r is greater than k, however, intrinsic value (V_0) will exceed book value. This conclusion is quite reasonable since the firm is assumed to earn a higher rate on new investment than that required by the market. On the other hand, if r is less than k, intrinsic value (and, therefore, market value) will be less than book value.

Not surprisingly, therefore, stocks typically sell at a price different from book value. A firm is not likely to earn a return on new investment exactly equal to the market-required return for investment in its stock over any extended period of time.

A growth firm, in terms of the above logic, can be defined as a firm earning a higher rate of return on new investments (r) than market-required return for investment in its stock (k). A declining firm would be one where $k > r$.

Growth models.   To assume that dividend payments would be constant into perpetuity is unrealistic. Dividends do change over time, reflecting corporate success or failure and market factors. Stocks are usually purchased with the anticipation of corporate success and dividend growth, and models have been developed by Gordon[8] and Lerner and Carleton[9] which incorporate a constant growth assumption. A constant growth assumption may itself be questionable but can be considered in the sense of

---

8 M. J. Gordon, *The Investment, Financing and Valuation of the Corporation* (Homewood, IL: Richard D. Irwin, 1962).

9 Eugene M. Lerner and Willard T. Carleton, *A Theory of Financial Analysis* (New York: Harcourt, Brace & Worlds, 1966).

an estimated long-run average growth for purposes of generating an intrinsic value estimate.

Let the dividend received on a particular stock at time $t = 0$ be D_0 (the current dividend). Suppose that dividends will grow at a constant rate, g, forever. The dividend at any future point in time, t, therefore, is simply:

$$D_t = D_0(1 + g)^t. \tag{3.11}$$

Substituting Equation (3.11) into Equation (3.10) and simplifying, we obtain

$$PV = D_0 \left[\sum_{t=1}^{\infty} \frac{(1 + g)^t}{(1 + k)^t} \right]. \tag{3.12}$$

Provided that the discount rate, k, is larger than the growth rate, g, it can be shown that Equation (3.12) is mathematically equivalent to[10]

$$PV = \frac{D_1}{k - g}, \tag{3.13}$$

where D_1 is the dividend to be received at time $t = 1$, or at the end of one holding period.

Discounting dividends rather than earnings.   Earnings not paid out in dividends are retained. When retained earnings are invested in profitable projects, the added earnings produce opportunities for higher future dividends. A present value approach, therefore, considers the earnings potential that results from the reinvested earnings by taking account of the future dividends generated. It would be double-counting to discount both present earnings and future dividends that result from earnings retention.

Implicit consideration of capital gains.   A shareholder who sells his or her stock might well realize capital gains as well as receiving dividends. Capital gains are considered in the above growth model, consistent with the assumed dividend growth rate and constant discount rate. To illustrate, assume Firm A pays a $1 dividend at the end of the first year of holding the stock (D_1), and dividends are expected to grow at a constant rate of 8 percent. Further assume that opportunity cost of a particular

---

10 For proof see Lerner and Carleton, ibid., pp. 105–108.

investor is 14 percent. The intrinsic value of Firm A stock at this moment, according to equation (3.13), is

$$PV_a = \frac{D_1}{k-g} = \frac{1}{.14-.08} = \frac{1}{.06} = \$16.67$$

Let us determine the present value of the stock five years from now, utilizing the same growth and discount rate assumptions:

$$PV_5 = \frac{D_6}{k-g}.$$

The expected dividend at the end of year five (D_6) is

$$D_6 = \$1(1+g)^5 = \$1(1.08)^5 = \$1(1.46933) = \$1.46933$$

The value of Firm A stock at the end of year five would, therefore, be

$$PV_5 = \frac{D_6}{k-g} = \frac{\$1.46933}{14-.08} = 24.488.$$

Discounting the expected cash flows generated by holding the stock for five years, we arrive at a consistent present value of $16.67, as calculated below:

End of Period	Cash Flow		Discount Factor	Present Value
	Dividend	Sales Price		
1	1.0000	—	.87719	0.87719
2	1.0800	—	.76947	0.83103
3	1.1664	—	.67497	0.78729
4	1.2597	—	.59208	0.74584
5	1.3605	24.4888	.51937	13.42535
Total Present Value				16.66667

We have ignored the impact of taxes in the above calculations, which will be introduced in our discussion of a finite holding period below.

Dividend policy and stock valuation. Miller and Modigliani argued that the value of a firm is not affected by the dividend policy of that firm in a world without taxes or transaction costs.[11] Let us illustrate this argument in terms of a dividend growth valuation model.

---

11 M. Miller and F. Modigliani, "Dividend Policy, Growth and the Valuation of Shares," *The Journal of Business* (October 1961), pp. 411–433.

Consider a firm that expands its capital (C) each year by retaining a portion of earnings (b). Profit for this firm can be defined in terms of the rate earned on capital (r), or as rC_0. Capital one year hence would equal capital at the beginning of the year (C_0) plus retained earnings brC_0. The rate of growth in capital can then be expressed as

$$g = \frac{C_1 - C_0}{C_0} = \frac{[C_0 + brC_0] - C_0}{C_0} = \frac{brC_0}{C_0} = br. \tag{3.14}$$

The rate of growth in dividends, in accordance with the above assumptions, also equals br:

$$g = \frac{D_1 - D_0}{D_0} = \frac{[(1 - b)r(C_0 + brC_0) - [(1 - b)rC_0]}{(1 - b)rC_0} \tag{3.15}$$

Now, we restate equation (3.13) in terms of earnings per share (e) and an assumed dividend payout ratio ($1 - b$).

$$V_0 = \frac{e_1(1 - b)}{k - br}, \text{ since } g = br. \tag{3.16}$$

If one further assumes that the firm exactly earns the rate required by the market on new investments in accordance with capital budgeting literature ($k = r$), the valuation equation can be restated as follows:

$$V_0 = \frac{e_1(1 - b)}{k - bk} = \frac{e_1(1 - b)}{k(1 - b)} = \frac{e_1}{k} \tag{3.16a}$$

Under these assumptions, dividend policy is irrelevant (it has no effect on the valuation of the firm) since b cancels out.

The above conclusion obviously does not follow when r and k differ or when taxes and transaction costs are considered. Ross, moreover, points out that a firm is valued on the basis of the *perceived* stream of cash flow that an investment in that firm will generate, and that changes in dividend policy could well alter the market's perceptions[12] and thus affect the firm's valuation. For example, if the dividend were reduced, the market might well interpret this reduction as implying a reduction in future profitability, resulting in the sale of shares and downward pressure on market price and intrinsic value estimations. The relation between k and r does appear to be

12 S. A. Ross, "The Determination of Financial Structure: The Incentive-Signaling Approach," *The Pell Journal of Economics* (Spring 1977), pp. 23–40.

the critical variable when trying to assess the likely impact of dividend policy changes on stock values.

Finite horizons and valuation.   Investors have the opportunity to sell their stock at any time, and they likely perceive of their investment horizons as limited to some finite period. A model that assumes an infinite horizon would not, therefore, serve as a very useful basis for stock selection or as a check on the reasonableness of estimations that enter into portfolio selection.

A limited holding period model, by contrast, assumes a sale of the stock being valued at the end of an assumed holding period. The present value, in this context, is the sum of the present values associated with the dividends received during a holding period, plus the present value of the sales price at the end of the holding period:

$$PV = \sum_{t=1}^{T} \left[\frac{D_t}{(1+k)^t} \right] + \frac{P_T}{(1+k)^T}, \tag{3.17}$$

where P_T is the expected sales price. Equation (3.17) can be rewritten in terms of earnings per share as follows:

$$PV = C_0 l \sum_{l=1}^{T} \frac{(1+g)^t}{(1+k)^t} + \frac{C_0 M_c (1+g)^T}{(1+k)^T}, \tag{3.17a}$$

where

C_0 = current earnings per share,
g = the anticipated compound annual growth rate of earnings per share,
l = the proportion of earnings paid out as dividends in each holding period,
M_c = the multiplier applied to earnings per share in the terminal year to determine selling price,
k = the appropriate discount rate.

Equations (3.17) and (3.17a) can be modified to account for the effects of taxation. To illustrate, suppose that:

1. A stock is purchased at year-end 1978 at $95 per share;

2. Dividend income is taxed at a 50 percent rate and capital gains at an effective rate of 20 percent (in accordance with capital gains tax law in effect prior to the Tax Reform Act of 1986);
3. Earnings per share at the time of purchase are $9.50, and are expected to grow at a compound annual rate of 6 percent;
4. The company pays out 55 percent of earnings in the form of dividends each year;
5. The stock will be sold at the end of the third year, and a price–earnings ratio of 15 is expected to apply to the stock at the time of sale;
6. A rate of 8 percent after taxes is available in alternative investment opportunities felt to be of equivalent risk.

Based on these assumptions, the present value of the stock is found to be $130.40, by means of the following sample calculation:

Year	Earnings Per Share	Dividends	After-Tax Dividend	After-Tax Proceed from Sale	Present Value Factor at 8 Percent	Present Value of Cash Flow
1978	9.50					
1979	10.07	5.54	2.77		.926	2.565
1980	10.67	5.87	2.94		.857	2.520
1981	11.31	6.22	3.11	154.72*	.794	125.317
Present Value of Stock						130.402

*The expected selling price of $169.65 (15 × $11.31) less the capital gains tax of $14.93 [$74.65 (capital gain) × .4 × .5].

The model described by Equation (3.17a) may be used in sensitivity analysis; that is, the estimates of C_0, g, k, and T can be varied one at a time, or in combination, to determine the sensitivity of the valuation estimate to changes in these parameters. The model does not require a constant growth rate or discount rate assumption. The problem for the analyst is determining the expectations stated in 1 through 6 above. The analytical framework developed in the remainder of the book is utilized to develop such expectations.

Growth duration. The longer one projects an above-average growth rate for calculated dividends and earnings, the higher will be the present value of the stock as calculated by any of the models discussed above. There is always some combination of growth rate and growth period that will justify any current market price. This point is made nicely by an illustrative valuation of IBM stock by Williamson.[13] In 1968, IBM sold at about $320 per share; 1967 earnings were $5.80 per share, and dividends were $2.17 per share. Consistent with recent growth, Williamson predicted earnings per share of $7 for 1968. He initially forecast a 16 percent earnings growth rate for 10 years, followed by indefinite growth of 2 percent and a dividend payout rate of 40 percent, which were in line with experience for IBM over the previous 10 years. Using a discount rate of 7 percent, he calculated an intrinsic value of $172.94. Noting that this represented about one-half of the current market value, Williamson said, "It does not seem sensible to predict only 10 years of above-average growth for IBM, so I extended my growth forecast to 20 years." Now the intrinsic value came to $432.66—well above the market. When a 10 percent discount rate was substituted for the 7 percent rate, and a growth rate of 16 percent for 20 years, however, Williamson found an intrinsic value of only $205.73.

Clearly, a growth model is quite sensitive to changes in the parameters included. The illustration shows the importance of not being carried away by enthusiasm that may prevail from time to time in the market and the tenuous nature of intrinsic value estimates.

Limitation of dividend valuation models.   The models discussed to this point are all subject to a number of simplifying assumptions that limit the accuracy of intrinsic value estimates. These limitations are briefly summarized as follows:

1. The intrinsic value estimate is no more accurate than the estimates of earnings and dividends underlying that valuation. Experience suggests that earnings growth rates can vary markedly over time, and firms do change their dividend policies. The problem of forecasting earnings and dividends will be discussed in more depth later in the book.

2. The discount rate (k) is typically held constant for the period covered by the model. In actuality, required market rates change over time, and the risk-class of a given firm may also change. In either situation, the assumption of a constant (k) would not be valid. The discount rate

---

13 J. Peter Williamson, *Investments: New Analytic Techniques* (New York: Praeger, 1971), pp. 155–159.

chosen should represent what the investor could earn in alternative instruments of equivalent risk. It is the required return of the investor.

3. Either earnings growth is assumed into perpetuity, or a terminal value representing the expected sales price of the stock at some predetermined time is made. The declining present value of far-distant streams does lessen the importance of errors in the estimation of such streams when a hold into infinity is assumed. However, the difficulty lies in imagining how accurate estimates can be made over such long horizons. When a finite holding period is assumed, the question arises as to how one determines that holding period in advance. Even if the holding period could be estimated accurately, one still faces the difficult problem of estimating the market value of the stock at the end of the holding period.

4. Growth is assumed to be financed through retained earnings. This assumption ignores the possible use of debt, new stock issues, and other sources of funds that could finance growth in assets and earnings.

5. Constant growth rate assumptions are often used. The rate then supposedly represents an average compound growth expected over the holding period. There is the danger of relying too much on the past when estimating this growth rate, especially when the firm has experienced high recent growth than can rarely be sustained indefinitely. This point is illustrated in the discussion of the valuation of IBM stock above.

6. After-tax cash flows could be estimated by assuming the tax bracket rate that will be applicable to the investor for each annual holding period. The appropriate tax bracket will depend, however, on the total income of the investor and the tax deductions available, not just on investment income. Such estimates are, of course, subject to error.

One would not, therefore, anticipate a high degree of accuracy in intrinsic value estimates when the inherent limitations of the valuation models are considered. The models do serve to clarify the relationship between the key factors that affect stock valuation, however. They also offer a way of studying the reasonableness of the assumptions that seem to underlie market values at a given point in time, thereby providing a constant framework for relative comparisons of securities. The importance of valuation efforts lies more in the discipline and organized structure it provides for making buy and sell decisions than in the numbers generated.

PRICE–EARNINGS RATIOS

A price–earnings ratio, as typically reported, is simply the result of dividing the current market price of a company's common stock by the most recent twelve-months' earnings per share. The ratio reflects what a perspective investor must currently pay to buy one dollar of reported earnings of the company.

Price–earnings ratios can change daily as market price changes and should not be mistaken as indicators of intrinsic value. They do suggest the esteem in which a company is held by the market at a moment of time, but are not indicative of whether or not the stock is overpriced based on assumptions about future earnings, risk, and opportunity costs, as are estimates of intrinsic value.

Price–earnings ratios may, in fact, give a distorted view of relative value due to different accounting techniques that may be used by different firms, thereby making reported earnings noncomparable.[14] Also, a price–earnings ratio may be temporarily high because earnings are currently low and the market expects a return to higher earnings levels. Moreover, price–earnings ratios reflect *historical earnings* while the investor is concerned with future earnings.

PRICE–EARNINGS RATIOS AND VALUATION

Some practicing analysts seem to prefer using a modified price–earnings ratio as a multiplier of earnings, rather than present value techniques, to generate an intrinsic value estimate.[15] In this approach, earnings are represented by an estimated average future earning per share, often referred to as "normalized earnings per share." Normalized earnings per share (e_n) has been defined as the "level of net income which would prevail currently if the economy were experiencing mid-cyclical conditions.[16] The determinations of normalized earnings per share, therefore, involves a consideration

---

14 We will have a good deal to say about problems of accounting techniques and noncomparability of earnings later in this book.

15 R. A. Bing, "Survey of Practitioners' Stock Evaluation Methods," *Financial Analysts Journal* 26, no. 2 (May–June 1971), pp. 55–60.

16 Volkert S. Whitbeck and Manown Kisor, Jr., "A New Tool in Investment Decision Making," *Financial Analysis Journal* 19, no. 3 (May–June 1963), p. 57.

of the earnings experience of a firm over a previous business cycle and an evaluation of current and expected market and cost conditions. In effect, then, it involves the same earnings forecasting efforts that would be needed to generate present value estimates.

The multiplier (P/e_n) is primarily determined by the riskiness of the firm and the expected rate of growth in earnings. It is often assumed that the Dow-Jones Industrial Average represents a cross-section of stocks with average risk and growth prospects, and the stock under study is given a multiplier that would be higher than the average for that index if it has higher-than-average growth prospects unless the higher growth is coupled with substantially greater risk.

An estimate of intrinsic value is then provided as follows;

$$V_o = e_n \, (P/e_n)$$

Those who favor this approach feel that the serious limitations underlying the earnings and dividend forecasts required by present-value techniques make such calculations not worth the effort. It must be remembered, however, that the P/E multiplier approach is merely a short-cut method where the impact of growth, risk and dividend policy is supposedly captured in one statistic (Pe_n). The real benefit gained in the valuation effort is the assessment of those underlying factors affecting value in an organized way, not the valuation estimate itself. The writer, therefore, believes that the present-value approach should be used.

Statistical Approaches to Estimating Intrinsic Value

The valuation formula for an assumed constant growth model, as already developed, can easily be converted to a price–earnings form by dividing both sides of the equation by earnings as follows:

$$P = \frac{D}{(k - g)}$$

therefore $P/_E = \dfrac{D/_E}{k + g}.$

Differing price–earnings ratios among companies should, therefore, be explainable in terms of differing dividend policies (D/E), growth rates (g), or risk-adjusted, market-required returns (k). Several authors have attempted to use statistical techniques, namely multiple regression analysis, to estimate the appropriate price–earnings ratio at a moment in time for these varying forces.[17]

Whitbeck and Kisor, for example, obtained estimates of dividend payout ratios, earnings growth rates and the variation (standard deviation) of those earnings growth rates (a proxy for risk) from selected security analysts for 135 stocks. They then used multiple regression techniques to define the average relationship between each of these variables and price–earnings ratios as of June 8, 1962. They found that each of the three variables studied had the expected sign and appeared to be significant. The regression results were as follows:

Theoretical P/E Ratio = 8.2 + 1.5 (Growth Rate)
+ 6.7 (Dividend Payment Ratio)
−.2 (Standard Deviation)

The usefulness of the model was tested by computing the theoretical P/E ratio for each individual stock based upon their projected dividend payments, earnings variability, and growth, and then classifying the stocks into overvalued and undervalued stocks in terms of a comparison of their actual and theoretical P/E ratios. It was found that the undervalued group consistently outperformed the S&P 500 on the basis of rate of return over four quarters, while the overvalued group consistently underperformed the S&P 500. The results were encouraging.

Unfortunately, the Whitbeck–Kisor, and other such statistical models built upon regression techniques, have been plagued by instability in the regression coefficients over time, and have also been sample sensitive. For this reason, the models have not been widely used by practitioners. The idea is interesting, but the forecasting ability of the models has not been established. We can only encourage further research in this area for the present.

SUMMARY

Stock valuation efforts represent an attempt to uncover the relationships that exist among the variables which affect the prices of financial assets, and to provide a systematic way of considering these forces relative to current market price when selecting financial assets for a portfolio. The

---

17 For example, see Volkert S. Whitbeck and Manown Kisor, Jr., ibid., pp. 55–62; or Burton G. Malkiel and John G. Cragg, "Expectations and the Structure of Share Prices," *American Economic Review* 60, no. 4 (September 1970), pp. 601–617.

central idea underlying present-value approaches is that a security is worth the discounted present value of all future cash flows generated through its purchase.

Some practitioners prefer using a price–earnings multiplier and forecasted earnings to generate intrinsic value estimates. The price–earnings multiplier approach is, however, merely a short-cut method where the impact of growth, risk, and dividend policy is supposedly captured in that multiplier.

It is important to recognize that, under conditions of uncertainty, intrinsic values can never be precise. Valuation models provide a systematic approach for assessing the impact of changing economic and company factors, through their effect on earnings, dividend policies, and risk, on the prices of financial assets. It is the understanding gained in the analysis that is important and useful, not the intrinsic value estimate in and of itself. We will be concerned with developing the information needed to effectively utilize valuation models to study these underlying relationships during the remainder of this book.

Appendix to Chapter 3

TABLE 3–A
Present Value of $1 Received at the End of the Year

Years Hence	1%	2%	4%	6%	8%	10%	12%	14%	15%	16%	18%
1	0.990	0.980	0.962	0.943	0.926	0.909	0.893	0.877	0.870	0.862	0.847
2	0.980	0.961	0.925	0.890	0.857	0.826	0.797	0.769	0.756	0.743	0.718
3	0.971	0.942	0.889	0.840	0.794	0.751	0.712	0.675	0.658	0.641	0.609
4	0.961	0.924	0.855	0.792	0.735	0.683	0.636	0.592	0.572	0.552	0.516
5	0.951	0.906	0.822	0.747	0.681	0.621	0.567	0.519	0.497	0.476	0.437
6	0.942	0.888	0.790	0.705	0.630	0.564	0.507	0.456	0.432	0.410	0.370
7	0.933	0.871	0.760	0.665	0.583	0.513	0.452	0.400	0.376	0.354	0.314
8	0.923	0.853	0.731	0.627	0.540	0.467	0.404	0.351	0.327	0.305	0.266
9	0.914	0.837	0.703	0.592	0.500	0.424	0.361	0.308	0.284	0.263	0.225
10	0.905	0.820	0.676	0.558	0.463	0.386	0.322	0.270	0.247	0.227	0.191
11	0.896	0.804	0.650	0.527	0.429	0.350	0.287	0.237	0.215	0.195	0.162
12	0.887	0.788	0.625	0.497	0.397	0.319	0.257	0.208	0.187	0.168	0.137
13	0.879	0.773	0.601	0.469	0.368	0.290	0.229	0.182	0.163	0.145	0.116
14	0.870	0.758	0.577	0.442	0.340	0.263	0.205	0.160	0.141	0.125	0.099
15	0.861	0.743	0.555	0.417	0.315	0.239	0.183	0.140	0.123	0.108	0.084
16	0.853	0.728	0.534	0.394	0.292	0.218	0.163	0.123	0.107	0.093	0.071
17	0.844	0.714	0.513	0.371	0.270	0.198	0.146	0.108	0.093	0.080	0.060
18	0.836	0.700	0.494	0.350	0.250	0.180	0.130	0.095	0.081	0.069	0.051
19	0.828	0.686	0.475	0.331	0.232	0.164	0.116	0.083	0.070	0.060	0.043
20	0.820	0.673	0.456	0.312	0.215	0.149	0.104	0.073	0.061	0.051	0.037
21	0.811	0.660	0.439	0.294	0.199	0.135	0.093	0.064	0.053	0.044	0.031
22	0.803	0.647	0.422	0.278	0.184	0.123	0.083	0.056	0.046	0.038	0.026
23	0.795	0.634	0.406	0.262	0.170	0.112	0.074	0.049	0.040	0.033	0.022
24	0.788	0.622	0.390	0.247	0.158	0.102	0.066	0.043	0.035	0.028	0.019
25	0.780	0.610	0.375	0.233	0.146	0.092	0.059	0.038	0.030	0.024	0.016
26	0.772	0.598	0.361	0.220	0.135	0.084	0.053	0.033	0.026	0.021	0.014
27	0.764	0.586	0.347	0.207	0.125	0.076	0.047	0.029	0.023	0.018	0.011
28	0.757	0.574	0.333	0.196	0.116	0.069	0.042	0.026	0.020	0.016	0.010
29	0.749	0.563	0.321	0.185	0.107	0.063	0.037	0.022	0.017	0.014	0.008
30	0.742	0.552	0.308	0.174	0.099	0.057	0.033	0.020	0.015	0.012	0.007
40	0.672	0.453	0.208	0.097	0.046	0.022	0.011	0.005	0.004	0.003	0.001
50	0.608	0.372	0.141	0.054	0.021	0.009	0.003	0.001	0.001	0.001	

(continued)

TABLE 3–A *(concluded)*

Years Hence	20%	22%	24%	25%	26%	28%	30%	35%	40%	45%	50%
1	0.833	0.820	0.806	0.800	0.794	0.781	0.769	0.741	0.714	0.690	0.607
2	0.694	0.672	0.650	0.640	0.630	0.610	0.592	0.549	0.510	0.476	0.444
3	0.579	0.551	0.524	0.512	0.500	0.477	0.455	0.406	0.364	0.328	0.290
4	0.482	0.451	0.423	0.410	0.397	0.373	0.350	0.301	0.260	0.226	0.198
5	0.402	0.370	0.341	0.328	0.315	0.291	0.269	0.223	0.186	0.156	0.132
6	0.335	0.303	0.275	0.262	0.250	0.227	0.207	0.165	0.133	0.108	0.088
7	0.279	0.249	0.222	0.210	0.198	0.178	0.159	0.122	0.095	0.074	0.059
8	0.233	0.204	0.179	0.168	0.157	0.139	0.123	0.091	0.068	0.051	0.039
9	0.194	0.167	0.144	0.134	0.125	0.108	0.094	0.067	0.048	0.035	0.026
10	0.162	0.137	0.116	0.107	0.099	0.085	0.073	0.050	0.035	0.024	0.017
11	0.135	0.112	0.094	0.086	0.079	0.066	0.056	0.037	0.025	0.017	0.012
12	0.112	0.092	0.076	0.069	0.062	0.052	0.043	0.027	0.018	0.012	0.008
13	0.093	0.075	0.061	0.055	0.050	0.040	0.033	0.020	0.013	0.008	0.005
14	0.078	0.062	0.049	0.044	0.039	0.032	0.025	0.015	0.009	0.006	0.003
15	0.065	0.051	0.040	0.035	0.031	0.025	0.020	0.011	0.006	0.004	0.002
16	0.054	0.042	0.032	0.028	0.025	0.019	0.015	0.008	0.005	0.003	0.002
17	0.045	0.034	0.026	0.023	0.020	0.015	0.012	0.006	0.003	0.002	0.001
18	0.038	0.028	0.021	0.018	0.016	0.012	0.009	0.005	0.002	0.001	0.001
19	0.031	0.023	0.017	0.014	0.012	0.009	0.007	0.003	0.002	0.001	
20	0.026	0.019	0.014	0.012	0.010	0.007	0.005	0.002	0.001	0.001	
21	0.022	0.015	0.011	0.009	0.008	0.006	0.004	0.002	0.001		
22	0.018	0.013	0.009	0.007	0.006	0.004	0.003	0.001	0.001		
23	0.015	0.010	0.007	0.006	0.005	0.003	0.002	0.001			
24	0.013	0.008	0.006	0.005	0.004	0.003	0.002	0.001			
25	0.010	0.007	0.005	0.004	0.003	0.002	0.001	0.001			
26	0.009	0.006	0.004	0.003	0.002	0.002	0.001				
27	0.007	0.005	0.003	0.002	0.002	0.001	0.001				
28	0.006	0.004	0.002	0.002	0.002	0.001	0.001				
29	0.005	0.003	0.002	0.002	0.001	0.001	0.001				
30	0.004	0.003	0.002	0.001	0.001	0.001					
40	0.001										

TABLE 3–B

Present Value of $1 Received Annually at the End of Each Year for N Years

Years (N)	1%	2%	4%	6%	8%	10%	12%	14%	15%	16%	18%
1	0.990	0.980	0.962	0.943	0.926	0.909	0.893	0.877	0.870	0.862	0.847
2	1.970	1.942	1.866	1.833	1.783	1.736	1.690	1.647	1.626	1.605	1.566
3	2.941	2.884	2.775	2.673	2.577	2.487	2.402	2.322	2.283	2.246	2.174
4	3.902	3.808	3.630	3.465	3.312	3.170	3.037	2.914	2.855	2.798	2.690
5	4.853	4.713	4.452	4.212	3.993	3.791	3.605	3.433	3.352	3.274	3.127
6	5.795	5.601	5.242	4.917	4.623	4.355	4.111	3.889	3.784	3.685	3.498
7	6.728	6.472	6.002	5.582	5.206	4.868	4.564	4.288	4.160	4.039	3.812
8	7.652	7.325	6.733	6.210	5.747	5.335	4.968	4.639	4.487	4.344	4.078
9	8.566	8.162	7.435	6.802	6.247	5.759	5.328	4.946	4.772	4.607	4.303
10	9.471	8.983	8.111	7.360	6.710	6.145	5.650	5.216	5.019	4.833	4.494
11	10.368	9.787	8.760	7.887	7.139	6.495	5.988	5.453	5.234	5.029	4.656
12	11.255	10.575	9.385	8.384	7.536	6.814	6.194	5.660	5.421	5.197	4.793
13	12.134	11.343	9.986	8.853	7.904	7.103	6.424	5.842	5.583	5.342	4.910
14	13.004	12.106	10.563	9.295	8.244	7.367	6.628	6.002	5.724	5.468	5.008
15	13.865	12.849	11.118	9.712	8.559	7.606	6.811	6.142	5.847	5.575	5.092
16	14.718	13.578	11.652	10.106	8.851	7.824	6.974	6.265	5.954	5.669	5.162
17	15.562	14.292	12.166	10.477	9.122	8.022	7.120	6.373	6.047	5.749	5.222
18	16.398	14.992	12.659	10.828	9.372	8.201	7.250	6.467	6.128	5.818	5.273
19	17.226	15.678	13.134	11.158	9.604	8.365	7.366	6.550	6.198	5.877	5.316
20	18.046	16.351	13.590	11.470	9.818	8.514	7.469	6.623	6.259	5.929	5.353
21	18.857	17.011	14.029	11.764	10.017	8.649	7.562	6.687	6.312	5.973	5.384
22	19.660	17.658	14.451	12.042	10.201	8.772	7.645	6.743	6.359	6.011	5.410
23	20.456	18.292	14.857	12.303	10.371	8.883	7.718	6.792	6.399	6.044	5.432
24	21.243	18.914	15.247	12.550	10.529	8.985	7.784	6.835	6.434	6.073	5.451
25	22.023	19.523	15.622	12.783	10.675	9.077	7.843	6.873	6.464	6.097	5.467
26	22.795	20.121	15.983	13.003	10.810	9.161	7.896	6.906	6.491	6.118	5.480
27	23,500	20.707	16.330	13.211	10.935	9.237	7.943	6.935	6.514	6.136	5.492
28	24.316	21.281	16.663	13.406	11.051	9.307	7.984	6.961	6.534	6.152	5.502
29	25.066	21.844	16.984	13.591	11.158	9.370	8.022	6.983	6.551	6.166	5.510
30	25.808	22.396	17.292	13.765	11.258	9.427	8.055	7.003	6.566	6.177	5.517
40	32.835	27.355	19.793	15.040	11.925	9.779	8.244	7.105	6.642	6.234	5.548
50	39.196	31.424	21.482	15.762	12.234	9.915	8.309	7.113	6.661	6.246	5.554

(continued)

TABLE 3–B *(concluded)*

Years (N)	20%	22%	24%	25%	26%	28%	30%	35%	40%	45%	50%
1	0.833	0.820	0.806	0.800	0.794	0.781	0.769	0.741	0.714	0.690	0.667
2	1.528	1.492	1.457	1.440	1.424	1.392	1.361	1.289	1.224	1.165	1.111
3	2.106	2.042	1.981	1.952	1.923	1.868	1.816	1.696	1.589	1.493	1.407
4	2.589	2.494	2.404	2.362	2.320	2.241	2.166	1.997	1.849	1.720	1.605
5	2.991	2.864	2.745	2.689	2.635	2.532	2.436	2.220	2.035	1.876	1.737
6	3.326	3.167	3.020	2.951	2.885	2.759	2.643	2.385	2.168	1.983	1.824
7	3.605	3.416	3.242	3.161	3.083	2.937	2.802	2.508	2.263	2.057	1.883
8	3.837	3.619	3.421	3.329	3.241	3.076	2.925	2.598	2.331	2.108	1.922
9	4.031	3.786	3.566	3.463	3.366	3.184	3.019	2.665	2.379	2.144	1.948
10	4.192	3.923	3.682	3.571	3.465	3.269	3.092	2.715	2.414	2.168	1.965
11	4.327	4.035	3.776	3.656	3.544	3.335	3.147	2.752	2.438	2.185	1.977
12	4.439	4.127	3.851	3.725	3.606	3.387	3.190	2.779	2.456	2.196	1.985
13	4.533	4.203	3.912	3.780	3.656	3.427	3.223	2.799	2.468	2.204	1.990
14	4.611	4.265	3.962	3.824	3.695	3.459	3.249	2.814	2.477	2.210	1.993
15	4.675	4.315	4.001	3.859	3.726	3.483	3.268	2.825	2.484	2.218	1.995
16	4.730	4.357	4.033	3.887	3.751	3.503	3.283	2.834	2.489	2.216	1.997
17	4.775	4.391	4.059	3.910	3.771	3.518	3.295	2.840	2.492	2.218	1.998
18	4.812	4.419	4.080	3.928	3.786	3.529	3.304	2.844	2.496	2.219	1.999
19	4.844	4.442	4.097	3.942	3.799	3.539	3.311	2.848	2.496	2.220	1.999
20	4.870	4.460	4.110	3.954	3.808	3.546	3.316	2.850	2.497	2.221	1.999
21	4.891	4.476	4.121	3.963	3.816	3.551	3.320	2.852	2.498	2.221	2.000
22	4.909	4.488	4.130	3.970	3.822	3.556	3.323	2.853	2.498	2.222	2.000
23	4.925	4.499	4.137	3.976	3.827	3.559	3.325	2.854	2.499	2.222	2.000
24	4.937	4.507	4.143	3.981	3.831	3.562	3.327	2.855	2.499	2.222	2.000
25	4.948	4.514	4.147	3.985	3.834	3.564	3.329	2.856	2.499	2.222	2.000
26	4.956	4.520	4.151	3.988	3.837	3.566	3.330	2.856	2.500	2.222	2.000
27	4.964	4.524	4.154	3.990	3.839	3.567	3.331	2.856	2.500	2.222	2.000
28	4.970	4.528	4.157	3.992	3.840	3.568	3.331	2.857	2.500	2.222	2.000
29	4.975	4.531	4.159	3.994	3.841	3.569	3.332	2.857	2.500	2.222	2.000
30	4.979	4.534	4.160	3.995	3.842	3.569	3.332	2.857	2.500	2.222	2.000
40	4.997	4.544	4.166	3.999	3.846	3.571	3.333	2.857	2.500	2.222	2.000
50	4.999	4.545	4.167	4.000	3.846	3.571	3.333	2.857	2.500	2.222	2.000

P A R T

FUNDAMENTAL ANALYSIS

Chapter Four

Analysis of the Economy and Stock Price Aggregates

Fundamental analysis begins by determining the state of the economic environment and the implications of that environment for investment decisions. Growth is the focal point when analyzing equity investments, since growth in earnings and cash flow is expected to provide the basis for growth in dividends and stock prices.

The dividend yield on common stocks often is substantially lower than the current yield that can be obtained through long-term commitments, such as bonds. Accordingly, a stock can only be a desirable investment if one expects the growth in stock price to more than cover the gap in bond current yields and stock dividend yields. It is important, therefore, that the analyst form some judgment as to future long-term secular growth of the economy and its major components, and also an opinion concerning the cyclical outlook for the economy.

Economic and demographic analysis provides a background for industry and company analysis. Economic analysis also provides a background for estimating levels of interest rates and the long-term trend of price–earnings ratios. The analyst also would hope to spot sectors of the economy that appear to offer better-than-average profit opportunities and relate that information to specific companies. For example, in the 1950s demographic data suggested a change in the growth and age composition of the U.S. population. The percent of the population represented by the young and that represented by the old were expected to rise significantly, while the middle-age group remained static or declined a bit. Professor Grodinski, based on these data, recommended the purchase of Levi-Strauss (which manufactured clothing favored by the young) and the sale of Botony (which manufactured suits for the middle-aged businessman). Following those recommendations proved to be quite profitable. He also favored purchase of healthcare industry stocks, because of the expected growth in the older-age group that was being increasingly supported financially by the federal government. During 1995, healthcare company stocks (such as drug companies) rose sharply as a fear that restrictive price legislation and increased government control seemed no longer likely. Again, healthcare stocks proved to be profitable investments if purchased when prices were depressed and P/E ratios were at historical lows.

The future is unlikely to be a mirror of the past, but reviewing the past offers an understanding of the interaction among important variables and forms a base for making projections. We will, therefore, first review the long-term past record in an effort to overcome illusions held by some investors whose judgment is based on relatively short experience.

ANALYSIS OF THE ECONOMY

Investment performance is associated intimately with the economic activity of the nation. Stocks typically perform well when the economy is strong and prosperous. Not all industries and companies prosper equally, and the investor eventually must assess the impact of a changing economic environment on particular companies.

Underlying Determinants of the Level of Economic Activity

The broadest measure of economic activity is the Gross Domestic Product (GDP), which represents the value of the aggregate amount of goods and services produced in a national economy. The GDP can be viewed as an aggregate sales index, since the marketplace is the touchstone for measuring value.

Changes in the level of the GDP can be studied by considering the four basic variables underlying the level of economic activity listed below:

1. The anticipated growth of the employed labor force.
2. The trend in average number of hours worked per week.
3. The trend in output per hour worked, which is an indicator of labor productivity.
4. The change in the price level.

The first three factors determine the anticipated change in the real GDP, while the price level factor relates the analysis to the current GDP.

The above framework typically underlies GNP forecasting models, and has been used by Lacy Hunt in his *CM&M Economic Commentary*. The commentary forecast a 2.5 percent annual growth rate for the spring quarter 1987 for real GDP, and noted that two main factors supported that projection. "First, the index of aggregate hours worked rose at a 2.2 percent annual rate. Only a modest 0.3 percent rate of increase in productivity is needed in order for our GDP forecast to be achieved. This is well within recent experience. Productivity rose at a 0.4 percent annual pace in the first quarter and by an average 0.6 percent in 1985 and 1986. Second, with April and May data already reported, industrial production apparently gained at a 2.2 percent rate in the second quarter versus a better 3.2 percent rate in the first quarter."[1]

Investors can review well-known GDP prediction models in terms of their underlying assumptions for the basic variables, as is done above.

The long-term record of economic growth. Real GDP has grown at a 3.02 percent annual growth rate from 1960 through 1994, and GDP in current dollars grew at a 7.87 percent rate over the same period (see Table 4–1). The growth calculations were made using data in *The President's Economic Report for 1994*, Tables B–1 (page 274) and Table B–2 (page 276). *The President's Economic Report* offers a wealth of information on the economy and interesting discussions of economic prospects. Growth rates have been a bit higher since 1960, than if measured from 1929.

Table 4–1 also shows that the growth rate for industrial production, as measured by the Federal Reserve Board Index, has been consistently higher than the growth rate for real GDP. Moreover, cyclical fluctuations have been much wider for industrial production than for real GDP. The cycles of industrial productiion, the author believes, may have greater significance to an investor than the cycles of GDP which are so often referred to in the newspaper. Table 4–2 contrasts the industrial production and GDP cycles.

Business Cycles and the Investor

Cyclical patterns and trends are as important to the investor as are longer secular trends. Actually, the business profits and stock market cycles since 1961 appear to have been major factors causing many investors to question

---

[1] Lacy H. Hunt, *CM&M Economic Commentary*, "Outlook Update," CM&M Group, Inc., New York, July, 1987.

TABLE 4–1
Growth Rates for Gross Domestic Product (GDP) and
Industrial Production: Selected Periods

Years	Compound Growth Rate In		
	GDP Real (%)	GDP Current Dollar (%)	Federal Reserve Board Index of Industrial Production (%)
1929–94	2.95	6.64	NA
1933–94	3.30	8.18	NA
1939–94	3.45	8.15	4.20
1960–94	3.02	7.87	3.38
1960–90	3.08	8.26	3.47
1960–85	3.15	8.60	3.70
1960–80	3.30	8.67	4.04
1960–75	3.30	7.81	3.76
1960–70	3.84	7.01	4.88
1960–65	4.62	6.48	6.29
1980–94	2.50	6.73	2.45
1980–90	2.63	7.43	2.34
1980–85	2.53	8.32	2.34
1985–94	2.49	5.85	2.52
1985–90	2.73	6.55	2.35
1990–94	2.20	4.98	2.74

the desirability of investment in common stocks in the late 1970s and early 1980s. For example, an investment in a portfolio of common stocks in 1968 that behaved as did the Standard & Poor's composite stock index would have shown a loss in 1969, 1970, 1971, 1974, 1975, 1977, and 1978. The portfolio would have grown at a compound annual rate of only 3.83 percent over the 17-year period ending at year-end 1985. In view of the high inflation experienced during the 1970s, this was not an exciting perform- ance. Stock prices began to rise sharply in late 1985, however, rewarding the patient investor. Market indexes reached a new record in 1995, reaching 4500 for the Dow-Jones Industrial Index by June 16, 1995. Interest in common stock investment was again strong, as we experienced one of the longest continued economic growth periods in our history.

TABLE 4–2
Business Cycles and Cycles of Industrial Production

	Business Cycles				Industrial Production		
	Through	*Peak*	*Duration (Months) Peak to Peak*		*Through*	*Peak*	*Duration (Months) Peak to Peak*
	Jan. 1893					Mar. 1892	
1.	June 1894	Dec. 1895	35	1.	Oct. 1893	Nov. 1895	44
2.	June 1897	June 1899	42	2.	Sept. 1896	June 1900	55
3.	Dec. 1900	Sept. 1902	39	3.	Oct. 1900	July 1903	37
4.	Aug. 1904	May 1907	36	4.	Dec. 1903	May 1907	46
5.	June 1908	Jan. 1910	32	5.	May 1908	Mar. 1910	34
6.	Jan. 1912	Jan. 1913	36	6.	Jan. 1911	Jan. 1913	34
7.	Dec. 1914	Aug. 1918	67	7.	Nov. 1914	May 1917	52
8.	Mar. 1919	Jan. 1920	17	8.	Mar. 1919	June 1920	32
						Feb. 1920	
9.	July 1912	May 1923	40	9.	Apr. 1921	May 1923	39
10.	July 1924	May 1926	41	10.	July 1924	Mar. 1927	46
11.	Nov. 1927	Aug. 1929	34	11.	Nov. 1927	July 1929	28
12.	Mar. 1933	May 1937	93	12.	July 1932	May 1937	34
13.	June 1938	Feb. 1945	93	13.	May 1938	Nov. 1943	78
					No Trough		
14.	Oct. 1945	Nov. 1948	45		Determined	July 1948	
15.	Oct. 1949	July 1953	56	14.	Oct. 1969	July 1953	60
16.	May 1954	Aug. 1957	49	15.	Apr. 1954	Feb. 1957	43
17.	Apr. 1958	Apr. 1960	32	16.	Apr. 1958	Jan. 1960	35
18.	Feb. 1961	Dec. 1969	116	17.	Feb. 1961	Sept. 1969	116
19.	Nov. 1970	Nov. 1973	47	18.	Nov. 1970	Nov. 1973	50
20.	Mar. 1975	Jan. 1908	74	19.	Mar. 1975	Mar. 1979	64
21.	July 1980	July 1981	18	20.	Jan. 1980	July 1981	28
22.	Nov. 1982	July 1990	108	21.	Nov. 1982	July 1990	108
23.	Mar. 1991			22.	Mar. 1991		

Source: *Business Conditions Digest* (January 1987)

TABLE 4–3
Business Cycles Expansions and Contractions in the United States 1854–94

| | Duration in Months | | | |
| | Contraction (Trough from Previous Peak) | Cycle | | |
Business Cycle Reference Dates		*Expansion (Trough to Peak)*	*Trough from Previous Trough*	*Peak from Previous Peak*
December 1854. . June 1857.	. . .	30	. . .	. . .
December 1858. . October 1860 . . .	18	22	48	40
June 1861 . . . . . . April 1865	8	46	30	54
December 1867. . June 1869.	32	18	78	50
December 1870. . October 1873 . . .	18	34	36	52
March 1879. . . . . March 1882	65	36	99	101
May 1885 . . . . . . March 1887	38	22	74	60
April 1888. . . . . . July 1890	13	27	35	40
May 1891 . . . . . . January 1893 . . .	10	20	37	30
June 1894 . . . . . . December 1895 .	17	18	37	35
June 1897 . . . . . . June 1899.	18	24	36	42
December 1900. . September 1902.	18	21	42	39
August 1904 . . . . May 1907.	23	33	44	56
June 1908 . . . . . . January 1910 . . .	13	19	46	32
January 1912. . . . January 1913 . . .	24	12	43	36
December 1914. . August 1918. . . .	23	44	35	67
March 1919. . . . . January 1920 . . .	7	10	51	17
July 1921. . . . . . . May 1923.	18	22	28	40
July 1924. . . . . . . October 1926 . . .	14	27	36	41
November 1927. . August 1929. . . .	13	21	40	34
March 1933. . . . . May 1937.	43	50	64	93
June 1938 . . . . . . February 1945 . .	13	80	63	93
October 1945. . . . November 1948 .	8	37	88	45
October 1949. . . . July 1953	11	45	48	56
May 1954 . . . . . . August 1957. . . .	10	39	55	49

(continued)

TABLE 4–3 *(concluded)*

| Business Cycle Reference Dates | Duration in Months | | | |
| | Contraction (Trough from Previous Peak | Expansion (Trough to Peak) | Cycle | |
			Trough from Previous Trough	Peak from Previous Peak
April 1958 . . . . . . April 1960	8	24	47	32
February 1961 . . . December 1969 .	10	106	34	116
November 1970 . . November 1973 .	11	36	117	47
March 1975 . . . . . January 1980 . . .	16	58	52	74
July 1980 . . . . July 1981	6	12	64	18
November 1982 . . July 1990	16	104	28	108
July 1980 . . . . July 1981	6	12	64	18
November 1982 . . July 1990	16	104	28	108
March 91	8		112	
Average, all cycles:				
1854–1982 (30 cycles)	18	33	51	[1]51
1854–1919 (16 cycles)	22	27	48	[2]49
1919–1945 (6 cycles)	18	35	53	53
1945–1982 (8 cycles)	11	45	56	55
Average peacetime cycles:				
1854–1982 (25 cycles)	19	27	46	[3]46
1854–1919 (14 cycles)	22	24	46	[4]47
1919–1945 (5 cycles)	20	26	46	45
1945–1982 (6 cycles)	11	34	46	44
Average, all cycles				

Note: Underscored figures are the wartime expansions (Civil War, World Wars I and II, Korean War, and Vietnam War), the postwar contractions, and the full cycles that include the wartime expansions: [1]29 cycles, [2]15 cycles, [3]24 cycles, and [4]13 cycles.

Source: U.S. Department of Commerce, Bureau of Economic Analysis, *Business Conditions Digest,* January 1987, p. 104.

The length of particular business cycles has varied, as shown in Table 4–3. Each cycle reflects particular characteristics that determine its length. It is useful to examine past cycles. Many economists might have had a better forecasting record had they considered the average length of past cycles—three-year minimum, five-year maximum. The mean length of the 30 cycles, 1854–1986, either from trough to trough or peak to peak was 51 months.

Since the 1930s there have been only three expansions that exceeded five years in length. The 1938–45 period reflected World War II and should be considered an aberration. The 1961–69 expansion was peculiar in that it included a mini-recession in 1967 that ended a 1961–66 corporate profits expansion of 83 percent, even though the economic expansion continued to December 1969. Corporate profits after taxes did not exceed the 1966 level until 1972—a major factor explaining the poor stock market performance during the period 1966–71. Therefore, of significance to investors, the profits recovery and expansion that began in the first quarter of 1961 ended in 1966 (5 years), not in 1969. The market discounted and signaled in advance this major profits change when it declined 27 percent in 1966. The market declined an additional 37 percent from December 1968 to May 1970, in anticipation of the 1970 decline in corporate profits. The long economic expansion ending in July 1990 (108 months from peak to peak) led to rapid growth in stock prices which continues in June 1995. This long upward growth cycle (from peak to peak) has roughly matched the 1961–69 cycle.

Daniel Gressel notes that post–World War II business cycles were mainly monetary or demand induced in nature. "In a typical pattern, the Federal Reserve prints money, interest rates decline, aggregate demand increases, aggregate supply increases to meet the demand, and inflation increases. With output running above potential and rapidly increasing inflation, the Federal Reserve is forced to tighten credit conditions. The interest rates increase, aggregate demand falls, aggregate supply falls to meet new lower demand and inflation falls."[2]

One could have felt at the beginning of 1994 that we were in a market environment similar to other tightening phases, since commodity prices were rising and interest rates had nearly doubled. Mr. Gressel, however, directs our attention to the Austrian economists investment-led explanation of the business cycle, emphasizing reductions in cost or increases in supply through technological breakthroughs as the explanation of a growth cycle. The rate of return on capital increases because of this. Dramatic enhancements in computers have led to cost reductions, union activity has lessened and the U.S. has been lowering trade barriers leading to greater mobility of

2 Daniel Gressel, *The Wall Street Journal*, Monday, June 19, 1995, p. A10.

capital. "If our expansion is dominated by these cost-reducing factors, instead of the typical demand-increasing factors,"[3] then recent sharp increases in stock prices (through June, 1995) is understandable. Investors must consider the causes underlying cycles and their implications for future profit growth. The anticipated behavior of corporate profits is the important variable.

It is interesting to note that the stock market typically reached bear market lows every four calendar years (not every 48 months) in 1949, 1953, 1957–58, 1962, 1966, 1970, 1978, and 1982. This reflects the constant repetition of the business and profits cycle recurring on the average of every three to five years. This pattern has been interrupted in the current long economic growth cycle, possibly demonstrating the investment-led explanation of the business cycle discussed above. Competitive firms, however, can keep expanding until they eventually overinvest, leading to the end of the long growth cycle. It would not, therefore, be surprising to see a return to the three- to five-year profit cycle in the future.

CORPORATE PROFITS

Corporate after-tax profit data go back only to 1929. For earlier data we used figures that link Cowels Commission earnings per share data to Dow-Jones Industrial Average stock indexes. The long-term record of growth for corporate profits, GDP, and stock prices is portrayed in Tables 4–4 and 4–5.

Over very long periods of time, corporate profits have grown at a faster rate than for real GDP and current GDP, though the growth rates were quite close for current GDP during the 1970–1994 period. Corporate profits both before and after have risen significantly as a percentage of real GDP since 1960, and have risen especially rapidly after 1980. When contrasted to nominal GDP, however, which is a more meaningful comparison, profits have risen as a percentage of GDP since 1986, but are well below figures recorded in the 1960s. The varying percentage of corporate profits to GDP over time show that the profit record has been more erratic than that of GDP and industrial production statistics. Remember, it is the profit record that is important for stock prices and dividends.

There have been only four five-year periods of strong corporate earnings growth, measured on a before-tax basis, during the years 1910–86. Earnings

---

3 Daniel Gressel, op.cit.

TABLE 4–4
Growth in Corporate Profits, GDP, and Stock Prices:
Compound Growth Rates, 1871–1994

Years	GNP and Profit Data			
	Current Dollar GNP (%)	*Real GNP (%)*	*Current Dollar Profits, All U.S. Corporations*	*Cowles Commission Earnings Linked to Dow-Jones Industrial Average Earnings Per Share (%)*
1871–1929	6.10	4.0	NA	2.4
1881–1980	6.31	3.6	NA	3.0
1929–1977	6.20	3.1	4.6	3.7
1929–1980	6.55	3.1	5.5	3.5
1933–1980	8.54	4.1	a	8.8
1933–1985	8.55	3.9	a	a
1970–1985	9.56	2.6	9.2	7.2
1933–1994	8.18	3.3	a	
1970–1994	8.22	2.62	8.59	
1980–1994	6.73	2.5	8.55	

Years	Stock Price Data		
	Dow-Jones Industrial Average (%)	*Current Dollars*	
		Standard & Poor's 500 (%)	*Standard & Poor's 400 (%)*
1871–1929	NA	NA	NA
1871–1980	NA	NA	NA
1929–1977	3.9	3.9	4.5
1929–1980	10.9	3.0	3.6
1933–1980	11.4	5.5	6.2
1970–1985	3.8	5.5	5.7
1933–1994	11.28	6.55	
1970–1994	6.97	7.38	
1980–1994	10.9	10.15	

aProfits were negative in 1933. Therefore, no meaningful calculation is possible.

TABLE 4-5
Corporate Profits and Gross Domestic Product (GPD) 1960–1994

Year	Real GDP	Current Dollar GDP	Corporate Profits Before Taxes				Corporate Profits After Taxes			
					% of GDP				% of GDP	
			$	Real	Nominal		$	Real	Nominal	
1960	1,970.8	513.3	50.7	2.57	9.88		28.0	1.42	5.45	
1961	2,023.8	531.8	51.6	2.55	10.31		28.8	1.42	5.42	
1962	2,128.1	571.6	59.6	2.80	10.43		35.6	1.67	6.23	
1963	2,215.6	603.1	65.1	2.94	10.79		38.9	1.76	6.45	
1964	2,340.6	648.0	72.1	3.08	11.13		44.1	1.88	6.81	
1965	2,470.5	702.7	82.9	3.36	11.80		52.0	2.10	7.40	
1966	2,616.2	769.8	88.6	3.39	11.51		54.9	2.10	7.13	
1967	2,685.2	814.3	86.0	3.20	10.56		53.3	1.98	6.55	
1968	2,796.9	889.3	92.6	3.31	10.41		53.2	1.90	5.98	
1969	2,873.0	959.5	89.6	3.12	9.34		49.9	1.74	5.20	
1970	2,873.9	1,010.7	77.5	2.70	7.67		43.1	1.50	4.26	
1971	2,955.9	1,097.2	90.3	3.05	8.23		52.6	1.78	4.79	
1972	3,107.1	1,207.0	103.2	3.32	8.55		61.3	1.97	5.08	
1973	3,268.8	1,349.6	116.4	3.56	8.62		67.1	2.05	4.97	
1974	3,248.1	1,458.6	104.5	3.22	7.16		52.7	1.62	3.61	
1975	3,221.7	1,585.9	121.9	3.78	7.69		71.0	2.20	4.48	
1976	3,380.8	1,768.4	147.1	4.35	8.32		82.8	2.45	4.68	

(continued)

TABLE 4-5 *(concluded)*

Year	Real GDP	Current Dollar GDP	Corporate Profits Before Taxes			Corporate Profits After Taxes		
			$	% of GDP Real	% of GDP Nominal	$	% of GDP Real	% of GDP Nominal
1977	3,533.3	1,974.1	175.7	4.97	8.90	102.6	2.90	5.20
1978	3,703.5	2,232.7	199.7	5.39	8.94	116.2	3.14	5.20
1979	3,796.8	2,488.6	202.5	5.33	8.14	114.5	3.02	4.60
1980	3,776.3	2,708.0	177.7	4.71	6.56	92.9	2.46	3.43
1981	3,843.1	3,030.6	182.0	4.74	6.01	100.9	2.63	3.33
1982	3,760.3	3,149.6	151.5	4.03	4.81	88.4	2.35	2.81
1983	3,906.6	3,405.0	212.7	5.44	6.25	135.4	3.47	3.98
1984	4,148.5	3,777.2	264.2	6.37	6.99	170.2	4.10	4.51
1985	4,279.8	4,038.7	280.8	6.56	6.95	184.2	4.30	4.56
1986	4,404.5	4,286.9	271.6	6.17	6.34	165.1	3.75	3.85
1987	4,539.9	4,539.9	319.8	7.04	7.04	192.8	4.25	4.25
1988	4,718.6	4,900.4	365.0	7.74	7.45	228.0	4.83	4.65
1989	4,838.0	5,250.8	362.8	7.50	6.91	221.5	4.58	4.22
1990	4,897.3	5,546.1	380.6	7.77	6.86	241.9	4.94	4.36
1991	4,867.5	5,724.8	390.3	8.02	6.82	259.2	5.33	4.53
1992	4,979.3	6,020.2	405.1	8.14	6.73	265.4	5.33	4.41
1993	5,134.5	6,343.3	485.8	9.46	7.66	312.5	6.09	4.93
1994	5,432.3	6,736.9	560.3	10.31	8.32	354.7	6.53	5.27

Source: *Economic Report of the President, 1995.*

rose 83 percent between 1925 and 1929, helping to fuel the strong growth in stock prices during that period. Profits then fell sharply during the Depression of the 1930s, and did not recover to the 1929 level until 1947–48. Corporate profits grew slowly during the period 1947–48 through 1960–61, rising only from $31.8 billion in 1948 to $51.6 billion in 1961—a compound annual rate of 3.8 percent per year. Profits then rose at a compound annual rate of 11.42 percent, to $88.6 billion dollars, during the five-year period ending in 1966, fueling a sharp rise in stock prices. Corporate profits then fluctuated around the 1966 level—only 90.3 billion in 1971—until 1973, when before-tax profits rose to $110.4 billion. Profits continued to rise sharply after 1973, though at a slower rate than in the 1961–66 period. Profit growth slowed markedly by 1982, and then resumed as stock prices rose to new records. The market appeared to anticipate a drop in future profit growth in October 1987, and, as previously suggested, fundamental factors supported such concern.

COMMON STOCK PRICE PERFORMANCE

Common stock prices trended downward during the period 1881–1898, reflecting flat corporate earnings. During the period 1899–1906, stock prices rose, reflecting a significant rise in corporate earnings. The stock price index then did not rise above its 1906–09 level until the 1925–29 bull market 16 years later, reflecting higher wartime earnings during the 1915–20 period. It then took 25 years before the price index again reached its 1929 level, in 1954. While investors may be correct in the long run, that may be too long a time for purposes of realistic investment decisions. In the 16 years from 1950 to 1966, stock prices rose spectacularly—the Dow-Jones Industrial Average from 160 to 1000 and the Standard & Poor's 400 (425) Industrials from 16 to 100.

History soon proved that the rapid growth in stock prices during the 1950–66 period would not be sustained. During the 1968–81 period, stock prices tended to move up and down around a horizontal trend line. An upward trend began again in 1982 and continued, with some downward interruptions into early 1987, before falling calamitously in October 1987. Stock prices then resumed their rise, culminating in record-breaking highs by June 1995. Stock prices also have become increasingly volatile, resulting in increased risk, especially where liquidity is important. This must be considered when planning a portfolio.

Price–Earnings (P/E) Ratios

Price–earnings (and price–dividend) ratios began to rise after 1955, reaching a high P/E ratio of 20.33 in 1961, suggesting market confidence in future corporate growth and expectations of relatively low risk levels for stock investors (see Table 4–6). They then fluctuated in a range of 17 to 18 during the years 1962 through 1972 before dropping sharply for the remainder of the 1970s to 1947–51 levels. P/E ratios really did not recover until 1983, but then rose sharply in the 1990s until 1994. The relatively high level of P/E ratios present in 1995 suggest caution in stock selection.

As previously noted in Chapter 3, price–earnings ratios can change daily as market prices change and should not be mistaken as definitive indicators of intrinsic value. Also, they may give a distorted view of relative value for a given company because of different accounting techniques used by different firms. Still, they do suggest the esteem in which a company is held by the market at a moment in time, and may be useful in suggesting when speculation or exaggeration of potential bad news is unduly affecting stock values in general. We do recommend that investors watch the historical level of both market average and company P/E ratios. Finally, in an investment induced (as opposed to aggregate-demand induced) economic cycle, they could well be a bit historically high, reflecting stronger than usual long-term growth opportunities.

Valuation logic and aggregate P/E ratios. Our study of valuation in Chapter 3 taught us that the value of any financial asset is the capitalized value of earnings, which provides the cash flows that are discounted. Investors can be said to have determined value by multiplying a capitalization rate (P/E ratio) by earnings. This raises the question, however, as to why P/E ratios vary so much from year to year (see Table 4–6).

In Chapter 3, we showed that a present-value dividend model could be converted into a price–earnings model of the following form:

$$P/E = \frac{D/E}{K - g}$$

The explanation for differing price–earnings ratios over time and among companies can be sought, therefore, by exploring the following three variables:

1. The dividend payout ratio D/E, or dividends divided by earnings.

TABLE 4–6
Mean Earnings–Price and Dividends–Price Ratios (%)
Standard and Poor's 500 Index

Year	Price–Dividend Ratio	Price–Earnings Ratio
1955	24.51	12.58
1956	24.45	13.25
1957	22.99	12.67
1958	25.19	16.05
1959	30.96	17.30
1960	28.82	16.95
1961	33.56	20.33
1962	29.67	17.18
1963	31.55	18.18
1964	33.22	18.80
1965	33.33	17.89
1966	29.41	15.08
1967	31.25	17.45
1968	32.57	17.64
1969	30.86	16.45
1970	26.11	18.35
1971	31.85	18.48
1972	35.21	18.18
1973	32.68	14.04
1974	22.37	8.63
1975	23.20	10.93
1976	26.53	11.24
1977	21.65	9.27
1978	18.94	8.31
1979	18.28	7.43
1980	19.01	7.90
1981	19.23	8.36
1982	17.21	8.62
1983	22.73	12.45
1984	21.55	9.98
1985	23.53	12.32
1986	28.65	16.42
1987	32.47	18.25
1988	27.47	12.48
1989	28.99	13.50
1990	27.70	15.46
1991	30.86	20.88
1992	33.44	23.70
1993	35.97	22.42
1994	35.46	16.92*

*Third quarter 1994

2. The risk-adjusted market-required rate of return on a stock or group of stocks (k). This represents the return required by investors to purchase the given stock or group of stocks.

3. The expected growth rate of dividends for the stock (g).

Historical data concerning dividend payout ratios is available, but the other two factors are more difficult to assess.

Determining (k): The required rate of return.   It is generally agreed that three basic factors determine the required rate of return (k): the risk-free rate of return demanded in that economy, the expected rate of inflation, and a risk premium.

The risk-free rate reflects the basic time value of money, assuming no probability of default and no inflation. Logically, the real risk-free rate should be determined by the real growth rate of the economy, which in turn is a function of underlying investment opportunities and the funds and resources available to take advantage of such opportunities.

The real growth rate of the U.S. economy generally has ranged from about 2.5 percent to 4.5 percent, and would likely be stable over long periods of time since the basic factors that determine real growth are slow to change.

The expected rate of inflation, however, can vary markedly from period to period, affecting the value of financial assets through its effect on k. The higher the expected rate of inflation, the higher will be k. Estimation of the expected rate of inflation is, therefore, also a critical factor affecting stock prices.

Determining (g): The growth rate of dividends.   Growth in dividends is determined by the growth of earnings, though the dividend growth rate also would be affected by changes in the dividend payout ratio. Growth in earnings can be studied by analyzing its underlying determinants.

While gross revenues (mainly sales) are the basic source of funds to a corporation, there may be revenue growth without a correlated growth in earnings. Sales prices may rise, but costs may rise faster, as has occurred in many industries at times since 1966. We must concentrate, therefore, on growth in earnings as the base supporting rising equity values.

Investors, when analyzing profitability, typically concentrate on earnings per share which is considered a more meaningful basic statistic for investment analysis than aggregate earnings. Growth in total dollar earnings may not translate into growth in earnings available to support share value. In fact, earnings per share could fall as reported earnings after taxes rose, because of an increase in the number of shares outstanding that exceeded the percentage increase in reported earnings (earnings dilution). Growth in earnings per share can be the result of either growth in the rate of return on stockholders' equity or growth in the total equity per share (book value per share), or both, as shown below, where EAC equals "earnings available to common stockholders" (earnings after taxes less preferred dividends):

$$\frac{EAC}{Common\ Equity} \times \frac{Common\ Equity}{Number\ of\ Shares} = \frac{EAC}{Number\ of\ Shares}$$

Over any extended period of time, there must be an increase in total invested capital to provide increases in earnings per share. Simply to generate an increased rate of return on a more-or-less stable capital base would be unusual. Growth in book value per share is the result of either earnings retention, the sale of additional stock at prices in excess of book value, or the repurchase of outstanding shares at a cost below book value per share. American corporations have, on average, raised about two-thirds of the funds used through earnings retention. A fast-growing corporation will, therefore, typically offer a low dividend payout ratio and, conversely, a high earnings retention rate.

It can be shown, using valuation models, that the rate of growth in earnings per share is the product of the rate of return earned on owners' equity times the proportion of earnings retained. This does assume, however, that past rates earned on owners' capital can at least be maintained. Moreover, it implies that if corporations in the aggregate (say in terms of the Dow-Jones Industrial Average or the Standard & Poor's Indexes) retain 45 percent of earnings on average and earn 11½ percent on owners' equity on average, earnings per share will grow for this group at about 5.18 percent per year (.45 × .115). This relationship is sometimes referred to as the sustainable rate of growth for a firm.

Return on owners' equity can be further analyzed by observing the following relationships:

$$\frac{EAC}{Total\ Assets\ (TA)} \times \frac{Total\ Assets\ (TA)}{Owners'\ Equity} = \frac{EAC}{Owners'\ Equity}$$

Thus, the two basic determinants of return on owners' equity are the return on total assets and the proportion of assets financed by owners' as opposed to creditors' funds.

Finally, we can usefully observe that return on total assets has two basic determinants:

$$\frac{EAC}{Net\,Sales} \times \frac{Net\,Sales}{Total\,Assets} = \frac{EAC}{Total\,Assets}$$

Let us now use the framework we have developed to assess the basic factors affecting the growth of dividends.

Dividend and profit growth analysis. Dividend growth can be expected to relate to a firm's earning growth over time. Accordingly, we have presented data for the basic factors underlying earnings growth for the Standard & Poor's 400 Stocks in Table 4–7. Total asset data was not available prior to 1976, limiting the data gathered.

Steady increases in book value per share over the period studied have supported earnings-per-share growth. Retention of earnings per share is the factor most commonly leading to increases in book value per share. The retention rate for all U.S. corporations was about 47–50 percent during the years 1965–72, and it seems reasonable to assume this also was true for the Standard & Poor's 400 Stocks. Beginning in 1973, the retention rate increased to the 57–63 percent range, and stayed in that range until 1981. The retention rate then dropped sharply, but the impact of this drop is somewhat mitigated by the sharp decrease in the inflation rate for the U.S. economy. The drop in retention rate, in and of itself, could suggest lowered business confidence in the prospects for future investment and slower profit growth in the future. This drop had not discouraged investors prior to September 1987 as stock prices rose to new records, but in October 1987 the Dow-Jones Index fell by over 30 percent in a week. Negative factors such as the trade deficit, the U.S. government deficit, and rising interest rates, coupled with programmed trading, took their toll.

Equity and asset turnovers tend to increase during inflation. The equity turnover did rise sharply to relatively high levels during the 1970s and early 1980s, when inflationary pressures were strong. Fortunately, equity turnovers remained high during the period 1982–85, though inflation fell. Firms are using their equity capital efficiently, at least in an historical sense. The rise in equity turnover is encouraging, but it must be noted that it occurred during one of the longest, continuous economic expansions on record. Firms may find it difficult to maintain such turnovers in the face of intense foreign competition and a possible slowdown in the economy.

After-tax profit margins fell sharply after 1979, to almost one-half of what they were in 1965. This is an adverse factor for investors. The question is, is the drop permanent or only fleeting? One could hypothesize that rising union power and increased foreign competition had permanently reduced

TABLE 4–7
Factors Underlying Earnings per Share and Dividend Growth, 1965–1985

Year	Return on Owner's Equity (EAC/OE) (%)	Book Value Per Share (OE/# of Shs.)	Return on Asset Invests (EAC/TA) (%)	Leverage Factor (TA/OE) (%)	Equity Turnover (Sales/OE) (%)	After-Tax Profit Margin (EAC/Sales) (%)	Turnover & Assets (Sales/TA) (%)	Retention Rate (%)
1965	12.64	43.50			1.85	6.82		
1966	12.88	45.59			1.94	6.64		
1967	11.76	47.78			1.92	6.12		
1968	12.27	50.21			2.02	6.07		
1969	11.86	51.70			2.10	5.65		
1970	10.28	52.65			2.09	4.92		
1971	10.80	55.28			2.14	5.04		
1972	11.71	58.34			2.21	5.30		
1973	14.15	62.84			2.37	5.96		
1974	14.17	67.81			2.69	5.28		
1975	12.11	70.84			2.61	4.63		
1976	13.91	76.26	66.64	2.09	2.58	5.42	1.23	60.3
1977	13.91	82.21	65.94	2.11	2.65	5.27	1.25	58.3
1978	14.50	89.34	66.73	2.17	2.74	5.30	1.26	59.1
1979	16.29	98.71	73.92	2.20	2.88	5.68	1.31	63.3
1980	14.65	108.33	65.43	2.23	2.96	4.95	1.32	59.2
1981	14.12	116.06	63.20	2.24	2.91	4.87	1.29	57.9
1982	10.82	118.60	47.05	2.31	2.74	3.96	1.18	45.5
1983	11.78	122.32	51.38	2.28	2.66	4.41	1.16	50.0
1984	13.98	123.99	57.95	2.37	2.92	4.75	1.23	58.2
1985	11.34	126.20	43.87	2.53	2.91	3.85	1.15	48.5

EAC = Earnings Available to Common Shareholders   OE = Owner's Equity   TA = Total Assets

Source: Author's calculations based on data provided in the *Financial Summary* published by Compustat Services Inc., Volume 6, Denver, Colorado, Standard & Poor's 400 Composite, November 6, 1986.

profit margins. National income data does suggest a real transfer from the corporate sector to government and individual sectors of the economy over the past decade. It is interesting to note that Kessel and Alchian found that the average increase in equity was greater for firms with lower wage ratios.[4] The relative importance of wages to total costs is worth considering when analyzing a firm, especially if inflation is anticipated. It is important to note, however, that the inflation rate fell sharply in the 1980s. Real returns, therefore, were not falling as fast as the dropping margin would suggest.

Professor Reilly examined the relationship between profit margins for the Standard & Poor's 400 stocks and the rate of inflation as measured by the Consumer Price Index for the period 1960–82.[5] The correlation was –0.60. He also considered the annual percentage changes in the two series, and the correlation was –0.11. One would expect profit margins to fall as inflation rose, and vice-versa. This did not work out in the 1970s, but the margin did fall sharply in 1985 when the rate of inflation had fallen. Inflation is bad for stocks since it brings about rising interest rates, a rising k, and therefore falls in stock values.

An increase in oil prices in mid-1987, rising wholesale prices, federal deficits, pressure on interest rates, and intense foreign competition all suggest that one cannot anticipate a rise in margins in the near term. This is adverse for investors. On the other hand, the relatively low inflation rate in mid-1987, the markedly increased inflow of foreign funds to our financial markets, and the continuing economic expansion should affect stock prices favorably. One cannot, however, be confident that inflow of foreign funds will not slow down and possibly leave the U.S. stock market if the dollar continues to fall and the trade and government deficits are not corrected.

INTEREST RATES

An interest rate is the price paid for loanable funds. It represents the required return, at a given moment, for a particular type of debt security, and is determined by the interaction of the supply of and demand for loanable funds.

---

[4] R. A. Kessel and A. A. Alchian, "The Measuring and Validity of the Inflation-Induced Drag on Wages Behind Prices," *American Economic Review* 50, no. 1 (March 1960), pp. 43–66.

[5] Frank K. Reilly, *Investment Analysis and Portfolio Management*, 2d ed. (Chicago: The Dryden Press, 1985), p. 387.

There are numerous alternatives available competing for the investor's dollar. Investors seek the highest return possible for the level of risk accepted when committing funds. It is important, therefore, that investors be aware of the pattern of yields available at any given time, and also that they understand why interest rates, and other yields, vary over time. If, for example, one makes the mistake of investing heavily in long-term bonds just before a sharp rise in the general level of interest rates, he or she will suffer serious losses in terms of capital and/or the current yield received on funds committed. Understanding the past will help develop a better feel for the future.

The Structure of Interest Rates

There is not just one interest rate, but a complex structure of interest rates that describes the pattern of interrelations of various maturities and risks, and reflects changing patterns in the demand for and supply of loanable funds. Typical short- and long-term yield patterns are shown in Figure 4–1 and 4–2. Generally, all interest rates move in the same direction, with short-term rates moving over a wider range. The longer the maturity, the higher the rate. There are exceptions, however. Short-term rates have exceeded intermediate-term rates and even longer-term rates. Also, within each maturity category, quality ratings differ. The higher the quality grade, the lower the rate.

One must be careful when comparing reported yields on tax-exempt securities with securities on which the interest received is taxable. Yields are reported on a before-tax basis; therefore, tax-exempt securities appear to offer much lower yields. Depending on one's tax bracket, however, the after-tax yield may be higher on the tax-exempt securities. Investors should use after-tax yields, based on their particular tax status, when making investment decisions. Call protection and marketability also affect interest rate patterns.

In periods of economic growth, yields on lower-quality debt issues tend to move closer to yields on high-grade issues. In periods of economic contraction, the yields on low- and high-grade issues tend to move further apart. This narrowing and widening of the yield spread can be observed in Figure 4–2. This change in yield patterns generally has been explained in terms of changes in investor psychology that take place over the economic cycle. The optimism that is generated during a long economic upswing is thought to cause investors to become less concerned about financial or default risk, while the pessimism associated with recessions is thought to

FIGURE 4-1
Short-Term Interest Rates: Money Market Discount Rate, Effective Date of Change; All Others, Quarterly Averages

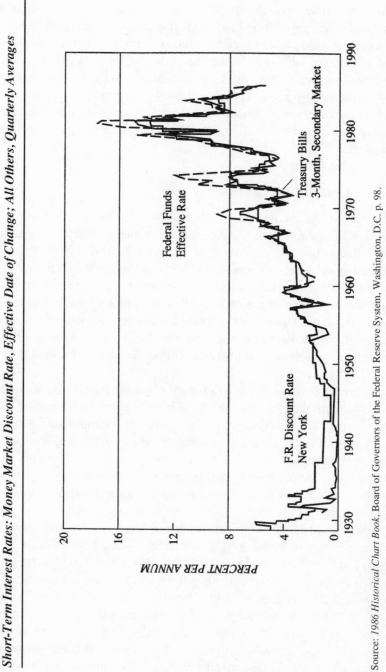

Source: *1986 Historical Chart Book*, Board of Governors of the Federal Reserve System, Washington, D.C. p. 98.

have the opposite effect. This suggests investors could profit by acquiring more-risky bonds during an economic downswing, when the added yield offered to take the higher risk is at a peak, and then concentrate on selecting high-quality securities at or near the peak of the economic cycle. One should watch the changing risk premiums over time and keep the patterns in mind when selecting bonds.

Interest rate patterns reflect demand and supply factors at work in the financial markets. The higher the demand, given a fixed supply of funds, the higher the level of rates, and vice-versa. The demand curve for loanable funds is subject to greater volatility than is the supply curve, and is more important in establishing rates. Salomon Brothers and Bankers Trust of New York publish excellent annual studies of the demand and supply factors, and forecast changes for the next year.

The Federal Reserve and Interest Rates

The Federal Reserve, in carrying out its policy decisions, enters the market on either the demand or supply side, thereby affecting interest rates, especially in the short-term markets. In periods of strong economic expansion, the Fed is likely to be worried about rising inflationary pressures. Demand for available funds tends to rise sharply during an expansion and is likely to exceed the supply of funds available, leading to rising rates. The Fed tends to restrict growth in the money supply during such a period to combat inflationary pressures. Conversely, in periods of economic contraction, demand for funds tends to fall, and the Fed typically allows the money supply to grow, leading to falling interest rates.

A major reason why interest rates for different maturity categories may move temporarily in different directions is that there are different supply and demand forces operative in the various segments of the financial market. Funds do not always move easily from one maturity category to another. Moreover, the Fed tends to concentrate its actions in the short end of the market, leading to greater volatility for shorter maturities.

Expectations of future rates are quite important when planning investment policy.

Historical Record of Interest Rates and Prices of Debt Instruments

In our chapter on valuation, we showed that bond prices and interest rates will vary inversely. Figure 4–2 shows the long-term secular trends that have

FIGURE 4-2
Long-Term Bond Yields, Quarterly Averages

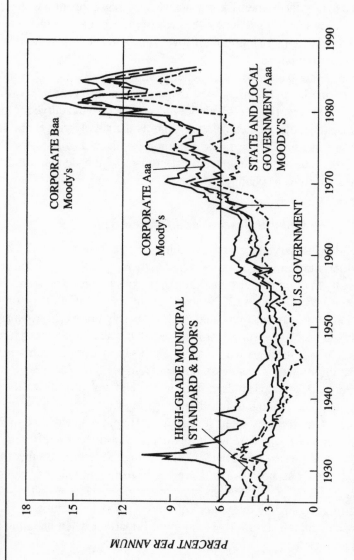

CORPORATE Baa
Moody's

CORPORATE Aaa
Moody's

STATE AND LOCAL
GOVERNMENT Aaa
MOODY'S

U.S. GOVERNMENT

HIGH-GRADE MUNICIPAL
STANDARD & POOR'S

PERCENT PER ANNUM

18
15
12
9
6
3
0

1930   1940   1950   1960   1970   1980   1990

Source: *1986 Historical Chart Book*, Board of Governors of the Federal Reserve System, Washington, D.C. p. 97.

developed in interest rates since 1925. Actually, there have been three major secular trends since 1900:

1. From 1900 to 1920, a secular rise in interest rates and corresponding decline in bond prices occurred.
2. From 1920 to 1946 a secular decline in interest rates and corresponding rise in bond prices occurred.
3. From 1946 to 1981, a secular rise in interest rates and corresponding decline in bond prices was experienced.

Since 1981, we have experienced a sharp drop in the general level of interest rates and, accordingly, bond prices have risen. Interest rates began to rise again after 1988, only to fall a bit after 1990.

Prior to the 1920s, an absolute low for bond yields in the United States was reached in 1899, when the average yield of municipal bonds (New England) and prime corporate bonds fell to between 3.07 and 3.20 percent. From 1899 to 1920, bond yields rose substantially, to 5.56 percent by May 1920.

Bond yields were at 5.50 percent in May 1930, and fell to 2.3 percent in April 1946. The yields on U.S. Government securities, however, were maintained by pegging operations conducted by the Federal Reserve during World War II, and we can learn little from this pattern. The problems that arose with the pegging operations suggest that we would not undertake such operations again, unless we were involved in a major war.

The period 1946 to 1981 saw a secular rise in interest rates, interrupted only temporarily during various economic recessions. Interest rates surpassed all previous highs, going above 16 percent in both long- and short-term markets by 1981. The sharp upswing in rates from 1978 to 1981 was accompanied by a sharp rise in the inflation rate, which reached double-digit levels. A relatively restrictive monetary policy was adopted by the Fed and large federal budget deficits were incurred, helping explain the sharp rise in interest rates. Inflation expectations are an important determinant of the level of interest rates. Interest rates fell sharply after 1981, leading to gains for bond investors.

Generally, higher yields can be found in the secondary markets (in which previously issued bonds are traded) when bond prices generally are rising, and in the new issues market when bond prices are declining. This occurs because price adjustments usually are reflected first in new issues. Inventories of bonds tend to grow in dealers' hands during declining markets (rising yields), and new issue prices are adjusted quickly downward to assure sale and avoid burdensome inventory levels. At the same time, most dealers are hesitant to mark down inventoried bonds unless the market shows real evidence of further deterioration. In rising markets, sales are brisk and dealers have no hesitancy to raise prices on new issues.

Nominal and Real Interest Rates

To represent cost or return, interest rates should be related to the rate of change in prices. One who has earned a total return of 14 percent from an investment in debt securities during a given year when the price level rose 10 percent has a net increase of only four percent in the purchasing power of the portfolio. The 14 percent return is referred to as the nominal rate of interest, while the four percent gain in purchasing power is referred to as the real rate of interest.

The real rate of interest and the rate of inflation, therefore, jointly determine the nominal rate of interest. The real rate of interest may be estimated by subtracting the quarterly percentage increase in the price level from the quarterly rate on three-month Treasury bills. Investors should concentrate on and be influenced by expected real rates of return when making investment decisions.

The real rate of interest has been volatile over the last two decades. The real rate is likely to decrease during recessions because there is a substantial amount of unused capital available and, therefore, a low return to capital. The real rate is likely to increase during periods of economic growth since capital is employed intensively and there is a need to expand the capital base.

Unexpected changes in the rate of inflation can also cause changes in the real rate. If financial markets expect a rising rate of inflation in the future, they will increase the nominal rates demanded for funds to maintain real returns. When unexpected changes occur, however, nominal interest rates will not initially correctly reflect the changes. For example, an unexpected increase in the inflation rate will tend to cause real rates to fall.

The real rate of interest, therefore, can be volatile, reflecting both changes in the strength of the economy and faulty inflationary expectations. The real rate tends to be low during recessions and high during periods of economic strength.

The Term Structure of Interest Rates

The term structure of interest rates seeks to explain the interrelationships between yield and maturity. A pattern of yield differentials that exists between securities that differ only in regard to maturity defines a particular yield structure. Risk or taxability are other factors that can cause yield differentials to exist.

The yield structure on U.S. Government securities is not affected by differences in financial risk or taxability, and is, therefore useful as a proxy for constructing a yield curve at a moment in time. The yield curves so constructing are represented in Figure 4–3, and show the diversity that has been experienced in the market. Why do these disparate configurations occur?

The May 1967 curve is a classic example of an upward-sloping curve that occurs typically in a recessionary period when interest rates are low. This shape can be explained in terms of expectations as to the future course of interest rates. When short-term rates are expected to rise in the future, it is desirable to stay short to facilitate reinvesting at the rising rates. Borrowers would prefer to invest long-term, locking in what they believe will prove to be relatively low rates. Demand for funds is concentrated, therefore, in the long end of the market, while the supply of funds moves toward the short-term market, explaining the rising curve. Risk considerations also would suggest a rising curve, since as maturity increases, price volatility increases, and so does the possibility of unexpected adverse events.

A declining curve was present in December 1969. Such a curve tends to exist when interest rates are at relatively high levels and are expected to decline. Borrowers then prefer to borrow short to refinance as rates fall, thereby concentrating demand in the short-term end of the market. Lenders prefer to lend long to lock in what they feel are historically high rates. Thus short-term rates rise to long-term levels. Moreover, high rates typically occur when the economy is strong, and the Fed will likely be restricting the money supply through operations in the short end of the market.

The humped-back curve (May 1970) tends to occur when interest rates are high and about to retreat to more normal levels. A flat-yield curve (June 1965) rarely exists over any period of time. It is a transitional structure usually followed by higher interest rates.

Money Supply Data

It is agreed that money and monetary policy influence economic activity, although the degree and direction of the influence is still controversial.

Monetarists stress the importance of control of the money supply in controlling output, employment, and inflation. They point out that changes in the growth of the money supply are highly correlated with changes in the

FIGURE 4–3
Yield Structure on U.S. Government Securities

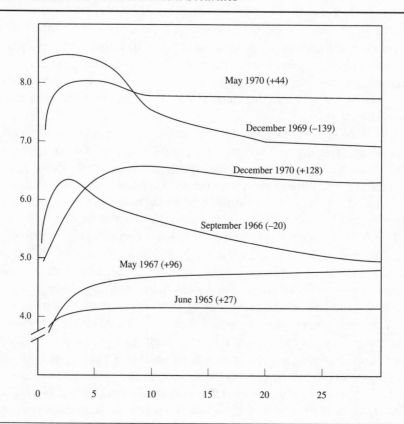

rate of total spending.[6] *Other economists argue that, in the long run, the* level of the money supply affects prices, but has no sustained effects on output.

The Fed is the main institution determining and implementing monetary policy using the following tools: (1) open market operations, which is the buying and selling usually of short-term government securities that affects the level of bank reserves and therefore the money supply; (2) changes in reserve requirements; and (3) changes in the discount rate, which is the rate

---

[6] The discussion is based on Lawrence K. Roos, "An Insider's View of Innovations and Monetary Policymaking: Implications for the Economy," *The CFA Study Guide I (Charlottesville, VA: The Institute of Chartered Financial Analysts, 1984), pp. 114–19.*

at which banks can borrow from the Fed. Investors should, therefore, be interested in Fed policy and statements made by the Fed. Publications of the Saint Louis Federal Reserve Bank are an excellent source of monetary data.

Several studies have found that money supply changes lead stock prices.[7] There is evidence, however, supporting the contention that the market anticipates changes in monetary growth, which means that investors cannot use past changes in the money supply to plan purchases and sales of securities.[8] The investor can utilize monetary data to develop a feel for the trend of the economy and interest rates rather than to pinpoint market action. This is useful, however, for purposes of developing profit expectations.

INFLATION AND COMMON STOCK

Persistent increases in the cost of living since World War II have reduced seriously the purchasing power of funds committed to fixed-income securities, and of idle cash balances. Common stocks often are suggested as an inflation hedge, based on assumed continued growth in corporate earnings and dividends and, therefore, the stock's value. In an effort to review the effectiveness of common stocks as an inflation hedge, Table 4–8 contrasts the change in price, earnings per share, and dividends per share for the Standard & Poor's 500 Stock Index against that of the Consumer Price Index (CPI) over the period 1933–93.

Table 4–8 shows that stock prices rose substantially more than did the CPI over the entire period studied, and dividends paid also rose substantially more. Common stocks, on average, did offer an effective inflation hedge over the entire time period, in fact offering substantial growth in real wealth. The data prepared by Robert Doyle and discussed in Chapter 1 further supports this conclusion.

However, the rise in stock prices during the period 1967–86 did not compensate for the loss in purchasing power suggested by the CPI, but would do so if growth in dividends is allowed for. Moreover, stocks did not offer an effective hedge when 1970 is the base year. An analysis such as this is deficient on two accounts. First, a stock average is not a realistic

---

7 For example, see Kenneth Homa and Dwight Jaffe, "The Supply of Money and Common Stock Prices," *The Journal of Finance* (December 1971), pp. 1045–66.

8 Michael Rozoff, "The Money Supply and the Stock Market—The Demise of a Leading Indicator," *Financial Analyst Journal* (September–October 1975), pp. 18–27.

TABLE 4–8
Growth in Stock Prices, Earnings per Share, and Dividends—
Standard & Poor's 500 Stocks: Selected Periods 1933–1993

	Standard & Poor's 500 Stocks			
Years	Year-End Price	Earnings per Share	Dividends per Share	Consumer Price Index
1933	10.10	0.44	0.44	38.8
1935	13.43	0.76	0.47	41.1
1940	10.58	1.05	0.67	42.0
1945	17.36	0.96	0.66	53.9
1950	20.41	2.84	1.47	72.1
1955	45.48	3.62	1.64	80.2
1960	58.11	3.27	1.95	88.7
1961	71.55	3.19	2.02	89.6
1965	92.43	5.19	2.72	94.5
1966	80.33	5.55	2.87	97.2
1967	96.47	5.33	2.92	100.0
1970	92.15	5.13	3.14	116.3
1975	90.19	7.96	3.68	161.2
1976	107.46	9.91	4.05	170.5
1977	95.10	10.89	4.67	181.5
1980	135.76	14.82	6.16	246.8
1982	122.55	12.64	6.87	289.1
1984	167.24	16.64	7.53	311.1
1985	210.68	14.63	7.90	322.2
1986	242.17	14.48	8.28	328.4
1987	247.06	17.50	8.81	339.8
1988	277.72	23.76	9.76	353.9
1989	353.40	22.90	11.05	371.0
1990	330.22	21.34	12.10	391.0
1991	417.09	15.97	12.20	407.5
1992	435.71	19.09	12.38	419.8
1993	466.45	21.88	12.58	432.3
	Compound Annual Growth Rates			
1933–1986	6.18	6.80	5.69	4.11
1945–1986	6.64	6.84	6.36	4.51
1950–1986	7.11	4.63	4.92	4.30
1960–1986	5.64	5.85	5.72	5.16
1967–1986	4.96	5.40	5.64	6.46
				(continued)

TABLE 4–8 *(concluded)*

| | Standard & Poor's 500 Stocks | | | |
Years	Year-End Price	Earnings per Share	Dividends per Share	Consumer Price Index
	Compound Annual Growth Rates			
1970–1982	2.40	7.80	6.74	7.88
1980–1986	10.13	–0.39	5.05	4.88
1970–1977	0.76	11.35	5.83	6.56
1933–1993	6.60	6.72	5.74	4.10
1945–1993	7.10	6.68	6.33	4.43
1950–1993	7.55	4.86	5.12	4.25
1960–1993	6.51	8.62	5.81	4.92
1967–1993	6.25	5.58	5.78	5.79
1970–1982	2.40	7.80	6.74	7.88
1980–1993	9.95	3.04	5.65	7.69
1970–1977	0.45	11.35	5.83	6.56
	Percentage Change			
1933–1986	2298	3191	1782	746
1945–1986	1295	1408	1155	509
1960–1986	317	343	325	270
1967–1986	151	172	184	228
1975–1986	169	82	125	104
1980–1986	79	–0.3	34	33
1970–1982	33	137	119	149
1970–1975	–0.2	55	17	39
1933–1993	4518	4872	2759	1014
1945–1993	4446	2179	1806	702
1960–1993	702	569	545	387
1967–1993	383	310	330	332
1975–1993	417	175	242	268
1980–1993	243	47	104	75
1970–1982	33	137	119	149
1970–1975	–0.2	55	17	39

proxy for an individual or many institutional portfolios. Second, the CPI may not represent the effect of inflation on a particular individual or a particular institution.

The early states of an inflationary period commonly are marked by large increases in the supply of money and credit, and thus by relatively low interest rates. Prices tend to rise faster than the money supply, reflecting inflationary anticipations, and the real supply of money then begins to decline. Interest rates rise sharply. The resulting tight liquidity situation and high interest rates are reflected in lower values for many financial assets, especially those offering fixed payouts to the holders. However, once the inflation rate begins to level off or starts to decline, even though prices continue to rise, stocks should begin to show more favorable price rises in line with expected growth in earnings and dividends. Thus, stocks perform poorly during an accelerating phase of inflation (e.g., the 1970–80 period), but may more than offset the effects of inflation, provided that corporate profits and dividends grow at a rate exceeding the average rate of inflation.

Alchian and Kessel[9] stress the importance of whether the firm is a net monetary debtor or creditor in evaluating its prospects for serving as an effective inflation hedge. A *monetary asset* is defined as an asset whose market value is independent of changes in the price level, such as money, accounts and notes receivable, and fixed-income securities that were purchased. A *monetary liability* is defined as a liability whose amount is independent of changes in the price level, i.e., denominated in dollars and payable in terms of the contractual amount no matter what happens to the price level during the time the debt is owed. Therefore, while banks are large debtors and would tend to gain during an inflationary period by repaying these debts with depreciated dollars, they are even larger creditors and lose when repaid with depreciated dollars. Therefore, on average, bank stocks have not proven to be good inflation hedges. Also, banks are characterized by large amounts of labor per dollar of invested capital, and wage costs for banks have tended to rise faster during inflationary periods than have the prices charged for bank services.

In summary, an accelerating period of inflation is not good for stock prices. Restrictive monetary and fiscal policies used to restrain inflationary pressures lead to relatively high interest rates, reduced real demand, and lower volumes of output. While unemployment often results, organized labor is able to increase dollar wage costs, and unit production costs tend to increase. Competition and political pressure make it difficult to raise prices sufficiently to maintain nominal, let alone real, profit margins, and corporate profits tend to decline in real terms. History does suggest that when inflation rates slow down appreciably, stock prices move up substan-

---

[9] Armen A. Alchian and Reuben A. Kessel, "Redistribution of Wealth through Inflation," *Science* 130, no. 3375 (September 4, 1959), pp. 535–539.

tially from lows recorded during the height of the inflation. When and if inflation rates recede, future returns on stocks are likely to be a function of corporate earnings and dividend growth, which in turn depend on the ability of corporations to earn an adequate return on invested capital. Notice the poor performance of the stock price index during the high inflation years of 1967–77.

Chapter Five

Financial Statements: A Basic Raw Material of Fundamental Analysis

A tendency toward an underlying continuity in business affairs makes the financial record, as portrayed in accounting reports, the logical point of departure for the projections needed for valuation estimates and risk analysis. Accounting reports call attention to the problems and the opportunities that confront an enterprise. Accounting has been defined as "the process of identifying, measuring, and communicating economic information to permit informed judgments and decisions by users of the information."[1]

Four major financial statements useful for investment analysis are outputs of the accounting system: (1) the balance sheet; (2) the income statement; (3) the statement of owners' equity (or retained earnings); and (4) the statement of changes in financial position. These statements and accompanying text are the main sources of financial information for persons outside the business organization. They attempt to summarize, in three or four pages, the activities of a business over a specified period of time (the income statement, statement of changes in financial position, and statement of owners' equity) or at a moment in time (the balance sheet). The statements portray where the firm is currently, and the operating results for the accounting period by which the firm arrived at this position.

One must recognize, however, that accounting language has many dialects. Words may not have the same meaning when used in accounting as

---

1 Charles J. Woelfel, Ezra Solomon and John J. Pringle, *Introduction to Accounting and Finance* (Malvern, OH: American Institute for Property and Liability Underwriters, 1978), p. 7.

in nonaccounting usage. For example, value, as applied to long-life assets in accounting, is historical costs less amounts recovered through charges to the income account, not current market value, replacement value, or liquidation value of that asset. Also, judgment often plays an important role in determining accounting values. Moreover, the rules that underlie the keeping of accounting records have changed over time in response to a changing society. One must, therefore, exercise caution when making comparisons of accounting data through time or between companies.

ACCOUNTING PRINCIPLES

The word *principle* has been defined as "a general law or rule adopted or professed as a guide to action; a settled ground or basis of conduct or practice."[2] The most authoritative source of accounting principles is the set of opinions of the Accounting Principles Board of the American Institute of Certified Public Accountants (AICPA). Also, the Financial Accounting Standard Board (FASB) from time to time issues Statements of Financial Accounting Standards, which represent authoritative expressions of generally accepted accounting principles. The financial reports of most companies of any substantial size are examined by certified public accountants who apply these principles. The Securities and Exchange Commission (SEC) also is an authoritative source of accounting principles, and their pronouncements generally have been consistent with the opinions of the Accounting Principles Board. Finally, some accounting principles have gained acceptance through widespread use.

Accounting principles do not, however, prescribe exactly how each detailed event should be recorded. Acceptable alternatives often are available for recording an event, such as LIFO or FIFO (last in, first out; first in, first out) for determining inventory costs, allowing judgment on the part of the accountant in reporting data. An analyst, accordingly, will not know the precise meaning of all the items on the financial statements without determining which of the equally acceptable possibilities has been selected for reporting purposes. Absolute uniformity in accounting data, over time or between firms, should not be assumed. The complex and varied nature of business operations and a rapidly changing economy suggest a need for flexibility in reporting, which is offered within the framework of principles developed for accounting.

---

[2] AICPA, *Accounting Terminology Bulletin*, no. 1, p. 9.

BASIC CONCEPTS

Basic concepts that underlie the preparation of financial statements, and that form the foundation on which accounting principles were built, are reviewed below.

The Money Measurement Concept

A standard of measure is needed to bring financial transactions together in a meaningful way. It would not be useful to present a list of the pounds of raw material in inventory, and the number of trucks, acres of land, and number of buildings owned. We need a way of expressing these things in terms that reflect value and that can be added and subtracted. The monetary unit becomes the common denominator allowing us to express the combined value of the many different assets and to measure the effect of operating policies on the well-being of the firm and its shareholders.

Adopting the money measurement concept does impose a severe limitation on accounting reports. For example, while changing laws, aggregate economic events, a strike, or the health of the firm's president all affect the future market value of a company, they are not recorded or accounted for specifically in the financial statements of that company. An analyst must seek information not found in the accounting reports to lend meaning to an investment analysis.

The usefulness of accounting data is reduced seriously when the value of money fluctuates. Sales and profits could increase in dollars during an inflationary period, when in terms of purchasing power the business is suffering real losses. We shall discuss inflation-adjusted accounting data and other implications of inflation for investment analysis at appropriate places in this book.

The Business Entity Concept

Accountants prepare statements for business entities, which are separate and distinct from the owners of that entity. At times analysts may be interested in something larger than the business entity. For example, a creditor can sue and collect from an individual's personal assets for a business debt, where that individual is the proprietor or a partner in the business. While the accounting records and statements would reflect only the business transactions, the creditor certainly could be interested in the personal assets of the principals.

A corporation is, by definition, a legal entity separate from the owners (stockholders). One corporation, however, might own a large block of stock of another corporation, and a share of stock in that company really shares in a broader interest than the individual corporate entity. The accountant may combine the businesses for accounting purposes and present a set of what are called consolidated financial statements.

The Going Concern Concept

Accounting assumes that a business will continue to operate for an indefinite period of time. The accountant, therefore, does not attempt to measure the current worth of the business. The accountant views himself or herself as a financial historian. Acquired but unused resources are not shown at their current value to a buyer, but at cost.

The success or failure of a business only can be determined by accumulating all transactions from the opening of the business until its liquidation. It would not, however, be feasible to await liquidation to judge the success or failure of current operating policies. While accounting for the success or failure of a business in midstream carries inaccuracies with it, since many transactions and commitments will be incomplete on any given date, an attempt must be made. The going concern convention recognizes this need.

Analysts must understand that a great deal of estimation enters into the process of preparing periodic accounting reports, introducing uncertainty into the interpretation of these reports. Some examples of the estimates necessary are:

1. The determination of the cost of inventory used in the production process and the valuation of inventory not yet used.
2. An estimation of possible losses that will be encountered in the collection of receivables or in other at-risk transactions.
3. The life and salvage value of assets, underlying the determination of depreciation expense.
4. The method to be used in estimating depreciation expense.
5. The extent of future warranty claims.

As noted above, assets typically are entered in the accounting records at the price paid to acquire them, thereby assuring objective determination of value. This historical cost is the basis for all subsequent accounting for the asset.

The worth of an item obviously may change over time, and the values recorded for assets in the balance sheet do not therefore reflect current worth or what an asset could be sold for. One cannot value a business by looking at the total value listed for assets in the balance sheet. A capitalization of the net earnings these assets generate, as estimated in the income statement, would form a more useful basis for estimating the current value of a business. Actually, valuation of a firm is related more usefully to cash flows generated through the investment of funds than to reported accounting profits.

Cost values for assets often are systematically reduced over the estimated life of a long-term asset for balance sheet purposes by processes called *depreciation, depletion,* or *amortization.* At the same time, that portion of historical cost charged as depreciation, depletion, or amortization expense for the current period is deducted from net total revenues to determine profit in the income statement. Also, if a long-term expenditure (such as the prepayment of five years of premiums for an insurance policy) is made, the expenditure would be set up as the value of the asset in the balance sheet, and one-fifth of that amount would be recognized each year for five years as insurance expense in the income statement. All expenditures are not expenses for purposes of determining net income. Thus, cash flow and reported profit are two different things.

Note that if a company pays nothing for an item, that item usually will not appear in the accounting records. Thus, the knowledge, contacts, and skill of employees and the good reputation of the company may be important assets to that company and have real value if that company were sold, but they do not appear on the financial statements since a cost has not been incurred. As another example, the death of a key executive could have an important effect on the value of that company's stock. The accounting records, however, will not be affected by this event.

The Dual-Aspect Concept

Accounting is governed by the principle of double-entry bookkeeping—the duality of every business transaction. All assets of the business are owned (claimed) by someone, either owners or creditors. Regardless of the number of transactions the firm engages in, this duality and balance prevails at all times. The duality is expressed in the basic accounting equation:

Total assets = Total liabilities + Owners' equity

When an asset is acquired by an entity, one of the following must also occur:

1. A liability is incurred, thereby increasing creditors' claims.
2. Ownership claims increase, since they were the source of the funds used to make payment.
3. Another asset was disposed of and is the source of the funds used in payment.

The duality of the transaction is clear.

To illustrate, assume a firm were created, borrowed $25,000 from a bank, and sold common stock for $50,000. The firm's balance sheet would then appear as follows:

Assets		Liabilities and Equity	
Cash	$75,000	Bank Loan	$25,000
		Owners' Equity:	
		Common Stock	50,000
	$75,000	Total	$75,000

Now assume that $25,000 is used as a down payment to acquire a building costing $100,000, with the remaining $75,000 borrowed through a mortgage loan. Further assume $25,000 is used to acquire inventory that the firm intends to resell. The balance sheet will now appear as follows:

Assets		Liabilities and Equity	
Cash	$25,000	Bank Loan	$ 25,000
Inventory			
(at cost)	25,000	Mortgage Loan	75,000
Building	100,000	Total Debt	$100,000
		Owners' Equity	
		Common stock	50,000
	$150,000		$150,000

Finally, let us assume that one-half of the inventory is sold for $20,000 in cash. Actually, revenues and expenses for a given accounting period are recorded separately, and the net effect of these items, in terms of the profit earned or loss incurred, is transferred to the retained earnings account on the balance sheet. We will, unrealistically, assume that no costs were incurred in generating the $20,000 of revenue, other than the cost of the inventory. We will not even recognize depreciation of the building for purposes of this illustration. We merely want to highlight the relation between the income statement and the balance sheet as reflected through changes in the retained earnings account. It would be useful to create the new balance sheet:

Assets		Liabilities and Owners' Equity	
Cash	$ 45,000	Bank Loan	$ 25,000
Inventory	12,500		
(at cost)		Mortgage Loan	75,000
Building	100,000	Total Debt	$100,000
		Owners' Equity	
		Common Stock	50,000
		Retained Earnings	7,500
	$157,500		$157,500

The retained earnings represent the profit on the sale of the inventory ($20,000 – $12,500).

Full Disclosure

Accountants are required to disclose all the facts that would have significant influence on the judgment of a user of their reports. Accounting policies, such as the inventory costing system used or the handling of a pension plan, must be disclosed in the footnotes to the annual report. Analysts should read and digest the footnotes before beginning to analyze the financial statements.

When an accounting method departs from the official position of the Financial Accounting Standards Board, that departure must be disclosed, along with justification for using the method chosen.

Accountants are expected to summarize and highlight key information in their reports. The full-disclosure concept can be violated by excessive disclosure.

Accrual Basis

Accounting records typically are kept on an accrual rather than a cash basis. Under an accrual system, revenue is recognized when earned and expenses are recognized when incurred, rather than when cash is received or expended. The use of the accrual basis requires a number of adjustments at the end of the accounting period, such as the determination of the amount of prepaid interest to remain in the balance sheet account and the amount to be recognized as expense during the current accounting period. Also, expenses that have been incurred during the current accounting period, but will not be paid until the next accounting period, must be recognized in the year in which those expenses were incurred. This would be accomplished by making a year-end adjustment entry, debiting, for example, wages expense (an expense in the income statement) and crediting accrued wages payable (a current liability in the balance sheet). Accordingly, reported profits and cash flow are two different things. Since users of financial statements are interested in both, the accountant prepares an income statement and then a summary cash flow statement.

Consistency

The consistency doctrine requires that the same treatment be given to comparable transactions from period to period. This allows users to compare accounting data and reports over time and study trends. For example, if a firm has chosen to use the FIFO inventory costing system in the past, it is expected to continue using that system in the future.

At times, a particular company does have a need to change a particular accounting method. Such a change can be made, but the justification for the change must be disclosed along with an explanation of the effects of the change on the financial statements. The justification and the explanation of effects are presented in the footnotes to the financial statements in the year in which the change occurs. Firms are not required to repeat this information in future years, which could mislead a user of the statements attempting to make comparisons through time. Accordingly, if an unusual change in data occurs between two given years, it is desirable to review the financial reports of the years involved to determine if a change in accounting methods occurred.

Accounting for Inflation

Businesspeople, financial analysts, and accountants have long realized that traditional financial statements prepared on the historical cost basis for measuring income and asset values produce misleading results when prices are changing. The inflation rate in the United States prior to the 1970s was relatively low, however, and many felt that the year-to-year changes in accounting data brought on by such inflation were insignificant and could best be estimated by the analyst.

The late 1970s were marked by unprecedently high inflation rates that led to strong pressures for change, resulting in the reporting of inflation-adjusted data in company annual reports. The SEC, in Accounting Series

Release 190 in 1976, required the nation's largest nonfinancial corporations to report, in their 10-K filings, estimates of the extent to which undervaluation of inventory and plant and equipment resulted in understatement of expenses and overstatement of profit in the income statement. Although not a comprehensive restatement of financial data to reflect the impact of inflation, the data generated were believed by many analysts, to offer a more useful suggestion of true earning power.

Financial Accounting Standards Bulletin No. 33 (adopted September 1979) required the disclosure in annual reports of two different types of inflation-adjusted financial data by publicly held corporations with total assets of more than $1 billion or inventories and property and equipment valued at $125 million. Inflation-adjusted data and their limitations are discussed in much greater detail in Chapter 7, after the subjects of depreciation and inventory accounting are more fully developed.

CONSOLIDATED STATEMENTS

Practically all large corporations are holding companies with subsidiaries and/or affiliates. A subsidiary is a corporation controlled by a parent company, the latter owning at least 50 percent of the voting stock of the subsidiary. To file a consolidated tax return, the parent must own at least 80 percent of the voting and nonvoting common stock of the subsidiary. The definition of an affiliate is not so precise. Affiliates include corporations that are controlled effectively, even though there is less than a 50 percent ownership.

Consolidated statements view all the companies involved as though they were a single entity. Accordingly, all assets, liabilities, and earnings or losses are combined with corresponding items in the financial statements of the parent company, after elimination of all intercompany transactions. Where the parent owns less than 100 percent of the subsidiary's common stock, the minority interest of outsiders is recognized in an owners' equity account.

Why consolidate? When income statements are not consolidated, only the dividend income from subsidiaries is included in the parent's balance sheet. When no dividends are received, therefore, there is no recognition of subsidiary earnings in the income statement of the parent company, resulting in understatement of the income in which the stockholders of the parent company have an interest.

To illustrate, assume Company X reports net earnings of $2,000,000 for the year and has 500,000 shares of common stock outstanding. Company X has therefore earned $4 per share. Further, assume that Company X owns 100,000 shares of the 150,000 shares of common stock of Company Y, and that Company Y earned $3 per share for the year. If Company Y paid no dividends for that year, none of its earnings would be reflected in an unconsolidated statement for Company X. Actually, two-thirds of the $450,000 of earnings of Company X, or $300,000, belong to Company X. Company X could, after all, have required Company Y to pay a dividend since it effectively controls Company Y. The analyst should therefore recognize that an investor in Company X has interest in earnings of $4.60 per share (the $300,000 spread over the 500,000 shares), not $4 per share.

Extent of consolidation. The annual report indicates whether statements are consolidated and the extent of their consolidation. It may state that "all subsidiaries are consolidated," or "all subsidiaries are consolidated except X financial subsidiary," or "all domestic subsidiaries are consolidated, but not foreign subsidiaries." Financial subsidiaries, even if owned 100 percent, often are not included in a consolidation because they have a large debt-to-equity ratio, which could make debt appear excessive on an operating parent's consolidated statement. A finance company, because of the liquid nature of its assets, is assumed to be able to safely carry a higher debt-to-equity ratio.

Reasons for not consolidating a subsidiary, other than the debt problem relative to consolidating a finance subsidiary, might be:

1. Where control was felt to be temporary, such as when the parent expects to dispose of the stock of the subsidiary in the near future.
2. Where there is uncertainty as to income, such as with foreign subsidiaries facing restrictions on conversion and repatriation of funds. Future taxes on repatriations also inject an uncertainty.

BASIC METHODS FOR ACCOUNTING FOR OWNERSHIP IN OTHER CORPORATIONS

Three methods may be used to account for ownership in a subsidiary:

1. Consolidated financial statements.
2. Equity method.
3. Cost method.

Consolidation and the equity method differ in the details recorded in the financial statements. Under the equity method the investment in a subsidiary initially is recorded at cost.[3] The carrying amount in subsequent statements is adjusted to recognize the investor's share of the earnings or losses of the subsidiary. Dividends received, for example, reduce the carrying amount of the investment. APB Opinion No. 18 requires that, in applying the equity method, any difference between the cost of an investment and the investor's equity in the net assets of the invested at the date of the investment be accounted for as if the invested were a consolidated subsidiary. Accordingly, the cost of investment would first be allocated to the investor's share of the invested's net identified assets and liabilities on the basis of the fair value. Only the excess of the cost of the investment over the sum of the amounts so allocated should be amortized over a period not to exceed 40 years as a reduction of the amount recognized each period by the investor as its equity in the earnings or losses of the invested.

Under the cost method, the investment in a subsidiary is recorded at cost, and income is recognized only if it is received by the parent as dividend distributions.

Limitations of Consolidated Statements

The major limitation of consolidated statements is their failure to report distinct information about the assets, liabilities, revenues, and expenses of the separate companies included in the consolidation. The individual statements for the separate entities that have been consolidated usually are not reported separately. Forecasting would be facilitated by showing the independent statements of the entities so as to reflect the varied resources, activities, and prospects of the several entities that have been combined.

Moreover, ratio analysis based on consolidated statements can deceive the analyst, since nonhomogeneous groupings often are reported. For example, a loss operation could be counterbalanced by a profitable one in a given year, when neither has strong prospects for the future. Earning power could then be overestimated.

---

3 APB (Accounting Principles Board) Opinion No. 18 covers the procedures that should be followed in applying the Equity Method.

Business Combinations

Acquisitions, mergers, and consolidations are common occurrences today. Two conflicting approaches have been developed to account for such events, the "pooling of interest" and "purchase" approaches.

Under the *pooling of interests* method, the former ownership interests continue (pooling assumes an exchange of voting securities), and assets and liabilities of the constituents are carried on the statement of the combined entity at their recorded accounting values. The *purchase method* views the combination as the acquisition by one entity of another. Assets and liabilities are recorded at cost, based on fair values at the date of acquisition (not recorded accounting costs). Moreover, the pooling method picks up income of the constituents for the entire fiscal period in which the combination occurs, while under the purchase method the acquiring entity picks up the income of the acquired entity only from the date of acquisition.

The rationale that accountants use in distinguishing pooling of interests from purchase combinations often may not be relevant to the analyst who is attempting to determine true recurring earnings. Room for abuses and loose interpretations are present under accounting rules when accounting for business combinations.[4] For example, broad latitude is possible in applying the rules of valuation and appraisal, and that can lead to understatement of asset values and, concomitantly, the understatement of costs and overstatement of income as those assets are depreciated.

Professors Briloff and Engler illustrate the effects of the pooling method by considering the companies shown in Table 5–1.[5]

Had the above acquisitions been recorded on the purchase basis, the acquiring companies would have reflected substantially higher values for the assets acquired. Accordingly, future costs related to the depreciation or amortization of those assets would have been substantially higher, leading to lower reported profits. Ratios used in analyzing profitability, liquidity, and long-term solvency would, therefore, be significantly different if the pooling approach, rather than the purchase method, were used.

---

[4] Professor Abraham J. Briloff illustrates many of the potential abuses in articles first appearing in 1967 in the *Financial Analysts Journal* and *Barrons.*

[5] A. J. Briloff and C. Engler, "Accountancy and the Merger Movement: A Symbiotic Relationship," *The Journal of Corporation Law* (Fall 1979).

Table 5–1
Data Highlighting Significant Effects of the Pooling Method (Millions of $)

Name of Acquiring and Pooled Company (Year of Acquisition)	Market Value of Share Issued in Acquisition	Book Value of Acquired Company	Unrecorded Value and Assets
Pepsico, Inc. and Taco Bell (1978)	$ 139	$ 36	$ 103
General Electric Co. and Utah International, Inc. (1976)	2,130	640	1,490

Interim Reports

Analysts must recognize the seasonal nature of corporate income when reviewing quarterly, semi-annual, or nine-month statement data. An analyst could be misled badly if he or she merely multiplies quarterly figures by four- or six-month figures by two to represent a year. When there is an important seasonal element, it would be estimated by reviewing past years' data, and current data should be adjusted accordingly.

Moreover, an analyst must recognize that corporations usually make adjustments only at the end of the year. These adjustments, therefore, are not reflected in interim statements.

INTRODUCTION TO THE BASIC FINANCIAL STATEMENTS

Useful approaches for analyzing the data offered in each of the four major statements will be developed in Chapters 6 through 11. At this point, we briefly review the structure and content of each statement, using the *1987 Annual Report* of Du Pont for illustrative purposes.

The Consolidated Income Statement

Table 5–2 reproduces the income statement as it appeared in the 1987 Annual Report for Du Pont. Total expenses incurred in operating the company are broken into major expense categories, and the total ($27.132 billion in 1987) is deducted from total revenues generated in a given year ($30.792 billion in 1987) to determine "Earnings before Taxes." Note that taxes other than income taxes were deducted as an expense category for

TABLE 5–2
Financial Statements—Consolidated Income Statement
(Dollars in millions, except per share)

	1987	1986	1985
Sales	$30,468	$27,148	$29,483
Other income	324	273	382
Total	30,792	27,421	29,865
Cost of goods sold and other operating charges . .	17,150	15,129	17,898
Selling, general and administrative expenses	2,716	2,350	2,077
Depreciation, depletion and amortization	2,225	2,119	1,796
Exploration expenses, including dry hole costs and impairment of unproved properties	459	550	561
Research and development expense	1,223	1,156	1,144
Interest and debt expense	435	438	513
Taxes other than on income	3,085	2,656	2,282
Gains from sales of businesses	(161)	(140)	(27)
Loss on restructuring of investments	—	178	226
Early retirement program expense	—	—	200
Total	27,132	24,436	26,670
Earnings before income taxes	3,660	2,985	3,195
Provision for income taxes	1,874	1,447	2,077
Net income	$1,876	$1,538	$1,118
Earnings per share of common stock	$ 7.39	$ 6.35	$ 4.61

Source: E. I. DuPont de Nemours and Company, *1987 Annual Report*, p. 26.

purposes of determining the earnings before income taxes. Income taxes are then deducted to determine "Net Income," which is earnings after income taxes. The net income represents the earnings available to common stockholders for purposes of determining earnings per share.

Investors often seek more detail than is provided in a summary income statement. Additional information can be gained from the notes to the financial statements, investment manuals (such as *Standard & Poor's, Moody's,* and *Value Line*), and analyses prepared by brokerage firms and other investment professionals. Practicing analysts may visit companies to gain additional data. We will suggest a general format useful for purposes of analyzing the income statement in Chapter 6.

For example, the *1987 Du Pont Annual Report* offers sales and operating income data by major industry segments and by geographical areas for 1987, 1986, and 1985. Moreover, the performance of each industry segment during the 1987 year and contrasted to 1986 and its outlook are discussed separately in an early section of the report. This information would be useful when attempting to forecast revenues and profits. It is important to remember that financial statements report on past history, while it is the future success and profitability of the company that will determine the success of an investment in that company.

The footnotes to the financial statements also discuss the accounting policies adopted by Du Pont and offer details on particular debt securities outstanding. Selected financial data adjusted for the effects of changing prices also are contained in the report.

The Balance Sheet

Note that assets are listed in the Balance Sheet (Table 5–3) in order of their liquidity. Liquidity refers to the length of time it normally takes to convert assets to cash through revenue-generating operations. Typically, cash acquired by a company is invested in inventory and plant and equipment. The inventory is then sold on credit terms, becoming accounts receivable, at a price that includes recovery of all costs including depreciation of plant and equipment and a profit. As receivables are collected, we are back to cash, which can be used to maintain the productive base of the company, replenish inventories needed in the production process, and finance growth through profits.

An appropriate balance of liquid versus relatively nonliquid assets is needed. If an excess of liquid assets is held, the opportunity for profit is sacrificed. An inadequate amount of liquid assets, however, may lead to an inability to pay bills and bankruptcy.

Liabilities are listed in the order in which they must be paid. The stockholders' equity represents residual claims on assets. The amount shown ($14.244 billion in 1987) need never be paid by the firm to anyone. It represents the owners' claim on assets, calculated on the basis of the original cost of those assets less charges to the income account to date (or book value). The amount of liabilities relative to the amount of equity for a firm is important to analysts, as it is an indicator of risk and leverage.

The Consolidated Statement of Stockholders' Equity

A potential stockholder would have interest in what caused the changes in stockholders' equity from year-to-year. For example, did an increase in stockholders' equity result from the sale of new stock or from the retention

TABLE 5-3

Financial Statements—Consolidated Balance Sheet (Dollars in millions)

December 31	1987	1986
Assets		
Current Assets		
Cash and Marketable Securities	$ 756	$ 584
Accounts and Notes Receivable	4,376	3,771
Inventories	4,342	4,253
Prepaid Expenses	479	352
Total Current Assets	9,953	8,960
Property, Plant and Equipment*	33,400	31,859
Less: Accumulated Depreciation, Depletion and		
Amortization	17,546	16,162
	15,854	15,697
Investment in Affiliates	541	469
Other Assets	1,861	1,607
Total	$28,209	$26,733
Liabilities and Stockholders' Equity		
Current Liabilities		
Accounts Payable	$ 2,422	$ 2,346
Short-Term Borrowings and Capital Lease Obligations . . .	1,641	1,625
Income Taxes	388	183
Other Accrued Liabilities	1,689	1,482
Total Current Liabilities	6,140	5,636
Long-Term Borrowing	3,018	3,227
Capital Lease Obligations	84	89
Other Liabilities	1,827	1,669
Deferred Income Taxes	2,801	2,648
Minority Interests in Consolidated Subsidiaries	95	90
Stockholders' Equity (See page 28)	14,244	13,374
Total	$28,209	$26,733

* Includes oil and gas properties accounted for by the successful efforts method of accounting.

Source: E. I. DuPont de Nemours and Company, *1987 Annual Report*, p. 27.

of earnings? The statement of stockholders' equity (Table 5–4) answers questions of this type.

Stockholders' equity is broken into four separate accounts: preferred stock, common stock, paid-in capital, and retained earnings. Preferred stock has a preference as to dividends at a stipulated rate that must be paid in any given year, before any dividends may be paid to the common stockholders.

TABLE 5–4

Financial Statements—Consolidated Statement of Stockholders' Equity
(Dollars in millions, except per share)

	1987	1986	1985
Preferred Stock, without par value—cumulative			
23,000,000 shares authorized; issued at December 31:			
$4.50 Series—1,672,594 shares (callable at $120) . . .	$ 167	$ 167	$ 167
$3.50 Series—700,000 shares (callable at $102)	70	70	70
	237	237	237
Common Stock, $1.66 ⅔ par value;			
300,000,000 shares authorized; issued			
at December 31: 1987—238,833,676;			
1986—239,978,627; 1985—240,636,707	398	400	401
Additional Paid-In Capital			
Balance at Beginning of Year	4,535	4,492	4,455
Common Stock			
Issued for Acquisition	—	42	—
Issued in Connection with Compensation			
and Benefit Plans	57	38	37
Repurchased and Retired	(37)	(37)	—
Balance at End of Year	4,555	4,535	4,492
Reinvested Earnings			
Balance at Beginning of Year	8,202	7,529	7,142
Net Income	1,786	1,538	1,118
	9,988	9,067	8,260
Preferred Dividends	(10)	(10)	(10)
Common Dividends (1987—$4.40;			
1986—$3.05; 1985—$3.00)	(792)	(734)	(721)
Total Dividends	(802)	(744)	(731)
Common Stock Repurchased and Retired	(132)	(121)	—
Balance at End of Year	9,054	8,202	7,529
Total Stockholders' Equity	$14,244	$13,374	$12,659

Source: E. I. DuPont de Nemours and Company, *1987 Annual Report*, p. 28.

Also, preferred stock typically has a preference to funds generated in the sale of company assets in the event of liquidation of the company. Most preferred stocks do not share in company earnings beyond their preference dividend and, therefore, do not have the growth potential associated with common stock.

Stock accounts, preferred or common, typically are kept at par value, which has no relation to the current market value of the stock. Note that Du Pont has a par value of $1.66 ⅔ per share while the common stock sold at over $80 per share in June 1988. When stock is sold originally by the company at a price in excess of par value, the additional payments are credited to paid-in capital. In June 1988, the market value of the 238,833,676 shares of Du Pont common stock outstanding as of December 31, 1987, would have been approximately $20 billion dollars (238,833,676 × $85/share), well in excess of the approximately $5 billion shown in the capital stock and paid-in capital accounts of Du Pont. It is important to recognize that accounting values do not represent market values.

The retained earnings account is the summation of all earnings of Du Pont since the company first began to operate, less all dividends paid out to stockholders and all charges made directly to the retained earnings account rather than to the income account. The amount shown for 1987 ($9.054 billion), however, has already been invested in the assets listed on the balance sheet. It is not a cash fund that could be used to pay dividends or expand operations.

Statement of Changes in Financial Position

This statement (Table 5–5) often is referred to as the statement of sources and uses of funds, or a cash flow statement. It shows how funds were obtained by the company during the year and how these funds were used. It is constructed by determining changes in balance sheet accounts from the prior year to the year being studied, and adjusting these data for fund flows that can be identified but are not accounted for accurately by balance sheet changes.

The statement is designed to answer the following types of questions:

1. How much of required capital to support continuing operations and growth was the firm able to generate internally and what amount did the firm have to raise in the money and capital markets?
2. How has the firm invested funds generated through operations and access to the money and capital markets?
3. Were externally raised funds in the form of equity or debt?
4. Has the firm been building up liquid assets to support an expanded level of operations or is it becoming less liquid?
5. Is the output of the company selling well or is it building up in inventory?
6. Are receivables being collected on time?

TABLE 5–5

Financial Statements—Consolidated Statement of Changes in Financial Position (Dollars in millions)

	1987	1986	1985
Cash and Marketable Securities at Beginning of Year	$ 584	$ 583	$ 674
Cash Provided by Operations			
Net Income	1,786	1,538	1,118
Depreciation, Depletion and Amortization	2,225	2,119	1,796
Increase in Deferred Income Taxes—Noncurrent	153	305	716
Dry Hole Costs and Impairment of Unproved Properties	272	372	347
Loss on Restructuring of Investments	—	178	226
Early Retirement Program Expense	—	—	200
Other Noncash Charges and Credits—Net	132	5	(15)
Cash Flow from Operations—Before Changes in Working Capital	4,568	4,517	4,388
Changes in Working Capital*			
Decrease (Increase) in Current Assets			
Accounts and Notes Receivable	(605)	273	(230)
Inventories	(89)	(380)	(81)
Prepaid Expenses	(127)	24	(5)
Increase (Decrease) in Current Liabilities			
Accounts Payable	76	(204)	105
Income Taxes	205	(248)	(139)
Other Accrued Liabilities	207	(125)	47
Increase in Working Capital	(333)	(660)	(303)
Net Decrease (Increase) in Working Capital from Major Acquisitions and Sales of Businesses . .	96	(110)	—
Increase in Working Capital—Excluding Major Acquisitions and Sales of Businesses	(429)	(550)	(303)
Cash Provided by Operations	4,139	3,967	4,085
Dividends Paid to Stockholders	(802)	(744)	(731)
Investment Activities			
Capital Expenditures			
Additions to Property, Plant and Equipment	(3,035)	(2,737)	(3,046)
Investment in Affiliates	(177)	(202)	(33)
Major Acquisitions			
Working Capital	—	(149)	—
Other Net Assets	—	(1,032)	—
After-Tax Proceeds from Sales of Businesses	447	179	21
Miscellaneous—Net	(88)	(136)	(306)
Cash Used for Investment Activities	(2,853)	(4,077)	(3,364)

*Excluding Cash and Marketable Securities, and Short-Term Borrowings and Capital Lease Obligations.

TABLE 5–5 (concluded)

	1987	1986	1985
Financing Activities			
Increase in Short-Term Borrowings and			
Capital Lease Obligations	$ 16	$902	$121
Changes in Long-Term Borrowing and			
Capital Lease Obligations			
Increases	115	642	237
Reductions	(329)	(610)	(478)
Increase (Reduction) in Borrowing and			
Capital Lease Obligations	(198)	934	(120)
Common Stock			
Issued for Acquisition	—	43	—
Issued in Connection with Compensation and			
Benefit Plans	58	40	039
Repurchased and Retired	(172)	(162)	—
Cash Provided by (Used for) Financing Activities .	(312)	855	(81)
Cash and Marketable Securities at End of Year . . .	$756	$584	$583
Increase (Decrease) in Cash and Marketable			
Securities	$172	$1	$(91)

Source: E. I. Du Pont de Nemours and Company, *1987 Annual Report*, p. 29.

Chapter Six

Analysis of the Income Statement: General Approach and Revenue Analysis

For many years, major emphasis has been placed on the income state-ment, not only in the case of common stock analysis but also in the case of bonds, private placements, and preferred stock analysis. The margin of safety for fixed-income security holders is provided by a corporation's earnings and cash flow. The value of the business reflects the amount that can be earned on the invested capital and the cash flow generated by that firm. Therefore, the analyst must determine a true earnings base of recurring earnings from which growth and volatility of earnings and dividends may be projected. All a common stockholder can receive from an investment are dividends and/or capital appreciation. Both are dependent on future earn-ings—and expectations by investors of future earnings and dividends.

INFORMATION PROVIDED BY THE INCOME STATEMENT

Security analysts seek information from the income statement in answering the following questions:

1. What is the true recurring earnings base that serves as a starting point for generating useful projections of future performance?

2. How has the company performed over a relatively long time horizon (10 years of data often are studied to encompass a business cycle), and in the recent past? What factors underlie the revenue and cost trends exhibited?

3. Is earnings growth consistent or is the company in decline? Do the earnings patterns from year to year display significant variability? If so, what causes this variability?

4. How does the company being analyzed compare with the earnings growth of the economy and the industry in which it participates? How does the company compare with competitors in terms of revenue, cost behavior, and profitability?

5. Does the company appear to have good control of costs?

The focal point of common stock analysis is on growth and profitability of the firm.

INCOME STATEMENT STRUCTURE

The most fundamental accounting principle applied to the income statement is that which requires the matching of revenues and expenses. As we discussed in Chapter 5, revenue is recognized when it is realized, not when the cash is received. The matching concept requires the recognition of all costs that are associated with the generation of the revenue reported in the income statement. Many subjective judgments are required of accountants in matching costs and revenues, leading to potential limitations of an analysis and possibly misleading conclusions if not properly considered by the analyst.

Income Statement Format

Balance sheet format is standardized in annual reports, but this is not true for the income statement. An analyst will find it useful to recast the income statement he wishes to study in the general form suggested in Table 6–1. Hopefully, more detailed information actually will be available, such as the major expense items making up the total of cost of goods sold, and that detail should be shown in the recast statements.

A spreadsheet of the company's income statements for about 10 years should be prepared to develop a feel for trends, revenue, and cost behavior

TABLE 6–1
Analytic Format for Income Statement

Major Divisions	Comments
Gross sales and revenue	Sometimes not given.
Sales return and allowances and cash discount	Sometimes not given.
Net sales or revenues	Often the first item in the income statement. SEC requires a breakdown of profits for each industry segment for which sales comprise 10 percent of the total. Also a breakdown of sales and earnings by broad geographic areas outside the United States.
Other income	Listed here in the AICPA* recommended form; but if it is material and nonrecurring, it is preferable to list below under extraordinary items.
Cost of goods sold	Rarely broken down into its components. It is useful to have detail on the components.
Gross profit	Net sales less cost of goods sold.
Gross profit margin	Percentage of gross profit to sales calculated by analyst.
Selling expenses	Promotion, selling, and distribution expenses.
General administrative expenses	Salaries, wages, office supplies, insurance, taxes other than income taxes, etc.
Profit from operations	Profit from operations in dollars and as a percentage of operating profit margin calculated by the analysts by dividing net operating profit by net sales.
Other income	Nonoperating income such as dividends and interest income typically are listed here. When it is regular and recurring in nature, the AICPA recommends showing it where indicated above; but if the items are substantial, analysts prefer that it be located here in the statement.
Other expenses	Nonoperating expenses such as bond interest, note interest, amortization, and bond discount.
Income before income taxes	
Income taxes	Federal and foreign income taxes.
Income before extraordinary items	Usually nonrecurring items of material amount, net of applicable income tax. Major items should be explained.
Extraordinary income and extraordinary expenses	

(continued)

---

* AICPA (American Institute of Certified Public Accountants).

TABLE 6–1 *(concluded)*

Major Divisions	Comments
Net income	Net income–profit margin; net profit divided by sales
Retained earnings at beginning of year	
Cash dividends on common stock	Also preferred dividends if any.
Cash dividends as percentage of net income	Payout ratio.
Retained earnings at end of year	

Per share of common stock:
  Income before extraordinary items
  Extraordinary items net of taxes
  Final net income
  Dividends	

over time.[1] Ten years usually is long enough to include a complete economic cycle. The spreadsheet can be entered in a computer, using Lotus 1-2-3® or a similar spreadsheet program, to facilitate analysis.

The analyst should determine and enter true recurring earnings for each year in the spreadsheet, which may be different than reported earnings. The analyst must reorganize and adjust for possible lack of uniformity in the accounting data (e.g., changes in methods used for reporting inventory) when preparing such a spreadsheet, to assure comparability of data.

ANALYSIS OF KEY ITEMS ON THE INCOME STATEMENT

The determination of net income involves two basic steps: (1) revenues attributable to the period reported must be separated from those that would be credited properly to other periods, and (2) the costs that were incurred in generating these revenues must be determined directly or by assignment to income statement accounts. The remainder of this chapter and chapters

---

[1] Standard & Poor's Compustat tapes contain income statements data and useful ratios covering many years for a large selection of companies. These data could facilitate preparation of spreadsheets.

7 and 8 are devoted to an analysis of the major items that require careful attention by the analyst. The relationship between items in the income statement usually is explored by means of ratio analysis, which will be discussed separately in Chapter 10.

Recognition of Revenue

Under the accrual system, the rules governing recognition of revenues appear straightforward. The rules, however, are subject to exceptions and a variety of interpretations that could mislead an analyst. For example, a profit is deemed to be realized when a sale is made, unless a serious question exists about the collectability of the resulting receivable. The judgment as to the noncollectability of a receivable may, however, be based on conservative or liberal assumptions. Not all banks agreed on the collectability of loans to Third World countries in 1987, and the extent of loan loss reserves set up for such loans can vary from bank to bank. Since the charge made to set up a loan loss reserve (or a bad debts reserve for a corporate receivable) reduces reported income for the period, reported profits by individual banks may not be comparable in terms of judging relative efficiency or future profitability.

The Focus Points of Analysis

Analysts have long stressed growth in demand for a company's products as important to successful investment. Growth in earning power, not sales per se, is the desired objective. Cost behavior, therefore, is important. Continued growth in profits over long periods of time, however, is not likely unless sales are growing. Cost economies usually are not repeated on a yearly basis.

The aim of sales analysis is to project revenues for possibly the next three to five years as a basis for generating cost and profit expectations. When studying historical revenue data, the analyst should be concerned with the size, trend, composition, and underlying determinants of those revenue patterns.

For the purposes of developing future sales forecasts, the analyst could:

1. Calculate the compound growth rate in sales over a period of about 10 years, to ensure including the effects of the business cycle.
2. Calculate a standard deviation around the average of the above data to assess the stability of revenue patterns over time.

3. Observe the resistance of company sales to negative economic and other factors.

4. Assess the major factors underlying the sales pattern observed.

Footnotes and discussion in the body of the financial report may offer information useful in estimating the physical sales volume. The analyst also can adjust reported sales data by utilizing a price index, such as the Consumer Price Index (CPI). An index adjustment will not generate physical volume figures, but the approximations of physical patterns generated can be useful.

Market Share Analysis

Analysts typically compare the sales patterns for a given company with those of its principal competitors and appropriate aggregate data (such as the GDP). Charting can be a helpful tool.

For purposes of growth comparisons, one should use semilogarithmic-scaled graph paper. Arithmetic-scaled paper can give misleading results, since equal space on a chart reflects equal absolute quantities, not rates of growth. Semilogarithmic-scaled paper represents equal percentage change (not absolute) by equal space changes. Growth is best measured in terms of percentage change, not absolute change, to avoid differing base problems.

For example, assume sales for Firm A grew from $1 million to $10 million over a 10-year period, while sales for Firm B grew from $90 million to $100 million over the same time period. If sales are charted on arithmetic scale paper, two parallel lines are shown, suggesting no difference in growth. Obviously, Firm A had had a much larger relative growth (25.9 percent compound annual growth rate for Firm A, compared to about 1.6 percent compound annual growth rate for Firm B). Charting on semilogarithmic-scaled paper would clearly show this, since the space from 1 to 10 is much deeper than the space from 90 to 100.

The slope of the sales line on a semilogarithmic-scaled chart and the changing character of that slope indicates the stability or the accelerating or decelerating nature of the demand for the company's products.

Sales Growth and Input-Output Analysis

Above-average sales growth for a company usually is predicated on expected rapid growth of the industry in which the company operates. A company may, however, accomplish above-average growth by gaining an increased share of total industry demand. Forecasting end-use demand for a company's products is therefore useful.

The heart of any really sophisticated system of forecasting demand on the basis of past demand–supply relationships rests on input–output tables. Input–output tables indicate how much each industry requires of the production of each other industry in order to produce each dollar of its own output. The various industrial subdivisions are listed both vertically and horizontally, similar to an intercity mileage chart on a road map. The individual inputs into a given industry are read vertically, while the industry's dollar sales to other specific industries are read horizontally. The U.S. Department of Commerce publishes these tables on an infrequent basis in the *Survey of Current Business*.

Product mix and market-share data can be important in spotting a growth company. For example, it was agreed in the 1970s that semiconductor producers emphasizing transistors would have a slower growth rate than those whose major product was integrated circuits. Moreover, those integrated circuit producers who specialized in devices that were particularly applicable to computers could be expected to grow more rapidly.

Trends and Common Size Statements

Common size statements can be useful for purposes of analyzing trends and the changing relationship between financial statement items. In a common size statement, all items in that statement are expressed as a percent of a base figure. For example, all items in each year's income statement could be presented as a percentage of net sales. By reviewing several years of such statements, one could observe changes in the relative importance of cost items, and how cost items vary as sales change.

Horizontal analysis is also a useful tool. In horizontal analysis, each item in the income statement is expressed as an index number calculated by dividing a given year's number by the number of a base year. Data on automobile companies is utilized to illustrate the process in Table 6–2. Net operating revenues increased by 76 percent from 1975 to 1981 for General Motors. This may sound impressive, until one notes that GNP increased 91 percent over the same time period. In other words, sales for General Motors grew at a rate below the economy's average during this time period, no doubt reflecting the rapid rise in sales of foreign car companies. During the period 1975–85, General Motors was the only U.S. automobile company to equal or exceed the growth of GNP. Interestingly, it is Ford Motor Company that adapted most effectively to changing demand and supply conditions in

TABLE 6–2
Horizontal Analysis of Operating Revenues for Automobile Companies

Company	Millions of $							Index Number (1975 = 100)						
	1975	1980	1981	1982	1983	1984	1985	1975	1980	1981	1982	1983	1984	1985
American Motors	2,552.6	4,039.9	2,588.9	2,878.4	3,271.7[1]	4,212.5	4,039.9	100	158	101	113	128	165	158
Chrysler	11,598.4	9,225.3	10,821.6	10,044.9[1]	13,240.4	19,572.7	21,255.5	100	80	93	87	114	169	183
Ford	24,009.1	37,085.5	38,247.1	37,067.2	44,454.6	52,336.4[1]	52,774.4	100	154	159	154	185	218	220
General Motors	35,724.9	57,728.5	62,698.5	60,025.6	74,581.5	83,889.8[1]	96,371.6[2]	100	162	176	168	209	235	270
Gross National Product (billions of dollars)	1,598.4	2,732.0	3,052.6	3,166.0	3,401.6	3,774.7	3,988.5	100	171	191	198	213	236	250

[1]Data include discontinued operations.

[2]This year's data reflect an acquisition or merger.

Source: Company data obtained from Standard & Poor's Industry Surveys, Autos—Auto Parts, Basic Analysis October 30, 1986 (Section 2), p. A95. GNP data obtained from *Statistical Abstract*, 1987.

the automobile market in recent years. Table 6–2 would not have suggested this. Remember, the key to successful investing is looking ahead.

We also could have contrasted growth of unit sales for individual car companies against growth in the total number of cars sold in the United States, emphasizing real growth by means of index numbers. One also could observe the reaction of sales of particular companies to changes in the general economic environment through horizontal analysis.

Installment Sales

Many companies recognize the entire profit for an installment sale when the sale is made, assuming the company is reasonably certain it will be paid. Certain types of sales may, however, result in periodic installment payments which could stretch over several years (e.g., a land development company). One could then raise the question as to the number of payments that would have to be received before the buyer has a sufficient stake to make continued payments relatively certain. The American Institute of Certified Public Accountants (AICPA) has issued standards governing the accounting for installment sales, but some companies may follow practices that are more conservative than the required standards while other companies follow only the minimally acceptable standards.

For tax purposes, companies typically report only actual income as payment is received. The effective tax rate, calculated for the company by dividing taxes paid by net income, therefore may well be lower than the applicable corporate rate would suggest. In other words, profits reported to stockholders typically are higher than the profits reported to the IRS when installment sales are involved. It would be helpful if corporations provided an estimate of the deferred taxes, and made adequate provisions for uncollectable receivables arising through installment sales.

Conglomerates and Sales Breakdowns

Analysts of diversified businesses face the problem of separating and understanding the impact that the different individual segments of the business have on the operational results of a firm. Opportunities for growth will vary among the different product lines, and this must be taken into account when forecasting sales and profitability. Analysts require information that is broken down to represent homogeneous groupings whose characteristics are similar in terms of growth potential, variability, and risk. A sample of the type of such a breakdown by Du Pont is shown in Table 6–3.

TABLE 6-3
Industry Segment Information

1987	Agricultural and Industrial Chemicals	Biomedical Products	Coal	Fibers	Industrial and Consumer Products	Petroleum Exploration and Production	Petroleum Refining Marketing and Transportation	Polymer Products	Consolidated
Sales to Unaffiliated Customers[1]	$3,979	$1,266	$1,770	$5,261	$3,284	$2,066	$9,031[2]	$3,811	$30,468
Transfers between Segments	575	7	58	91	63	1,066	305	135	—
Total	$4,554	$1,273	$1,828	$5,352	$3,347	$3,132	$9,336	$3,946	$30,468
Operating Profit	$ 708	$ 44	$ 234	$1,019	$ 383	$ 882	$ 154	$ 587	$ 4,011
Provision for Income Taxes	(270)	4	(80)	(462)	(142)	(782)	—	(240)	(1,972)
Equity in Earnings of Affiliates	25	—	3	67	(59)	—	23	2	61
After-Tax Operating Income	$ 463[3,4]	$ 48	$ 157	$ 624	$ 182	$ 100[6]	$ 177[7]	$ 34[3]	$ 2,100[8]
Identifiable Assets at December 31	$2,889	$1,417	$2,629	$3,502	$2,649	$5,080	$4,066	$2,874	$25,106[9]
Depreciation, Depletion, and Amortization[10]	$ 307	$ 85	$ 195	$ 334	$ 162	$ 900	$ 153	$ 249	$ 2,456
Capital Expenditures[11]	$ 323	$ 127	$ 127	$ 501	$ 279	$ 932	$ 213	$ 444	$ 3,035

(continued)

TABLE 6–3 (continued)

1986	Agricultural and Industrial Chemicals	Biomedical Products	Coal	Fibers	Industrial and Consumer Products	Petroleum Exploration and Production	Petroleum Refining Marketing and Transportation	Polymer Products	Consolidated
Sales to Unaffiliated Customers[1]	$3,396	$1,150	$1,501	$4,786	$2,839	$1,926	$7,893[2]	$3,657	$27,148
Transfers between Segments	538	5	38	63	81	902	318	158	—
Total	$3,934	$1,155	$1,539	$4,849	$2,920	$2,828	$8,211	$3,815	$27,148
Operating Profit	$ 347	$ 123	$ 189	$ 946	$ 297	$ 389	$ 623	$ 471	$ 3,385
Provision for Income Taxes	(128)	(32)	(59)	(447)	(100)	(448)	(227)	(207)	(1,648)
Equity in Earnings of Affiliates	22	—	(3)	43	(28)	—	18	2	54
After-Tax Operating Income	$ 24[12]	$ 88[13]	$ 130	$ 542[14]	$ 169[15]	$ (59)[16]	$ 414[1]	$ 266	$ 1,791[8,18]
Identifiable Asset at December 31	$2,954	$1,197	$2,700	$3,061	$2,440	$5,169	$3,904	$2,724	$24,149[9]
Depreciation, Depletion and Amortization[10]	$ 394	$ 63	$ 154	$ 319	$ 133	$ 960	$ 136	$ 261	$ 2,489
Capital Expenditures[11]	$ 310	$ 95	$ 136	$ 443	$ 263	$ 781	$ 233	$ 399	$ 2,737

(continued)

TABLE 6—3 (concluded)

1985	Agricultural and Industrial Chemicals	Biomedical Products	Coal	Fibers	Industrial and Consumer Products	Petroleum Exploration and Production	Petroleum Refining Marketing and Transportation	Polymer Products	Consolidated
Sales to Unaffiliated Customers[1]	$3,396	$1,150	$1,501	$4,786	$2,839	$1,926	$ 7,893[2]	$3,657	$27,148
Transfers between Segments	480	1	18	24	50	1,299	627	106	—
Total	$3,868	$1,017	$1,535	$4,507	$2,830	$4,758	$10,088	$3,485	$29,483
Operating Profit	$ (176)	$ 61	$ 188	$ 345	$ 284	$2,128	$ 434	$ 269	$ 3,533
Provision for Income Taxes	125	—	(57)	(131)	(98)	(1,804)	(177)	(97)	(2,239)
Equity in Earnings of Affiliates	18	—	—	29	(5)	—	18	1	61
After-Tax Operating Income[19]	$ (33)[20]	$ 61	$ 131	$ 243	$ 181	$ 324	$ 275	$ 173	$ 1,355[8]
Identifiable Assets at December 31	$2,364	$ 747	$2,559	$2,686	$1,909	$5,706	$ 4,196	$2,835	$23,002[9]
Depreciation, Depletion and Amortization[10]	$ 277	$ 57	$ 145	$ 260	$ 119	$ 786	$ 123	$ 228	$ 2,059
Capital Expenditures[11]	$ 332	$ 82	$ 129	$ 351	$ 257	$1,113	$ 289	$ 392	$ 3,046

[1] Sales of refined petroleum products of $8,126 in 1987, $7,018 in 1986, and $8,701 in 1985, exceeded 10 percent of consolidated sales.

[2] Excludes crude oil and refined product exchanges and trading transactions.

[3] Agricultural and Industrial Chemicals includes $31 gain and Polymer Products included $69 gain from side of U.S. high density polyethylene business and related ethylene facilities.

4. Includes gain of $31 from sale of a chlorine and caustic soda production facility.

5. Includes $28 write-off of inactive coal mines.

6. Includes $28 charge for abandonment of marginal domestic producing properties and $14 write-off of previously capitalized exploratory well costs; also reflects $45 benefit from settlement of certain sales contracts.

7. Includes $29 benefit from adjustment of prior year tax provisions.

8. The following reconciles After-Tax Operating Income to Net Income:

	1987	1986	1985
After-Tax Operating Income	$2,100	$1,791	$1,355
Interest and Other Corporate Expenses Net of Tax*	(314)	(253)	(237)
Net Income	$1,786	$1,538	$1,118

*Includes interest and debt expense and other corporate expenses such as exchange gains and losses, minority interests in earnings of consolidated subsidiaries, and amortization of capitalized interest. Also includes $40 charge in 1987 and $13 charge in 1986 for debt restructurings.

9. The following reconciles Identifiable Assets to Total Assets:

	1987	1986	1985
Identifiable Assets at December 31	$25,106	$24,149	$23,002
Investment in Affiliates	541	469	280
Corporate Assets	2,562	2,115	1,858
Total Assets at December 31	$28,209	$26,733	$25,140

10. Includes depreciation on research and development facilities, impairment of unproved properties and, in 1986 and 1985, depreciation reflected in loss on restructuring of investments.

11. Excludes investment in affiliates.

12. Includes charge of $76 associated with the planned dismantlement of chlorocarbons and chloralkali facilities, partially offset by gains of $31 on the sale of the company's 50 percent interest in Condea Chemi GmbH, a German affiliate, and $13 on the sale of the sodium silicates business.

13. Includes gain of $15 from sales of technology.

14. Includes gain of $30 on the sale of the "Reemay" and U.S.-based "Typar" businesses.

15. Includes benefit of $12 on withdrawal from the commercial propellants business.

16. Includes $45 benefit from adjustment of prior year tax provisions partly offset by a $35 write-off of an investment in a petroleum concession in the Gulf of Suez.

17. Includes $45 benefit from adjustment of prior year tax provisions.

18. Includes $54 reduction due to the Tax Reform Act of 1986.

19. Includes Early Retirement Program expense as follows:

Agricultural and Industrial Chemicals	$24
Biomedical Products	8
Coal	(4)
Fibers	49
Industrial and Consumer Products	18
Petroleum Exploration and Production	(14)
Petroleum Refining, Marketing and Transportation	(13)
Polymer Products	31
Total	$99

20. Includes loss of $66 attributable to the withdrawal from the company's investment in Syngas Company and the shutdown of an associated methanol plant, loss of $22 due to the shutdown of an ethylene production unit, and loss of $32 on disposition of DuPont Canada's interest in Petrosar Limited.

See Industry Segment Reviews for a description of each industry segment. Products are transferred between segments on a basis intended to reflect as nearly as practicable the "market value" of the products.

Source: E. I. Du Pont de Nemours and Company, *1987 Annual Report*, pp. 38 & 39.

The *1987 Du Pont Annual Report* also offered seven pages of discussion, reviewing past performance of each industry segment shown in Table 6–3 and commenting on the outlook for each segment. Du Pont also offered data covering capital expenditures, investment, employment, sales, net income, and net assets by major geographic areas in its 1980 annual report, but such data was not offered in the 1987 report.

The degree of disclosure of product line breakdown varies widely among companies. There are numerous difficulties, including problems of allocating overhead and interdivisional transfer pricing, in preparing such data. Moreover, management is reluctant to divulge information that might help competitors.

SFAS14[2] was issued by the Financial Accounting Standards Board (FASB) in 1976, establishing disclosure requirements concerning information about operations in different industries, foreign operations, and major customers. Companies are required in their annual reports to offer breakdowns of significant segments in terms of revenues, operating profit, and identifiable assets. Also, the method of accounting for transfer pricing and cost allocations are to be disclosed. A segment is significant if sales, operating profit, or identifiable assets are 10 percent or more of the combined accounts for all of a company's industry segments.

While disclosure of information on business segments is helpful, one must recognize the many judgments necessary for preparing such data, which limit its usefulness. Cost allocations often are arbitrary, and there are no generally accepted principles governing such allocations. Information on business segments must be treated as highly qualitative, and one must not attribute undue accuracy to such data.

Calculating Growth Rates

Analysts typically calculate compound annual growth rates, based on the logic of compound interest, when studying long-term trends in sales and other variables. A compound annual growth rate is that rate which, if applied each year for a given number of years to a beginning balance, will cause the balance to grow to the known ending value. Relatively inexpensive hand calculators, such as the Texas Instrument Business Analyst II, will make such calculations.

---

2 SFAS14, "Financial Reporting for Segments of a Business Enterprise."

One should always use a compound annual growth rate for time series, rather than a simple average growth rate. A simple average growth rate typically will overstate the growth experienced. To illustrate, assume sales for a given company rose from $2,000,000 to $3,000,000 over 10 years. The compound annual growth rate is 4.14 percent, calculated as shown below:

$$\begin{matrix} \text{Compound Annual} \\ \text{Growth Rate} \end{matrix} = \sqrt[n]{\frac{TV_n}{TV_0}} - 1$$

where:

TV_n = Total Value at End of Time Period

TV_0 = Total Value at Beginning of Time Period

n = Number of Years in Time Period

$$\sqrt[10]{\frac{3,000,000}{2,000,000}} - 1$$

$$1.0414 - 1 = .0414$$

The average growth rate is 5 percent (50 percent/10), which overstates the annual growth rate experienced.

If distortion is feared because of an atypical beginning or ending number, one might average data to determine the beginning and ending numbers, adjust any given year's data to a more "normal" level, or determine the rate based on regression analysis where all data are utilized.

Regression Analysis

Regression analysis is a valuable statistical technique that can yield useful insights when used properly. We can only introduce the subject in this book, and suggest that those not familiar with the tool review a statistics textbook.

Regression analysis can be used to examine the relationship between variables, either in a cross-sectional or a time series analysis. An analyst, for example, could, in a simple regression analysis, assess the strength of the relationship between disposable personal income and a company's sales. The correlation coefficient generated is a measure of the degree of association between the dependent and independent variables. Moreover, the regression line developed through such an analysis could be used as a beginning framework for generating a sales forecast. Actually, in generating a sales forecast, more than one independent variable might be used in the regression analysis (multiple regression). Curvilinear and multiple regression techniques may provide better forecasts if the relationship is not linear or depends on more than one independent variable.

As one becomes more sophisticated in analysis, the cost increases and may not justify the added expenditure of time and money. Also, underlying relationships can change markedly over time. Computers eliminate the need for manual calculations, however, and make the mathematical work simple.

Nonrecurring Items

Net income should reflect all operating items related to the current period, with segregation and disclosure of extraordinary and nonrecurring items. Nonrecurring gains and losses arise for reasons outside the regular course of business and are not expected to be repeated in future years. Therefore, nonrecurring revenues should not be included in a forecast of future revenues. Events which occurred in past years that can result in nonrecurring income are tax adjustments and/or tax forgiveness, litigation and claims and/or renegotiation, an accounting charge or change in accounting estimates, or a prior-period adjustment such as could result from foreign currency translations and adjustment. A sale of assets also could result in nonrecurring revenues, since a company does not often sell productive assets such as plant and equipment. Another example would be the proceeds of life insurance policies on key company officers. Where possible, the results of nonrecurring events should be placed in the year in which the event occurred to better understand year-to-year changes in revenues and income. For example, a tax refund received in 1987 for overpayment of 1986 and 1985 taxes should be handled by restating the revenues, costs, and income for 1986 and 1985. The adjustment is necessary to properly review trends over time. Of course, if the nonrecurring items are small, it is not necessary to make such adjustment.

Discontinuation of a product line or sale of a segment of the business can result in a large-magnitude nonrecurring item. The discontinuation or sale may well be the result of unprofitable operation in that segment of the business, and may include large termination benefits for employees. The effect on the future operations of the company must be analyzed carefully.

INDUSTRY ANALYSIS AND PERFORMANCE

While a broad holding of stocks (such as those included in the Standard & Poor's 500 Index) would have recorded little or no capital gains over various time periods after 1966, a portfolio invested in selected industry grouping could have shown excellent performance. The 46 Moody's Industry Groups reviewed in Table 6–4 shows that about half did as well as or better than the published market averages over the period 1957–59 to February 1981. Of the 35 Standard & Poor's Industry Groups shown in Table 4-6, again about half did as well as or better than the S&P 500 Index over the period 1985–1993. The performance of individual industry groups varies widely over any time period reviewed.

A firm's profits typically are affected by economy-wide factors (e.g., interest rates and price-level fluctuations), by factors specific to the product line or industry areas in which the firm operates, and by factors specific to the firm itself (e.g., quality of management and locational factors). Therefore, a part of the revenues and earnings of a corporation is determined by industry forces. It is important to attempt to assess which groups are likely to perform most favorably over the next 5–10 years.

Industry Growth and the "Life Cycle"

Some writers, notably Julius Grodinsky[3] drew a rough parallel between industry growth and the human life cycle. They point out that when new industries are born, there often is a rush by many companies to enter the field in this period of initial and rapid growth. This is followed by a shakeout period, with only a relatively few survivors, and by a continuing period of strong growth, although the rate of growth is slower than in the initial period. Grodinsky described these first two periods as (1) the pioneering stage, and (2) the expansion stage. Finally, industries are expected to stop growing, either living a relatively stable existence for an extended period of time or dying.

Grodinsky pointed out the great risk of selecting stocks in the pioneering stage, where little information about participants may be available. There is little or no past record to guide investors or aid in preparing future projections. Some suggest participating in the pioneering stage by buying stocks of many companies in the new industry, thereby spreading the risk.

---

3 Julius Grodinsky, *Investments* (New York: The Ronald Press, 1953), Part II.

TABLE 6–4
Market Price Trends for Industry Groups Based on Standard & Poor's Data

Industry—S&P Index	Base Year	1985	1990	1993	Compound Percentage Growth 1985-93
Oil Well Equip & Serv.	1941–43—100	1108.8	1862.9	1747.9	5.85
Electronics—Defense	1983—100	96.8	142.9	252.4	12.73
—Instrumentation	1970—10	69.8	55.4	126.8	7.75
—Semiconductors	1970—10	48.2	58.1	179.5	17.86
Broadcast Media	1941–43—10	1851.2	4239.6	7760.0	19.62
Cosmetics	1957—10	68.6	174.0	290.6	19.78
Beverages (Soft Drinks)	1941–43—10	259.8	824.3	1464.8	24.13
Health Care (Drugs)	1941–43—10	400.9	1077.2	1202.2	14.71
Health Care (Composite)	1987—100	—	174.0	262.0	NC
Tobacco	1941–43—10	205.2	953.6	1017.9	22.16
Publishing	1941–43—10	1102.0	1287.3	2161.1	8.78
Machinery	1941–43—10	164.8	227.1	380.8	11.04
Machine Tools	1941–43—10	131.1	58.1	97.6	NC
Office Equip. & Supplies	1982—100	164.4	149.2	291.3	7.41
Beverages (Alcoholic)	1941–43—10	138.4	296.2	343.1	12.02
Railroads	1941–43—10	141.2	197.9	313.3	10.48
Airlines	1982—100	183.9	235.1	278.0	5.30
Insurance (Prop. & Cas.)	1941–43—10	285.6	348.8	464.6	6.27
Insurance (Life)	1941–43—10	695.6	793.3	1415.5	9.29
Foods	1941–43—10	245.6	612.7	764.3	15.25
Aerospace	1941–43—10	303.8	362.8	544.1	7.56
Auto Parts	1970—10	27.8	24.5	61.7	10.48
Automobiles	1941–43—10	113.2	118.8	251.9	10.52
Building Materials	1941–43—10	128.4	158.7	342.2	13.04
Chemicals (Composite)	1992—100	—	157.4	231.3	NC
Banks (Composite)	1982—100	158.1	109.7	234.9	9.99
Retail Stores (Composite)	1941–43—10	101.8	188.7	321.0	15.44
Natural Gas	1941–43—10	334.2	408.7	415.1	2.75
Electrical Equip.	1941–43—10	639.3	841.0	1353.1	9.83
Textiles	1941–43—10	123.1	168.2	206.2	6.66
Financial (Misc.)	1970—10	24.7	26.0	53.5	10.14
Containers (Metal & Glass)	1941–43—10	106.3	228.2	444.1	19.57
Paper & Forest Prod's	1941–43—10	437.7	634.5	932.4	9.91
Retail (Food Chains)	1941–43—10	141.3	420.1	533.5	18.07
Retail (Gen. Mdse)	1970—10	16.0	28.3	49.8	15.25
S&P 500 Index	1941–43—10	186.8	334.6	451.4	11.66

Reprinted with permission of Standard & Poor's, a division of The McGraw-Hill Companies.

Grodinsky and the author feel the average investor is better served by concentrating on companies whose major product lines are in the second or third stage (especially the second stage). Moreover, we believe this analysis, while useful, must be brought into context with security price. Many stocks during the second phase (the growth phase) may sell at relatively high price–earnings (P/E) ratios that more than discount their growth potential.

AN ILLUSTRATED REVENUE ANALYSIS

An industry analysis lays the basis for analyzing company performance and future revenue prospects. A well-prepared analysis of Deere and Company, dated January 1981 and constructed by Jerry Anderson, while at Sanford C. Bernstein & Co., Inc., is used with permission of that company for illustrative purposes.

The report began with historical and forecast data for the United States agricultural tractor market as shown in Tables 6–5 and 6–6. Continued growth in the 40 p.t.o. (power take-off, the standard measure for agricultural tractor horsepower in the United States) was forecast, as well as continued expansion of the four-wheel-drive segment. While the under-40 p.t.o. segment was expected to expand rapidly over the forecast period, 1984–85 was expected to represent a peak in unit sales, as a fall-off in replacement demand was anticipated after that peak was reached. The under-40 p.t.o. market was dominated by Japanese manufacturers at the time of preparing the report, because of cost advantages and a paucity of U.S. manufacturing capacity for small diesel engines.

Deere's Industrial Position and Strategic Orientation

Among domestic manufacturers, Deere was believed to be the leader in every major segment of the two- and four-wheel-drive tractor market. Under-40 p.t.o. tractors were sourced from Yanmar, a Japanese vendor, and this source was considered safe for the future.

Deere's strategy for continued market leadership and penetration was based on two elements: (1) product quality, and (2) low-cost manufacture. Deere also maintained a highly efficient and highly regarded network of retail dealers, considered one of its greatest competitive advantages. Deere, at the time of the report, was thought to be the industry's lowest-cost producer of agricultural tractors in the domestic market. Financial plans were prepared and appeared to offer adequate and reasonable cost financing

TABLE 6–5
United States Agricultural Tractor Market—Industry Unit Sales

U.S. Horsepower Classification	1979	1980E	1981E	1984E
Under 30	41,820	38,015	42,000	53,000
30–39	7,477	6,725	7,600	9,690
40–49	17,055	16,300	16,575	16,975
50–59	12,632	11,850	12,550	13,710
60–69	14,788	12,700	13,100	12,700
70–79	6,790	5,565	6,525	6,695
80–89	11,460	9,510	11,150	11,480
90–99	2,275	1,910	2,175	2,250
100–119	15,022	12,150	14,400	15,085
120–139	25,910	20,600	23,800	23,500
140–159	11,407	9,475	10,600	10,925
160–179	4,728	3,925	4,450	4,885
Over 180	5,468	4,825	5,200	6,540
Total Two-Wheel Drive	176,832	153,650	170,125	188,235
170–199	4,944	4,550	5,350	6,565
200–249	4,926	4,100	4,625	5,535
250+	1,585	1,650	1,685	2,155
Total Four-Wheel Drive	11,455	10,400	11,600	14,255
Total Market	188,287	164,050	181,785	202,490

Source: Farm & Industrial Equipment Institute and Bernstein estimates. Sanford C. Bernstein & Co., Inc., New York, *Deere & Company,* January 1981, p. 18.

TABLE 6–6
Summary—Agricultural Tractor Market—Industry Model
Mix Analysis and Forecast

	1979	1980E	1981E	1984E
Under 40 p.t.o. Horsepower	26.18%	27.27%	27.28%	31.36%
40–99 p.t.o. Horsepower	34.53	35.25	34.15	31.51
100–139 p.t.o. Horsepower	21.74	19.97	21.01	19.05
Over 140 p.t.o. Horsepower	11.47	11.11	11.14	11.04
Total Two-Wheel Drive	93.92%	93.60%	93.58%	92.96%
Four-Wheel Drive	6.08%	6.40%	6.42%	7.04%
Total U.S. Market	100.00%	100.00%	100.00%	100.00%

Source: Bernstein estimates. Sanford C. Bernstein & Co., Inc., op. cit., p. 19.

TABLE 6–7
Research & Development Expenditures as a Percentage of Sales

Fiscal Year	Deer & Company	Allis- Chalmers	Caterpillar Tractor	Clark Equipment	Inter- national Harvester	Massey- Ferguson
1977	3.8%	3.4%	3.8%	1.2%	2.7%	1.9%
1978	3.7	3.4	3.6	1.3	2.6	1.6
1979	3.8	3.0	3.7	1.5	2.6	1.5
Three-Year Average	3.8	3.3	3.7	1.4	2.6	1.7
1979 Dollar Expenditure (millions)	$188.1	$58.9	$283.0	$26.3	$217.8	$44.3

Source: Corporate reports and Bernstein estimates. Sanford C. Bernstein & Co., Inc., op. cit. p. 22.

for purposes of carrying out the strategies. Research and development also was considered to be a vital part of the company's overall strategy. Deere was spending a larger percentage of sales revenues on research and development than its major competitors at the time of the report, as shown in Table 6–7.

MARKET PENETRATION FORECAST

Tables 6–8 and 6–9 compare Deere's market position in 1979 with its competitors. Table 6–10 shows Deere's 1979 and projected penetration in the U.S. market for agricultural tractors.

In the under-40 p.t.o. segment, Deere was expected to increase its share substantially on the strength of new product introductions. Limited gains were expected in the 40–99 p.t.o. and 100–139 p.t.o. segments because of market, and competitive factors. Both the 40–99 p.t.o. and 100–139 p.t.o. segments were expected to decline in relative importance to the entire market and Deere was expected to direct its attention elsewhere. Also, competitors were in the process of introducing new, more competitive models in these markets.

A significant increase in market share for Deere was expected in the four-wheel-drive segment of the market based on introduction of a new model and the relieving of capacity constraints.

TABLE 6–8
Two-Wheel Drive Agricultural Tractors, Estimated Domestic Market Share—1979

Company	40–99 H.P.	100–140 H.P.	Over 140 H.P.	Total Market
Allis-Chalmers	2%	2%	2%	6%
J. I. Case	3	3	2	8
Deere & Company	14	14	17	35
Ford Motor Company	9	2	0	11
International Harvester	8	7	4	19
Massey-Ferguson	9	1	1	11
White Motor	2	2	1	5
Other	4	1	0	3
Total	51%	32%	17%	100%

Source: Bernstein estimates. Sanford C. Bernstein & Co., Inc., op. cit., p. 23.

TABLE 6–9
Four-Wheel Drive Agricultural Tractors, Estimated Domestic Market Share—1979

Company	Estimated Market Share
Allis-Chalmers	7%
J. I. Case	14
Deere & Co.	29
Ford Motor Company	1
International Harvester	18
Massey-Ferguson	2
White Motor	5
Versatile	8
Steiger[1]	16
	100%

[1] Includes only those units marketed under the Steiger brand name.

Source: Bernstein estimates. Sanford C. Bernstein & Co., Inc., op. cit., p. 23.

The North American market for combine harvesters was believed to be in a mature phase. Total unit sales were expected to decline by about 1.0 percent per year over the 1979–84 forecast period. The same trends that

TABLE 6–10

United States Agricultural Tractor Market, Deere & Company Unit Sales

U.S. Horsepower Classification	1979E	1980E	1981E	1984E
Under 30	6,600[1]	6,045[1]	6,720[1]	9,145[1]
30–39	n/m[1]	100[1]	380[1]	725[1]
40–49	3,000[2]	2,895[2]	2,910[2]	2,970[2]
50–59	2,275[2]	2,135[2]	2,225[2]	2,435[2]
60–69	2,390	2,050	2,100	2,055
70–79	3,250	2,645	3,065	3,145
80–89	4,475[2]	3,710[2]	4,350[2]	4,705[2]
90–99	2,150	1,815	2,020	2,025
100–119	5,300	4,280	5,150	5,505
120–139	12,250	9,735	11,305	11,515
140–159	5,650	4,690	5,300	5,680
160–179	0	0	0	0
Over 180	3,250	2,895	3,225	4,185
Total Two-Wheel Drive	50,590	42,995	48,750	54,090
170–199	1,150	1,160	1,470	1,935
200–249	2,200	1,845	1,990	2,490
Over 250	0	0	0	110
Total Four-Wheel Drive	3,350	3,005	3,460	4,535
Total Market	53,940	46,000	52,210	58,625

[1] Comprises models sourced from Yanmar.

[2] Comprises units sourced from the Deere & Company factory in Mannheim, Germany.

Source: Bernstein estimates. Sanford C. Bernstein & Co., Inc., op. cit., p. 26.

were influencing the agricultural tractor market were felt to be operative in the combine harvester market—namely, the increase in size of the average farm and farmers' need for productivity improvements to offset inflationary cost increases. Estimates were prepared for unit sales of both rotary and conventional combines for the North America and export markets, and for Deere's share of these markets. Moreover, Deere was expected to introduce a new large-size rotary combine after 1984, following the next expected domestic agricultural equipment market cycle decline. During the interim, efforts of major competitors to concentrate on the rotary end of the market were expected to enable Deere to further its penetration of the conventional combine market.

Deere entered the construction and industrial equipment market for two reasons: (1) this market typically has a cycle that does not coincide with the agricultural equipment cycle, and (2) manufacturing both types of equipment provides an increased opportunity for vertical integration into the manufacture of a variety of shared components. Deere was working to increase product-line depth and breadth via progressive new product introductions and to take advantage of market segmentation. Deere was expected to expand its market share and experience revenue growth and profitability in this area of operations.

Historical and Forecast Summary

Each segment discussed above was analyzed extensively in this 123-page report. The report includes 91 tables and analyzes both revenues and costs by plant location and geographical areas. We are only summarizing the approach for illustrative purposes. The report concludes by presenting year-by-year forecasts by manufacturing plant, a historical and forecast consolidated income statement, a forecast balance sheet, and a forecast cash flow statement. Since we are interested in revenues analysis, the historical and forecast income statement is presented as Table 6–11.

The revenue estimates developed consider the basic five factors suggested by Michael Porter[4] somewhat modified and enlarged:

1. The threat of new entrants to the major markets served by Deere.
2. The threat posed by substitute products or services.
3. The possible entry of new products under analysis by the company.
4. The rivalry among existing firms serving the markets important to Deere, and Deere's present and expected position in those markets.
5. Deere's strategy for maintaining its leadership position in its markets, and its financial and other abilities to carry out these strategies.
6. The position in the life-cycle analysis approach of the major product lines of Deere.

We will postpone discussing cost estimates developed in this report until a framework for cost analysis has been developed. At that time, we will not only discuss cost and profit estimates, but offer a valuation estimate for Deere as of January 1981, using a dividend capitalization model.

---

4 Michael Porter, *Competitive Strategy: Techniques for Analyzing Industrial and Competitors* (New York: The Free Press, 1980).

TABLE 6–11
Deere & Company Consolidated Income Statement—Historical and Forecast ($ Million)

	1973	1974	1975	1976	1977	1978	1979	1980E	1981E	1984E
Total Sales	$2,003.0	$2,495.1	$2,955.2	$3,133.8	$3,604.0	$4,155.0	$4,933.1	$5,304.0	$6,263.3	$9,239.9
Interest and miscellaneous income	$ 45.7	$ 43.5	$ 39.5	$ 49.2	$ 56.3	$ 74.4	$ 81.8	$ 80.0	$ 87.7	$ 129.3
Foreign exchange gain	1.6	4.3	0.0	0.3	0.0	0.0	0.5	0.0	0.0	0.0
Total Revenues	$2,050.3	$2,542.9	$2,994.7	$3,183.3	$5,660.3	$4,229.4	$5,015.4	$5,384.0	$6,351.0	$9,369.2
Cost of goods sold	1,479.5	1,932.5	2,273.3	2,316.2	2,686.9	3,142.3	3,794.6	4,207.2	4,898.4	7,139.9
Gross profit	$ 523.5	$ 562.5	$ 681.9	$817.5	$917.1	$1,012.7	$1,138.5	$1,096.8	$1,364.9	$2,100.0
Selling, general and administrative	$ 189.5	$ 223.5	$ 274.6	$ 316.2	$ 347.6	$ 377.5	$ 444.4	$ 508.0	$ 572.9	$ 774.4
Research and development	73.9	86.1	98.0	108.4	137.5	155.0	188.1	201.5	248.0	361.1
Operating income	$ 260.1	$ 253.0	$ 309.3	$ 392.9	$ 432.0	$ 480.2	$ 506.1	$ 387.3	$ 544.0	$ 964.5
Interest expense	$ 27.4	$ 34.9	$ 67.4	$ 56.8	$ 63.5	$ 86.4	$ 95.5	$ 183.5	$ 162.1	$ 238.0
Foreign exchange loss	0.0	0.0	17.2	0.0	13.6	53.9	0.0	0.0	0.0	0.0
Miscellaneous expense	4.8	4.8	5.2	4.4	3.2	4.3	3.8	5.0	6.5	10.0
Total expense	$1,775.1	$2,281.8	$2,735.7	$2,802.0	$3,252.4	$3,819.4	$4,526.6	$5,105.2	$5,887.9	$8,523.4
Pretax income	$ 275.2	$ 261.1	$ 259.0	$ 381.3	$ 407.9	$ 410.0	$ 489.0	$ 278.8	$ 463.1	$ 845.8
Income taxes	121.1	112.3	103.7	165.4	181.9	184.5	214.9	117.6	208.4	380.6
Net income	$ 154.1	$ 148.8	$ 155.3	$ 215.9	$ 226.0	$ 225.5	$ 274.1	$ 161.2	$ 254.7	$ 465.2
Equity income	$ 14.4	$ 15.5	$ 23.8	$ 25.7	$ 29.6	$ 39.3	$ 36.5	$ 45.6	$ 45.0	$ 79.0
Net income	$ 168.5	$ 164.3	$ 179.1	$ 241.6	$ 255.6	$ 264.8	$ 310.6	$ 206.8	$ 299.7	$ 544.2
Net per share—primary	$ 2.88	$ 2.78	$ 3.01	$ 4.04	$ 4.24	$ 4.38	$ 5.12	$ 3.34	$ 4.72	$ 8.50
Net per share—fully diluted	$ 2.88	$ 2.78	$ 2.98	$ 3.89	$ 4.07	$ 4.20	$ 4.90	$ 3.27	$ 4.72	$ 8.50

Source: Corporate reports and Bernstein estimates.

Chapter Seven

The Income Statement: Cost of Goods Sold and Related Cost Items

Many income statements offered by firms today separate the results achieved through regular operations from those produced by non-operating and/or extraordinary activities of the company. Moreover, expenses often are classified by functions, e.g., the cost to produce goods, selling expenses, administrative expenses, and other expenses. This facilitates year-by-year comparisons of key expense categories and forecasting efforts.

We will concentrate on items affecting the cost of goods sold in this chapter, ending with a discussion of inflation adjusted accounting data. The analysis of other expense items will be covered in Chapter 8.

COST OF GOODS SOLD

At the moment that net income is increased by revenues derived from the sale of a product, it is also decreased by the costs associated with producing that product. If one thinks of a cashier in a supermarket, it is not difficult to understand that it would not be feasible to record the cost at the same time as sales value is running up for every item sold.

Accountants determine the total cost of goods sold for a period by a process of deduction. The value of inventory on hand at the beginning of the period is added to that acquired during the period to determine the total cost for all goods available for sale. Those units still on hand at the end of the period obviously were not sold. Accordingly, the value of goods on hand at the end of the period is determined by means of a physical inventory and subtracted from the costs of goods available for sale to determine the cost of goods sold figure used in the income statement.

Inventory Valuation and Price Level Changes

Inventory, in accordance with accounting standards should be valued "at cost or market, whichever is lower." Application of this rule, however, requires the determination of cost.

If prices were constant, the determination of cost of goods sold would be simple. Prices to acquire units of inventory do change, however, and one must determine which particular units were sold to match costs and revenues. To illustrate the problem, assume the data shown below.

	Number of Units	*Cost per Unit*	*Total Cost*
Beginning inventory	140	$12	$1,680
Purchase, February 26	70	18	1,260
Purchase, June 13	70	22	1,540
Purchase, September 28	70	28	1,960
Purchase, December 12	70	35	2,450
Available for sale	420		$8,890
Units sold	220		
Units in ending inventory	200		

How are the units sold and those in ending inventory valued? The two most widely used methods for assigning these costs are first-in-first-out (FIFO) and last-in-first-out (LIFO).

FIFO Method. The FIFO method is based on the assumption that the first merchandise acquired is the first merchandise sold. The ending inventory, therefore, consists of the most recently acquired goods. This method may be adopted by any business, regardless of whether or not the actual physical flow of inventory corresponds to the assumption of selling the earliest-acquired goods first. The key to calculating the cost of goods sold is determination of the value of the ending inventory of 200 units that was determined by physical count. The value of the ending inventory is $5,730, calculated as follows:

70 units purchased December 12	$2,450
70 units purchased September 28	1,960
60 units purchased June 13 (@ $22/unit)	1,320
200 units	$5,730

Cost of goods sold is $3,160 calculated as follows:

Beginning inventory	$1,680
Plus Purchases	7,210
Cost of goods available for sale	$8,890
Less ending inventory	$5,730
Cost of goods sold	$3,160

LIFO method.   Under this method, the most recently acquired goods are assumed to be sold first, and the ending inventory consists of "old" goods acquired through the earliest purchases. Such a flow assumption seems to match the actual flows in the oil industry, for example, since oil enters the storage tanks at the top and this newest oil is drawn first as oil is taken from the tank.

For purposes of measuring income, the flow of costs may be more significant than the actual flow of goods. LIFO seems realistic in this context since costs stated in more current dollars are matched against revenues stated in relatively current dollars.

The value of the ending inventory under the LIFO method is $2,760, calculated as follows:

140 units, Beginning Inventory	$1,680
60 units, February 26 Purchase	1,080
200 units	$2,760

Cost of goods sold is $6,130, calculated as follows:

Beginning Inventory	$1,680
Plus Purchases	7,210
Cost of goods available for sale	$8,890
Less ending inventory	−2,760
Cost of goods sold	$6,130

Comparison of costing methods.   Assuming that net sales for the period were $13,200, the gross profit as reported under each of the above methods is shown below:

	FIFO	LIFO
Net sales	$13,200	$13,200
Less costs of goods sold	3,160	6,130
Gross profit	$10,040	$ 7,070

It is apparent that during a period of rising prices the use of LIFO will result in lower reported profits and, therefore, the firm will incur a lower income tax liability than under FIFO If prices were to fall, then the firm using FIFO would report the lower profits and higher cost of goods sold. Current tax laws practically allow any business firm to adopt LIFO, regardless of the actual flow of goods through the firm, and many firms have adopted the method since the 1950s. A firm that uses LIFO for financial reporting purposes also must use that system for tax purposes.

Profits appear to be more volatile when FIFO rather than LIFO costing is used to determine ending inventory values. This occurs because FIFO accounting tends to cause inventory profits to be added to regular operating profits when prices are rising since current cost is not matched with current revenue. The opposite will occur during a recession, thus increasing volatility. Where selling prices are less flexible than new material prices, however, profits may not be more volatile under FIFO than under LIFO.

It is agreed that profits are overstated in real terms by FIFO (or average cost) as opposed to using the LIFO system during an inflationary period. This is because "old" inventory costs that do not reflect current replacement costs are matched against revenues stated in current dollars that fully reflect current selling prices. It is important to understand that a significant portion of reported net income of companies using the FIFO method may be inventory profits that will melt away as inventory must be replaced in the future.

Finally, LIFO could show illusory profits if a firm does not replenish inventory in a given year and digs into the "old" cost LIFO reserve to meet sales at current prices. The firm will have to restock eventually at the higher current replacement cost, causing a sharp decline in future profits. This can occur, for example, when a firm faces an extended strike by employees and attempts to continue sales from existing inventory.

Expenditures Included in Inventory

Management has a great deal of flexibility in determining what expenses will be capitalized in the inventory accounts and which expenses will be written off directly as cost of the period. For example, if the personnel department was housed in the building used for administrative staff, the expenses associated with its operation are likely to be written off directly as part of administrative expense. If the personnel department staff were housed in an operating plant, at least part of the expenses of its operation are likely to be capitalized in the inventory account. A liberal interpretation of the question of capitalizing versus expensing such costs could improve reported income for a given period. Moreover, different decisions as to whether to capitalize in the inventory account or directly expense could distort comparability of reported income data between companies or through time.

Decreasing-Cost Industries

In a decreasing-cost industry, such as semiconductors and possibly computers, LIFO, rather than FIFO, will report higher profits during a period of generally rising prices. Since the reporting of lower profits saves taxes, it is not surprising to note that, in 1984, only 38 percent of firms in those industry groups used the LIFO method.

Adjusting Noncomparable Inventory Data

Where inventories are not a significant asset, the analyst need not be overly concerned about differences in inventory costing systems through time for a company or when comparing different companies. In many cases, however, misleading conclusions may be drawn if the analyst is not careful to adjust when different systems are used.

The footnotes to the financial statements, unfortunately, rarely facilitate an accurate adjustment, unless a company has just switched from one method to the other. Where a company has changed inventory costing methods, they must report the dollar-and-cents impact on inventory, cost of goods sold, taxes, and profits in the financial report of that year. This data need not be repeated, however, in future annual reports. When contrasting two companies using different inventory costing methods, the analyst can only subjectively adjust the data of one to the system used by the other company. Sometimes, to facilitate an adjustment, analysts assume that the gross profit margin percentages would have been the same if the companies had used the same inventory costing procedures. This is not a useful technique, however, since this will wash out differing efficiencies between companies that the analyst is looking for.

FASB Statement No. 33[1] requires that large corporations disclose what it would cost to replace their inventories at year-end and what their cost of goods sold would be if computed using current replacement cost at the date of sale. These data can help the analyst better frame reasonable adjustments where two companies use different inventory costing systems.

For comparative purposes, either the LIFO or FIFO firm could be adjusted to the system used by the other firm. We have indicated above our

---

[1] Financial Accounting Standards Board Statement No. 33, "Financial Reporting and Changing Prices" (Stamford, CT, 1979).

TABLE 7–1
Illustrative Adjustment of Selected Data from the 1985 Annual Report of Maytag Company to a FIFO Approach (Millions of Dollars)

	1985	1984
1. LIFO reserve	37.3	39.1
2. Inventories (LIFO)	78.5	77.7
3. Total = FIFO inventories	115.8	116.8
4. Cost of sales	432.9	421.5
5. Stockholders' equity (LIFO)	256.6	228.9
6. Stockholders' equity (FIFO)	276.7	250.0
7. Net income (LIFO)	71.8	63.1
8. Net income (FIFO)	70.8	

FIFO stockholders' equity = [(1 – tax rate) × (LIFO reserve)] + LIFO stockholders' equity. The tax rate was 46% at the time of this example.

FIFO net income = [(1985 LIFO reserve – 1984 LIFO reserve) × (1 – tax rate)] + 1985 LIFO net income.

Source: S. Cottle, R. Murray, and F. Black, *Graham and Dodd's Security Analysis*, 5th ed., (New York: McGraw-Hill Inc., 1988) pp. 206–207.

preference for LIFO reporting on the grounds that this system reports more meaningful profit data. Therefore, it would seem best to adjust the firm using FIFO to the LIFO approach. Unfortunately, one is likely to find that available information facilitates adjustment of the LIFO company to a FIFO basis, using current replacement cost information.

Data for the Maytag Company in Table 7–1, as prepared by Cottle, Murray, and Block, illustrate the adjustment process, based on recognizing that LIFO inventory plus LIFO reserve equals FIFO inventory.

Balance Sheet Effects

Finally, it is important to recognize that the choice of an inventory costing system also affects the balance sheet. A period of sustained inflation tends to cause assets to be valued in the balance sheet at amounts substantially below their current replacement cost, especially when the LIFO costing system is used. This occurs because inventory is carried at "old" costs to acquire, which deviate more and more from current replacement cost as the inflation continues. Accordingly, a company using LIFO may have a low current ratio relative to a company using FIFO when the liquidity of the two companies is the same.

Changes in Inventory Accounts

It can be interesting to note how each of the three basic inventory accounts change over time. For example, assume one noted that Raw Materials Inventory was declining while Finished Goods Inventory was increasing. This could be favorable, if it meant that the firm was increasing the holdings of finished goods to meet rising demand and decreasing the supply of raw materials to reflect new efficiencies in the inventory handling and production process. It could also suggest increasing difficulty in selling finished goods and adjustment of the raw materials inventory position to bring it in line with falling demand, which would be an unfavorable scenario.

DEPRECIATION

Depreciation of production facilities would be a cost entering into the determination of cost of goods sold, but depreciation of sales office space properly would be shown as a selling expense. Depreciation may, therefore, affect the determination of several major subdivisions of the income statement.

> Depreciation accounting is a system of accounting which aims to distribute the cost . . . of tangible capital assets, less salvage (if any) over the estimated useful life of the unit (which may be a group of assets) in a systematic and rational manner. It is a process of allocation (of cost), not of valuation. Depreciation for the year is the portion of the total charge under such a system that is allocated to the year. Although the allocation may properly take into account occurrences during the year, it is not intended to be a measurement of the effect of all such occurrences.[2]

Because the accounting charge for depreciation does not represent a corresponding outlay of cash, some investors and analysts have implied that depreciation is not a real expense by using the terms "cash earnings per share" or "cash flow earnings per share" and have even substituted these terms for "net earnings per share." Strong criticism of this position by the AICPA, the NYSE, and the Financial Analysts Federation has reduced sharply the use of these terms in brokerage houses and annual corporate reports.

---

[2] "Review and Résumé," *Accounting Terminology Bulletin* No. 1 (New York: American Institute of Certified Public Accountants, 1953), p. 25.

Since fixed assets, particularly plant and equipment, represent such a substantial outlay, it would be impractical to write them off entirely as an expense charged against the income of the year in which they are purchased, especially since benefits from their use will be received over an extended period. Furthermore, as soon as it is purchased, a fixed asset begins to depreciate. To ignore this fact would be to experience a gradual loss of capital without any reflection on the books of account. Accountants consider the original cost of a fixed asset to be a prepaid expense that must be amortized during the service life of the asset by regular periodic charges to the depreciation expense account. After deduction of the annual charge, the remaining amount is the unamortized cost; but in no way, except by coincidence, does this amount represent the economic value of the asset at that time.

Basis for Depreciation: Replacement Value versus Original Cost

Inflation, which has long been a problem, has led many to advocate a policy of substituting replacement cost for original cost as the basis for determining depreciation charges in the income statement. Corporate management especially has been vocal in this regard. The basic function of depreciation charges is to amortize the cost of a capital asset over its useful life. Management is concerned with a second function: providing the funds needed for replacement of assets after they have worn out or become obsolete technologically. Depreciation charges do not provide a company with cash. However, they are tax deductible and they do protect cash generated by sales operations from the burden of taxes.

When replacement costs have risen far above original cost, prudent business management must recognize this capital erosion and set aside the additional funds necessary to continue a business in operation. Such funds must be provided from retained earnings, because the income tax laws do not recognize the inflation situation. Income taxes must be paid on the capital lost through inflation, which makes the problem of maintaining a company's capital doubly difficult.

Other countries (e.g., The Netherlands, Chile, and Brazil) with more rapid inflation than the United States have changed their tax laws in various ways to prevent the gradual liquidation of capital investment through payment of income taxes on capital eroded by inflation; asset values are raised yearly and depreciated on the new values.

A change to replacement cost would change fundamental concepts of accounting, since it would represent a breaking away from the basic idea that balance sheets and expense accounts are based on monetary cost and not on economic values. The cost basis of measurement has the advantages of: (1) uniformity of interpretation of the values to be entered in the balance sheet and the charges to be entered in the income account, and (2) objectivity. Accountants question whether a system based on an attempt to measure replacement values, with its loss of objectivity, has additional advantages that more than offset the advantages of the cost basis. Other questions are raised, such as whether the assets are replaced with like assets or superior ones that justify part of the higher cost, whether the assets will in fact be replaced as technology changes, and whether current or future customers should pay for the replaced equipment.[3]

In June 1969 the AICPA issued APB Statement No. 3, "Financial Statement Restated for General Price Level Changes." This statement, which still reflects the AICPA thinking at this writing, is quoted in part as follows:

> The Board believes that general price-level financial statements or pertinent information extracted from them present useful information not available from basic historical-dollar financial statements. General price-level information may be presented in addition to the basic historical statement, but should not be presented as the basic statements.[4]

This view was reiterated by the AICPA in its "Fundamental Statement" published in October 1970. Firms are not currently required to present general price-level information in annual reports.

Magnitude of Depreciation

Two major reasons why investors and analysts need to devote so much attention to depreciation are: (1) the magnitude of depreciation, and (2) the leeway that management can exercise in reporting depreciation—that is, the lack of uniformity in reporting depreciation in published reports. The magnitude of depreciation is evident when it is related to corporate profits as is done in Table 7–2. This table shows that depreciation in absolute terms

---

3 See *Accounting Research Bulletin,* no. 43, published in 1953, for both the majority view and the dissenting view of a special committee appointed by the AICPA.

4 APB Statement No. 3, "Financial Statement Restated for General Price-Level Changes," *Journal of Accountancy* (September 1969), pp. 62–68.

TABLE 7-2

Absolute Importance of Depreciation and Relative Importance of Cash Flow[a] of All U.S. Corporations (Billions of Dollars), 1946–1986

Year	(1) Capital Consumption Allowances (Depreciation Only)	(2) Capital Consumption Adjustment	(3) Capital[b] Consumption Allowances Including Capital Consumption Adjustment	(4) Profits Before Taxes	(5) Profits Tax (Income Tax Liability)	(6) Profits After Taxes	(7) Total Cash Flow I Capital Consumption (Depreciation Only) Plus Profits After Taxes (Col 1 + 6)	(8) Undistributed Profits (Profits After Dividends)	(9) Net Cash Flow II Capital Consumption Allowances (Depreciation Only) Plus Undistributed Profits (Col 1 + 8)	(10) Capital Consumption Allowances (Depreciation Only) As % of Cash Flow II (Col 1/9)
1946	4.7	2.7	7.4	24.6	9.1	15.5	20.2	9.9	14.6	32.2
1947	5.8	3.4	9.2	31.5	11.3	20.2	26.0	13.9	19.7	29.4
1948	7.0	3.9	10.9	35.2	12.4	22.8	29.7	15.7	22.7	30.8
1949	8.0	3.8	11.8	28.9	10.2	18.7	26.7	11.5	19.5	41.0
1950	8.8	4.0	12.8	42.6	17.9	24.7	33.5	15.9	24.7	35.6
1951	10.3	4.6	14.9	43.9	22.6	21.3	31.6	12.8	23.1	44.6
1952	11.5	4.5	16.0	38.9	19.4	19.5	31.0	10.7	22.2	51.8
1953	13.2	4.1	17.3	40.5	20.3	20.2	33.4	11.5	24.7	53.4
1954	15.0	3.2	18.2	38.1	17.6	20.5	35.5	11.4	26.4	56.8
1955	17.4	2.1	19.5	48.4	22.0	26.4	43.8	16.1	33.5	51.9
1956	18.9	3.0	21.9	48.6	22.0	26.6	45.5	15.5	34.4	54.9
1957	20.9	3.3	24.2	46.9	21.4	25.5	46.4	14.0	34.9	59.9
1958	22.0	3.4	25.4	41.1	19.0	22.1	44.1	10.8	32.8	67.1
1959	23.6	2.9	26.5	51.6	23.6	28.0	51.6	15.8	39.4	59.9
1960	25.2	2.3	27.5	48.5	22.7	25.8	51.0	13.0	38.2	66.0
1961	26.6	1.8	28.4	48.6	22.8	25.8	52.4	12.5	39.1	68.0
1962	30.5	-1.2	29.3	53.6	24.0	29.6	60.1	15.2	45.7	66.7
1963	32.5	-2.1	30.4	57.7	26.2	31.5	64.0	16.0	48.5	67.0
1964	34.5	-2.8	31.7	64.7	28.0	36.7	71.2	19.4	53.9	64.0

(continued)

TABLE 7–2 (concluded)

1965	37.5	−3.8	33.7	75.2	30.9	44.3	81.8	25.2	62.7	59.8
1966	40.6	−3.9	36.7	80.7	33.7	47.0	87.7	27.6	68.2	59.5
1967	44.1	−3.7	40.4	77.3	32.5	44.8	89.0	24.7	68.8	64.1
1968	48.1	−3.7	44.4	85.6	39.3	46.3	94.3	24.2	72.3	66.5
1969	52.9	−3.5	49.4	83.5	39.7	43.8	96.7	21.2	74.1	71.4
1970	56.6	−1.5	55.1	71.5	34.5	37.0	93.6	14.1	70.7	80.1
1971	60.9	−0.3	60.6	82.0	37.7	44.3	105.2	21.3	82.2	74.1
1972	67.9	−2.5	65.4	96.2	41.4	54.8	122.5	30.0	97.9	69.4
1973	73.8	−1.9	71.9	115.8	48.7	67.1	140.9	39.3	113.1	65.3
1974	81.7	2.9	84.6	126.9	52.4	74.5	156.2	43.6	125.3	65.2
1975	88.7	12.2	100.9	123.5	50.2	73.3	162.1	41.0	129.7	68.4
1976	97.1	14.7	111.8	156.9	64.7	92.2	189.2	56.4	153.5	63.3
1977	104.7	7.2	111.9	171.7	69.2	102.5	207.2	61.4	166.1	63.0
1978	136.4	13.5	149.9	203.6	83.0	120.6	257.0	86.3	222.7	61.2
1979	155.4	15.9	171.3	225.0	87.6	137.4	292.8	102.5	257.9	60.3
1980	175.4	17.2	192.6	214.4	82.3	132.0	307.4	94.6	270.0	65.0
1981	206.2	16.8	223.0	209.3	81.2	128.1	334.3	77.3	283.5	72.7
1982	222.0	1.1	223.1	152.4	59.2	93.2	315.2	38.8	260.8	85.1
1983	231.2	33.2	264.4	178.4	75.8	102.6	333.8	39.6	270.8	85.4
1984	256.6	41.0	297.6	205.4	93.6	111.8	368.4	44.7	301.3	85.2
1985	268.2	58.1	326.3	191.3	91.8	99.5	367.7	30.2	298.4	89.9
1986	280.3	56.6	336.9	202.0	103.5	98.5	378.8	22.3	302.6	92.6

[a]In 1976 the Bureau of Economic Analysis of the U.S. Department of Commerce completed a benchmark revision of the National Income and Product accounts. The depreciation measure included in the NIPAs of the revision is based on current-cost valuation and the straightline depreciation formula. The new measure of depreciation will not be appropriate for all uses. For example, in studies of the effects of tax policies, the old measure probably would be required. Accordingly, in addition to the new series, the NIPAs will continue to show tax return-based depreciation for corporations and non-farm sole proprietorships and partnerships. Also, several variants based on consistent accounting will be provided regularly in the Survey of Current Business so that users can judge the effects of depreciation formulas, service lives, and valuations and, if they desire, substitute an alternative for the NIPA measure.

[b]The adjustment of the previous estimates of capital consumption allowances to the new basis and the associated changes in the profit-type incomes, which are net of capital consumption allowances, is accomplished by a new entry labeled capital consumption adjustment. This entry equals the previous measure of capital consumption (based on tax return information) less the new measure (based on consistent accounting and valued in current prices).

Source: U.S. Department of Commerce, various issues of *Survey of Current Business.*

has risen from $4.7 billion annually in 1946 to $280.3 billion for 1986. Furthermore, in relative terms, depreciation as a percentage of Cash Flow I (depreciation plus net profits) ranged between 46 percent and 58 percent between 1960 and 1986, and depreciation as a percentage of Cash Flow II (depreciation plus undistributed profits after dividends) ranged between 59 percent and 93 percent in the same period. The major uses of cash flow are for:

1. Corporate dividends and debt amortization, including sinking fund payments;

2. Required increases in working capital; and

3. Capital budget programs, repurchase of company securities, etc.

In broad terms, cash flow represents the basic protection offered investors for both dividends and debt service requirements, including sinking funds and amortization.

Methods of Reporting Depreciation

Although corporate laws and accounting principles require that corporations make some charge for depreciation, corporate management is permitted numerous alternatives in the manner in which it amortizes the cost of fixed assets over their useful life on its books and in published reports.

The straight-line method provides for the regular distribution of the original cost of fixed assets, less their estimated salvage value, over their estimated service lives. In addition to the straight-line method of depreciation, the Internal Revenue Code permitted two other depreciation methods: the declining-balance method and the sum-of-the-years-digits method in a 1954 tax revision.

The declining-balance method permits a taxpayer to use a rate of depreciation, not exceeding twice the straight-line rate, on the original cost (unadjusted for salvage value) less accumulated depreciation. The Code permitted a taxpayer to change at any time from the declining-balance method to the straight-line method since charging all original cost as depreciation under the declining-balance method is impossible arithmetically. The straight-line rate would be based on a realistic estimate of the remaining life of the property at the time of the switch.

The sum-of-the-years-digits method is somewhat more complicated. The annual depreciation deduction is calculated by applying a changing fraction to the original cost of the property less the estimated salvage value. The

TABLE 7–3

Annual Depreciation Charge for a Fixed Asset Costing $1,000 with No Expected Salvage Value and an Estimated Useful Life of Five Years

Year	Straight-Line Method	Declining-Balance Method	Sum-of-the-Years-Digits Method
1	$200	$400	$333.33
2	200	240	266.67
3	200	144	200.00
4	200	108*	133.33
5	200	108*	66.67

*It is assumed that the taxpayer switched to straight-line depreciation in the fourth year.

numerator of the fraction is the number of useful years of life remaining for the property, what it will be in the first year, in the second year, etc. The denominator is the factorial sum of the estimated useful life of the property and may be calculated by using Equation (7.1) below:

$$D = \frac{N(N+1)}{2} \qquad (7.1)$$

where

D = the denominator of the fraction used to calculate
the annual depreciation charge

N = the number of years of useful life of the asset.

For a fixed asset with an estimated life of five years, the fractions used would be 5/15, 4/15, 3/15, 2/15, and 1/15.

The annual depreciation charges under the three depreciation methods are contrasted in Table 7–3. Obviously, the reported earnings for a given year would be different if companies did not use the same depreciation method, and therefore would not be comparable unless adjustments were made.

Accelerated Cost Recovery System (ACRS)

Prior to 1981 taxpayers could compute depreciation using either: (1) the facts and circumstances method, or (2) the class life system. These methods gave taxpayers great flexibility in calculating depreciation, and led to possible abuse by tax authorities.

The Economic Recovery Tax Act of 1981 substantially revised the method of computing depreciation by introducing the ACRS, which is still used today. Taxpayers have virtually no choice under this system in selecting a useful life for depreciation property, and salvage value is ignored. The Tax Reform Act of 1986 provided less liberal write-offs, especially of real estate, but retained the ACRS approach. The shorter depreciable lives mandated by ACRS do introduce another factor that can cause taxable income to differ from reported accounting income since different depreciating methods may be used for purposes of preparing financial statements and tax returns.

The new system relies on pre-1981 Asset Depreciation Range (ADR) guidelines. Assets are assigned to one of six categories, or to one of two classes of real property as shown in Table 7–4.

FLOW-THROUGH METHOD AND NORMALIZING METHOD OF REPORTING DEPRECIATION

Since 1954, most corporations have reported publicly on a straight-line basis to stockholders, while taking advantage of the rapid amortization permitted under the Code for tax purposes. Until fiscal 1968, income statements in annual reports of numerous corporations reported depreciation by the flow-through method, which annually flows through the full tax savings to net income. However, other corporations reported depreciation by the normalizing method, making a charge in the income account equivalent to the tax savings and thus washing out the benefits of the tax savings as far as the final net income reported in their published income statements. In statements, the charge for deferred taxes usually is included in the total item entitled "Federal Income Taxes."

In December 1967, the AICPA stated categorically that the deferred method of tax allocation should be followed.[5] An exception to insistence on the deferred method would be allowed for regulated companies, such as public utilities, where particular regulatory authorities may require the use of flow-through accounting.

Those who favor normalizing state that the use of rapid amortization for tax purposes will result in lower taxes being paid in the earlier years of the life of the assets than under the straight-line method because of higher

---

5 "Accounting for Income Taxes," *Opinions of the Accounting Principles Board* no. 11 (New York: American Institute of Certified Public Accountants, 1967).

TABLE 7–4
Accelerated Cost Recovery System (ACRS)

ACRS Class and Method	ADR Midpoint	Special Rules
3-year, 200% declining balance	4 years or less	Includes some race horses. Excludes cars and light trucks.
5-year, 200% declining balance	More than 4 years to less than 10	Includes cars and light trucks, semiconductor manufacturing equipment, qualified technological equipment, computer-based central-office switching equipment, some renewable and biomass power facilities and research and development property.
7-year, 200% declining balance	10 years to less than 16	Includes single-purpose agricultural and horticultural structures and railroad track. Includes property with no ADR midpoint.
10-year, 200% declining balance	16 years to less than 20	None.
15-year, 150% declining balance	20 years to less than 25	Includes sewage treatment plants, telephone distribution plants and comparable equipment for two-way voice and data communication.
20-year, 150% declining balance	25 years or more	Excludes real property with ADR midpoint of 27.5 years or more. Includes municipal sewers.
27.5-year, straight-line	N/A	Residential rental property.
31.5-year, straight-line	N/A	Nonresidential real property.

Source: Tax Reform 1986, Arthur Andersen & Company, 1987, p. 112.

depreciation charges, but that in later years depreciation will be less than straight-line rates; taxes will therefore be higher than in the earlier years. Total taxes for the entire life of the assets should be the same under either straight-line or rapid amortization. Therefore, tax savings are temporary and deferred until later years of lower depreciation charges. Those holding this viewpoint, including the AICPA and the SEC, therefore wish to eliminate any effect of tax savings on net income in the earlier years of the asset's life.

Those who have advocated the flow-through method, including numerous state public utility commissions (not the SEC), have argued that as long as a company is regularly expanding and purchasing fixed assets, the new assets will have the advantage of rapid amortization, therefore offsetting the declining depreciation on older assets. The lower taxes paid in the earlier years, therefore, are not deferred to later years, but payment will be deferred indefinitely. Therefore, there will be a constantly increasing "deferred taxes" account on the balance sheet.

Although depreciation is a real expense, it does not involve an outlay of cash in the period charged; therefore, the sales revenues allocated to the depreciation charges do represent a tax-protected source of funds to the business enterprise. While the total depreciation charged over the life of the asset is not affected by the method used, the greater amounts of revenues protected in early years by the declining-balance method and sum-of-the-years-digits method have a higher present value than funds that might be protected in later years. Rapid amortization is similar to an interest-free loan from the Treasury Department. Generally firms do not have access to other sources of funds with no greater risk or cost than the funds provided by depreciation. Therefore, acquiring an increased amount of funds through depreciation tends to lower the cost of capital to the firm.

Adequacy of Depreciation Charges

Depreciation charges often are substantial, and the estimates made have a material effect on the reported profits or loss of a given year. Profits are overstated when depreciation charges understate the actual using up of assets during the productive process. Depreciation charges can be understated by increasing the estimated life of the asset beyond that over which the asset is useful economically, or overstating salvage value. For example, several American airlines extended the depreciable life of their aircraft between 1968 and 1970, thereby reducing annual depreciation expense and increasing reported earnings at a time when airline earnings generally were depressed.

Accountants cannot know in advance how long an asset will last or what its salvage value will be. The depreciation expense charged in the income statement is a rough estimate of cost and does not allow for the effects of inflation. Determining the adequacy of depreciation charges is difficult. The following tests are suggested:

1. The consistency of the rate of depreciation charged over time can be explored by studying depreciation as a percentage of gross plant assets and sales over an extended period of time.

2. Depreciation rates of a given company should be compared to those utilized by similar companies.

A study by Price Waterhouse found that current-cost depreciation exceeded historical-cost depreciation by 37 percent in 1980 and averaged 31 percent from 1980 to 1983.[6] This suggests that income, based on historical accounting, has been overstated, as there was inadequate provision for replacement of fixed assets. Analysts should keep this in mind when reviewing the adequacy of depreciation charges and comparing income data.

DEPLETION

The depletion allowance, for tax purposes, represents recognition of the fact that operations of companies with wasting assets result in a decrease in the value of their natural resources as these are used up. Depletion is the accounting term applied to the amortization of the cost of exhaustible natural resources such as minerals, metals, and standing timber.

Wasting Asset Companies

The majority of wasting asset companies, such as mining companies, depreciate their fixed assets through cost depreciation charges to a depreciation expense account. However, for their wasting assets they use percentage depletion accounting. Also, these wasting asset companies have large *exploration* and development costs. A comparative cash flow analysis, because of heavy depletion charges and encompassing special tax treatment for these development costs, is as essential as net income analysis for wasting asset companies and has been used for such companies for many years.[7]

---

6 *Inflation Accounting* (New York: Price Waterhouse & Co., 1981).

7 On the companies' own books and for public reporting purposes on charges for depletion, they deduct that percentage of the cost of the natural resource property which the mineral (or the resource) extracted bears to the total resource content. This is known as the "units-of-production" method. This method is also applied to calculate the depreciation on equipment, such as cars, where their service life is governed by the same factors.

Percentage Depletion Method

This method[8] differs from normal depreciation methods, and therefore from the cost amortization method, in that allowable depletion charges are based on gross income instead of on the cost of reserves. Percentage depletion is used only for income tax purposes, not for financial statements made available by the company to the public. Percentage depletion is calculated by multiplying the allowable percentage for the particular mineral in question by the gross income from the property, but it is limited to 50 percent of the taxable or net income from the property. The gross income under Treasury regulations is not the same as the gross income of the taxpayer as defined in other sections of the Internal Revenue Code. Rather, according to the Treasury, it must be calculated separately. It is the amount for which the mineral is sold if the sale takes place in the vicinity of the property in the form in which the mineral is sold by basic producers; or it is the calculated value at the basic state of production in case it is sold later in a more advanced state, for example, after processing.

Exploration and Related Costs

Under the Internal Revenue Code, the taxpayer has the choice of accounting for exploration costs not in excess of $400,000 by either (1) charging them off currently as incurred, or (2) considering them as a deferred charge to be deducted proportionately as the extracted minerals that result from the exploration are sold. All such expenditures may be capitalized. Any excess exploration costs must be capitalized. Such deductions are in addition to depletion allowances, but they must be considered when the taxpayer is calculating net income to determine the 50 percent limitation for percentage depletion.

---

8 Sec. 613. Percentage Depletion, Internal Revenue Code General Rule: In the case of mines, wells, and other natural deposits listed in subsection (b), the allowance for depletion under Section 611 shall be the percentage, specified in subsection (b), of the gross income from the property, excluding from such gross income an amount equal to any rents or royalties paid or incurred by the taxpayer in respect of the property. Such allowances shall not exceed 50 percent of the taxpayer's taxable income from the property computed without allowance for depletion. In no case shall the allowance for depletion under Section 611 be less than if computed without reference to this section (i.e., not less than the cost method).

Exploration and Development Costs: Gas and Oil

Partly due to public resentment against the big oil companies, effective January 1, 1975, the percentage depletion allowance for gas and oil wells (with certain exceptions) was repealed. The repeal affected all tax years after 1974. The 1975 Energy Policy and Conservation Act directed the Securities and Exchange Commission to come up with oil and gas industry accounting standards by December 22, 1977. The Financial Accounting Standards Board held a four-day hearing in New York in the spring of 1977 on financial accounting for the extractive industries. There was almost even division between those who wanted the full-cost method and those who wished the successful-efforts method. On July 19, 1977, the FASB proposed (FASB No. 19) that the successful-efforts method be used "for financial statements for fiscal years beginning after June 15, 1978...(and that the standards) be applied retroactively through the restatement of financial reports for prior periods.[9]

Smaller oil and gas firms objected strongly to FASB No. 19, and the Department of Energy suggested that companies that had been using the full-cost method could reduce their exploration activities because of the unfavorable earnings impact associated with successful-efforts accounting. The SEC then issued three Accounting Series Releases, adopting both a form of the successful-efforts approach and a full-costing approach, and suggesting a yet-to-be-developed method (reserve recognition accounting).[10]

Depletion and Depreciation Reserves
Distributed to Stockholders

Unfortunately, the income tax regulations confuse the status of depreciation and depletion reserves that are accumulated. These regulations state that "a distribution made from (charged to) a depletion or depreciation reserve based on the cost or other basis of the property, instead of being charged to retained earnings, will not be considered as having been paid out of the earnings of the property." Therefore, such distributions to stockholders are

---

9 Peter B. Roche, "Successful-Efforts Method for Reporting Oil and Gas Search Costs Backed by Panel," *The Wall Street Journal*, July 20, 1977, p. 8.

10 See "Adoption of Requirements for Financial Accounting and Reporting Practices for Oil and Gas Producing Activities," *Accounting Series Release*, no. 253 (Washington, DC: SEC, August 1978); "Requirements for Financial Accounting and Reporting Practices for Oil and Gas Producing Activities," *Accounting Series Release*, no. 257 (Washington, D.C.: SEC, 1978); and "Oil and Gas Producers Full Cost Accounting Practices," *Accounting Series Release* no. 258 (Washington, D.C.: SEC, 1978).

not taxable as ordinary dividends. However, the regulations clearly state that such reserves are "not a part of surplus out of which ordinary dividends may be paid." Such distributions are considered to be liquidating dividends because they represent a return of capital and not a distribution of earnings. Numerous tax-exempt dividends result, and prior to 1972 this was the major reason for the tax-exempt status to the recipient of a portion of dividends paid by many public utility companies.

AMORTIZATION OF INTANGIBLES

In addition to the major noncash charges for depreciation and depletion in the income statement, the amortization of intangibles such as goodwill, patents, and trademarks represents noncash charges in the income account.

Intangible Assets

The following statements are pertinent to the classification and amortization of intangible assets:

Intangible assets are classified in APB Opinion No. 17, Par. 12, as follows:

(a) Those having a term of existence limited by law, regulation, or agreement, or by their nature (such as patents, copyrights, leases, licenses, franchises for a fixed term, and goodwill as to which there is evidence of limited duration);

(b) Those having no such limited term of existence and as to which there is, at the time of acquisition, no indication of limited life (such as goodwill generally, going value, trade names, secret processes, subscription lists, perpetual franchises, and organization costs.[11]

When a corporation decides that a type (b) intangible may not continue to have value during the entire life of the enterprise, it may amortize the cost of such intangible by systematic charges against income despite the fact that there are no present indications of limited existence or loss of value which would indicate that it has become type (a) and despite the fact that expenditures are being made to maintain its value.[12]

---

11 "Inventory of Generally Accepted Accounting Principles for Business Enterprises," *Accounting Research Study*, no. 7 (New York: American Institute of Certified Public Accountants, 1965), p. 54.

12 Ibid., p. 155.

The problem of determining the time over which the values recognized for intangibles are consumed is a difficult one, and differing judgments can lead to noncomparability of reported income data by different companies.

Goodwill. Goodwill, and the accounting for goodwill has become important to analysts with the tremendous merger movement that has occurred since World War II. The costs of acquisitions often have been well in excess of the book value of the assets acquired, and a balancing item of goodwill has been added in the balance sheet. The AICPA requires that the item of goodwill be amortized annually as a charge against income over a period of not more than 40 years. Since firms may write off choosing any time span within the 40-year period, profit comparability can be distorted.

Capitalizing versus Expensing

Expenditures for items where the benefits are expected to be received over a period longer than one year typically are capitalized (recorded in asset accounts), and the total recorded is depreciated or amortized over the life of the asset. Where the benefit is expected to be received within a year, the cost of the item is directly charged to an expense account and fully reduces reported profit of that year. Many items are not easily labeled as short or long term, and some companies may capitalize a given item while other companies expense it. This can lead to non-comparability of reported profits.

Capitalized Items and Deferred Expense Items

There are numerous items that a corporation may expense in its tax return but capitalize in its published balance sheet. Many companies have followed a similar procedure in regard to advertising and promotional expenses. Analysts are cynical about capitalization and deferral of expense items. For example, when companies defer items that more properly should be currently expensed, the result is higher reported profit. For 1968, United Air Lines cushioned its decline in profits by deferring to later years the costs of training pilots, mechanics, and ground crews to handle new equipment. Estimates were that such deferrals of expenses amounted to $9 to $10 million. The analyst must make adjustments, increasing reported expenses and decreasing reported profits for these and similar expense items that should be expensed in the current year rather than deferred to later years.

Other items that are capitalized in annual reports, but expensed in tax returns, are intangible drilling costs of oil and natural gas producers and exploration and development expenses of mining companies. These all raise a problem for the analyst attempting to place different companies on a comparable base.

Another item that must be mentioned is interest charged to construction credit, which is capitalized by public utility companies in their published statements but is expensed in their income tax reports. This item will be examined in detail in Chapter 12.

One further item should be mentioned because it is often capitalized in published balance sheets while being expensed in tax reports to the IRS. This is the item of cost applicable to start-up and related expenses for new plants. The analyst may decide that if the company is regularly expanding, capitalizing such expenses in the company's published reports is justifiable. This item will almost always be expensed in the tax report. The reverse item is cost of plant closing, which should be reported separately before extraordinary items.

FASB Number 33: Inflation-Adjusted Data

Financial Accounting Standards Bulletin No. 33 required the disclosure in annual reports of two types of inflation-adjusted data by publicly held corporations with total assets of more than $1 billion, or whose inventories and property, plant, and equipment are valued at more than $125 million dollars. Each of the types of inflation-adjusted data is discussed briefly below. These data were required from 1979 through 1986, but became voluntary in 1987. Many companies still provide estimates.

Constant-dollar data. Constant-dollar data are derived by restating historical accounting data in dollars of current purchasing power. The historical stated accounting value is multiplied by a fraction, the numerator of which is the current consumer price index for urban items, and the denominator the index that prevailed at the date related to the amount being restated. For example, assume an asset was acquired for $15,000 on January 1, 1975. It would be restated in terms of December 31, 1980, dollars as follows:

$$\frac{1980\ \text{Index}}{1975\ \text{Index}} \times \$15{,}000 = \text{Cost of the asset in terms of 1980 dollars}$$

$$\frac{261.5}{161.2} \times \$15{,}000 = \$24{,}333$$

Raising the value of a depreciable asset affects the income statement as well as the balance sheet, since depreciation expense also would be increased, thereby lowering reported profits.

The actual preparation of constant-dollar financial statements is more complex than illustrated above. To restate historical statements, one must distinguish between monetary and nonmonetary items. A monetary item is cash or any claim receivable or payable in a specified number of dollars. When the price level rises, each dollar purchases less in terms of real goods and services. A holder of monetary assets, therefore, loses in real terms since the number of dollars will remain fixed. Nonmonetary assets tend to behave in the opposite manner, since the number of dollars that can be obtained through sale of such assets tends to rise during inflation. It is preferable, therefore, to hold nonmonetary assets rather than monetary assets during a period of inflation. The value of nonmonetary assets is raised accordingly, as in the illustration above, to recognize the rising value; the purchasing power loss of monetary assets also must be recognized.

One who incurs monetary liabilities gains when prices rise, since the obligations are repaid with dollars of lesser purchasing power than those acquired when the obligation was assumed. Index adjustments are, therefore, also made to recognize such gains, and the gain on monetary liabilities is offset against the loss on monetary assets to determine whether the firm had a net gain or loss on monetary items.

Constant-dollar adjustments do provide objectively and consistently determined estimates from company to company on the impact of inflation. This enhances comparability of such data. Unfortunately, however, such estimates can be misleading. Constant-dollar data assumes that the impact of inflation falls equally on all firms and classes of assets and costs, which is not correct. Using a single index to adjust the historical data of all firms would hide the effects of changing technology, supply and demand shifts that may well be related to the inflation phenomena, and the impact of successful or unsuccessful management in meeting the problem brought on by inflation. In short, one could say that such data are better than nothing, assuming the user understands their limitations. In all cases, such data should be used with caution.

Current-value data.   Proponents of this approach are interested in what the business is worth now rather than historical past accounting values. They argue the value of assets should be stated in terms of the present value of the future receipts these assets can be expected to generate, or as the cost of replenishing the assets at today's prices. The latter method is used by most firms to prepare supplementary current-value inflation-adjusted data in accordance with requirements of FASB No. 33.

Such estimates seem more useful than index-number–adjusted data, but they also suffer serious analytical drawbacks. The differing impact of inflation on firms and on classes of assets and costs is estimated. The computation of current value or cost, however, is subjective since many assets do not have a ready market price and might be replaced with a different type of asset or not replaced at all. Accounting rules do allow considerable flexibility in determining current-value estimates, and certainly comparing data prepared by different companies will be difficult. In short, the accuracy of current cost estimates is open to serious question. Still, the estimates of management offer possible insights into the impact of inflation on business firms that were not available formerly to analysts.

Tables 7–5 and 7–6 offer illustrations of the reporting of inflation-adjusted data by E. I. Du Pont Company. The income reported after inflation adjustments is less than one-half of the income reported on a historical-cost basis. The higher effective tax rate is incurred by the company when inflation-adjusted data are considered. Finally, note that inflation-adjusted earnings per share (constant dollars) did not cover the dollar dividend paid per share in 1980. This has important cash flow implications, and shows that profits were overstated significantly on a historical-cost basis.

TABLE 7–5

E. I. Du Pont Company—Comparative Historical Dollar, Constant Dollar,
and Current Cost Income Statements, 1980 (Dollars in Millions)

	As Reported in the Primary Statements (Historical Dollars)	General Inflation (Average 1980 Constant Dollars)	Adjusted for Changes in Specific Prices 1980 Current Costs)
Sales	$13,652	$13,652	$13,652
Other Income	149	149	149
Total	13,801	13,801	13,801
Cost of goods sold and other operating charges	10,293	10,420	10,437
Selling, general, and administrative expenses	1,466	1,466	1,466
Depreciation and obsolescence	804	1,156	1,109
Interest on borrowings	110	110	110
Total	12,673	13,152	13,122
Earnings before income taxes and minority interests	1,128	649	679
Provision for income taxes	402	402	402
Earnings before minority interests	726	247	277
Minority interests in earnings of consolidated subsidiaries	10	10	10
Income from continuing operations	$ 716	$ 237	$ 267
Effective income tax rate	36%	62%	59%
Gain attributable to holding net monetary liabilities		$ 85	$ 85
Income including gain attributable to holding net monetary liabilities	$ 716	$ 322	$ 352
Increase in value of inventories and net plants and properties held during the year			
Measured in constant dollars			$ 1,290
Measured by current costs*			1,050
Excess of constant dollar over current cost increase			$ 240

*At December 31, 1980, current cost of inventories was $3,300, and current cost of plants and properties, net of accumulated depreciation and obsolescence, was $8,281.

Source: 1980 Annual Report of E. I. Du Pont.

TABLE 7–6
*E. I. Du Pont Company—Comparison of Selected Financial Data in Histori-
cal Dollars, Constant Dollars, and Current Costs**
*(Dollars in Millions, Except Per Share; All Constant Dollar and Current Cost
Data in Average 1980 Dollars)*

	1980	1979	1978	1977	1976
Sales					
Historical dollars	13,652	12,572	10,584	9,435	8.361
Constant dollars	13,652	14,272	13,368	12,830	12,103
Income from continuing operations					
Historical dollars	716	939	787	545	459
Constant dollars	237	620	585	522	421
Current costs	267	554			
Earnings per share from continuing operations					
Historical dollars	4.83	6.42	5.39	3.69	3.10
Constant dollars	1.55	4.21	3.97	3.50	2.81
Current costs	1.76	3.75			
Effective income tax rate	36%	37%	41%	44%	44%
Historical dollars	62%	50%	54%	52%	55%
Constant dollars	59%	53%			
Current costs					
Gain attributable to holding net monetary liabilities	85	102	109	109	77
Earnings per share including gain attributable to holding net monetary liabilities	4.83	6.42	5.39	3.69	3.10
Historical Dollars	2.13	4.92	4.73	4.25	3.34
Constant Dollars	2.34	4.46			
Current Costs					
Excess of constant dollar over current cost increase in value of inventories and net plants and properties	240	—	—	—	—
Stockholder's equity at year-end	5,690	5,312	4,760	4,317	4,030
Historical dollars	10,251	10,273	9,832	9,491	9,203
Constant dollars	10,365	10,585			
Current costs					*(continued)*

*Current cost data have not been developed for years prior to 1979.

TABLE 7–6 *(concluded)*

	1980	1979	1978	1977	1976
Debt ratio (%) at year-end	21%	20%	22%	26%	27%
Historical dollars	12%	12%	14%	17%	19%
Constant dollars	12%	12%			
Current costs					
Dividends paid per common share					
Historical dollars	2.75	2.75	2.42	1.92	1.75
Constant dollars	2.75	3.12	3.05	2.61	2.53
Market price per common share at year-end	42.00	40.38	42.00	40.13	45.04
Historical dollars	40.11	43.34	51.09	53.21	63.78
Constant dollars	246.8	217.4	195.4	181.5	170.5
Average DPI-U (1967 = 100)					

Source: 1980 Annual Report of E. I. Du Pont.

Chapter Eight

Analysis of the Income Statement: Operating Expenses and Other Items

S elling, administrative, other expenses and taxes must be deducted from gross profit (and other income added) to determine net income. These expenses are not identifiable specifically with or assigned to production. Some costs may be included here because they are difficult to allocate; it is, therefore, possible that a part of some of these expense items should affect production costs.

OPERATING EXPENSE

The main classifications under operating expenses in the income statement are selling, general, and administrative expenses. Expenses related to storing and displaying merchandise for sale, advertising, sales salaries, and delivery costs are the main items included under selling expenses. General and administrative expenses include: costs related to the operation of the general offices, costs of the accounting department, costs of the personnel office, and the costs of the credit and collections department. Certain expenses may be listed separately under operating expenses, including depreciation, depletion and amortization, maintenance and repair expenses, research and development (R&D) expenses, rental expenses, costs of exploration, and employee benefit payments (mainly pension costs), though they should have been part of the determination of cost of goods sold.

The analyst should calculate each of the listed expenses as a percentage of sales, as is done in preparing common size statements, which were discussed in Chapter 6. This will highlight the changing importance of expense items, trend patterns, and how costs relate to sales activity. A useful comparison also can be made between the behavior of individual expense items relative to sales, both over time and with industry composite figures.

MAINTENANCE AND REPAIRS

The significance of maintenance and repair costs will vary with the amount invested in plant, equipment, and productive activity. These costs typically are composed of both fixed and variable elements. While it is useful to look at their behavior in relation to sales, one should not make much of this comparison—a consistent relationship with sales is not to be expected. Also, it is useful to look at annual maintenance and repair costs in relation to total plant and equipment. Unfortunately, maintenance and repair expense is not always presented separately in the financial statements.

These costs are discretionary and can be postponed within limits. Unfortunately, management may be tempted to postpone needed maintenance and repairs when revenues are falling to maintain the level of income reported to stockholders. This can lead to continued future deterioration in profits. The analyst should assure himself/herself that reasonable amounts are being spent to maintain competitive facilities.

Inadequate maintenance and repairs can shorten the useful lives of assets, thereby invalidating depreciation expense charges, which are related to useful-life estimates.

RENTAL EXPENSES

A large number of corporations have chosen to lease rather than purchase assets. Lease rental costs, therefore, can become important expense items. Where a long-term lease is involved, the resulting rental expense can be characterized as a required series of payments over many years that include elements of both principal amortization and interest expense. To an important extent, the payment requirements on a long-term lease are equivalent to fixed charges incurred when debt is utilized to acquire an asset, and the fixed-charge obligation of a lease can force a company into financial difficulties just as readily as can fixed charges on funded or other debt.

An analyst should determine the future minimum lease payments required, both for capital leases and operating leases, and relate the payment requirements to expected cash flow to ensure that the firm has not overcommitted itself.

EXPLORATORY EXPENSES

Exploratory expenses, including intangible drilling and development costs, are a major expense item for oil, gas, and mining companies. Many companies charge off exploration costs currently, arguing that the future benefits are too uncertain to justify capitalizing such expenditures. Some companies, however, capitalize all development costs and amortize them over future periods. This can create a noncomparability problem when assessing the profitability of two companies using the different techniques.

For example, Standard Oil of California sold at a price–earnings ratio of about 12.5 during the years 1954–56, while Amerada Petroleum sold at a price–earnings ratio of about 25. One could ask, why were investors willing to pay twice as much for a dollar of reported earnings of Amerada? The answer seems to lie solely in the way intangible drilling costs were handled.

Amerada chose to expense all such costs in the year incurred. Standard Oil of California chose instead to capitalize such costs and write them off over the life of the leasehold, which was then averaging 10 years. Amerada reported a net income ranging from $22 to $24 million over the years 1954–56 and also reported intangible drilling costs ranging from $25 to $27 million over the same years. If one were to convert Amerada data to the system used by Standard Oil of California, they would report only about one-tenth of the intangible drilling costs actually reported each year. This would double reported profits, and the price–earnings ratios based on the adjusted data would then be about the same. It seems the market did make such adjustments.

FULL-COST VERSUS SUCCESSFUL EFFORT METHODS

We discussed the full-cost and successful efforts methods in Chapter 7. These methods now govern accounting in the oil and gas industry. Under the successful efforts method, the costs associated with unsuccessful attempts to find gas and oil are charged immediately against earnings, while the costs associated with successful drillings are capitalized. Full-cost accounting capitalizes all exploratory expenses and amortizes them as the resources actually are produced. A growing company doing a large amount of exploration will report lower earnings under the successful efforts method (similar to Amerada above) and probably appear more volatile.[1]

PENSION COSTS

Pension plans come in a variety of shapes, sizes, and formats. Let us first distinguish between defined contribution and defined benefit plans.

A defined contribution plan is one in which the firm's contribution rate is fixed—usually in terms of covered wages and salaries. Once a company has made the required contribution, it has no liability for additional payments. The recognition of the required contribution as expense, therefore, assures proper recognition of pension costs in the income account.

A defined benefit plan, by contrast, "is one where the benefits are established in advance by formula and the employer contributions are treated as variable."[2] The estimation of the size of the pension obligation is difficult and subject to great uncertainty in terms of what the company actually will be obligated to pay in the future. A large number of plans today are of the defined benefit type.

Under a defined benefit plan, the employer's commitment is to fund a future benefit, often defined in terms of the last three to five years of salary. The required annual contribution to the plan is not fixed, but is being redefined constantly in terms of changing wage rates, earnings rates of the fund, and other variables. Whether or not present employees will live long enough to collect benefits, how long they will collect benefits, the future salary rate that will determine benefit levels, and the earnings rate that will be experienced on pension plan assets, has been estimated to lead to defendable pension plan expense estimates that could be as much as five times as large as others. The required annual contribution to the plan is not fixed, but constantly is being redefined in terms of changing wage rates, the earnings rate of the fund, and other variables.

Accounting for Defined Benefit Plans

When a firm establishes a defined benefit plan, it commits itself to two undetermined costs: (1) past service costs that arise because of contracted

---

[1] For example, when Texaco switched to the "successful efforts" method in 1975, estimates were that full-cost accounting had increased reported profits by $500 million over the preceding 10 years.

[2] Dan M. McGill, *Foundations of Private Pensions* (Homewood, IL: Richard D. Irwin, 1975), p. 98.

obligations to employees for years served before either the founding of a plan or a change in the plan, and (2) current period costs as required by the plan. APB Opinion 8 and FASB Statement No. 87 (issued in December 1985) are the basic guides to accounting for pension costs.

APB Opinion 8 establishes both a floor and ceiling in terms of items that must be included when determining pension costs. This leaves, however, a large area for different cost determinations by different companies. Moreover, there appeared to be little uniformity in the information covering pension plans and costs provided in footnotes, and often far too little detail for purposes of evaluating the reasonableness of the annual charge actually made by a company. Footnotes typically provided information covering the actuarial present value of vested and nonvested accumulated plan benefits, the plan's assets at market value, and the interest assumption used. No information was available concerning salary projections or the age distribution of the workforce, an important component of ultimate liability.

SFAS 36 required that accumulated benefits be disclosed in annual reports. Accumulated benefits are the amount workers would be entitled to if they stopped working for the company at the date of the financial statements. Statement 87 requires a more suitable number for an ongoing firm—the estimate of benefits earned for services rendered to date based on future pay rates, not today's level. Moreover, it requires all companies to use the "projected unit credit" actuarial cost method. This method includes salary progression estimates that would result from inflation, promotion, and productivity gains. Also, limitations are placed on the freedom to select actuarial assumptions.

Finally, current accounting requirements call for amortization of prior service costs and of actuarial gains and losses over the remaining service lives of the existing employees, rather than the 30- or 40-year write-off period that had been used typically. Statement 87 should result in more realistic and comparable pension plan cost estimates among companies. Still, an analyst must recognize two things when evaluating pension charges and pension plans:

1. A defined benefit plan places an uncertain constraint on the future earnings of a firm in terms of the amount available to owners and managers.

2. Reported profits can be distorted in a comparative sense because of different assumptions used in determining annual charges, both over time and between companies.

Actuarial Funding Formulas

These formulas are driven by two primary variables:

1. The interest rate assumption, which represents the annual rate of return that the actuary expects the pension fund assets to earn.
2. The wage assumption, which represents the annual rate at which covered wages are expected to grow.

The higher the interest rate assumption and the lower the wage growth assumption, the smaller will be the reported unfunded pension liability and the lower the required company contribution. In actuality, the setting of these assumptions is more art than science, making it difficult to compare pension costs between firms and to judge the adequacy of the costs charged for funding purposes.

Prior Service Charges

Accounting views prior service costs as an expense that should be spread over subsequent years, even though the liability could be immediate. The analyst should include such charges as an ordinary charge against income and such charges should not be run through the inventory accounts. These charges will require regular cash disbursements by the company to the pension plan in the future and represent a constraint on future income growth.

Impact of Inflation

In a world of uncertain future inflation rates and changing social patterns, the benefit package that a firm is required to fund is difficult to define precisely before the fact. The purpose of a pension program is to provide not merely so many unadjusted dollars of income at retirement, but rather an amount that is sufficient to fund some target standard of living for the retiree. This will be reflected in union bargaining and wage scales upon which the benefits are based.

Each generation is blessed with the task of funding the promises and/or miscalculations of the previous generation. In order for one generation of producers and wage earners to subsidize a previous one, in the form of benefits improvements, output must be growing at a rate that is sufficient to fund the resulting benefits. If output (and firm income) does not grow at the required rate, just two alternative possibilities remain: (1) the pension system must renege, or (2) there must be a continuous relocation of wealth flowing from producers to nonproducers and denigration in the claim that producers have on the fruits of their own labor or capital. In the face of declining worker productivity in the 1970s, declining birth rates, and increased life expectancies, investors have ample justification for concern with the effect of pension plan obligations on their future well being.

An analyst must consider the elasticity of demand for a firm's products and the resulting ability to pass on rising costs related to inflation and improved benefits. Rising pension claims act as a constraint on future firm income and, therefore, deserves careful analysis.

Termination of a Pension Plan and Risk Profiles

The *Employment Retirement Income Security Act* (ERISA) of 1974 provides that the sponsor of a plan who terminates that plan at a time when pension fund assets are not sufficient to fund that portion of vested benefits that are guaranteed by the Pension Benefit Guarantee Corporation (PBGC) is liable to PBGC up to a limit of 30 percent of net worth.[3] This "converted employer pension obligations from gratuities to corporate liabilities enforceable at law."[4] Accordingly, ERISA changed the risk profile of firms that offered pension plans. Market risk profiles will be higher:

1. The more closely related future benefit levels are to inflation-related variables.
2. The narrower a firm's equity cushion.
3. The narrower the spread between marginal revenue and cost.
4. The more variable the firm's total revenue function.
5. The higher the degree of statistical relationship between a firm's total revenue function and the status of business conditions in general.

An investor should require a higher potential return for a firm that has a higher-risk profile, and avoid firms where the risk exceeds his capacity to accept.

Firms may, and have, terminated pension plans where the value of the assets in the pension fund exceeded the level of guaranteed benefits plus

---

3 Modifications of the act to increase this limit have been considered, but Congress has not taken action to date.

4 Patrick Regan Treynor and William Priest, *The Financial Reality of Pension Funding Under ERISA* (Homewood, IL: Dow Jones–Irwin, 1976), p. VII.

0.3 times the market value of the firm's equity. The firm, under these conditions, can walk away from its pension liabilities and gain assets. PBGC must make up the deficit. This part of the law may well be changed in the future. Two studies have shown positive returns to shareholders around the time of such a termination.[5]

Other Employee Benefits

Accounting requires the disclosure of the costs of past employment benefits (OPEB). The costs of health and life insurance benefits are the main components of these costs, and such benefits usually continue after an employee reaches retirement and often include the spouse and children. These costs are potentially large and should receive careful consideration in terms of the liability they create and their impact on future income.

These costs typically are accounted for on a pay-as-you-go basis; this could substantially underestimate future liability and place a constraint on income. Cottle, Murray, and Block recommend multiplying the annual expense reported by a company by a factor between 10 and 15 (with the factor rising with age of the workforce), to estimate the balance sheet liability.[6] They feel this reasonably estimates the liability over the working lives of the employees and allows for inflation.

Research and Development Costs

Research and development costs are difficult to properly account for because:

1. The ultimate results are highly uncertain.

2. A long time can occur between the initiation of a research project and the determination of its ultimate success or failure.

Such expenditures are often substantial and must be considered when analyzing current income and forecasting future profits.

---

5 J. Van Der Heis, "The Effect of Voluntary Terminations of Oversized Defined Benefit Pension Plans on Shareholder Wealth," *The Journal of Risk and Insurance* (1987), and M. J. Alderson and K. C. Chan, "Excess Asset Reversions and Shareholder Wealth," *Journal of Finance* (March,1986).

6 Sidney Cottle, Roger Murray, and Frank Block, *Graham and Dodd's Security Analysis*, 5th ed. (New York: McGraw-Hill Book Company, 1988), p. 193.

FASB Statement Number 2 concludes that, subject to certain exceptions, all Research and Development (R&D) costs should be charged to expense in the year incurred. This does seem to conflict with the accounting principle of matching costs and revenues, since it does not match the expenses with the potential future benefits the firm hopes to generate.

The analyst should attempt to judge the success of past R&D expenditures and the likelihood of future successes when evaluating a firm. It is the future that is of importance when evaluating a common stock, and accounting for R&D expenses is not helpful in this regard. Evaluation of the potential future success generated by R&D outlays requires information on the types of research performed, the outlays by category, the technical feasibility of projects being undertaken, and the quality of the research staff. It is also useful to know the company's success–failure experience in the past.

Interest Expense

Interest costs generally are expensed when incurred, except in the case of public utilities and industries such as real estate.

Interest related to construction may be capitalized by public utilities. Utilities cannot include funds raised for purposes of planned construction in their rate base while those funds are a part of current assets, on which they are permitted to earn a fair rate of return. If the matter were left at that point, the utilities would be paying the cost for the funds, but would not be permitted to capitalize the interest costs on funds raised for construction prior to the time that useful fixed assets are available and added to the rate base.

Investors should realize that the interest charged to construction credit items is temporary in nature, and will disappear as soon as the funds actually are invested in fixed assets. Ideally, as soon as this occurs, the company will begin to earn a fair return on the additional plant and equipment, and the additional earnings will replace the amount that was added previously to earnings for interest charged to construction credit. It is, however, a noncash item and the situation may not be ideal.

Assume that the interest charged to construction credit items was equal to $0.25 per share this year as part of total reported earnings of $2.25 ($2 per share being earned on the old property). Next year the item is lost. If earnings on the old property rise by 8 percent, then earnings on the old property would rise from $2 per share to $2.16 per share. If no additional earnings flow from the new property, the earnings per share will be reported as $2.16 next year versus $2.25 this year. If earnings on new property were $0.09 per share, then earnings per share would be reported as $2.25 in each year. If earnings per share on the new property exceed $0.09 per share, then an increase in earnings per share, compared to last year, will be reported. An analyst must consider this item when forecasting income and for purposes of deciding whether or not management's expansion plans were desirable for the owners. This item also must be considered when calculating interest or fixed charges coverage ratios, as we will discuss in Chapter 11.

BREAK-EVEN ANALYSIS AND LEVERAGE

Cost analysis is concerned with the relationship between sales, costs, and profits. The analyst wants to know how costs vary as sales and output levels change, and the effect of those variations on the profitability of the firm.

A framework known as break-even analysis has been developed to explore those relationships. It is based on classifying costs into fixed and variable cost categories. Fixed costs are those that do not change with changes in the level of output. Variable costs are those that change as the level of output changes. For example, the preparing of the plates for each page of this book are a fixed cost, since the total fixed cost will be the same whether one book is printed or five thousand books are printed. The paper used is a variable cost that will tend to vary directly and proportionately with the number of books produced.

An Illustrative Break-Even Analysis

The break-even point is that level of output at which neither a profit is earned nor a loss incurred. This could only occur where total revenues equal total costs. To illustrate, let us assume that the sales price for a unit of product sold by the firm is $5 and that fixed costs total $2,000, while variable costs are $2 per unit and vary in direct proportion to changes in the level of output. Under these conditions, the firm will break even if it sells 666⅔ units, calculated as follows when X equals the number of units at break-even:

$$\text{Total revenues} = \text{Total costs}$$
$$\text{Total revenues (R)} = \text{Fixed costs (F)} + \text{Variable costs (V)}$$
$$\$5X = \$2000 + \$2X$$
$$\$3X = \$2000$$
$$X = 666\tfrac{2}{3} \text{ Units}$$

FIGURE 8–1
Illustrative Straight-Line Break-Even Chart

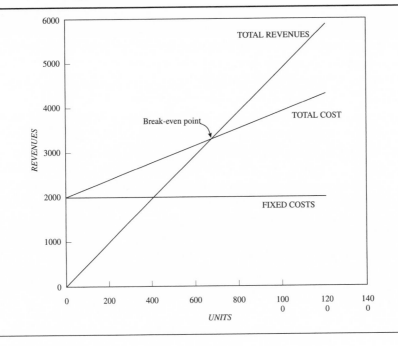

This can also be represented in a diagram (see Figure 8–1).

Only after a company moves beyond the break-even point does it realize a profit, and the break-even point is, therefore, important.

Limitations of Break-Even Analysis

The above illustration assumed that all costs could be classified as either fixed or directly and proportionally variable throughout time.

First, there are costs that are semivariable, that is, they are fixed over a certain range of outputs and then vary. In the long run, all costs are probably variable since plant scale can be changed. Therefore, break-even estimates built on the basis of a simplified analysis could only be useful, even in the estimating sense, over limited time periods. A straight line will not represent a semivariable cost, as it assumes a constant rate of change. An example of a semivariable cost might be the cost associated with a generator used to produce electric power. That cost could be fixed up to a certain number of units of output (capacity for that generator) and then rise sharply as a new generator must be brought on line to continue to expand output.

Second, the sales price was assumed constant no matter how many units were assumed sold. A firm might have to lower price to sell additional units, and a straight line would not then represent the change in total revenues as sales changed. Some type of curve, based on the elasticity of demand for the firm's products, would likely represent total revenue behavior as sales change.

The total cost curve also would be represented more realistically by a curve than a straight line. Economies of scale are likely to cause total cost to increase at a decreasing rate, at least to the point of diminishing returns. Moreover, as noted above, all costs probably are variable in the long run.

Finally, break-even analysis requires that the variable components of expense be separated from the fixed components. Accounting data is not segregated in this fashion, and even internal management of a firm finds this a difficult task. An outside analyst could only crudely approximate such breakdowns based on past experience.

Still, the break-even framework can be useful if its limitations are recognized and its applications kept in proper perspective.

Some Applications of Break-Even Analysis

Leverage is present whenever a firm has fixed costs. Once a firm develops a volume of sales that is sufficient to cover its fixed costs, further increments in sales will result in a more-than-proportionate increase in profitability. However, this is a two-edged sword. If sales fall below the break-even level, profits will fall more than in proportion to the drop in sales. A firm that has a high proportion of fixed costs is then risky when an analyst fears an economic downturn, and interesting if an economic expansion is expected.

Also, the higher the level of fixed costs relative to variable costs, the higher the break-even point, but the greater the rate of profit increase once sales exceed the break-even level. Moreover, a company with a higher degree of operating leverage could appear to be an exceptional growth company in a booming economy. The sharp increase in earnings could, however, be temporary and rapidly disappear in a cyclical economy. If one observed the increase in profits without reference to leverage of the firm, they could draw an incorrect conclusion about the long-run profitability of the firm.

Contribution Margin

The contribution margin is what remains of the sales price after deducting variable cost per unit. It is important as fixed costs must be met from this margin before a profit can be earned. From our break-even illustration above, the contribution margin is $3 per unit. If sales exceed 666⅔ units (the break-even point), profits will expand at a rate of $3 per unit sold. This, of course, is based on the oversimplification that straight-line assumptions can be utilized. Such assumptions, while not accurate, may provide useful ballpark estimates.

Keep in mind that changes in sales mix or the efficiency of a firm will result in a different profit change for a given sales volume estimate than the profit margin would suggest. Still, a useful estimate may be obtained at minimum cost by using straight-line assumptions, and the analyst can vary that estimate subjectively to allow for greater reality.

AN ILLUSTRATIVE COST ANALYSIS

For illustrative purposes, we return to our review of an analysis of Deere & Company issued by Sanford C. Bernstein & Co., Inc., in January, 1981. We discussed their analysis and forecast of revenues at the end of Chapter 6. We will review their analysis of costs and their profit forecasts in this chapter, and suggest a valuation for the stock that could have been prepared based on the data generated in the report.

"The key to a financial analysis of Deere & Company is an understanding of the company's revenues and cost structure for either a single product line or a group of closely associated product lines. As the factories are treated as profit centers, manufacturing costs specific to each factory may be estimated. . . . Further, the costs and profitability generated by the sales branches, as a total group, may be estimated."[7] The analyst chose to separate costs into fixed and variable components, and use these estimates with revenue estimates to review past profit contribution and forecast future profit contribution for each major cost center. The analyst did have the advantage of detailed data gathered in field visits that would not necessarily be part of the annual report.

The Waterloo Tractor Works

Let us review the study of and forecasts for a particular cost center, namely the Waterloo Tractor Works. Revenues expected to be generated by this

---

7 Sanford C. Bernstein & Co., Inc., Report (New York: 1981), p. 106.

TABLE 8–1

North American Agricultural Tractors—Waterloo ($ million)

	1979E	1980E	1981E	1984E
Net sales	$1,020.0	$1,021.7	$1,288.0	$1,840.0
Direct labor	33.0	33.2	41.9	59.8
Direct materials	480.0	485.3	618.2	883.3
Variable manufacturing overhead	112.0	127.6	146.3	207.1
Total variable manufacturing costs	$ 625.0	$ 646.1	$ 806.4	$1,150.2
Variable SG&A-allocated	$ 20.0	$ 21.4	$ 25.8	$ 33.7
Total variable costs	645.0	667.5	832.2	1,183.9
Variable profit	375.0	354.2	455.8	656.4
Fixed manufacturing overhead	112.0	124.5	144.4	211.6
Fixed SG&A-allocated	68.0	71.6	86.3	112.8
Total fixed costs	$ 180.0	$ 196.1	$ 230.8	$ 324.4
Operating profit[1]	$ 195.0	$ 158.1	$ 225.0	$ 332.0

[1]Before allocation of net miscellaneous items.

Source: Bernstein estimates, Bernstein Report, op. cit., p. 34.

plant were forecast based on the data presented in Chapter 6. The estimates for selected years are presented in Table 8–1.

Fiscal 1980 results were expected to reflect the dampening effects of cyclical economic conditions as well as other adverse factors, such as the Soviet grain embargo. Fixed costs were expected to rise in reaction to both inflationary trends in personnel costs and higher levels of depreciation and amortization. The expectation of higher levels of depreciation and amortization were based on expected capital expenditures designed to expand capacity and enhance manufacturing efficiencies. While the expected increase in fixed costs would raise the break-even point, it would also increase the degree of operating leverage. Increased operating leverage would accelerate profit growth as long as sales were expanding, and decrease profits if sales declined. Accordingly, operating profit margins were expected to show a sharp decline in 1980 to about 15.53 and then rise to about 17.5 percent in 1981.

Total variable costs were expected to rise by 12.9 percent per year over the forecast period (1980–84), mainly because of a rise in direct material cost, the largest component of variable costs, and also in direct labor costs.

Rises in revenues after 1980 are expected to offset these cost increases, keeping the relationship between total operating costs and sales steady.

Consolidated Income Statement

An historical and forecast consolidated income statement was presented in Table 6–11 in Chapter 6. This statement was prepared on the basis of the data gathered and analyzed for each major cost center. For example, the forecasts for 1984 by cost center and for the total company are presented in Table 8–2. The following highlights of the financial forecasts were noted in the report:[8]

1. Return on investment was expected to recover strongly from 1980s depressed level, but to remain below the levels achieved in the 1973–1979 period. The analysis of return on investment is summarized in Table 8–3. This is a useful check on the reasonableness of the assumptions underlying their forecasts. The erosion of return relative to 1973–79 derives from expected continued pressure on net margins in North American operations.

2. Return on equity is forecast to recover to just under 19 percent by 1984, modestly above the 17.7 percent recorded in fiscal 1979, but generally below the returns achieved during most of the 1970s.

3. Total dividend payments are projected to rise by 14.2 percent per year through 1984, as shown below:[9]

	Earnings per Share	Dividends per Share	Payout Ratio
1980	$3.27	$1.875	57.3%
1981	4.72	2.050	43.4
1982	6.00	2.300	38.3
1983	7.50	2.600	34.7
1984	8.50	3.000	35.3

Dividends per share were $1.55 in 1979 and $0.66 in 1973. The report then noted that "if economic conditions are such that our earnings and cash flow projections are not realized, dividend growth will be reduced accordingly." The report also noted that management felt strongly that financial leverage should be constrained to protect

---

8 Sanford C. Bernstein & Co., Inc., op. cit., p. 100–01.

9 Sanford C. Bernstein & Co., Inc., op. cit., p. 102.

TABLE 8–2
Deere & Company—Fiscal 1984 Forecast ($ Million)

	Waterloo	Harvester Works	Implement & Other	Construction & Industrial	Total North American Manufacturing	Mannheim	Zweibrucken & Other	Total Overseas Manufacturing	Total Deere & Company
Net Sales	$1,840.3	$1,157.0	$2,672.0	$1,772.0	$7,441.3	$986.1	$812.5	$1,798.6	$9,239.9
Direct Labor	59.8	52.1	100.2	88.6	300.7	49.3	35.7	85.0	385.7
Direct Materials	883.3	538.0	1,456.2	779.7	3,652.2	43.0	414.4	907.4	4,564.6
Variable Manufacturing Overhead	207.1	167.8	340.0	265.8	980.6	140.5	126.1	266.6	1,247.2
Total Variable Manufacturing Costs	$1,150.2	$ 757.9	$1,896.4	$1,134.1	$4,938.5	$682.8	$576.2	$1,259.0	$6,197.5
Variable SG&A Allocated	$ 33.7	$ 21.1	$ 48.9	$ 32.5	$ 136.3	$ 18.1	$ 14.9	$ 32.9	$ 169.2
Total Variable Costs	$1,183.9	$ 779.0	$1,945.3	$1,166.5	$5,074.8	$700.9	$591.1	$1,291.9	$6,366.7
Variable Profit	$ 656.4	$ 378.0	$ 726.7	$ 605.5	$2,366.5	$285.2	$221.4	$ 506.7	$2,873.2

(continued)

TABLE 8-2 (concluded)

	Waterloo	Harvester Works	Implement & Other	Construction & Industrial	Total North American Manufacturing	Mannheim	Zweibrucken & Other	Total Overseas Manufacturing	Total Deere & Company
Fixed Manufacturing Overhead	$ 211.6	$ 145.2	$ 360.7	$ 290.8	$1,008.4	$167.6	$117.5	$ 285.1	$1,293.5
Fixed SG&A Allocated	112.8	70.9	163.8	107.6	456.2	60.4	49.8	110.3	566.4
Total Fixed Costs	$ 324.4	$ 216.1	$ 524.5	$ 399.4	$1,464.5	$228.1	$167.3	$ 395.4	$1,859.9
Operating Profit[1]	$ 322.0	$ 161.9	$ 202.2	$ 206.1	$ 902.1	$ 57.1	$ 54.1	$ 111.2	$1,013.3
Net Miscellaneous Items									136.1
Unallocated SG&A									31.3
Equity Income									0.0
Pretax Income									$ 848.8
Taxes									380.6
Net Inc-Consol Group									$ 465.2
Equity Income									79.0
Net Income									$ 544.2
Earnings Per Share									$ 8.50

[1] Operating profits before allocation of net miscellaneous items.

Note: Totals may not add due to rounding.

Source: Corporate reports and Bernstein estimates. Berstein Report, op. cit., p. 110.

TABLE 8–3
Deere & Company—Analysis of Return on Investment and Capital Self-Sufficiency[1]

	Net Margin[2]	×	Capital Turnover[3]	=	Return on Investment	+	Effect of Financial Leverage	=	Return on Equity	×	Retention Rate	=	Reinvestment Rate	−	Growth in Operating Investment	=	Equity Capital Required as % of Equity Base[4]
1973	9.2%		1.75		16.1%		6.9%		23.0%		75.6%		17.4%		1.3%		16.1%
1974	7.4		2.15		15.9		3.8		19.7		72.1		14.2		24.4		(10.2)
1975	7.4		2.05		15.2		5.5		20.7		69.7		14.4		23.7		(9.3)
1976	8.7		1.68		14.6		5.7		20.3		74.3		15.1		10.3		4.8
1977	8.1		1.83		14.8		3.7		18.5		71.6		13.3		21.3		(8.0)
1978	7.5		1.74		13.1		3.6		16.9		68.0		11.5		10.5		1.0
1979	7.4		1.87		13.8		3.9		17.7		68.2		12.1		10.7		1.4
1980E	5.8		1.82		10.6		0.0		10.6		45.2		4.8		34.9		(30.1)
1981E	6.2		1.59		9.9		4.3		14.2		55.5		7.9		4.5		3.4
1984E	7.3		2.01		14.7		4.1		18.8		64.7		12.2		11.4		0.8

[1] All data based on beginning year balance.

[2] Pre-interest expense net of related taxes.

[3] Based on operating capital as defined in Table 84.

[4] Represents amount of equity, stated as a percentage of prior year net worth, needed to maintain constant capital ratios; positive number implies a reduction in financial leverage.

Source: Corporate reports and Berstein estimates, Berstein Report, op. cit., p. 117.

current debt ratings, even if dividend growth is reduced as a result. Still, the author of the report felt the dividend projections were reasonable.

4. The earnings retention rate was expected to fall below that in the 1970s when it reached a high of 75.6 percent. Capital expenditure programs were expected to be maintained, however.

An Illustrative Valuation Model

We will use the limited-hold present-value valuation framework, assuming a five-year hold ending at year-end 1984, for purposes of preparing a suggested valuation of Deere & Company stock as of January 1981. The following data are required to calculate intrinsic value for the stock:

1. Expected earnings per share and dividends per share over the period 1980–84. These estimates are provided above, as prepared by the analyst.
2. The expected tax rate for the investor. We will assume an effective rate for calculation purposes of 50 percent (the top bracket rate at that time) for ordinary income and 25 percent for capital gains. Note that intrinsic values would be different for different investors, depending on their tax circumstances.
3. The opportunity cost for the investor. There are several approaches suggested in the investment literature for estimating this variable. We will review these approaches below and arrive at an estimated discount rate.
4. The price at which an investor might have expected to sell the stock at the end of 1984. We will estimate this variable by multiplying expected earnings per share for 1984 by the price–earnings ratio we might have expected to exist at that time. Development of this estimate also will be discussed below.

Estimating the Appropriate Discount Rate

A common stock is a desirable purchase when an investor believes that the expected return generated from holding that stock exceeds the return required by the investor for the level of risk represented for that stock. It is an opportunity cost concept, based on answering the question, what could the stockholder earn on alternative investments of equivalent risk?

The Discounted Cash Flow Approach

One approach suggested in the literature is based on a manipulation of the hold-into-perpetuity valuation model as follows:

$$P = D_1/k - g$$

where

P = The intrinsic value estimate for the stock.

D_1 = The dividend expected to be received at the end of the first holding period.

g = The compound annual growth rate expected for dividends.

k = The appropriate discount rate.

Accordingly:

$$k = D_1/P + g$$

The expected dividend at the end of the first one-year holding period is relatively easy to estimate. Current market price of the stock at the time the estimate is being prepared could be logically used for P. The difficulty is estimating g. Two possible ways of estimating g are suggested below and related to the analyst's forecasts:

1. The historical growth rate for g could be used if earnings and dividend growth rates have been relatively stable in the past. Total dividends paid grew at a 15.6 percent compound annual rate from 1973 through 1980. Over a 10-year period ending in 1984, however, our analyst estimated the earnings growth rate as 11.5 percent, and felt that the growth rate could slow to 9 percent, assuming a GNP growth of 9 percent (3 percent real and 6 percent inflation), with the profitability estimate given. This could suggest a 10 percent growth estimate, assuming constancy in the dividend pay-out ratio. Remember, our purpose is more to illustrate the valuation process than to develop accurate estimates for Deere & Company.

2. Retention growth. The basic valuation model into perpetuity can be used to show that, in the model,

$$g = br$$

where

g = The growth rate expected for dividends.

b = The retention rate for the firm, calculated by dividing dividends per share by earnings per share.

r = The rate of return earned on owner's equity.

For steady-state profitability assumptions (average for the cycle), the analyst's projections would lead to the following:

$$g = (.65)(.177) = .115$$

This rate often is called the sustainable growth rate for a firm. Since it is higher than the historical estimate above, yet in line with a 10-year period, we would raise our growth rate expectation to 11–11.5 percent. Based on our work above, we would suggest calculating intrinsic value using an 11 percent growth rate.

The analyst preparing this report was more optimistic, projecting a 14.2 percent growth rate for dividends and a higher growth rate for earnings per share. Using a 14 percent rate for earnings per share and assuming an effective tax rate of 33 percent, the appropriate discount rate is 13 percent, calculated as follows:

$$k = \frac{D_1 + g}{P}$$

$$= \frac{2.05}{38} + .14$$

$$= .05 + .14 = .19$$

Adjusted for taxes = $.19 \times .67 = .13$

If a rate of 11 percent representing the sustainable growth rate is used, however, the suggested discount rate would be 11 percent ($.16 \times .67$). We have, accordingly, used an after-tax discount factor of 11 percent in Table 8–4 to calculate the intrinsic value of this stock.

The Capital Asset Pricing Model Approach

The literature also suggests using the Capital Asset Pricing Model Approach for estimating k. First, one would have to estimate a risk-free rate. The 90-day Treasury bill rate is often suggested as a proxy for the risk-free rate. The T-bill rate, however, varies markedly over time and is not truly riskless when one considers the need to roll over funds. Practitioners often use as a base rate the rate on long-term Treasury bonds rather than a risk-free rate, since common stocks are long-term securities, and Treasury bond rates are more stable. Also, long-term bonds reflect an opportunity cost an investor certainly would want to exceed, to accept the added risks associated with purchasing common stocks.

Brigham and Gapenski[10] note that Merrill Lynch publishes, on a regular basis, a forecast based on discounted cash flow methodology for the expected return on the market. They suggest subtracting the current long-term Treasury bond rate from Merrill Lynch's current market forecast to determine implied market risk premiums. To illustrate, assume that Merrill Lynch's reported expected return on the market at the end of 1980 were 20 percent, and the Treasury bond rate were 11 percent. The implied market risk premium would then be 9 percent. We would then determine the beta for Deere & Company and multiply it by the risk premium to estimate k. Assuming the beta for Deere & Co. were 1.2, then k would equal 10.8 percent. This would strengthen using a g of 11 percent rather than 11.5 percent.

One must remember, however, that we are trying to estimate investor's expectations (not necessarily those of Merrill Lynch), and professional analysts other than Merrill Lynch may have different market expectations. We, therefore, did not press to get accurate forecasts for 1980 since we are more interested in illustrating the methodology than in valuing Deere & Co.

Estimating the Sales Price for the Stock

A market price for a stock can be said to equal earnings per share times the price–earnings ratio at any given time. The report on Deere provided us with estimates of earnings and dividends per share that we will assume we accept as reasonable. We still must estimate the appropriate price–earnings ratio that we feel will prevail by year-end 1984. This estimate should be based on past history, our future expectations, and the market conditions we expect for year-end 1984. The average annual price–earnings ratio varied between 7 and 8 during the years 1972–79 and rose to 9.5 in 1980. The favorable expectations suggested in the report could justify an expectation of 10 in a price–earnings ratio for year-end 1984 as of January 1981. The actual price–earnings ratio was higher as earnings expectations for this

---

10 Eugene Brigham and Louis Gapenski, *Financial Management: Theory and Practice*, 5th ed. (New York: The Dryden Press, 1988), p. 226.

report were not realized. Let us assume a price–earnings ratio of 10, since we are estimating as of January 1981.

The Valuation Model

Based on the assumptions noted above, we would have determined an intrinsic value of $53.53 for Deere & Company calculated as shown in Table 8–4. These calculations also assume the investor receives the 1981 dividends and all dividends in succeeding years including 1984.

The intrinsic value estimate would have suggested purchasing the stock. Graham and Dodd, however, suggested a margin of at least 40 percent for intrinsic value over purchase price to cover forecasting errors. The margin here is only 13.89 percent ($53.53 – $47.47), and a purchase would not have been suggested if their rule had been applied. We suggest requiring a margin of at least 30 percent before purchasing a stock, and would not, therefore, have recommended purchase as of January 1981. The analyst's expectations were not realized since the stock sold at about $40 per share by year-end 1984, and earnings per share actually had fallen rather than risen. Our decision not to purchase, even with the favorable information developed in the research report, would have been a correct one. In 1988, however, the stock was again in favor with institutional investors, and rated highly in terms of timeliness by *Value Line* in their report.

TABLE 8–4
Calculation of Intrinsic Value for the Common Stock of
Deere & Company as of January 1981

Year	Earnings Per Share	Dividends Per Share	After Tax Dividend	Discount Factor @ 11%	Present Value of Dividends
1980	$3.27	—	—	—	—
1981	4.72	2.050	1.025	.9009	.9234
1982	6.00	2.300	1.150	.8116	.9333
1983	7.50	2.600	1.300	.7312	.9506
1984	8.50	3.000	1.500	.6587	.9881

Present Value of Expected Dividends   3.7954

Plus Present Value of Sales Price:

Expected Sales Price = 8.5×10 = $85.00

Expected Capital Gains

    ($85.00 – Purchase Price*) = $47.00

Expected Capital Gains Tax ($85.00 – 47.00) (.25)   = (9.50)

    $75.50

Present Value of Realized Cash Inflow $(75.50 \times .6587)$ = $49.7318

Intrinsic Value Estimate   = $53.5272

*Average Price for January, 1981.

Chapter Nine

Balance Sheet Analysis

It has long been recognized that, for most corporations, there is little correlation between the earning power value of a stock and its book value and between economic and market value of assets and their book value. Most investors and analysts pay little attention to book value in terms of valuing a business, except in the case of (1) financial corporations if stated asset values are assumed to be close to realizable market values; (2) public utilities because they are entitled (although not guaranteed) to earn a fair return on the fair value of assets used in the public service; and (3) on occasion, natural resource companies.

After World War II and until the 1970s, less and less attention had been paid to balance sheet analysis—we believe less attention than should have been paid. While it is true that the value of a business and particularly of its owner's equity rests largely on earning power and its quality, inadequate liquidity or an overburdensome debt can prevent future growth and possibly lead to bankruptcy. Corporate liquidity did shrink sharply in the 1970s, as shown by the fall in liquidity ratios in Figure 9–1. The ratio of liquid assets to short-term market debt and debt maturity ratios had fallen to historic lows by 1980. Based on current ratio and quick ratio data by industry groupings (see Table 9–1), liquidity has appeared to stabilize in recent years. The quick ratios seem adequate, suggesting little or no liquidity problems.

Inflation would encourage a sharp curtailment in liquidity since a holder of monetary assets loses during such a period. Moreover, firms would want to avoid holding excess liquid assets, since they could be losing profits that could have been gained by more effectively investing these assets. Still, the sharp drops in corporate liquidity during this period make corporations more vulnerable to a recession. Investors should carefully monitor these developments in relation to firms whose securities they are reviewing for potential purchase.

FIGURE 9–1

Cyclical Pattern of Debt Financing, Liquidity Ratios, and Debt Maturity Ratios for Nonfinancial Business Corporations

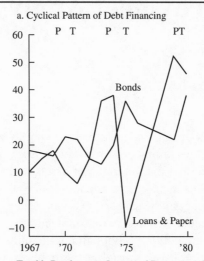

a. Cyclical Pattern of Debt Financing

Taxable Bonds versus Loans and Paper, annual
Net Increases in Amounts Outstanding, $ Billions.

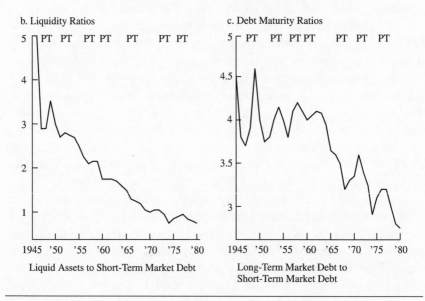

b. Liquidity Ratios

Liquid Assets to Short-Term Market Debt

c. Debt Maturity Ratios

Long-Term Market Debt to
Short-Term Market Debt

Note: P (Peak) and T (Trough) represent NBER Reference Cycle Peaks and Troughs.

Source: H. Kaufman, J. McKean, and D. Foster, *1981 Prospects for Financial Markets* (New York: Salomon Brothers, December 8, 1940), p 7.

TABLE 9–1
Liquidity Ratios—S&P Groups, 1988–93

	Current Ratio						Quick Ratio					
	1993	1992	1991	1990	1989	1988	1993	1992	1991	1990	1989	1988
Energy Composite	1.1	1.0	1.0	1.1	1.1	1.2	0.8	0.7	0.7	0.8	0.8	0.8
Aerospace	1.4	1.4	1.4	NA	NA	NA	0.7	0.6	0.5	NA	NA	NA
Building Materials	1.9	2.0	0.8	0.8	1.6	1.8	1.1	1.1	0.5	0.5	1.0	1.1
Chemicals	1.3	1.3	1.4	1.4	NA	NA	0.9	0.9	0.9	0.9	NA	NA
Communication Equip.	1.3	1.3	1.2	1.6	1.6	1.5	1.0	1.0	0.9	1.2	1.1	1.0
Computer Software & Serv.	2.2	2.0	1.9	1.9	2.1	2.2	2.2	NA	1.9	NA	NA	NA
Computer Systems	1.4	1.3	1.4	1.6	1.8	2.0	1.0	1.0	1.0	1.2	1.3	1.5
Electronics—Defense	1.8	2.1	2.2	1.4	1.4	1.4	1.7	1.7	1.8	1.0	0.9	0.9
Electronics—Instr.	1.5	1.5	1.6	1.5	1.5	1.7	0.9	1.0	1.1	1.0	1.0	1.1
Electronics—Semiconductors	1.8	1.8	1.7	1.7	1.7	1.7	1.4	1.5	1.3	1.2	1.3	1.2
Enginering & Constr.	1.3	1.3	1.5	1.3	1.4	1.1	1.0	1.0	1.1	1.0	1.0	0.7
Foods	1.2	1.2	1.2	1.3	1.3	1.4	0.7	0.7	0.7	0.7	0.7	0.8
Health Care—Composite	1.5	1.6	1.7	1.6	1.8	1.7	1.1	1.2	1.2	1.2	1.3	1.3
Health Care—Drugs	1.2	1.3	1.4	1.3	1.6	1.6	0.9	1.0	1.1	1.0	1.3	1.2
Machine Tools	1.7	1.9	1.9	2.0	2.1	2.0	1.1	1.3	1.0	1.1	1.1	1.1
Oil & Gas Drilling	4.0	3.0	2.1	3.8	3.4	0.5	3.7	2.6	2.0	3.6	3.2	0.5
Oil (Expl. & Prod.)	1.0	0.8	0.9	1.0	1.1	NA	1.0	0.8	0.9	0.9	1.1	NA
Oil (Composite)	1.0	1.0	1.0	1.0	1.1	1.2	0.8	0.7	0.7	0.8	0.8	0.8
Steel	1.4	1.3	1.3	1.6	2.0	1.8	0.8	0.8	0.7	0.9	1.3	1.2
Telecomm (Long Dist.)	1.1	1.1	1.1	1.1	1.1	1.3	1.0	1.0	1.0	0.9	0.9	1.0
Transportation (Composite)	0.8	0.7	0.7	0.7	0.8	0.9	0.7	0.6	0.6	0.6	0.7	0.8
Airlines	0.7	0.6	0.7	0.5	0.7	0.8	0.6	0.5	0.6	0.4	0.6	0.7
Truckers	1.1	1.2	1.1	1.1	1.1	1.1	1.1	1.2	1.1	1.0	1.1	1.1

Source: Standard & Poor's *Analyst's Handbook, 1994 Annual Edition.* Reprinted by permission of Standard & Poor's, a division of The McGraw-Hill Companies.

BALANCE SHEET DISCLOSURE

Investors must understand what balance sheets demonstrate. One examines a balance sheet to determine the company's current financial position, the amount and nature of invested capital, the sources of invested capital, the proportionate division of corporate capitalization, and, with the income statement, the rate of return earned on total assets, on total capitalization, and on stockholders' equity.

Balance Sheet Values

The word "value" is used in accounting to describe the figure at which an asset or liability is carried in the accounts, although the amount may represent something different than "value" as the word is used ordinarily. Accounting is based predominantly on cost, and assets usually are carried at cost or some modification of cost. For example, accountants report the original cost of fixed assets on the balance sheet, less amortization of that cost over the useful life of the asset. Inventories will reflect the cost to purchase the items included, unless current market value falls below that cost. Accounting values, therefore, are not intended to represent current market value, replacement value, or liquidation value of assets.

Accounting values are book values which signify only the amount at which an item is stated in accordance with the accounting principles related to the item. The term *book value* also is used to represent the total owners' equity shown in the balance sheet; book value per share is the owners' equity divided by the number of shares outstanding. Book value per share should not be thought of as an indicator of economic worth.

Balance Sheet Information Sought by Analysts

Balance sheet is a technical accounting term. "In this view, a balance sheet may be defined as a tabular statement or summary of balances (debit and credit) carried forward after an actual or constructive closing of books of account kept according to principles of accounting.[1] This is as far as accountants are willing to go. The investor must expect neither more nor

---

[1] *Accounting Research Study* no. 7 (New York: American Institute of Certified Public Accountants, 1965), p. 226.

less than this. A balance sheet does not purport to list economic or investment values, which are related more to cash flow and earning power of a firm.

The major types of information that the analyst seeks from the balance sheet are as follows:

1. The sources of funds that have been used to acquire the corporate assets:

    (a) The long-term funds invested by creditors (bondholders, private placement noteholders, equipment trust noteholders, etc.), by preferred stockholders, and by common stockholders. In the case of common stockholders, it includes earnings retained in the business (not paid out as dividends) and capital in excess of par.

    (b) The short-term funds supplied by banks, commercial paper houses, factors and trade creditors, etc.

    On the basis of the above information, the investor can calculate the proportion of invested capital contributed by creditors, preferred stockholders, and common stockholders and can determine such ratios as long-term debt to stockholders' equity. It is worthwhile for the investor to calculate the market value of the corporation's securities and the ratios of each component to the total capitalization so calculated. In this calculation, par value often is used for bonds and preferred stock, but market value is used for common stock: hence the term "total capitalization with common at market" (number of shares times market value).

2. The strength of the corporation's working capital position as indicated by the various working capital ratios. These ratios indicate the corporation's assumed ability to meet current liabilities, which are expected to be paid with current assets.

3. The assets of the corporation, which indicate the sources of the corporation's income and the manner in which capital was invested, as well as providing a base for assessing the adequacy of total assets and the mix of assets to support expected levels of operation.

4. Data for an analysis of the balance sheet combined with an analysis of the income statements to indicate:

    (a) The amount and the rate of return on total long-term capitalization (an excellent test of corporate management).

    (b) The rate of return on total assets.

(c) The rate of return on the stockholders' equity.

(d) A check of the retained earnings account in the balance sheet with the earnings reported over a period of years in the income statement. [Retained earnings at the beginning of the period plus earnings (less losses) for the entire period less dividends paid should give the total in the retained earnings account at the end of the period, except for charges or credits made directly to the retained earnings account that may not have been recorded in any income statement but that should have been disclosed in annual reports.]

In essence, the balance sheet when combined with income statement data offers a basis for a long-term study of earning power relative to asset mix and financial structure.

We will discuss the ratios mentioned above in much greater detail in Chapter 11.

ASSETS SECTION OF THE BALANCE SHEET

In considering assets in the balance sheet as offsets to the liabilities and capital, the analyst must recognize what asset figures really mean. The analyst should not be under the illusion that these offsets to liabilities and capital represent reliable estimates of economic value, except to some extent in the case of current assets; and, even in this case, book figures may be far removed from economic values, especially in the case of inventories.

Current Assets: Working Capital

Current assets of a business (also called circulating assets or working assets) represent its working capital. The character of a borrower's working capital has been of prime interest to grantors of credit. Bond indentures, credit agreements, and preferred stock agreements commonly contain provisions restricting corporate actions that would effect a reduction or impairment of working capital (and would impair ability to satisfy debt requirements). Such restrictions can affect future financing possibilities of a firm, with growth and dividend-paying capacity thereby affecting the common stockholders' interest. Net working capital is represented by the excess of current assets over current liabilities, and identifies the relatively liquid portion of total enterprise capital that constitutes a margin or buffer for meeting obligations within the ordinary operating cycle of the business.

For accounting purposes, the term *current assets* is used to designate cash and other assets or resources commonly identified as those that are expected to be realized in cash or sold or consumed during the normal operating cycle of the business. Thus, the term comprehends in general the following resources:

1. Cash available for current operations and items that are the equivalent of cash;
2. Inventories of merchandise, raw materials, goods in process, finished goods, operating supplies, and ordinary maintenance materials and parts;
3. Trade accounts, notes, and acceptances receivable;
4. Receivables from officers, employees, affiliates, and others, if collectible in the ordinary course of business, usually within a year;
5. Installment or deferred accounts and notes receivable if they conform generally to normal trade practices and terms within the business;
6. Marketable securities representing the temporary investment of cash; and
7. Prepaid expenses such as insurance, interest, rents, taxes, unused royalties, current paid advertising service not yet received, and operating supplies.

The ordinary operations of a business involve a circulation of capital within the current asset group. Expenditures are accumulated as inventory cost. Inventory costs, on sale of the products, are converted into trade receivables and ultimately into cash again. The average time intervening between the acquisition of materials or services entering this process and the final cash realization constitute an operating cycle.

Cash and Cash-Equivalent Items

Cash equivalent items include temporary investments of currently excess cash in short-term, high-quality investment media such as Treasury bills and Banker's Acceptances. There is little or no chance of loss in the event these items had to be liquidated.

Sometimes cash and cash-equivalent items are segregated arbitrarily and not included in current assets. If such segregated items have been excluded from current assets and if these items are, in fact, subject to the full control of management and not required to be segregated by regulations or contract agreements, the analyst should add them back to the current assets.

The firm is likely to operate a pension fund, and that pension fund could have cash items. We would not, however, consider these cash items as current assets. The company may be able to capture some or all of these assets through an "asset reversion" (where pension fund assets are excess), but such a process requires approval of the Pension Benefit Guarantee Corporation and typically is subject to long delays. The firm does not have ready access to this cash for corporate purposes.

Receivables

Receivables, less any allowance for doubtful accounts, are included as current assets on the grounds that the firm intends to convert them to cash in the ordinary operating cycle of the business. Receivables, accordingly, may be included as a current asset when the payment period runs beyond a year, as with installment sales discussed below. This must be kept in mind when judging the firm's ability to pay current liabilities.

The analyst must consider the nature of the receivables in terms of the characteristics of the industry and the company's business. The analyst should determine whether the receivables are proportionately larger than normal in respect to current assets for the type of business, and whether the deductions for estimated doubtful accounts are reasonable in terms of industry averages and firm experience. Schedule VIII of a firm's 10-K filing with the SEC offers useful information for purposes of evaluating the adequacy of the reserve for doubtful accounts of a firm, especially when compared with other firms operating in the same industry. Any information on the average age of receivables and trends in this respect is significant. Receivables turnover ratios (discussed in Chapter 11) are a useful analytical tool.

Installment Sales and Receivables

Various methods are used in accounting for installment sales. The following two methods are the most important:

1. Consider each collection on installment sales as both a recovery of cost and a return of profit to the same extent as the ratio of cost and profit at the time the sale was consummated. Such installment sales

are only taken up as income and considered as income for tax purposes in the period in which the receivables are actually collected.

2. Consider the full amount of installment sales as ordinary sales for the period in which the sales are first consummated, although income taxes will not be paid until the receivables actually are collected. In such cases, the analyst should make an estimate of the income taxes to be paid when the receivables are collected and should deduct these taxes from the receivables on the balance sheet.

The estimate for doubtful or uncollectible accounts must be reasonable in relation to receivables in the case of installment sales, and this is true if profits on installment sales are taken into income in the period that the sales are accomplished rather than when receivables are collected. If a corporation sells its installment notes to banks or finance companies, it should note whether they have been sold outright or on a "recourse basis." In the latter case, the corporation has a contingent liability, which usually is not shown in the balance sheet but is included as a footnote. The analyst must consider the size of these contingent liabilities and the likelihood of the contingency materializing in the light of industry and company experience and the character of the receivables.

Inventories

The analyst should, where possible, calculate inventory turnover. Unfortunately, a definitive ratio usually can be achieved by outside analysts only through an examination in terms of annual figures, dividing cost of goods sold by average inventory. Ideally, with respect to seasonal business, monthly sales at cost would be the most relevant, but annual figures are often the only ones available to investors.

Recessions, generally characterized as inventory recessions, result from excessive inventory build-ups during the previous expansion, and require working down. Wide fluctuation in the price structure has heretofore caused severe inventory problems, but the advent of computer controls combined with economic and market analysis has somewhat reduced the inventory problem. Still, in certain industries excessive inventories and inventory price fluctuations can cause serious financial problems, as in 1974 and 1975. Inventories in the following expansion were more tightly controlled.

The analyst also must consider the implications of FIFO and LIFO inventory accounting as applied to analysis between companies, and over a period of years for the same company, if company reports do not provide actual figures indicating the effect of a change from FIFO to LIFO or vice versa.[2] One must be careful to make appropriate adjustments when comparing two firms, one of which uses LIFO while the other uses FIFO. The firm using LIFO will report a lower profit and inventory than the firm using FIFO when there are no real differences.

Our study of the LIFO inventory costing technique in Chapter 6 showed that the inventory stated on the balance sheet is likely to include old costs which would not reflect current market values. We suggest, therefore, that the analyst add back the LIFO reserve to assets before calculating a current ratio, return on owners' equity or assets, or an inventory turnover. When projecting the likely profit margin for next year, however, it is better to keep the inventories on a LIFO basis since reported profit is then closer to economic or real profit.

Long-Term Investments: Noncurrent Assets

One of the noncurrent classifications applicable to assets is that of investments. Investments owned by business enterprises include shares of stock, bonds, and other securities, mortgages and contracts receivable, life insurance policies on the lives of officers that designate the company as beneficiary, and special funds to finance plant expansion or to retire long-term debt. Temporary investments are classed as current assets. Only long-term holdings of securities are classified as investments.

A basic accounting position on the reporting of long-term investments and noncurrent assets is quoted below.

> Long-term investments in securities should be carried at the lower of aggregate cost or market. When market quotations are available, the aggregate quoted amounts (and information as to whether aggregate cost or market is the carrying amount) should be disclosed. Investments in affiliates should be segregated from other investments.[3]

Fixed Assets

Fixed assets consist of land, plant, and equipment reported at cost less depreciation, i.e., amortization of cost. The process of depreciation is the

---

2 See the discussion of Inventory Accounting in Chapter 6.

3 Quoted from *Accounting Research Study*, no. 7, pp. 259–60, and APB Opinion No. 18, except for changes made by FASB Statement No. 12 (December 1975).

process of amortization of cost over the estimated life of the asset, and is in no sense a process of valuation, as discussed in Chapter 6.

The economic value of fixed assets is their earning power, which bears no necessary relationship to the amount at which they are carried in the books. In most cases, the going-concern value and the replacement value of fixed assets in recent years are well in excess of the amount at which the fixed assets are recorded in the company's books of account, as evidence by the willingness of acquiring companies to pay 1½ times book value or more in recent years.

Since it has been permissible to use one set of accounting rules when reporting to the IRS and another when reporting to stockholders, in the mid-1970s there was overreporting of profits to stockholders. By 1979, underdepreciation is said to have amounted to almost one-fourth of pretax profits in reports to stockholders and about half of that in reports to the IRS. Many said that the estimating of replacement costs might have the advantage to corporations of showing the IRS that the corporations' real profits didn't merit present taxes.

Wasting Assets

Natural resources are wasting assets. They are exhausted physically through extraction and, except for timber, they are irreplaceable. Until these resources are extracted from the land, they are classified as fixed assets; once they have been extracted, they are classified as inventories until sold.

Accepted practice in accounting for natural resources is as follows:

> When the presence of a natural resource is discovered subsequent to acquisition of the property, or when the extent of the deposit is determined to be materially more extensive than previously assessed, it is accepted practice to reconsider previous allocations of aggregate cost.
>
> The search for new resources is a continuing endeavor. . . . This endeavor necessitates large outlays for exploration, options, lease bonuses, advance royalties, abstract and recording fees, geological and geophysical staff expenses, and so forth. Even when the most advanced geological and geophysical technology is used to predict reserves, there is no assurance that resource deposits in paying quantities will be located, or that once located, the original estimates of the deposit will hold up. The uncertainty characteristic of extractive industries presents difficult problems of cost determination and allocation. It is accepted practice either to capitalize or expense the outlays mentioned above; but the majority practice is to capitalize the costs that are readily identifiable with the

successful acquisition of specific resources in paying quantities and to expense the others.[4]

Intangibles

Intangibles that appear in the balance sheet come from two sources: (1) intangible assets purchased outright, and (2) intangible assets developed initially in the regular course of business. Such assets have no physical existence and depend on future anticipated benefits for their value.

Intangibles purchased outright are intangibles (such as goodwill) that have been acquired in exchange for an issue of securities, for cash, or for other considerations. The AICPA stated in APB Opinion No. 17 (1970) that the costs of all intangible assets, including those arising from a "purchase" type of business combination, should be recorded as assets and should be amortized by systematic charges to income over estimated benefit periods, the period of amortization not to exceed 40 years.

Goodwill has been important in recent years as the result of the multitude of mergers and other acquisitions that have taken place. The acquiring corporation often pays more than book value for the assets acquired, and the difference is recorded as goodwill under the purchase-of-assets method. As explained earlier, the use of the "pooling-of-assets" method has been discouraged by AICPA pronouncements.

There may be intangible assets developed in the regular course of the business—for example, as the result of research and development or of advertising and promotion. With respect to research and development, the author of an AICPA-published study has stated that "the most practical treatment is to charge these expenditures to expense currently, for it is usually difficult to determine in advance the benefit that may result in future periods."[5] This position was adopted officially by the AICPA in Statement of Financial Accounting Standards No. 2. With respect to advertising costs incident to developing consumer preference for trademarks, tradenames, brand names, and brands, this author also has stated: "It is, however, impossible to delineate the portion of advertising costs that have expired in the production of current revenue from the portion that may be applicable to the future. Treatment as current expense is, therefore, accepted practice."[6]

---

[4] *Accounting Research Study*, no. 7, p. 258.

[5] Ibid., no. 7, pp. 265–66.

[6] Ibid., p. 266.

The questionable liquidity value of intangibles has led to the suggestion that such assets be eliminated from total assets and owners' equity when studying capital structure. These assets, however, may be among the most valuable owned by the enterprise, and it, therefore, seems inadvisable to eliminate them from consideration in a financial analysis. Goodwill, for example, should be supported by superior earning power, and this can be looked for. The accountant's value for intangibles in a balance sheet are highly questionable, but one should assess whether values beyond the physical assets of a business exist when assessing its common stock.

LIABILITIES AND CAPITAL SECTIONS OF THE BALANCE SHEET

The balance sheet furnishes information on the amount of funds raised from creditors, both short- and long-term obligations, and from owners (including retained earnings). Investors should analyze the long-term capitalization of the corporation (long-term debt plus owners' equity), by means of ratios, to indicate the degree of financial leverage being utilized by the corporation and rates of return being earned on capitalization. Short-term obligations should be analyzed in terms of the current assets and cash flow factors from which payment must come.

Current Liabilities

Current liabilities designate obligations that must be paid within one year from the date of the balance sheet. The current liability classification, however, is not intended to include a contractual obligation falling due at an early date that is expected to be refunded, or debts to be liquidated by funds that are carried in noncurrent asset accounts.[7] Liquidation of such liabilities reasonably could be expected to require the use of current assets or the creation of other current liabilities. Current liabilities are therefore related to current assets when assessing the possibility that the firm will experience liquidity problems. The ratios used in such an analysis are discussed in Chapter 11.

---

7 See "Restatement and Revision of Accounting Research Bulletins," *Accounting Research Bulletin*, no. 43, pp. 21–23, and amendment by SFAS No. 6 (May 1975), for a detailed and specific item-by-item discussion of the accounts included as current liabilities.

Long-Term Debt

This section consists of long-term obligations such as bonds, private-placement notes, equipment obligations, and term and time bank loans, the latter generally with maturities of one to eight years. The amounts that appear on the balance sheet generally can be assumed to state accurately the amount of long-term obligations currently outstanding. Notes to financial statements will furnish additional information about the debt contracts, such as restrictive clauses against charges to retained earnings for dividends and officers' salaries. Such restrictions are important to common stockholders, since they can limit financing opportunities to support growth and dividend payments.

Leases

In the post–World War II period, leasing has become a major method of financing the acquisition of property and equipment; annual rentals under leases run into billions of dollars. Leasing differs in technique, although often not in substance, from conventional purchase of assets.

FASB Statement No. 13 contains guidelines, which became effective January 1, 1977, for classifying leases and for accounting and reporting standards for each class of lease.

Before the FASB issued Statement 13 during 1976, the IRS had ruled, on May 5, 1975, that a lessor had to have at least 20 percent equity in the property leased in order to have the owner privilege of the investment credit. At that time, the SEC was requiring only footnote disclosure of lease obligations in financial statements. When Statement 13 called for capitalization on the balance sheet, the debt-to-equity ratio of companies making use of leasing was greatly affected. For this reason, Statement 13 permitted companies that had leases already in existence four years (until December 31, 1980) before requiring capitalization. However, in the spring of 1977 the SEC proposed requiring immediate retroactive application of FASB Statement No. 13 to existing leases in reports for fiscal years ending on or after December 1977. This was in the belief "that most of the data will have to be accumulated by the end of this year under other requirements and should be available at that time for restatement purposes."[8] If a company had difficulty resolving its restrictive clause problems, and therefore could not comply with requirements, it was to disclose that fact.

---

[8] See SEC Section of News Report, *Journal of Accountancy* (May, 1977), pp. 20–22.

According to FASB Statement No. 13, leases are classified as (1) capital leases, or (2) operating leases. Operating leases are those that the lessor will reacquire to lease again. They are to be accounted for as rental expense to the lessee and as rental income to the lessor.

Capital leases are defined under the following criteria:

1. The lease transfers ownership of the property to the lessee by the end of the lease term.

2. The lease contains a bargain purchase option.

3. The lease term is equal to at least 75 percent of the estimated economic life of the leased property. This criterion does not apply if the beginning of the term falls within the last 25 percent of the total estimated life.

4. The present value of the minimum lease payments at the beginning of the lease term equals 90 percent of the fair value of the leased property, less any related investment tax credit retained by the lessor.

5. If the lease meets any of these criteria, it must be capitalized by the lessee on the balance sheet as an asset and an obligation. If it doesn't meet any of these criteria, it is an operating lease and needn't be capitalized, according to the statement.[9]

Unfunded Pension Reserves: Past Service Cost

When a corporation establishes a pension fund, it accepts two costs: (1) past service costs that have not been funded, and (2) current pension costs based on current payrolls. Pension costs, and especially legislation to require vesting of pensions, were discussed in Chapter 8.

The problem as far as the balance sheet is concerned is that of past service costs—the unfunded pension costs covering the period prior to the inauguration of the pension plan. These funds were not set aside previously but would have been funded if a pension plan had been in effect. The amount of these unfunded pension costs often is substantial, and in the case of large corporations may amount to several billion dollars.[10] Investors Management Sciences, Inc., recorded, in their survey of 1976 corporate pension

---

9 Quoted directly from FASB section of News Report, *Journal of Accountancy* (January 1977), p. 7.

10 See "Unfunded Pension Liabilities: A Growing Worry for Companies," *Business Week* (July 18, 1977), pp. 86–88.

liability, that General Motors had $7.3 billion in unfunded past/prior service costs and $3 billion in unfunded vested benefits. IMS's survey covered 1,644 companies. These unfunded pension costs are a liability of the corporation. However, many pension fund agreements provide that annual payments to amortize unfunded pension costs may be skipped in years of poor earnings, sometimes for as many as three consecutive years.

However, the Accounting Principles Board of the AICPA stated that a major objective of Opinion No. 8 was to eliminate inappropriate fluctuation in recorded pension costs. It stated that "costs should not be limited to the amounts for which the company has a legal liability." The principles involved are that the pension cost accounting method should be applied consistently from year to year and that the amount recognized for past pension service costs should be relatively stable from year to year.[11] Opinion No. 8 does not require that certified statements disclose the amount of unfunded or otherwise unprovided-for past or prior service costs. However, the SEC does require such disclosure.

It is certainly true that the unfunded cost is, to a degree, a fluctuating type of liability and therefore should not have to be incorporated as a liability on the balance sheet proper. However, the requirement by the AICPA that the amount of the annual past pension service cost (amortized) should be stable from year to year should place the analyst on notice that the liability for past service costs is a liability that should be amortized in a relatively stable manner.

Preferred Stock Equity

If the corporation has preferred stock outstanding, the balance sheet will disclose the number of shares, the par or stated value per share, and the total dollar amount of the preferred stock. In the balance sheet, preferred stock is listed in the capital section along with the common stock. Although it is essentially an equity security, it is a strictly limited equity security.

The preferred stock is senior to the common stock. The amount shown on the balance sheet should represent the claim of preferred stock coming ahead of the common stock, but this is not always the manner in which it is reported. If the preferred stock has a par value or a stated value relatively close to its legal claim (for example, liquidating value) ahead of the common

---

11 Julius W. Phoenix, Jr., and William D. Bosse, "Accounting for the Cost of Pension Plans—More Information on APB No. 8, *Journal of Accountancy* (October 1967); and "Pension Reform," *Journal of Accountancy* (May 1972), p. 76.

stock, then the balance sheet closely reflects the actual situation. However, if the stated value is only a nominal amount and is not close to the claim of the preferred stock, then the preferred stock on the balance sheet (number of shares of preferred stock times the stated value) does not reflect the true situation. In addition, there may be dividend arrears, which, while they are not liabilities of the corporation, do represent a claim senior to the common stock. However, such arrearages usually are not shown on the balance sheet but are disclosed only as a footnote thereto.

In summary, if the balance sheet does not reflect the preferred stock's claim properly, the analyst should reconstruct the balance sheet so that it reflects the preferred claims that are senior to the common stock.

Common Stock Equity

Because the common stock is the residual claimant to the assets and the earnings of the corporation, the common stock section of the balance sheet is divided into three separate accounts: capital stock, retained earnings (formerly earned surplus), and capital paid-in in excess of par (or stated) value (formerly capital surplus).

There is considerable lack of uniformity in the manner in which common stock (and preferred stock) is reported in the balance sheet. Many analysts feel that the trend in recent years toward highly condensed statements supported by notes to financial statements has gone too far (e.g., giving only one summary figure for capital stock). Furthermore, in spite of the opinion[12]

---

12 Accounting Research Study No. 7, pp. 188–190 states:

67. While the terms capital surplus and earned surplus have been widely used, they are open to serious objection.

1. The term surplus has a connotation of excess, overplus, residue, or "that which remains when use or need is satisfied" (Webster), whereas no such meaning is intended where the term is used in accounting.
2. The terms capital and surplus have established meanings in other fields, such as economics and law, which are not in accordance with the concepts the accountant seeks to express in using those terms.
3. The use of the term capital surplus (sometimes called, paid-in surplus) gives rise to confusion. If the word surplus is intended to indicate capital accumulated by the retention of earnings, i.e., retained income, it is not used properly in the term capital surplus; and if it is intended to indicate a portion of the capital, there is an element of redundance in the term capital surplus.
4. If the term capital stock (and in some states the term capital surplus) be used to indicate capital which, in the legal sense, is restricted as to withdrawal, there is an implication in the terms surplus or earned surplus of availability for dividends. This is unfortunate because the status of corporate assets may be such that they are not, as a practical matter, or as a matter of prudent management, available for dividends.

that the term "surplus" should not be used because it has a "money in the bank" connotation that is misleading, a few corporations still use the term.

An authoritative writer[13] on accounting has suggested the following breakdown of the capital section of the balance sheet, although stating that "the detail breakdown . . . is not ordinarily shown in financial statements."

Stockholders' equity in capital invested
   Capital stock
      Preferred stock—5% cumulative; par value
         $100; authorized ___ shares; issued ___ shares   . . . . .
      Class A preferred stock—$2.00 cumulative;
         no par value, redeemable value $30; authorized
         and issued—shares   . . . . .
      Common stock—no par value; stated value $10;
         authorized ___ shares; issued ___ shares of
         which ___ are in treasury   . . . . .

   Capital paid-in excess of par, redemption and stated
      values of capital stocks

      Premium on preferred stock   . . . . .
      Arising from treasury stock
         transactions   . . . . .
      Paid-in on common stock
      Retained earnings capitalized on
         stock dividends   . . . .

---

68. In seeking terms more nearly connotative of the ideas sought to be expressed, consideration should be given primarily to the sources from which the proprietary capital was derived . . .

69. In view of the foregoing the committee in 1949 . . . recommending that, in the balance-sheet presentation of stockholders' equity:

1. The use of the term surplus (whether standing alone or in such combinations as capital surplus, paid-in surplus, earned surplus, appraisal surplus, etc.) be discontinued . . .

3. The term earned surplus be replaced by terms which will indicate source, such as retained income, retained earnings, accumulated earnings, or earnings retained for use in the business. In the case of a deficit, the amount would be shown as a deduction from contributed capital with appropriate description. That the term "surplus" should not be used because it has a "money in the bank" connotation that is misleading, a few major corporations still are using the term on their balance sheets.

13 Ibid., pp. 191–192.

Retained earnings:

Appropriated in amount equal to restriction
    under bank loan as to payment of
    dividends   . . . . .
Unappropriated   . . . .
    Total   . . . . .
Deduct cost of ___ shares of treasury stock   . . . . .
Stockholder equity   . . . . .

Chapter Ten

Earnings Per Share and Cash Flow Analysis

On Wall Street, the most significant figures used in reference to common stock are its earnings per share and its correlated ratio of market price to earnings per share (the P/E ratio). Accountants and financial analysts have criticized the undue emphasis often placed on earnings per share, especially when reviewed without consideration of accounting limitations inherent in the calculation and other income statement items. Moreover, reported net income and earnings per share are not good surrogates for cash flow from operations when considering full paying capacity and ability to finance company growth and operations.

The three major criticisms of the use of earnings per share figures by themselves are: (1) without correlation with an income statement review and analysis, it can lead to erroneous conclusions; (2) reported earnings per share may be noncomparable over time or between companies; and (3) it concentrates the investor's attention on a single figure without reference to other corporation data, which provide information on the sources and the nature of income and some basis for a reasonable projection of earnings and dividends. An analyst of financial statements should carefully review the income statement and adjust where needed to represent economic influences and comparable income over time and between firms.

CALCULATING EARNINGS PER SHARE

Earnings per share are calculated by dividing the earnings available to common stockholders (earnings after taxes less any required preferred stock dividends) by the weighted average number of common shares outstanding over the year for which the calculation takes place. Opinion No. 15[1] required two presentations of earnings per share when dilutive securities (convertible securities or securities with warrants) that can be used to purchase common stock are outstanding: (1) primary earnings per share and (2) fully diluted earnings per share. These two calculations recognize the potential for dilution of earnings per share, if the dilutive securities are utilized to acquire common stock. Moreover, Opinion 15 required that earnings per share or net loss per share must be reported separately for ordinary items, extraordinary items, and total earnings.

An illustrative calculation can clarify the meaning of primary and fully diluted earnings per share. Assume a company has outstanding 20 million shares of common stock (on average) and that common equity totals $400 million in the balance sheet. Further assume that there is $400 million of 5 percent preferred stock outstanding of which $200 million is convertible into 40 million common shares. Also assume there is $400 million of 10 percent long-term debenture bonds outstanding, of which $200 million is convertible into 30 million common shares. Finally, assume this company has a profit before interest charges and income taxes of $200 million and is subject to an effective income tax rate of 50 percent. The corporate tax rate today is lower than 50 percent, but the aim merely is to show the impact of taxes. Primary earnings per share for a company that has no dilutive securities outstanding would be the same as the usually determined earnings per share, or undiluted earnings per share. Fully diluted earnings per share (assuming all convertible securities are converted) and undiluted earnings per share for our illustrative company are shown in Table 10–1.

Primary earnings per share are calculated on the basis of the number of common shares actually outstanding plus shares that would be issued in a conversion when the convertible instruments are considered common stock equivalents by the accountant. They would be so considered when the cash yield on such convertibles is less than 66⅔ percent of the then-average AA corporate bond yield. Accordingly, in the above example, if all of the convertibles were considered common stock equivalents, then primary and fully diluted earnings per share would be the same. If none of the convertibles were considered common stock equivalents, then primary earnings per share would equal undiluted earnings per share. If a part of the convertible securities were considered common stock equivalents, then primary earn-

---

[1] "Earnings per Share," *Opinions of the Accounting Principles Board*, no. 15 (New York: AICPA, 1969).

TABLE 10–1
*Calculation of Undiluted and Fully Diluted Earnings per Share
(Millions of Dollars)*

	Undiluted		Fully Diluted
Earnings Before Interest and Taxes	$200		$200
Interest Expense* ($400 Million × .1)	40	($200 Million × .1)	20
	160		180
Taxes at 50%	80		90
Earnings After Taxes	80		90
Preferred Dividend ($400 Million × .05)	20	($200 Million × .05)	10
Earnings Available to Common	60		80
Number of Shares*	20		90
Earnings per Share	$ 3.00		$ 0.89

*The conversion of the $200 million of bonds resulted in the issue of an additional 30 million shares outstanding. The conversion of the $200 million of preferred stock resulted in the issue of an additional 40 million shares. The number of shares outstanding, therefore, increased by 70 million. Moreover, the interest expense and preferred dividends associated with instruments converted will no longer be paid and must be eliminated. This required an adjustment in taxes.

ings per share would fall between undiluted and fully diluted earnings per share. Though not illustrated, where options or warrants are considered to be common stock equivalents, the funds raised in their exercise are assumed to be used to purchase common stock at current market prices and retire it.

It is suggested that both primary earnings per share and fully diluted earnings per share be used when calculating an intrinsic value for a common stock. The analyst will then determine two intrinsic values and can use them as a range of potential value.

The Price–Earnings Ratio

A reported price–earnings ratio may be the current market price of the stock divided by (1) the latest available 12-months' earnings, (2) earnings projected for the next 12 months, (3) the average or midpoint of projected earnings for the next five or six years, or (4) the earnings expectation in a target year three to six years hence. The most commonly used denominator is the latest available 12-months' earnings.

P/E ratios are used commonly as indicators of relative value for various common stocks. P/E ratios can, however, give a distorted view of relative value due to different accounting techniques and definitions that may be employed by various firms or by the same firm over time, as already discussed in previous chapters. Moreover, a common stockholder is concerned with the future performance of the firm, while a P/E ratio is typically based on past performance. This is why estimates of future earnings are sometimes used in calculating such ratios. P/E ratios provide only a crude indicator of relative investment merit, and must be used with great caution. Still, they do provide an indication of market expectations if earnings are properly adjusted when calculating the ratio. The higher the expected growth rate and the less the volatility of earnings, the higher the P/E ratio awarded to a firm.

Low P/E-Ratio Stock Selection Approach

The low P/E approach to stock selection advocates choosing a representative group of companies from the bottom three or four deciles, or those with the lowest 30 to 40 percent of all P/E ratios. One must be careful when reviewing cyclical companies since they are likely to have very low P/E ratios when their earnings are at the cyclical trough. We would suggest calculating an average of the earnings over the cycle and using this as a reference point in interpreting their P/E ratios.

Another problem arises with companies that have loss years, since a meaningful P/E ratio cannot be calculated in such years. The analyst would have to consider the future prospects of these companies when selecting stocks. Fundamental analysis and valuation, as advocated in this book, provide useful tools to aid in implementing a low P/E-ratio selection approach, since they do consider the future and can handle the problems described above.

There is much support in the literature for the low price–earnings ratio approach to stock selection, as summarized briefly below:

1. Paul Miller performed a study at Drexel & Company of the price performance of the 30 Dow Jones stocks grouped by P/E ratios over the period 1937-69.[2]

   From the 30 stocks, two groups were selected for each year, the 10 lowest P/E-ratio stocks and the 10 highest. The two groups were also compared to the average for the 30 stocks. The results are summarized

---

2 See B. Graham, D. Dodd, and S. Cottle, *Security Analysis Principles and Technique,* 4th ed. (New York: McGraw Hill, 1962) pp. 468–477.

TABLE 10–2
Average Annual Percentage Gain or Loss on the Test Issues, 1937–1969

Period	Ten Low P/E Stocks	Ten High P/E Stocks	Thirty DJIA Stocks
1937–1942	–2.2%	–10.0%	–6.3%
1943–1947	17.3	8.3	14.9
1948–1952	16.4	4.6	9.9
1953–1957	20.9	10.0	13.7
1958–1962	10.2	–3.3	3.6
1963–1969	8.0	4.6	4.0

Source: Benjamin Graham, *The Intelligent Investor*, 4th ed.

in Table 10–2. The low P/E stocks clearly outperformed the high P/E stocks and the Dow-Jones Industrial Average.

2. David Dreman reported on extensive statistical studies supporting the low P/E stock selection approach in the 1979 edition of his book, *Contrarian Investment Strategy*. The results of his study of annualized compound rates of return for a sample of 1251 companies (70 percent of which were listed on the New York Stock Exchange) over the period 1968–1977 are summarized in Table 10–3.

TABLE 10–3
Annualized Compound Rates of Return, August 1968–1977

Stocks Ranked by P/E Multiples Decile*	1 Quarter	6 Months	1 Year	3 Years	Holding Original Portfolio for 9 Years
1 (Highest P/Es)	–2.64%	–1.06%	–1.13%	–1.4%	0.33%
2	0.92	1.62	0.56	–0.28	1.27
3	0.51	0.62	1.63	0.85	3.30
4	3.06	3.42	3.31	4.87	5.36
5	2.19	4.46	2.93	5.02	3.72
6	4.84	5.33	6.70	4.82	4.52
7	7.90	6.07	6.85	5.89	6.08
8	8.83	8.24	8.56	7.78	6.35
10 (Lowest P/Es)	14.00	11.68	10.26	10.89	7.89
Average return of sample = 4.75%.					

*Takes all stocks in study and divides them into ten groups according to the P/E ratio.

Source: David Dreman, *Contrarian Investment Strategy* (New York: Random House, 1979), p. 131.

3. Anthony Hitschler, David Good, John Peavy, and others have published articles offering similar support.

4. The author of this book recently completed a study (unpublished at this time) covering the period 1968–86 and using the P.D.E. Compustat tape which generated similar results to those found by David Dreman.

The cited studies offer strong support for the usefulness of price–earnings ratios as a screening tool in stock selection. Still, with the known limitations of such ratios, the selection process must probe much deeper, using fundamental analysis and valuation efforts. The author is convinced that the best values will be found among stocks sporting relatively low P/E ratios, but careful selection must be made to weed out the stocks that sport low P/E ratios because their future is not bright and/or their risk is high. The sound-value approach, based on the premise that no common stock should be purchased unless a careful industry and company analysis has been made, is still the approach recommended.

Low P/E-Ratio Out-of-Favor Approach

During business recessions, the stock market, in general, tends to be undervalued in terms of norms related to the long upward secular trend. Also, some groups and individual stocks, frequently of major companies and industries, decline more than the averages. While the greatest number of undervaluations are likely to occur near the bottom of bear markets, in any year there are usually some undervaluations available. Accordingly, a sound-value-approach investor can buy in both bull and bear markets. The out-of-favor approach does require the emotional stamina to go against the crowd and to exercise patience.

It may seem illogical to emphasize consideration of the purchase of stocks in industries and companies whose problems (perhaps serious ones) are obvious to all. However, a little thought would raise questions concerning a policy that would buy stocks when they are popular (suggesting high demand and price peaks) and sell them when they are unpopular (suggesting low demand and price troughs).

Basic Assumptions of the Low P/E Out-of-Favor Approach

The low P/E out-of-favor approach assumes that investors tend to exaggerate either prosperity and highly favorable current information and

TABLE 10–4
Selected Stock Prices, 1928–32

Security	Opening Price 3/3/28	High Price 9/3/29	Low Price 11/13/29	Low Price 1932
AT&T	$179\frac{1}{2}$	$335\frac{5}{8}$	$197\frac{1}{4}$	$70\frac{1}{4}$
Bethlehem Steel	$56\frac{7}{8}$	$140\frac{3}{8}$	$78\frac{1}{4}$	$7\frac{1}{4}$
General Electric	$128\frac{3}{4}$	$396\frac{1}{4}$	$168\frac{1}{8}$	$8\frac{1}{2}$
Montgomery Ward	$132\frac{3}{4}$	$466\frac{1}{2}$*	$49\frac{1}{4}$	$3\frac{1}{2}$
National Cash Register	$50\frac{3}{4}$	$127\frac{1}{2}$	59	$6\frac{1}{4}$
RCA	$94\frac{1}{2}$	505*	28	$2\frac{1}{2}$

*Adjusted for stock splits.

Source: Burton G. Malkiel, *A Random Walk Down Wall Street* (New York: W.W. Norton, 1975), pp. 38, 43.

likewise exaggerate problems that may beset a company. Growth stocks, accordingly, may be priced far above reasonable values based on future prospects, thereby including a heavy speculative element in the price of the stock. The behavior of a financial market is an expectations phenomenon, and unfortunately seems to reflect, at times, mob psychology rather than reasoned thought. Professor Malkiel has illustrated this in a thought-provoking discussion in his book, *A Random Walk Down Wall Street*.[3] How could one explain the sharp run-up in the prices of selected stocks, as shown in Table 10–4, only to be followed by extreme lows in 1932? Similar pricing situations are shown in 1961–62 (Table 10–5) and 1967–69 (Table 10–6). A more current illustration can be found in drug stocks during 1994–95. Changing waves of optimism and pessimism offer investment opportunities. The systematic use of valuation techniques and fundamental analysis should reduce the likelihood of being drawn in by fads and misplaced speculative fever, thereby avoiding including seriously overvalued securities in an investment portfolio.

All low price–earnings-ratio out-of-favor stocks do not, of course, represent undervaluations and sound investments. The investor must be convinced that the problems are temporary and there is a good probability that

---

3 Burton G. Malkiel, *A Random Walk Down Wall Street*, Chap. 2 and 3 (New York: W. W. Norton, 1975).

TABLE 10–5
Price Performance of a Few Selected Growth Stocks, 1961–62

	1961		1962	
Security	High Price	Price–Earnings Ratio	Low Price	Price–Earnings Ratio
IBM	607	80.7	300	34.4
Texas Instruments	$206\frac{3}{4}$	87.6	49	23.0
Microwave Associates	$60\frac{3}{8}$	85.0	8	12.7
Fairchild Camera	$88\frac{1}{4}$	42.0	31	13.1
Perkin-Elmer	$83\frac{1}{2}$	67.3	25	16.7

Source: Burton G. Malkiel, *A Random Walk Down Wall Street* (New York: W. W. Norton, 1975), p. 49.

there will be a recovery of earning power before investing. This assumption should be based on a careful analysis of the industry and company concerned.

An important advantage of the low P/E out-of-favor investing approach is that downside price risk for the stock is quite limited. The stock has usually declined significantly by the time it is considered for purchase, the

TABLE 10–6
Price Performance of Selected Conglomerates, 1967–69

	1967		1969	
Security	High Price	Price–Earnings Ratio	Low Price	Price–Earnings Ratio
Automatic Sprinkler	$73\frac{5}{8}$	51.0	$10\frac{7}{8}$	13.4
Litton Industries	$120\frac{3}{8}$	44.1	35	14.4
Teldynamics	$71\frac{1}{2}$	53.8	$28\frac{1}{4}$	14.2
Textron, Inc.	55	24.9	$23\frac{1}{4}$	10.1

Source: Burton G. Malkiel, *A Random Walk Down Wall Street* (New York: W. W. Norton, 1975), p. 63.

P/E ratio is below (often significantly below) that of the average stock, and the dividend yield tends to be relatively high for a stock. Accordingly, such a stock can be bought by dividend-yield-conscious investors as well as by strongly capital-appreciation-oriented investors.

CASH FLOW ANALYSIS

Cash flow is used typically on Wall Street, in the financial press, and in company reports to designate net earnings after taxes with depreciation, depletion, and other noncash expense items of the period added back. It is important to realize, however, that depreciation and depletion (and other noncash expenses) are real expenses, even though they did not require a cash outflow in the current period. Any attempt to downgrade the importance of depreciation or depletion as an expense can lead to an erroneous conception of true corporate earning power over time. Inability to generate adequate earnings after depreciation may lead to serious financial problems and inability to replace assets as they wear out or become obsolete. Remember, one must replace the asset base that is wearing out if one is to continue to produce income.

Depreciation or depletion are often considered a source of funds (and listed as such in a cash flow or funds flow statement) in the sense that funds generated by sales are not siphoned off by depreciation or depletion since no expenditures are currently made. But a situation where there is no profit before depreciation or where there is a loss before depreciation clearly emphasizes that depreciation by and of itself is not a source of funds. Sales revenues are the basic source of all funds derived from operations.

STATEMENT OF CHANGES IN FINANCIAL POSITION

Fragmentary information on sources and uses of funds and cash can be obtained from comparative balance sheets and income statements. A comprehensive picture of the cash flow of a business can only be gained, however, from a Statement of Changes in Financial Position, found in an annual report. This statement can provide information on such questions as:

1. How were the funds provided by operations, and from other sources, used in the business?

TABLE 10–7
Consolidated Statements of Changes in Financial Position—
Bell South Corporation

	For the Years Ended December 31,		
In Millions	*1986*	*1985*	*1984*
Funds from Operations:			
Net Income	$1,588.7	$1,417.8	$1,257.2
Add Expenses Not Requiring Funds Currently:			
Depreciation	1,935.6	1,802.2	1,535.8
Deferred Income Taxes	481.2	359.9	375.6
Investment Tax Credits	(69.9)	74.3	53.8
Deduct Income Not Providing Funds Currently:			
Interest Charged Construction	33.0	36.0	30.0
Total Funds From Operations	3,902.6	3,618.2	3,192.4
Less: Dividends Declared	954.6	847.1	766.0
	2,948.0	2,771.1	2,426.4
Funds from External Financing:			
Issuance of Common Stock	329.5	397.9	277.5
Increase (decrease) in Debt Due To:			
Issuance of Long-term Notes and Debentures	800.0	550.0	—
Short-term Borrowings—Net	(8.6)	(300.8)	341.4
Obligations Under Capital Leases—Net	11.7	11.3	123.2
Other	(142.2)	74.9	26.3
Total Funds from External Financing	990.4	733.3	768.4
Less: Retirement of Long-term Debt	1,350.0	45.0	—
Investment:*	(359.6)	688.3	768.4
Construction Expenditures (including $33.0, $36.0 and $30.0, Respectively, of Interest Charged Construction)	(2,835.1)	(2,624.1)	(2,274.0)
Purchase of Treasury Stock	—	(184.9)	—
Affiliates and Other	(199.7)	(8.8)	(1.0)
	(3,034.8)	(2,817.8)	(2,275.0)
Changes in Working Capital* (excluding current maturities of long-term debt, notes payable and deferred income taxes)			
Accounts Receivable	2.7	59.6	(539.7)
Material and Supplies	(32.9)	(7.4)	(135.2)
Other Current Assets	(78.7)	(5.3)	(156.1)
Accounts Payable	293.1	(203.2)	160.9
			(continued)

TABLE 10–7 *(concluded)*

In Millions	For the Years Ended December 31,		
	1986	*1985*	*1984*
Taxes Accrued	$ 95.4	$ (44.5)	$ (11.1)
Advance Billing and Customer Deposits	25.1	29.2	17.7
Dividends Payable	27.8	19.5	194.4
Interest and Rents Accrued	(37.3)	16.4	(11.2)
Other Current Liabilities	(62.1)	128.6	8.6
	233.1	(7.1)	(471.7)
Other Changes:*			
Deferred Charges and Other Assets	(24.4)	(18.6)	(54.0)
Other—net	179.9	(99.0)	50.9
	155.5	(117.6)	(3.1)
Increase (decrease) in Cash and Temporary Cash Investments	(57.8)	516.9	445.0
Cash and Temporary Cash Investments at Beginning of Period	1,008.1	491.2	46.2
Cash and Temporary Cash Investments at End of Period	$ 950.3	$1,008.1	$491.2

The accompanying notes are an integral part of these financial statements.

* ( ) Denotes a use of funds.

Source: Bell South Corporation, *1986 Annual Report*, p. 42.

2. Where did the funds come from to maintain dividends in the face of potential losses?
3. How did the business get the funds to accomplish the debt repayment that took place during the period?
4. What were the sources of increases in working capital during the period or what uses were made of withdrawals from working capital?
5. How did the company finance a large investment project, such as Atlantic Richfield's financing its drilling for oil in the North Slope of Alaska?

Moreover, analysts forecast future fund flows under varying assumptions to assess the ability of the firm to finance its growth plans, maintain its capital base, and reward owners. The "Consolidated Statement of Changes in Financial Position for Bell South Corporation" is offered for illustrative purposes in Table 10–7.

A CASH FOCUS

Statements of Changes in Financial Position often focus on explaining changes in working capital, but there are increasing demands that these statements focus on cash.[4] Analysts should concentrate on the nature of cash inflows and outflows to provide a better basis for assessing future cash flows. Previous chapters of this book offer numerous examples indicating that reported net income and cash flow are two different things, since the determination of net income is based on accrual accounting techniques. For example, depreciation is listed as an expense in a given year, thereby reducing reported profits, when there has been no corresponding cash outflow. Net income becomes an even less-adequate surrogate for assessing cash flow during inflationary periods. The gap between reported earnings and cash flow widens during inflationary periods, since a growing investment in receivables and inventories is not offset by corresponding increases in trade credit.

J. A. Largary, III, and C. P. Stickney reviewed W. T. Grant Co. during the 1966–75 period preceding its bankruptcy.[5] They noted that financial indicators such as profitability ratios and trends, turnover ratios, and liquidity ratios showed some downtrends, but provided no definite clues to the company's impending bankruptcy. A study of cash flows from operations, however, revealed that company operations were causing an increasing drain on cash, rather than providing cash. This necessitated increasing use of external financing, the required interest payments on which exacerbated the cash flow drain. Cash flow analysis clearly was a valuable tool in this case.

A financially healthy firm will generate cash from operations on a consistent basis. Professor Bernstein has pointed out that, "The unsuccessful firm will find its cash drained by slowdowns in receivables and inventory turnovers, by operating losses, or by a combination of these factors.[6] The investor should look for companies that report real earnings, not those that are the result of inflation; that have healthy cash flows; and that have sound reasons for assuming that these cash flows will continue in the future.

---

4 See "Objectives of Financial Reporting by Business Enterprises," *Statement of Financial Accounting Concepts*, no. 1 (Stanford, CT: Financial Accounting Standards board, 1978).

5 J. A. Largay III and C. P. Stickney, "Cash Flows, Ratio Analysis and the W. T. Grant Company Bankruptcy," *Financial Analysts Journal*, July–August, 1980, pp. 51–54.

6 Leopold A. Bernstein, *Financial Statement Analysis: Theory, Application, and Interpretation*, 3rd ed. (Homewood, IL: Richard D. Irwin, Inc., 1983), p. 405.

INFLATION AND CASH FLOW

Profits reported to stockholders during inflationary periods are in part real earnings and in part illusion. If the need to replace worn-out plant and equipment and inventories that were used to generate the cash inflows are considered, there may be no real profits. A real profit means that the firm has more real assets at the end of the period than when they began the period.

Richard Greene illustrates this problem effectively by contrasting Dow Chemical and Union Carbide:[7]

Take a look, for example, at Dow Chemical and Union Carbide, two giant chemical companies. Over the four years from 1976 to 1979, Dow showed earnings totaling about $2.5 billion. Over the same period, Union Carbide reported cumulative earnings of some $1.8 billion. It would appear that both firms were robust money-makers in the same league.

But, take it a step further and look at cash. Kidder, Peabody & Co. did this and, although Kidder's methodology is a bit controversial, the question is a matter of degree—not direction. Kidder came up with a number called discretionary cash flow. That's the figure representing how much money a firm has left to grow with—after taking out the amount necessary to maintain its property, plant and equipment, and dividends. Companies don't really set aside money to replace equipment but ultimately they have to put out the cash—and it's not going toward growth.

Dow's discretionary cash flow is at a healthy level with $924 million over the four-year period. But Union Carbide has a different story, negative discretionary cash flow of $663 million. That means, according to Kidder, Union Carbide was paying dividends for that whole period of time with borrowed money. It was, in effect, cannibalizing its capital structure to keep the stock price up. That's not a healthy habit. But it's common among the kind of huge firms you'd think would know better.

Calculating Cash Flow from Operations

One can estimate cash flow from operations by adding all noncash charges in the income statement (such as depreciation expense) to reported earnings after taxes, and deduct from this total all dividends paid and capital

---

7 Richard Greene, "Are More Chryslers in the Offing?" *Forbes,* February 2, 1981, pp. 69–73, as reported in William M. Bowen and Frank P. Ganucheau, *The Investor's Equation* (Chicago, IL: Probus Publishing Company, 1984), p. 111.

Table 10–8
Calculating Flow from Operations

A. Sales
  - + Decrease (– increase) in accounts receivable
  - + Cash collections on sales
  - + Other revenues (+ or – adjustments for noncash items)
  - = Total cash collections from operations

B. Cost of Goods Sold (excluding depreciation, amortization, etc.)
  - + Increase (– decrease) in inventories
  - + Decrease (– increase) in trade payables
  - + Operating Expenses
  - + Other Expenses (including interest)
  - + Increase (– decrease) in prepaid assets
  - + Decrease (– increase) in accrued liabilities
  - + Income Tax Expense (excluding deferred taxes)
  - + Decrease (– increase) in accrued taxes
  - = Total cash outflows from operations

C. Net Cash Flows from Operations = A – B

Source: Leopold A. Bernstein, op. cit., pp. 411–413.

---

expenditures. A healthy company should show a positive total for cash flow from operations over a five-year period.

Professor Bernstein suggests a more detailed approach to calculating cash flow from operations, as shown in Table 10–8. This offers a more complete basis for analysis of cash flow, since it considers changes in working capital as well as dividends and capital expenditures, and begins with sales rather than reported earnings.

SOME CHARACTERISTICS OF "GOOD" COMPANIES

Bowen and Ganucheau suggest the following list of characteristics of a "good" company for investment:[8]

---

[8] William M. Bowen, IV, and Frank P. Ganucheau, III, *The Investor's Equation,* op. cit., pp. 122–130.

1. The ability to raise prices to cover rises in costs, even in poor economic times. This requires that the company face a relatively inelastic demand. Companies that offer unique high-quality goods or services or are in oligopolistic market situations with little threat of new entry are most likely to meet this condition. One must be careful, however, since pricing power may be more than built into the price of the company's stock. Careful valuation analysis is still necessary.

2. The company shows unit, as well as dollar, growth in sales. In other words, the growth in sales is real.

3. Leverage, both operating and financial, is favorable.

4. The company is able to retain a high or above-average return on total assets and owners' equity.

5. Labor costs are low, in comparison to competitors.

6. Pension plans are funded adequately, and cash flow seems able to support future needs without hurting the return to owners.

7. Research and development efforts have been successful historically. For most companies, research and development expenses are not voluntary. Failure to maintain this effort often will lead to failure of the company, since the innovations introduced by competitors will cause their product and/or service offerings to become obsolete. A healthy cash flow is needed to support the research and development effort.

8. A relatively low fixed-cost base, as indicated by a relatively high ratio of sales to each dollar of average gross plant value for the industry the company operates in.

9. A high earnings retention ratio that supports company growth and sustains capital during inflationary times.

10. A healthy cash flow over an extended period.

Ratio analysis, to be discussed in the next chapter, will provide a useful tool, with cash flow analysis, for purposes of assessing the degree to which a company offers the above characteristics.

Chapter Eleven

Ratio Analysis

The major function of financial statement analysis is to disclose those significant relationships demonstrated by the past and present record of a company, so that a meaningful projection of the company's future performance probabilities and financial strength may be estimated. The ratios suggested in this chapter represent relationships that analysts have found useful over many years of experience. Suggested ratios will be grouped into four basic areas for analytical purposes:

1. Profitability ratios. These ratios break earnings per share into its basic determinants for purposes of assessing the factors underlying the profitability of the firm. They help assess the adequacy of historical profits, and to project future profitability through better understanding of its underlying causes.
2. Short-term solvency ratios. These ratios assess the ability of the firm to meet debts maturing over the coming year.
3. Long-term solvency and financial leverage ratios. These ratios assess the extent to which a firm relies on debt financing, and the ability of the firm to meet the fixed obligations brought about by debt financing.
4. Value ratios. These ratios deal with market price of the shares of the firm and its relation to relative value of a firm's stock.

Standards for a given ratio will vary according to operating characteristics of the company being analyzed and general business conditions; such standards cannot be stated as fixed and immutable. Experience plays an important role in setting such standards.

PROFITABILITY ANALYSIS

Profitability ratios are utilized to explore the underlying causes of a change in earnings per share. They show the combined effects of liquidity and asset and debt management on the profitability of the firm.

It is assumed that the analyst has made all adjustments deemed necessary to reflect comparable and true earning power of the corporation before calculating the ratios discussed below. It is important to stress that ratios are utilized to raise significant questions requiring further analysis, not provide answers. Ratios must be viewed in the context of other ratios and other facts derived from sources other than the financial statements. We have noted that cash flow analysis provided an indication that W. T. Grant was getting into financial difficulties when typical profit and liquidity ratios did not.

Underlying Cases of Growth in Earnings per Share

Profit is the ultimate measure of success of a firm, but it must be related to total assets and owner's investment to avoid being misled. For example, assume a firm with 1,000,000 common shares outstanding earned $1,000,000 after taxes. Earnings per share, assuming only that class of common stock outstanding, would be $1 per share. Now assume the company could earn an additional $500,000 after taxes by utilizing the funds raised through selling an additional 1,000,000 common shares. While total earnings would increase, this would not be advantageous to the stockholder. There are now 2,000,000 shares outstanding, and since earnings would be $1,500,000 after taxes, earnings per share would fall to seventy-five cents per share. Return on the total owners' investment also would fall. This suggests concentrating, at least initially, on earnings per share and its determinants rather than earnings after taxes.

The two basic determinants of earnings per share are the return on stockholders' equity and the book value per share, as shown by the equation below:

$$\text{Earnings Per Share} = \frac{\text{Earnings Available to Common (EAC)}}{\text{Average Number of Common Shares}} = \frac{\text{EAC}}{\text{Owners' Equity}} \times \frac{\text{Owners Equity}}{\text{\# of Shares}}$$

Owners' equity would cancel when multiplying, and one would be left with earnings per share.

Growth in Book Value per Share

How can a firm get growth in book value per share? There are three basic ways:

1. Retain earnings. When the firm retains earnings, owners' equity increases, but there is no change in the number of common shares outstanding. This assumes that the retained earnings can be utilized as effectively as past owners' equity has been; in other words, that the return on owners' equity is at least maintained.

    The growth rate in earnings supported by retained earnings can be calculated by multiplying the rate of return earned on owners' equity by the retention rate of the firm (retained earnings divided by earnings after taxes). A firm that earns 10 percent on its owners' equity and has a retention rate of 40 percent, builds a 4 percent growth rate for earnings per share. To illustrate, assume:

    > Earnings per share = 1
    > Book value per share = $10
    > Retention rate = 40%

    Forty cents will be retained of each $1 earned per share, increasing book value per share to $10.40. If the firm continues to earn 10 percent on the owners' capital ($1/$10), the earnings per share will rise to $1.04, or a 4 percent growth rate. If the rate earned on owners' capital fell because of the added production capacity, however, earnings per share could fall even with retention. For example, if return on owners' capital fell to 8 percent, the earnings per share would be only 83 cents ($.08 \times $10.40 = $.832$).

2. Buy back company stock at a price per share less than book value per share. The opportunity for a firm to do this can occur when there is a serious decline in the stock market, such as in 1974. Ford Motor and other firms did buy back shares in 1974, knowing that it would improve earnings per share for the remaining stockholders. Moreover, they believed there were not many profitable opportunities for investing the cash flow in added business assets.

3. Sell stock at a price above book value per share. Mergers can result in an increase in book value per share for the surviving company, since the book value of the acquired shares may be greater than the book value of the shares given in exchange.

While it is true that book value per share has no necessary relationship to market value per share, investors should follow what happens to book value since it is an important determinant of earnings.

Some analysts suggest adding the sustainable growth rate of a firm and its dividend yield and comparing this figure when assessing various firms. The total in future years must be greater, on a compound annual basis, than the difference between the yield offered by the bond and the dividend yield of the common stock to justify purchase of that stock. The price of a common stock is unlikely to offer the sustained rises needed if not supported by sustained earnings growth.

Return on Owners' Equity

It would be useful to review pages 80 through 86 at this point, to see a macro-application of the analytical framework we will develop for assessing returns on owners' equity. The equivalent of Table 4–7 can be prepared for a company as a basis for studying its profitability.

The two basic determinants of return on owners' equity are the return on total assets and the proportion of assets financed by owners as opposed to creditors. This is demonstrated in the equation below:

$$\frac{\text{Earnings Available to Common (EAC)}}{\text{Owners Equity}} = \frac{\text{EAC}}{\text{Total Assets}} \times \frac{\text{Total Assets}}{\text{Owners' Equity}}$$

Stockholders are the residual claimants to the profits earned after taxes less any preferred dividends (earnings available to common). The rate earned on the stockholders' invested capital (return on owners' equity) and the behavior of the basic components determining that return are the key criteria when selecting stocks.

Industry statistics on annual rates of profit on stockholders' equity before and after federal income taxes are presented in Table 11–1. Average rates of return on stockholders' equity for all U.S. corporations and the average profit earned per dollar of sales (the margin) are presented in Table 11–2. The figures offered can serve as crude benchmarks when studying individual companies. Remember, variations from average do not prove a firm will be a good or bad investment. They merely serve to suggest when caution and deeper investigation is necessary. Such investigation should center on likely future behavior suggested by past patterns, not merely historical experience.

TABLE 11-1

Annual Rates of Profit on Stockholders' Equity, by Division and Major Group

(Percent)

Industry	Income before income taxes[1,2]					Income after income taxes[2]				
	2Q 1993	3Q 1993	4Q 1993	1Q 1994	2Q 1994	2Q 1993	3Q 1993	4Q 1993	1Q 1994	2Q 1994
All manufacturing corporations	14.5	14.4	12.1	18.6	23.4	9.8	9.5	8.5	13.1	16.9
Nondurable manufacturing corporations	15.8	15.5	13.6	18.8	19.9	11.4	9.7	9.9	13.3	14.3
Food and kindred products[3]	24.4	23.4	18.0	26.5	24.5	16.5	15.2	12.3	18.4	17.0
Textile mill products	20.5	12.3	11.5	11.3	16.8	12.5	6.8	6.6	6.3	10.1
Apparel[4]	24.2	33.5	13.3	8.5	21.8	16.6	23.7	8.6	4.4	16.9
Paper and allied products	9.8	(10.6)	1.7	9.8	12.8	6.8	(15.2)	0.0	6.1	8.8
Printing and publishing	16.8	14.3	20.1	17.9	23.0	10.8	7.8	11.6	11.1	14.4
Chemicals and allied products	11.2	18.2	11.2	25.8	25.5	8.4	12.7	8.5	19.3	17.9
Industrial chemicals and synthetics[5]	17.1	2.2	3.1	17.4	19.8	13.5	0.7	2.5	13.2	13.7
Drugs[5]	30.3	37.9	12.8	40.3	30.3	23.3	28.7	10.7	30.3	20.8
Residual of chemicals[5]	(16.4)	19.9	20.6	21.4	28.1	(13.8)	12.6	14.2	15.8	20.6
Petroleum and coal products	11.7	13.0	13.7	9.6	8.5	10.4	9.4	13.1	7.1	8.1
Rubber and miscellaneous plastics products	25.3	18.2	13.7	15.8	28.4	18.7	12.3	8.8	11.9	21.4
Durable manufacturing corporations	13.1	13.1	10.5	18.5	27.2	7.8	9.4	6.8	12.9	19.7
Stone, clay, and glass products	33.3	17.3	(8.5)	(7.8)	26.6	29.7	14.1	(6.3)	(9.1)	19.0
Primary metal industries	13.7	5.4	(6.6)	13.0	18.6	11.6	2.5	(6.7)	9.1	13.9
Iron and steel[5]	29.4	4.8	(1.0)	17.5	24.3	24.3	1.6	(5.2)	13.3	18.3
Nonferrous metals[5]	5.4	5.7	(10.3)	10.2	14.7	5.0	2.9	(7.7)	6.3	11.0
Fabricated metal products	21.1	17.9	(5.9)	20.2	25.9	16.3	13.1	(8.7)	15.1	18.5
Machinery except electrical	(23.5)	3.7	6.5	10.7	19.7	(26.0)	1.4	3.7	7.4	15.1

(continued)

TABLE 11–1 (concluded)

(Percent)

Industry	Income before income taxes[1,2]					Income after income taxes[2]				
	2Q 1993	3Q 1993	4Q 1993	1Q 1994	2Q 1994	2Q 1993	3Q 1993	4Q 1993	1Q 1994	2Q 1994
Electrical and electronic equipment	21.2	19.0	16.3	20.6	26.4	15.6	12.6	11.3	14.3	18.0
Transportation equipment	30.9	10.8	25.9	31.6	43.8	21.3	9.7	18.9	21.6	31.3
Motor vehicles and equipment[5]	37.8	2.4	38.8	41.6	60.4	26.5	6.8	29.9	29.0	43.9
Aircraft guided missiles, and parts[5]	23.5	19.7	15.3	21.8	23.9	15.7	13.0	9.9	14.3	16.1
Instruments and related products	21.9	16.1	8.8	19.0	24.1	16.6	12.9	6.9	14.7	18.8
Other durable manufacturing corporations	26.0	24.2	17.7	22.0	28.9	18.1	16.5	11.4	15.4	20.5
Lumber and wood products[5]	34.1	27.0	18.3	28.3	37.1	24.7	19.4	12.5	20.5	27.0
Furniture and fixtures[5]	21.0	19.2	19.2	13.8	25.6	14.7	12.9	12.3	8.9	18.7
Miscellaneous manufacturing[5]	21.6	25.3	15.8	21.3	21.3	14.0	16.4	9.3	14.7	13.6
All mining corporations[6]	11.7	5.0	0.6	5.5	8.3	8.6	4.0	1.0	4.2	6.4
All retail trade corporations[6]	19.5	14.6	22.6	15.1	NA	12.7	8.7	12.0	8.7	NA
All wholesale trade corporations[6]	15.4	8.3	12.6	12.2	13.3	9.8	5.0	8.7	8.1	8.5

[1]Based on profit figures which include net income (loss) of foreign branches and equity in earnings (losses) of nonconsolidated subsidiaries net of foreign taxes.

[2]Some of the rates in this column have been revised since their first appearance. See footnotes to Tables 1.0—47.1.

[3]Includes tobacco industry.

[4]Includes leather industry.

[5]Included in major industry above.

[6]Mining, wholesale and retail trade data are the quarterly results of companies in those divisions drawn into the sample in the fall of 1993 with assets over $50 million. Data for manufacturing corporations represent the quarterly results of companies with assets over $250,000.

Source: Quarterly Financial Report for Manufacturing, Mining & Trade Corporations, Third Quarter 1993, U.S. Dept. of Commerce, 1994.

TABLE 11–2
Relation of Profit after Taxes to Stockholders' Equity and to Sales, all Manufacturing Corporations, 1947–94

Year or Quarter	Ratio of Profits after Income Taxes (Annual Rate) to Stockholders' Equity—Percent[1]			Profits after Income Taxes per Dollar of Sales—Cents		
	All Manufacturing Corporations	Durable Goods Industries	Nondurable Goods Industries	All Manufacturing Corporations	Durable Goods Industries	Nondurable Goods Industries
1967	11.7	11.7	11.8	5.0	4.8	5.3
1968	12.1	12.2	11.9	5.1	4.9	5.2
1969	11.5	11.4	11.5	4.8	4.6	5.0
1970	9.3	8.3	10.3	4.0	3.5	4.5
1971	9.7	9.0	10.3	4.1	3.8	4.5
1972	10.6	10.8	10.5	4.3	4.2	4.4
1973	12.8	13.1	12.6	4.7	4.7	4.8
1973: IV	13.4	12.9	14.0	4.7	4.5	5.0
New Series						
1973: IV	14.3	13.3	15.3	5.6	5.0	6.1
1974	14.9	12.6	17.1	5.5	12.7	6.4
1975	11.6	10.3	12.9	4.6	4.1	5.1
1976	13.9	13.7	14.2	5.4	5.2	5.5
1977	14.2	14.5	13.8	5.3	5.3	5.3
1978	15.0	16.0	14.2	5.4	5.5	5.3
1979	16.4	15.4	17.4	5.7	5.2	6.1

(continued)

TABLE 11-2 (concluded)

Year or Quarter	Ratio of Profits after Income Taxes (Annual Rate) to Stockholders' Equity—Percent[1]			Profits after Income Taxes per Dollar of Sales—Cents		
	All Manufacturing Corporations	Durable Goods Industries	Nondurable Goods Industries	All Manufacturing Corporations	Durable Goods Industries	Nondurable Goods Industries
1980	13.9	11.2	16.3	4.8	4.0	5.6
1981	13.6	11.9	15.2	4.7	4.2	5.1
1982	9.2	6.1	11.9	3.5	2.4	4.4
1983	10.6	8.1	12.7	4.1	3.1	4.9
1984	12.5	12.4	12.5	4.6	4.4	4.8
1986	9.5	7.5	11.5	3.7	2.9	4.6
1987	12.8	11.9	13.7	4.9	4.5	5.2
1988	16.1	14.3	17.9	6.0	5.2	6.7
1989	13.6	11.1	16.2	5.0	4.1	5.8
1990	10.7	8.0	13.4	4.0	3.0	4.9
1991	6.3	1.5	10.8	2.4	0.6	4.1
1992	2.2	-5.0	8.4	0.8	-1.7	3.1
1993	8.1	5.7	10.1	2.8	1.9	3.7
1994: I	13.1	12.9	13.4	4.7	4.2	5.1
II	16.9	19.7	14.3	5.7	6.1	5.2
III	16.4	16.4	16.5	5.6	5.4	5.9

Annual ratios based on average equity for the year (using four end-of-quarter figures). Quarterly ratios based on equity at end of quarter only.

Note—Based on data in millions of dollars.

Source: Department of Commerce, Bureau of the Census. Taken from the *Economic Report of the President*, (Washington, D.C.: United States Government Printing Office, 1988) p. 353.

Leveraged capital structures. Most firms have a leverage capitalization, meaning debt has been used as a source of funds. This will cause profits and the return to owners to be much more variable than if only equity capital were used to raise funds. The effects of financial leverage are compounded by the effects of operating leverage introduced by fixed operating costs. To illustrate, assume the following data for Temple Corporation:

1. The product of the firm is sold at $3 per unit.
2. Fixed costs are $180,000.
3. Variable costs are $1.50 per unit and vary in direct proportion.
4. The firm is capitalized as follows:
   (a) $300,000—10 percent debenture bonds.
   (b) Common equity equals $300,000 and there are 3,000 shares of common stock outstanding.
5. The firm currently is selling 160,000 units.
6. The effective income tax rate applicable to the firm is 40 percent.

The effect of a 10-percent increase in units sold and a 10-percent decrease in units sold is illustrated in Table 11–3. Earnings per share rose 80 percent when sales increased 10 percent, but fell by 80 percent when sales decreased by 10 percent.

When the firm is leveraged financially, the difference between the rate of return on total capital invested and the rate of return on common stockholders' equity indicates the effect of trading on the equity.

Where favorable financial leverage exists, the rate of return on common stockholder's equity will exceed the rate earned on total invested capital. A strong firm will show favorable leverage even when the economy is experiencing a downturn, and certainly over an economic cycle.

Return on Total Assets

As shown above, return on total assets is a key determinant of the return earned on owners' equity. There are two basic determinants of the return on total assets: (1) the cents of profit generated by each dollar of sales (the margin), and (2) the dollars of sales generated on average for each dollar of assets (the turnover of assets). This is demonstrated in the equation below:

$$\frac{\text{Net Earnings}}{\text{Total Assets}} = \frac{\text{Net Earnings}}{\text{Net Sales}} \times \frac{\text{Net Sales}}{\text{Total Assets}}$$

TABLE 11–3
Temple Corporation—The Determination of Earnings per Share for the Three Levels of Sales

Units Sold		144,000		160,000		176,000
Sales		$432,000		$480,000		$528,000
Less Costs						
Fixed Costs	$180,000		$180,000		$180,000	
Variable Costs	216,000		240,000		264,000	
Total Costs		396,000		420,000		444,000
EBIT[1]		$ 36,000		$ 60,000		$ 84,000
Less Interest Expense		30,000		30,000		30,000
Taxable Income		$ 6,000		$ 30,000		$ 54,000
Less Taxes		2,400		12,000		21,600
Earnings after Taxes		$ 3,600		$ 18,000		$ 32,400
Number of Shares		3,000		3,000		3,000
Earnings Per Share (EPS)		1.20		$6		$10.80

[1]EBIT = Earnings before Interest and Taxes

Percentage increase in EPS for 10 percent rise in sales:

$$\frac{10.80 - 6}{6} = \frac{4.80}{6} = 80\%$$

Percentage Decrease in EPS for 10 percent drop in sales:

$$\frac{6 - 1.2}{6} = \frac{4.80}{6} = 80\%$$

Return on total assets and the behavior of its components offers probably the most useful statistics for studying the operating efficiency of a firm.

Profit margin. Profit margin can be calculated in many ways to aid in studying operating efficiency of a firm. One can calculate and assess each of the following margin ratios:

1. Gross profit margin. This ratio is calculated by dividing gross profit by net sales. This ratio is a useful indicator of the productive efficiency on the plant floor of a firm. It should be analyzed in terms of its trend over time and in relationship to other companies operating in the same industry. As noted earlier, the method of inventory valuation used by the firm (e.g., LIFO versus FIFO) is important, and the analyst must be sure that the figures used for comparison are comparable.

2. Net operating margin. This ratio is calculated by dividing net operating income by net sales. It is the complement of the net operating
expense ratio, since the two when added must always equal 100
percent. This ratio indicates the percentage of sales dollars not used
up in the generation of the sales. In other words, this is the percentage
of sales dollars available to meet finance charges, pay taxes, and
provide for dividends and financing of corporate capital needs. Many
analysts consider this ratio of equal importance with the number of
times fixed charges are earned, when determining the quality of debt
obligations and the risk of leverage.

3. Before-tax and after-tax profit margins. The before-tax ratio is calculated by dividing the earnings before taxes by the net sales. It is a more
useful intermediate determinant of the return on assets than the
after-tax profit margin for purposes of assessing the efficiency with
which assets are used. Industry statistics for profits per dollar of sales
after taxes are given in Table 11–2.

The percentage of sales brought down to before-tax profit may be low
(as for a food chain), but if inventory turnover and capital investment
turnover are high the rate of return on assets may still be big. Conversely,
the before-tax margin may be relatively high (as for a public utility), but if
inventory and/or capital asset turnover are low, the return on assets may be
low. These ratios are components of the return on assets, and must be
interpreted in relation to asset turnovers. It is the return on capital committed
that is important to an investor, not how that return is generated. Breaking
the return on investment into its basic components, however, helps gain a
better understanding of the firm's operating record and provides a better
basis for forecasting.

The turnover of assets is calculated by dividing the net sales by the total
assets. There are numerous combinations of asset turnover and margin that
will yield a given return on assets. One should compare both the turnover
ratios and the margins over time for a company to that of competitive
companies, or companies in the same industry. Such an analysis, especially
when buttressed by information gained in the analysis of the economy, can
reveal weaknesses as well as the potential strength of a firm.

One must go beyond a mere calculation of these ratios and a comparison
to competitors. A weak margin suggests problems in controlling expenses
for a firm. Vertical and horizontal analysis can help explore these problems.
Vertical analysis is accomplished by dividing each expense item in the
income statement of a given year by net sales. One would expect expenses

to rise as sales rise. When a particular expense item, however, rises at a faster rate than sales, it should be explored carefully. In horizontal analysis, each expense item of a given year is divided by that same expense item in the base year. This allows exploring changes in the relative importance of expense items over time and the behavior of expense items as sales change.

Changes in asset turnover and expansion.   The turnover of assets may fall sharply when a firm undertakes a major expansion. The large asset investment involved causes this, since there has not yet been adequate time for these assets to generate the anticipated growth in sales that motivated undertaking the expansion. One must, therefore, be careful to review capital expenditures when assessing asset turnover ratios.

Leasing and the asset turnover ratio.   Leased assets usually are not recorded on the balance sheet, and are not, therefore, a part of the total assets shown on the balance sheet. Still, leased assets do result in sales. A rising or relatively high turnover ratio could, therefore, be generated by a firm that increases the use of leasing to acquire assets. This would not indicate more efficient use of asset investment.

Profitability Analysis and Physical Data Ratios

Analysts frequently calculate physical data ratios, and reduce them to a per share basis, to aid in studying profitability. These ratios are useful when calculated on the basis of specific characteristics of a given industry and used for comparing companies in that industry.

Physical reserves.   Reserves are of utmost importance to companies dependent on wasting assets for their operations (such as oil or timber companies). Reported reserves by major companies normally provide a conservative representation of such assets. The analyst should note the quality or grade of reserves as well as the quantity, with special attention to changes in grade from year to year. Changes from year to year indicate current extractive policy and possibly "high grading" (mining primarily the highest-grade ores in the deposit) in any given year.

Reserves of oil and gas, normally stated in terms of millions of barrels and billions of cubic feet, respectively, frequently are reported on a per share basis. The estimated value of reserves can be computed by multiplying the number of units in reserve by the going market price per unit. The value of reserves per share often is compared to current market price per share when looking for undervalued companies. This is not necessarily a valid indicator of value since market prices for the physical resource can rise or fall sharply in the future (witness oil).

Capacity. Producers and processors of various materials normally have specific productive or fabricating capacity that may be expressed in physical terms. These data can be reduced to a per share or a per employee basis for comparison between companies. Capacity also can be related to order backlogs, both in units and dollars. Persistent excess capacity often is a symptom of decline for a firm.

Production data. Production data in units can be related to capacity figures to assess whether or not excess capacity is present. This information should be compared to other firms in the industry. In companies concentrating principally on one type of product (e.g., crude oil, ingot steel, or copper), production data in units can be used to estimate selling prices, production costs, and profits per unit. Such data also help the analyst determine the effects of changes in costs and selling prices and the profit margins of the company.

Freight volume and other specialized ratios. Detailed information relative to volume, product composition, and geographical distribution of freight carried is valuable to the analyst in appraising the outlook for a transportation company such as a railroad, airline, trucking service, or barge line. Other examples of specialized physical ratios could be residential and commercial load for utilities, ton miles per dollar of debt for railroads, or the load factor for airlines.

SHORT-TERM SOLVENCY RATIOS

Short-term solvency ratios are used to judge the adequacy of liquid assets or the ability to meet short-term obligations as they come due. Firms go bankrupt, or get into financial difficulty, because they cannot pay obligations as they come due, not merely because they are not profitable. An investor should, therefore, assure himself or herself that liquidity problems are not likely to appear before buying a stock.

A complete analysis of the adequacy of working capital for meeting current liabilities as they come due and assessing management's efficiency in the use of working capital would require a thorough analysis of cash flows, sources and applications of funds, and forecasts of funds flows in future periods. Ratios can provide, however, a crude but useful assessment of working capital in many instances. We suggest using the five ratios listed below to assess the adequacy of working capital for a firm:

1. The current ratio.
2. The acid-test ratio.
3. The inventory turnover ratio.
4. The receivables turnover ratio.
5. The working capital turnover ratio.

Current ratio.   The current ratio is calculated by dividing current assets by current liabilities. It indicates the company's coverage of current liabilities by current assets. For example, if the ratio were 2:1, the firm could realize only one-half of the values stated in the balance sheet in liquidating current assets and still have adequate funds to pay all current liabilities.

For many years it has been rather loosely stated that, as a general rule, this ratio should be 2:1 or better. For all United States corporations, however, the ratio has only averaged about 1.85:1 in recent years, and seemed adequate.

A general standard for this ratio is not useful. Such a standard fails to recognize that an appropriate current ratio is a function of the nature of a company's business and would vary with differing operating cycles of different businesses.

A current asset is defined as any asset that is expected to be converted into cash in the ordinary operating cycle of a business. Inventory, therefore, is a current asset. In a tobacco or liquor company, inventory may be as much as 80 to 90 percent of current assets. Yet for a liquor company that inventory may have to age four years or more before it can be converted into a salable asset. Such a company typically would require a much higher current ratio than average to have adequate liquidity to meet current liabilities maturing in one year. For a public utility company where there is no inventory or receivables collection problem, a current ratio of 1.1 or 1.2 to 1 has proved satisfactory. We suggest looking at industry averages, rather than considering an overall standard, as produced by organizations such as Dun & Bradstreet or Robert Morris Associates. Such averages have their faults, but are preferable to general standards that do not recognize operating differences between companies.

The current ratio has a major weakness as an analytical tool. It ignores the composition of current assets, which may be as important as their relationship with current liabilities. Assume the current assets and current liabilities for a firm were as shown below.

Curent Assets		Current Liabilities	
Cash	$ 1,000	Accounts payable	$5,000
Receivables	1,000	Bank loans	2,000
Inventory	12,000		
Total	$14,000		$7,000

While this firm has a 2:1 current ratio, which would more than meet the average in many industries, one could question its liquidity. The inventory has not been sold yet and appears high relative to the total of current assets. Therefore, current ratio analysis must be supplemented by other working capital ratios.

Acid-Test (Quick) Ratio

Because the problem in meeting current liabilities may rest on slowness or even inability to convert inventories into cash to meet current obligations, the acid-test ratio is recommended. This is the ratio of current assets minus inventories, accruals, and prepaid items to current liabilities. This ratio does assume that receivables are of good quality and will be converted into cash over the next year. This ratio is only 2:7 in the above illustration, which would be low based on many industry averages.

The key to whether or not the firm in the illustration above will have liquidity problems is the salability of the inventory. If all the inventory can be sold and the resulting receivables collected over the next year, the liquidity is adequate. We therefore need a test of the salability of that inventory.

Inventory Turnover

The inventory turnover is computed by dividing the cost of goods sold by the average inventory investment for a year. Dun and Bradstreet industry ratios, unfortunately, use net sales as the numerator for this ratio, and that numerator would have to be used in the calculation if one wants to compare to their averages. The analyst is interested in determining the physical turnover of the inventory, and needs a numerator (cost of goods sold) that is calculated on the same basis as the inventory. Price changes could distort this ratio, as an indicator of physical turnover, when net sales are used as a numerator.

A low ratio suggests the possibility that investment in inventory is too high for the sales capacity of the business. This will hurt future profitability, both because of the interest costs incurred by borrowing to support the inventory investment and because of the storage costs.

On the other hand, a high ratio relative to the industry tends to suggest that inventories are too low. This often is an indication of overtrading. This can result in a serious financial collapse and even bankruptcy if sales activity slows down temporarily. Debt is incurred increasingly as sales rise, and there is no reserve to draw on when cash flows shrink. Moreover, sales might be lost by a firm because of inadequate selection for its customers.

The number of days' sales outstanding in inventory can be calculated by dividing the number of days in a year (365) by the inventory turnover ratio. For example, if the inventory turnover ratio were 12, the number of days sales outstanding would be about 30. This would mean that if the firm continued to sell at the same rate it has in the past, it would sell the entire inventory shown on the balance sheet in 30 days.

Receivables Turnover

The time needed to translate receivables into cash could be important for purposes of judging the adequacy of working capital. The receivables turnover can be determined by dividing the net credit sales by the total of accounts and notes receivable. Net sales typically is used as the numerator because information is not available as to the portion of sales that were on credit terms. This does tend to overstate the liquidity of receivables when cash sales are significant, as for a retailer.

The turnover may be converted into the number of days' sales outstanding in receivables by dividing the turnover figure into 365. One would expect the receivables turnover to be relatively in line with the firm's terms of sale. The ratio also should be reviewed over time. A high receivables turnover could make a relatively low current ratio acceptable, from a liquidity standpoint, and lead to a higher return on assets. On the other hand, a high turnover could suggest inadequate inventory for meeting customer's demands and/or an overly tight credit policy that is causing the firm to miss potentially profitable sales.

The average days' sales outstanding in receivables and in inventory can be combined to obtain an "average age of conversion" of noncash current assets into cash. The age of conversion is a rough indicator of the length of the operating cycle of the firm. These figures are useful when attempting to project cash flows.

CAPITALIZATION RATIOS

Analysts also calculate capitalization ratios to determine the extent to which the corporation is trading on its equity, the resulting financial leverage, and the degree of risk related to that leverage. These ratios can be interpreted only in the context of the stability of industry and company earnings and cash flow. The assumption is that the greater the stability of industry and company earnings and cash flow, the more the company is able to accept the risk associated with financial leverage, and the higher the allowable ratio of debt to total capitalization (the total dollar amount of all long-term sources of funds in the balance sheet).

In the case of new companies or companies in highly cyclical industries, the use of any long-term debt may be unsound. If the fixed charges required to service the debt are covered by a large margin when studied in relation to likely cash flows in recession years, the debt can be acceptable. A highly leveraged capital structure can offer high returns on assets and equity in boom periods, but lead to serious financial consequences in recession years as illustrated by the railroads and airlines in 1960–61, 1970–71, and 1974–75. This can result in low prices for the securities of such companies in recession years. However, if an investor believes the worst has been experienced and that a decided improvement in earning power can be expected, a commitment in these securities while the prices are depressed and P/E ratios are relatively low can be rewarding.

Capitalization ratios can be calculated by dividing total capitalization by each major component of the capitalization structure; that is, dividing by total long-term debt, preferred stock, and common equity. It is useful to calculate common equity at market as well as at book value for purposes of determining these proportions. A market calculation for common equity may indicate considerably more or less financial leverage than a book calculation.

The proportion can serve as a screening device. When the common equity represents 70 percent or more of total capitalization, there normally is no need to be concerned with the risk of leverage. An analyst could then better spend his time studying more critical problems revealed by his or her analysis.

Leases and the Stock Equity Test

Many corporations rent buildings and equipment under long-term lease contracts. Required rental payments are contractual obligations similar to bond coupon and repayment obligations. However, assets acquired through leasing may not be capitalized and shown in the balance sheet. Two companies, therefore, might work with the same amount of fixed assets and produce the same profits before interest or rental payments, but the one leasing a high proportion of its productive equipment could show significantly lower debt relative to total capitalization.

Stock Equity Tests and Standards

Standards only can be established in a general sense. An electric utility, for example, with highly stable and recession-resistant income can utilize more debt and preferred stock relative to equity than a company with more cyclical earnings, such as a steel or auto company. Debt could range from 50 to 65 percent of total capitalization, and up to 75 percent of total capitalization where preferred stock is included, for a public utility without suggesting excessive borrowing and leverage. A railroad or a highly cyclical company would raise serious questions if long-term debt was as much as 50 percent of total capitalization. We would suggest questioning the capital structure for a cyclical company if the long-term debt represented more than 35 percent of total capitalization. For a company less subject to the business cycle, such as a food company, long-term debt safely could approach 50 percent of total capitalization. The key is the stability of the company's income over the cycle.

EARNINGS COVERAGE TESTS

The earnings of a corporation are the basic source of cash flows. Coverage ratios are used to test the adequacy of cash flows generated through earnings for purposes of meeting debt and lease obligations.

Tests of the adequacy of earnings are applied to the past record of the company, although the future record is the one that will determine the soundness of the judgment exercised in buying a security. These ratios must, therefore, be interpreted in the light of the likelihood that the past financial record offers a reasonable indication of future performance.

Calculation of Earnings Available to Cover Fixed Charges

The calculation of an interest coverage or a fixed charges coverage ratio is simple: earnings available for paying the interest or the total fixed charges for a given year are divided by the annual interest expense and fixed charges.

Interest expense and rental expenses are tax deductible and, therefore, all earnings before taxes are available for paying such charges. The proper calculation is shown in equation form below:

$$\frac{E_t + I_t + R_t}{I_t + R_t}$$

where

E_t = earnings before taxes during year t

I_t = interest charges paid during year t

R_t = rental payments made under long-term leases during year t.

Financial reporting services report coverage after taxes and also show average before taxes. Corporate annual reports often report the amount available for interest after taxes rather than before, and many do not consider lease payments.

Minimum Standards for Fixed Charges Coverage Ratios

Suggested standards are based on experience and empirical studies relating the incidence of defaults over a number of years to such ratios.[1]

Different standards are in order for a highly cyclical company than for a stable company. Data suggest that average coverage over a business cycle should be eight or better to be classed as higher grade for a cyclical company, while the coverage ratio should not fall below four in any one year. For stable companies, an average coverage ratio of five or better and a minimum ratio of 2.5 in any year suggests relatively high quality.

VALUE RATIOS

Ratios based on market price per share of the company's common stock offer investors important measures of growth and stability of earnings, and a crude indicator of relative value.

---

[1] For example, see W. Braddock Hickman, *Corporate Bond Quality and Investor Experience* (New York: National Bureau of Economic Research, 1958).

Price–Earnings Ratio

The P/E ratio was discussed in Chapter 10, and we refer the reader to that discussion. The range of the P/E ratio for a particular company's stock over a five- to ten-year period should be related to the range for the appropriate Dow-Jones and Standard & Poor's indexes for the same years, as well as the ratios of companies in the same industry. This will suggest whether a stock is high priced or low priced in relation to earnings. We suggest a low P/E out-of-favor stock selection policy, and this ratio is an initial screen.

An investor should aim at purchasing growth stocks whose future performance has not been over-discounted in their market price. A P/E ratio screen can help spot such companies.

An undervalued stock selection strategy tends to be oriented cyclically and long term in approach. During economic recessions, the market tends to become undervalued in terms of any norm relative to the long-term secular trend of stock prices. At such times, the prices of the stocks of some major companies may decline more than the averages, but in many years there are likely to be some undervaluations. Following this approach does require the emotional stamina to go against the crowd, and the patience to wait for the crowd to appreciate the facts. History suggests that investors tend to exaggerate both pessimism and optimism.

Not all low P/E stocks represent undervaluations. Undervaluation is found when a company's earning power can be expected to recover or has been underestimated by the market. Risk tends also to be minimized by concentrating stock selection on low P/E companies. The adverse expectations of the market already are reflected in the current stock price, lessening the downside risk of such selections. Moreover, low P/E stocks tend to offer high divided yields, giving further downside protection if expectations are not realized.

Dividends per Share and Dividend Yield

The stability and growth of dividends on a compound annual basis should be calculated over the past five years, and explanations sought for significant changes in dividend payout policy. Dividend payout can be reviewed by dividing dividends per share by earnings per share. Also, it is useful to review dividends as a percentage of cash flow income over time.

Fundamental Analysis of Special Classes of Securities

Chapter Twelve

Regulated Industries: Utilities

The general legal and economic classifications of public utilities include, among others: (1) electric light and power companies; (2) companies supplying natural or manufactured gas, either pipeline companies or direct operating companies; (3) telephone, telegraph, and other companies supplying communication services; (4) companies supplying water; and (5) railroads and other transportation companies.

In the financial community, transportation companies are placed in a separate classification for separate analysis, and accordingly they will be discussed in the next chapter. Because electric utilities represent the major segment of investor interest in public utilities, they will be emphasized in this chapter. Space limitations permit only limited coverage of other types of utilities, such as gas, communication, and water companies, that are nonetheless of significant importance in the investment field.

THE PUBLIC UTILITY INDUSTRY

Public utility companies are required to meet the demands for service of all users, irrespective of fluctuation in demand. This requires maintenance of capacity to meet peak loads, with certain amounts of idle capacity at other times.

Characteristics of Public Utility Companies

Public utility companies can be identified by the following salient features:

1. They are affected with a public interest. Their service is a necessity for a large segment of the economy, and public utilities must meet public demand.
2. They operate under conditions where direct competition generally is not practical, although there may be competition between services, such as electric versus gas service for heating.
3. Because of the above factors, utilities are subject to broad regulation (especially rate regulation) by one or more governmental bodies or agencies.
4. Production of services is simultaneous with customer use and, unlike industrial companies, there is no inventory problem and a minimum of "receivables" problems. Receivables problems have been increasing, however, for urban utilities (such as Philadelphia Gas Co.), and this area, must be watched.

Territory served.   The territory served by a public utility is carefully defined by the franchises and certificates of necessity under which regulated companies operate. The analyst must carefully analyze the economics of the areas served as well as the geographic, physical, and atmospheric environment. Costs of operation, as for example maintenance for railroads, are generally affected by physical and atmospheric environment.

Capitalization and securities.   Regulators must approve the type of capitalization, the type of securities issued, and each sale of securities, including the method of sale and type of securities issued and their specific characteristics, as well as the use to which funds will be put.

Management.   Although management of regulated industries operates within a narrower decision scope than does management of industrial companies, management is still important, especially in its relations with the regulators and in the area of operations, such as efficiencies and ability and willingness to provide satisfactory service whenever and wherever needed. Labor relations are another important factor. Perhaps the most serious problem other than in the area of actual operations is public relations and related environmental problems.

Regulation of the Public Utility Industry

An analysis of a utility company should begin with an analysis of the regulatory climate, followed by an economic and financial analysis of the company. Unless the regulatory climate is satisfactory, the analyst should not proceed further. Earnings of utility companies actually are determined by regulatory authorities who must approve all rate changes.

Because utility companies often are natural monopolies that supply a necessary service to the public, they must be subject to government regulation. Electric utility companies are domiciled in the state in which they operate and are subject to regulation by state public utility commissions. States and local authorities with power delegated to them by their states regulate intrastate utilities.[1]

Regulation covers a broad area: rates, service rendered, purchase and sale of assets, issuance of securities, and a uniform accounting system. Utilities are required to conform to the uniform system of accounts to which most state utility commissions have subscribed. An excellent utility will make every effort to maintain good relations with its regulatory commission. However, it may have to apply to the courts for approval of rate increases, if the commission refuses to sanction equitable rates that would yield a fair return on the fair value of the property and that provide sufficient income to maintain the financial standing of the company's securities in the capital markets. The United States Supreme Court has the final decision in rate cases involving the question of fair return.

Franchises and certificates of necessity.   Contracts between the state (and local subdivisions) and public utilities authorize a particular utility to operate in a particular territory. Contracts may be perpetual, indeterminate, or limited in time. If a utility operates under a definitive term, questions may arise as the terminal date approaches concerning its renewal or at least the characteristics of the new contracts. A utility's bonds should not mature beyond the terminal date. In recent years, the trend has been toward indeterminate life franchises continuing as long as service is satisfactory.

Federal regulation.   Several agencies of the federal government are involved in the regulation of utilities, as outlined below.

---

[1] See Moody's *Public Utilities Manual* for information concerning regulating authorities and the National Association of Railroad & Public Utility Commissioners.

1. The Interstate Commerce Commission regulates the rates, service standards, financing, and accounting of railroads, trucking companies, and buses engaged in interstate business.

2. The Federal Energy Regulatory Commission regulates those electric utilities that use power from navigable streams as well as other users of these streams and rivers. It also governs utilities regularly transporting electricity and gas across state lines. Regulation includes approval of rates for electric power and gas crossing state lines, approval of mergers and securities acquisitions by such companies, and issuance of certificates for construction of interstate natural gas pipelines. Companies must file financial reports with the Energy Information Administration.

3. The Federal Communications Commission determines the rates and controls the accounts and basic practices of telephone and telegraph companies engaged in interstate commerce as they apply to the interstate activities of these companies.

4. The Securities and Exchange Commission, under the Public Utility Act of 1935, regulates public utility electric and gas holding companies that control operating companies in more than one state. Control is exercised over capital structures, financing, and accounting of registered public utility holding companies in conjunction with state regulation commissions and their subsidiary operating companies.

5. The Civil Aeronautics Board regulates the air transport industry with authority over routes, schedules, rates, services, safety standards, accounting, mergers and acquisitions, and intercorporate relations.[2]

6. Proposals in connection with the new U.S. Department of Energy were the first attempt by the federal government to regulate overall rates the U.S. charges on both a retail and wholesale basis, overriding state and local regulations. (Legislation recommended by House and Senate Conference, November–December 1977.)

The National Association of Railroad and Utility Commissions adopted a revised uniform system of accounts for electric and gas utilities in 1961. The Federal Energy Regulatory Commission requires essentially the same

---

[2] Effective early January 1978, Congress legislated deregulation of rates and routes for air cargo carriers. The Civil Aeronautics Board still has the power to alter "predatory" or "discriminatory" pricing. Deregulation of passenger fares was being proposed, as was deregulation of rates applying to interstate truck and bus companies. In all cases, the industries concerned were fighting deregulation of rates, claiming that cutthroat competition would result from deregulation.

system for hydroelectric companies and utility companies that come under its jurisdiction. Other types of utility companies also are required to use a uniform system of accounting. Uniform accounting is a real aid to financial analysis of utility companies because the analyst can assume that accounts identified by similar names represent identical items. However, although there is uniform accounting, there is a considerable divergence in actual accounting practices in published reports—for example, flow-through versus normalizing for depreciation methods, depending on state commissions.

Importance of regulation to investors.   It has been noted that the regulatory climate in which a utility must operate is of vital importance to the investor, especially because of the effect of regulation on rates and service standards and on rate of return on investment. The rates charged must be approved by the regulatory commission, and the rates charged times the units sold determine the gross income of the utility. The utility has control over its costs but not its revenues. An electric utility company is permitted to earn a fair return on the fair value of its property used in the public service, but is not guaranteed such a return.

The Hope Natural Gas decision by the United States Supreme Court in 1944 has been interpreted as releasing the regulatory commissions from the necessity of adhering to any specific method of determining the rate base. The method used by a commission in determining utility rate base valuation is no longer subject to judicial (U.S. Supreme Court) review. Rather, the overall effect of the rates charged on the company's credit standing in the capital markets has become the crucial issue. As most utilities are frequently in the capital markets to secure funds for expansion, the ability to secure their funds at a reasonable competitive cost is crucial and was so recognized by the Court (the cost-of-capital approach).

Methods of determining a fair rate of return vary widely. Some commissions use the accounting and statistical approach, while others have considered the rising cost of new money. There also is evidence in decisions of the recognition of "attrition" in earnings resulting from inflation (or the effect of inflation on the rate base).

Rate of return on rate base.   Utilities are permitted to charge rates that will produce the rate of return on their asset rate base approved by the regulatory commission. The allowed rate of return varies among states—the spread ranges from a low of 5 percent to a high of 10 percent, with an average range of 5 to 7 percent.

The relatively few growth utilities have had two major factors that contributed to growth in earnings greater than that of the industry overall: (1) a favorable regulatory climate—average rate of return above 7.3 percent—on their rate base; and (2) the advantage of operating in a rapidly growing area, such as Florida. Both factors need to be present. For example, in spite of the exceptionally rapid population and economic growth in California after World War II, the regulatory climate was not satisfactory, as the rate of return on the rate base tended to be held to an annual 5½ percent. On April 20, 1994, the California Public Utilities Commission announced a new proposal under which all electricity customers in that state would be allowed to choose the source of their electrical generation by January 1, 2002. Many investors view California as the bellwether for actions of regulators in other states. This was cited by Standard & Poor's as one reason for poor performance of electric utility stocks during the second-quarter 1994. Moreover, California electric utilities did not demonstrate nearly as high an earnings growth rate as did the Florida utilities in the post–World War II years, partly due to the regulatory environment, and this was reflected in stock prices.

The investor must know the rate of return permitted in the state where the utility under analysis operates, as well as whether there has been an up- or downtrend. The investor also should be familiar with the political climate in the state in regard to the utility commission or the probability of a change in the regulatory climate as a result of a changing political environment.

Of course, the rate base is as important as the allowed rate of return on the rate base. The investor should know the principle on which the commission calculates the rate base. For example, a rate base estimated on historical cost would be much lower than one based on reproduction cost or one that recognized the effect of inflation on property values.

Rate of return on investment. For electric utilities, rates of return on total invested capital and stockholders' equity were satisfactory up to 1970. However, during 1970–75 a serious lag developed between inflationary cost increases (particularly costs of fuel, construction, and interest for new financing and refinancing) and rate increases. As a result, the rates of return on investment and the amount available to meet fixed charges and provide a return for stockholders fell to unsatisfactory levels from the standpoint of the investor, and this was reflected in the securities markets, as shown by the sharp drop in utility stock prices during the years 1971–75 (see Figures 12–1 and 12–2). The number of times fixed charges were earned for the industry overall fell well below two times, interest costs rose

FIGURE 12–1
500 Composite versus Utilities

Source: Standard & Poor's *Analyst's Handbook, 1994* (New York: Standard & Poor's Corporation, 1994). Reprinted by permission of Standard & Poor's, a division of The McGraw-Hill Companies.

FIGURE 12–2
Utilities versus Electric Companies

Source: Standard & Poor's *Analyst's Handbook, 1994* (New York: Standard & Poor's Corporation, 1994). Reprinted by permission of Standard & Poor's, a division of The McGraw-Hill Companies.

TABLE 12–1
Profitability and Growth Measures, 1976–80

	Profits After Taxes to:		Five Year Average Growth in:	
	Stockholders' Equity	Total Capital	Sales	Earnings Per Share
Utilities Serving:				
The Northeast	11.5	6.6	12.9	3.3
The Midwest	11.8	6.2	15.1	2.1
The Southeast	12.1	6.6	16.1	2.9
The Southwest	14.0	7.4	19.8	6.0
The West	11.8	6.6	15.8	2.7
All Industry Medians	15.5	10.9	14.0	12.5

Source: "34th Annual Report on American Industry," *Forbes,* January 4, 1982, pp. 104–108.

to 9 to 10 percent, and common stocks of many utilities fell below book values and sold at yields as high as 10 to 11 percent. After 1975, substantial rate relief was granted in a majority of cases, and the rates of return began to return to satisfactory levels, which in time was reflected in the securities market (see Table 12–1). Electric company stocks have been rising in the 1990s, but at a significantly slower rate than utility stocks in general. Moreover, utility stocks in general have risen less than the S&P 500 composite.

Table 12–1 contrasts key profitability and growth measures for the utility industry and all corporations covered in a *Forbes* study. Table 12–2 updates this information for the utility industry and provides additional data, including forecasts. Figure 12–1 compares a price index for electric power company stocks to the Standard & Poor's 500 Stock Index.

It is not difficult to understand why utility stocks, on average, have such low P/E ratios, and that the prices of electric utility stocks are low relative to the S&P 500 Stock Index. They earn less on capital employed, and have shown insignificant earnings-per-share growth, especially since 1985. They are bought mainly on the basis of the high dividend yield these stocks offer, though substantial capital gains could have been made during the period 1980–85 when the operating expense ratio was dropping sharply.

TABLE 12–2
Key Financial Statistics and Ratios for Investor-Owned Electric Utilities

	1980	1984	1985	1986	1987	1988	1989	1990	1991	1992	1993	E 1994
Construction and Financing Requirements												
Construction expenditures (Million $)	28,235	35,285	33,294	31,023	27,035	23,630	24,760	24,187	23,360	24,246	25,209	25,903
AFUDC included above	4,365	7,923	6,941	5,659	3,893	2,711	2,241	1,708	1,132	1,347	944	832
New long-term financing (Million $)												
Debt	7,847	9,361	9,189	10,344	8,688	6,800	8,337	5,594	4,887	9,007	8,729	NA
Preferred stock	2,003	888	655	985	1,205	552	350	660	505	3,059	2,395	NA
Common stock	4,063	862	1,579	606	246	503	772	217	864	1,647	1,647	NA
Industry Financial Ratios												
Capitalization (%)												
Long-term debt	50.4	48.2	48.2	48.0	47.0	49.0	49.1	49.0	49.1	48.9	48.7	NA
Preferred stock	12.3	10.2	9.9	8.7	9.0	7.7	7.6	7.2	7.1	7.1	6.8	NA
Common stock	37.3	41.6	41.9	43.3	44.0	43.3	43.3	43.8	43.8	44.0	44.5	NA
S & P electric utility Price–earnings ratio (High–Low)	7.25– 5.80	6.88– 5.52	7.98– 6.70	10.29– 7.60	10.24– 7.85	11.0– 9.8	12.2– 9.7	14.2– 11.9	15.5– 12.3	14.1– 12.5	17.1– 14.6	NA
Average interest rate on long-term debt (%)	8.4	9.9	10.0	9.8	8.5	9.1	8.8	9.0	8.5	8.2	7.8	NA

(continued)

TABLE 12–2 (concluded)

	1980	1984	1985	1986	1987	1988	1989	1990	1991	1992	1993	E 1994
Return on common equity	11.4	14.5	13.8	13.7	13.0	10.3	10.1	9.2	9.6	10.1	9.7	NA
Growth in earnings per share— S&P Electric Utility Index (%)	3.1	7.5	1.6	1.3	1.0	(14.5)	10.5	(14.3)	6.2	11.4	(6.7)	NA
Income tax rate	29.4	36.6	37.0	30.9	35.0	32.9	34.6	34.5	34.5	35.0	35.0	NA
Dividend payout ratio	75.8	65.7	74.6	65.6	66.0	70.7	7 0.0	76.1	79.8	84.5	80.5	NA

Sources: Edison Electric Institute, Standard & Poor's *Industry Surveys, Utilities—Electric,* February 23, 1995, p. U36. Reprinted by permission of Standard & Poor's, a division of The McGraw-Hill Companies.

Utility stock prices are highly sensitive to interest rate changes, and investors can purchase them for capital gain purposes when they believe interest rates will decline significantly. Investors become much more interested in purchasing tangible assets when real interest rates are negative (nominal rates trail the rate of inflation) and inflation is high. Stocks and bonds tend to fall out of favor during such a period, especially where their earnings growth trails behind the inflation rate. This did occur during the 1970s. Utilities also were hurt during this period because inflation rates exceeded the rate at which utility assets were being depreciated, thereby eroding asset values.

The inflation rate and interest rates were lowered sharply in the 1980s, leading to more favorable conditions for utilities. This was reflected in their stock prices (see Figure 12–1) through 1985.

STOCK YIELDS AND INTEREST RATES

Investors in electric utility stocks were hurt as interest rates rose from third-quarter 1993 through third-quarter 1994. The yield on 30-year Treasury bonds was 7.8 percent on September 30, 1994, versus 5.9 percent a year earlier. The S&P Electric Utilities Stock Index fell 8.4 percent during the fourth quarter of 1993, and declined another 13.8 percent during the first quarter of 1994 while the S&P 500 had fallen only 4.4 percent. The index continued to perform poorly during the second quarter of 1994, and started to rebound in the third quarter, only to decline again in September when the New York Public Service Commission recommended rate cuts for Niagara Mohawk and Consolidated Edison.

MERGERS

Merger and acquisition activity is expected to continue in the electric utility industry, in an effort realize synergies and achieve cost savings in a difficult business environment highlighted by limited growth prospects for electricity demand. The regulatory authorities, however, are expected to make completing mergers difficult. Diversification into areas not related to the core energy business has not typically been successful. Electric utilities are now concentrating on diversifying into energy-related fields.

FIGURE 12–3
Dividend Payout Ratio of S&P Electric Utility Index

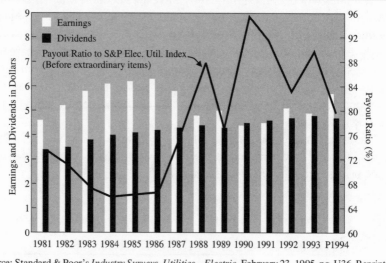

Source: Standard & Poor's *Industry Surveys, Utilities—Electric,* February 23, 1995, pg. U36. Reprinted by permission of Standard & Poor's, a division of The McGraw-Hill Companies.

P = Preliminary

DIVIDEND YIELD

Electrical utility stocks have typically offered relatively high dividend yields, offsetting relatively lower price growth for the securities. S&P reports that the industry's dividend payout ratio has, however, declined to 80.5 percent at December 31, 1993 (see Figure 12–3) from 84.4 percent a year earlier. The decline in dividend payout ratio continued during the first nine months of 1994, with the payout ratio falling to 76.7 percent by September 30, 1994. Dividend cuts were largely responsible for this development. Standard & Poor's expects dividend increases for this industry "to average only about 1.5 percent annually over the next several years."[3]

Increasing competition and a relatively difficult operating environment for this industry are likely to hold dividend payout ratios to the 70 percent to 76 percent range over the next several years. Investors should be concerned that dividends may be cut (or at least will not grow much) for companies whose payout ratios are 80 percent or higher.

---

3 Standard & Poor's *Industry Surveys, Utilities—Electric,* February 23, 1995, p. 37.

ANALYSIS OF GROSS REVENUES

The annual report of a public utility generally will provide, in the income statement or in a supplementary statement, a breakdown of revenues and KWHs by class of customer, as illustrated in Table 12–3 (see Operating Statistics). Other useful data also is contained in the Table. A utility is to a large extent the prisoner of its geographic, economic, and political environment—it may, at times, buy and/or sell electricity outside its territory. A reasonable balance between type of customer—residential, industrial, and commercial—is desirable.

Residential load. The residential load for utilities has demonstrated, in general, great stability and sustained growth. Years ago lighting was the major load, with the peak being in the evening and in December. Air conditioning now has become a major factor, causing loads to peak in the summer. Sales of electricity to residential customers by American Electric Power (AEP) rose fairly steadily over the period 1990–94, at a 4.72 percent compound annual growth rate. While severe winter weather in January 1994 and extremely hot June weather increased residential sales, the mild weather throughout the remainder of 1994, combined with increased competition in the wholesale market, held down growth for the year. Weather, therefore, is also an important, and impossible to predict, factor.

Commercial load. This load has demonstrated about as much stability for American Electric Power as the residential load, and grew at about 19 percent over the period 1990–94. Customer classification includes stores, restaurants, gasoline stations, retail establishments, and the financial industry. Commercial demand tends to vary as the economy of the area served varies. Growth in the economy should lead to continued growth in this area, but a slowdown in the economy would markedly slow growth. Some fear a slowdown in the financial sector could adversely affect this demand.

Industrial load. This load is less stable than the residential or commercial load in terms of the business cycle, and grows at a slower rate for American Electric Power. The instability is greatest if sales to the durable goods or capital goods areas represent a substantial portion of gross revenues. The investor should analyze the types of industrial service offered and the company's past record in this respect.

TABLE 12–3
American Electric Power at a Glance

	1994	1993	1992	1991	1990
Operating Statistics					
Net Generation	120,620	120,759	114,606	115,255	119,292
Net Purchased and Interchange Power	3,358	3,418	3,467	4,710	8,276
Total System Load (in millions of kwh)	123,978	124,177	118,073	119,965	127,568
Coal—Purchased (estimated)	40,597	36,065	35,055	31,086	34,624
—Mined by System Companies (estimated)	7,166	8,803	11,528	12,168	11,581
Total Coal Used (actual) (in thousands of tons)	47,763	44,868	46,583	43,254	46,205
System Capability					
—Coal	20,795	21,120	21,120	21,120	20,865
—Nuclear	2,110	2,110	2,110	2,110	2,130
—Hydro, pumped storage and other	854	854	854	854	854
—Contracted Purchases (Sales)	(89)	118	118	118	118
Total Capability at Year End (megawatts)	23,670	24,202	24,202	24,202	23,967
Transmission Lines (circuit miles)	21,906	21,916	21,856	21,722	21,730
Total System Peak Load (megawatts)	26,371	22,142	20,474	22,360	21,708
Heat Rate (Btu per kwh of net generation)	9,817	9,872	9,796	9,953	9,777

(continued)

1994 Retail Revenues by Operating Company

Indiana
Michigan 18.7%
Kentucky 5.3%
Appalachian 26.0%
1.7% Wheeling
19.9% Columbus Southern
1.7% Kingsport
26.7% Ohio

1994 Operating Revenues by Jurisdiction

Michigan 2.9%
Federal 13.2%
Indiana 13.4%
Kentucky 4.6%
1.5% Tennessee
12.2% W. Virginia
11.8% Virginia
40.4% Ohio

Sources of Energy Supplied

Nuclear 7.5%
Purchased & Net Inter-change 2.7%
0.8% Hydro & Other
89.0% Coal

TABLE 12–3 *(continued)*

	1994	*1993*	*1992*	*1991*	*1990*
Operating Revenues *(in thousands)*					
Residential	**$1,835,442**	$1,780,802	$1,663,348	$1,658,165	$1,526,377
Commercial	**1,217,921**	1,153,207	1,097,735	1,079,040	1,021,217
Industrial	**1,578,579**	1,514,691	1,506,234	1,431,395	1,431,659
Miscellaneous	**64,668**	62,879	67,507	68,653	67,444
Total Retail	**4,696,610**	4,511,579	4,334,824	4,237,253	4,046,697
Wholesale *(sales for resale)*	**714,076**	687,072	647,286	738,292	1,070,483
Other	**93,984**	70,191	62,682	71,066	60,440
Total Operating Revenues	**$5,504,670**	$5,268,842	$5,044,792	$5,046,611	$5,177,620
Energy Use *(in millions of kwh)*					
Residential	**28,818**	28,876	26,998	27,458	25,332
Commercial	**21,209**	20,711	19,661	19,704	18,608
Industrial	**43,579**	42,479	41,327	39,482	39,169
Miscellaneous	**1,201**	1,187	1,269	1,324	1,297
Wholesale *(Sales for resale)*	**21,907**	23,588	21,596	24,671	35,659
Total Energy Use	**116,714**	116,841	110,851	112,639	120,065
Average Annual Use Per Customer *(in kwh)*					
All Residential: AEP System	**11,491**	11,635	10,996	11,302	10,530
All Investor-Owned Utilities	**9,445***P*	9,380*P*	8,949	9,280	9,056
Average Annual Bill Per Customer					
All Residential: AEP System	**$731.85**	$717.57	$677.46	$682.51	$634.49
All Investor-owned Utilities	**829.43***P*	818.47*P*	772.58	784.80	740.04
Average Kwh Price Per Customer *(in cents)*					
All Residential: AEP System	**6.37**	6.17	6.16	6.04	6.03
All Investor-owned Utilities	**8.78***P*	8.73*P*	8.63	8.46	8.17
All Retail: AEP System	**4.95**	4.84	4.86	4.82	4.79
All Investor-owned Utilities	**7.15***P*	7.14*P*	7.08	7.01	6.77
All Customers: AEP System	**4.64**	4.45	4.49	4.42	4.26
Customers *(at Dec. 31)*	**2,874,304**	2,840,217	2,807,846	2,774,396	2,747,013
Shareholders *(at Dec. 31)*	**183,461**	194,019	204,170	206,584	213,152
Employees *(at Dec. 31)*	**19,660**	20,007	20,841	22,136	22,798

(P) Preliminary

(continued)

TABLE 12–3 *(continued)*

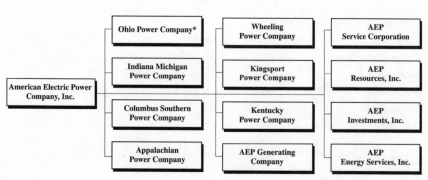

* Active Mining Subsidiaries—Central Ohio Coal Co., Southern Ohio Coal Co. & Windsor Coal Co.

Year Ended December 31,	1994	1993	1992	1991	1990
Income Statements Data *(in millions)*					
Operating Revenues	**$5,505**	$5,269	$5,045	$5,047	$5,178
Operating Income	**932**	928	883	918	861
Net Income	**500**	354	468	498	496

December 31,	1994	1993	1992	1991	1990
Balance Sheets Data *(in millions)*					
Electric Utility Plant	**$18,175**	$17,712	$17,509	$17,148	$16,652
Accumulated Depreciation and Amortization	**6,827**	6,612	6,281	5,952	5,588
Net Electric Utility Plant	**$11,348**	$11,100	$11,228	$11,196	$11,064
Total Assets	**$15,713**	$15,341	$14,277	$13,886	$13,596
Common Shareholders' Equity	**4,230**	4,152	4,246	4,222	4,167
Cumulative Preferred Stocks of Subsidiaries:					
Not Subject to Mandatory Redemption	**233**	268	535	535	535
Subject to Mandatory Redemption*	**590**	501	234	141	145
Long-term Debt*	**4,980**	4,995	5,311	5,029	4,927
Obligations Under Capital Leases*	**400**	284	300	273	290

(continued)

TABLE 12–3 *(concluded)*

Year Ended December 31,	*1994*	*1993*	*1992*	*1991*	*1990*
Common Stock Data:					
Earnings per Share	**$2.71**	$1.92	$2.54	$2.70	$2.65
Average Number of Shares Outstanding *(in thousands)*	**184,666**	184,535	184,535	184,535	187,064
Market Price Range: High	**$37⅜**	$40⅜	$35¼	$34¼	$33⅛
Low	**27¼**	32	30⅜	26⅝	26
Year-end Market Price	**32⅞**	37⅛	33⅛	34¼	28
Cash Dividends Paid	**$2.40**	$2.40	$2.40	$2.40	$2.40
Dividend Payout Ratio	**88.6%**	125.2%	94.6%	88.9%	90.3%
Book Value per Share	**$22.83**	$22.50	$23.01	$22.88	$22.58

*Including portion due within one year

Source: 1994 Report to Shareholders, American Electric Power, Pages 18, 19 and 21.

Street and highway lighting. This load is as stable as the residential load, but political pressures on rates can be serious.

Sales to other companies for resale. Utilities have built up a large network of interconnections, and consistently sell or purchase power. Such sales may show considerable instability and should be analyzed carefully.

Regional outlook. Utilities serving the industrial Midwest, the Far West, and the East Central areas are likely to realize good growth over the next few years because of the reasonably good growth in the industrial economy of those areas. This is likely to lead to increased off-system sales to utilities serving these areas to assure meeting demand.

Expenses

The major expense items in the income statement are fuel and purchased power, maintenance, depreciation, federal income taxes and other taxes. In the post–World War II years, the operating ratio for electric utilities (operating expenses divided by operating revenues) generally ranged from 78 to 83 percent until 1976, when it rose sharply to about 85 percent, reflecting higher costs not balanced by rate increases. Many utilities received substantial rate relief by 1980 and this ratio began to fall, settling in the 80–82 percent range since 1988 (see Table 12–5).

Edison Electric Institute reported that operating revenues were up 3.8 percent during the first nine months of 1994, but operating expense rose 5.5 percent during the same period. Maintenance expenses were up 5.1 percent during this period as a result of one-time charges for workforce reductions as companies continued to enhance their competitiveness. Purchased power and net interchange expenses were up 8 percent. There may, therefore, not be a long-term unfavorable change in the operating ratio. We would look carefully at any electric utility whose operating ratio exceeds 82–83 percent before purchasing its stock.

The Nuclear Problem

There have been substantial efforts by community groups to stall the licensing process for nuclear plants. The Shoreham plant, owned by Long Island Lighting Company, and the Seabrook station owned by Public Service of New Hampshire and 11 other utilities, are illustrative of the problems this can present. Congress recently expressed the sentiment that local officials should not be permitted to veto nuclear plant licenses. This should help bring resolution to the problem of bringing these plants into operation, though not many new ones have been built.

Investors should be cautious about acquiring the stock of an electric utility with nuclear plants facing political problems. They represent a costly investment, and the utility may not be allowed to include that investment in the rate base if they cannot operate the plants.

Allowance for Funds Used in Construction

This item is peculiar to utilities and often is a major expense item. The utility borrows funds and pays interest on these funds. The utility is permitted to capitalize a "reasonable" amount of interest and to show a noncash credit (income) item in its income statement for the same amount. If the amount is significant, the analyst must estimate what it will amount to over the next several years. The item ceases when the plant goes into operation, at which time it is hoped that additional income generated will offset the previous "Allowance for Funds Used in Construction" credit item in the income statement.

Income Available for Fixed Charges

In the income statement of regulated companies, the income available for fixed charges is "after taxes" because taxes were deducted in operating expenses. If the analyst wishes to calculate the coverage before taxes, income taxes must be added to the "income available for fixed charges." The income coverage should be at least two times. It fell below that level for the industry overall in years such as 1973–75, but rate increases caused it to recover. The analyst recommending utility securities in the years 1973–75 when they were selling at especially depressed prices and were distinctly out of favor had to feel reasonable assurance that rate relief was forthcoming, which indeed proved to be the case in most areas. The analyst also should calculate the coverage for fixed charges *plus* preferred dividends, allowing for the fact that preferred dividends are not tax deductible as is interest paid.

Comparative Financial Statistics

When considering purchasing a stock, including utilities, one should compare the companies' earnings records and key balance sheet relationships with appropriate industry data. The Standard & Poor's *Industry Surveys* and the *Analyst's Handbook* published by Standard & Poor's offer data for this purpose. Tables 12–4 and 12–5 contain per share data prepared by Standard & Poor's Corporation useful for comparative purposes. The industry surveys offer significant ratios for individual companies in the given industry.

Note that the industrials earned a much higher average return on book value per share than the electric utilities earned on net property per share (the equivalent). Also, the electricals pay out a higher proportion of earnings as dividends than do the industrials, and offer significantly higher dividend yields. The growth characteristics, however, suggest greater capital gains potential for the industrials. The key question for the investor is whether or not the growth already is reflected in the price of the stock when purchase is considered.

Suggested minimum standards for electric utility companies are presented in Table 12–6.

Utility Industry Diversification

In recent years, many utility companies have branched out from their traditional regulated businesses into new areas (primarily nonregulated

TABLE 12–4
Industrials

Per Share Data—Adjusted to stock price index level. Average of stock price indexes, 1941–1943 = 10

	Sales	Oper. Profit	Profit Margin %	Depr.	Income Taxes	Cash Flow	Earnings Per Share	Earnings % of Sales	Dividends Per Share	Dividends % of Earn.	Prices 1941–43 = 10 High	Prices Low	Price/Earn. Ratio High	P/E Low	Div. Yields High	Div. Yields Low	Book Value Per Share	Book Value % Return	Working Capital	Capital Expenditures
1963	68.50	10.73	15.66	3.04	3.51		4.24	6.19	2.36	55.66	79.25	65.48	18.69	15.44	3.60	2.98	38.17	11.11	17.64	4.41
1964	73.19	11.67	15.94	3.24	3.70		4.85	6.63	2.58	53.20	91.29	79.74	18.82	16.44	3.24	2.83	40.23	12.06	18.07	5.71
1965	80.69	13.11	16.25	3.52	4.14		5.50	6.82	2.82	51.27	98.55	86.43	17.92	15.71	3.26	2.86	43.50	12.64	18.80	6.87
1966	88.46	14.48	16.37	3.87	4.35		5.87	6.64	2.95	50.26	100.60	77.89	17.14	13.27	3.79	2.93	45.59	12.88	19.48	8.26
1967	91.86	14.28	15.55	4.25	4.11		5.62	6.12	2.97	52.85	106.15	85.31	18.89	15.18	3.48	2.80	47.78	11.76	20.74	8.35
1968	101.49	16.08	15.84	4.56	5.14		6.16	6.07	3.16	51.30	118.03	95.05	19.16	15.43	3.32	2.68	50.21	12.27	21.08	8.65
1969	108.53	16.63	15.32	4.87	5.14		6.13	5.65	3.25	53.02	116.24	97.75	18.96	15.95	3.32	2.80	51.70	11.86	21.05	9.70
1970	109.85	15.54	14.15	5.17	4.23		5.41	4.92	3.20	59.15	102.87	75.58	19.01	13.97	4.23	3.11	52.65	10.28	20.70	10.25
1971	118.23	17.22	14.56	5.45	4.98		5.97	5.04	3.16	52.93	115.84	99.36	19.40	16.64	3.18	2.73	55.28	10.80	22.61	9.96
1972	128.79	19.39	15.06	5.76	5.90		6.83	5.30	3.22	47.14	132.95	112.19	19.47	16.43	2.87	2.42	58.34	11.71	24.41	10.08
1973	149.22	23.64	15.84	6.25	7.59		8.89	5.96	3.46	38.92	134.54	103.37	15.13	11.63	3.35	2.57	62.84	14.15	26.49	11.65
1974	182.10	27.97	15.36	6.86	10.22		9.61	5.28	3.71	38.61	111.65	69.53	11.62	7.24	5.34	3.32	67.81	14.17	28.47	14.65
1975	185.16	26.63	14.38	7.36	9.40		8.58	4.63	3.72	43.36	107.40	77.71	12.52	9.06	4.79	3.46	70.84	12.11	30.47	14.43
1976	202.66	29.23	14.42	7.58	10.21		10.69	5.27	4.22	39.48	120.89	101.64	11.31	9.51	4.15	3.49	76.26	14.02	31.89	14.92
1977	224.24	32.20	14.36	8.53	11.14	19.94	11.45	5.11	4.95	43.23	118.92	99.88	10.39	8.72	4.96	4.16	82.21	13.93	33.28	17.02
1978	251.32	36.19	14.40	9.64	12.14	22.65	13.04	5.19	5.37	41.18	118.71	95.52	9.10	7.33	5.63	4.53	89.34	14.60	34.88	19.70
1979	292.38	42.01	14.37	10.82	14.02	27.08	16.29	5.57	5.92	36.34	124.49	107.08	7.64	6.57	5.53	4.76	98.71	16.50	36.32	26.44

(continued)

TABLE 12-4 (concluded)

Per Share Data—Adjusted to stock price index level. Average of stock price indexes, 1941–1943 = 10

	Sales	Oper. Profit	Profit Margin %	Depr.	Income Taxes	Cash Flow	Earnings Per Share	Earnings % of Sales	Dividends Per Share	Dividends % of Earn.	Prices 1941-43 = 10 High	Prices 1941-43 = 10 Low	Price/Earn. Ratio High	Price/Earn. Ratio Low	Div. Yields High	Div. Yields Low	Book Value Per Share	Book Value % Return	Working Capital	Capital Expenditures
1980	327.36	43.08	13.16	12.37	13.67	28.45	16.12	4.92	6.49	40.26	160.96	111.09	9.99	6.89	5.84	4.03	108.33	14.88	36.52	29.86
1981	344.31	44.50	12.92	13.82	12.95	30.52	16.74	4.86	7.01	41.88	157.02	125.93	9.38	7.52	5.57	4.46	116.06	14.42	35.98	33.03
1982	333.86	42.67	12.78	15.30	10.95	28.46	13.20	3.95	7.13	54.02	159.66	114.08	12.10	8.64	6.25	4.47	118.60	11.13	34.41	31.30
1983	334.07	45.57	13.64	15.67	12.12	30.41	14.77	4.42	7.32	49.56	194.84	154.95	13.19	10.49	4.72	3.76	122.32	12.07	36.55	25.24
1984	379.70	51.50	13.56	16.31	14.15	34.40	18.11	4.77	7.51	41.47	191.48	167.75	10.57	9.26	4.48	3.92	123.99	14.61	38.94	30.08
1985	398.42	53.23	13.36	18.19	13.68	33.44	15.28	3.84	7.87	51.51	235.75	182.24	15.43	11.93	4.32	3.34	125.89	12.14	39.32	31.42
1986	387.76	51.02	13.16	19.41	11.01	33.91	14.53	3.75	8.14	56.02	282.77	224.88	19.46	15.48	3.62	2.88	124.87	11.64	40.30	29.58
1987	430.45	58.89	13.68	20.21	13.96	40.46	20.28	4.71	8.72	43.00	393.17	255.43	19.39	12.60	3.41	2.22	134.19	15.11	45.39	27.59
1988	486.92	74.31	15.26	23.59	15.00	50.13	26.59	5.46	9.80	36.86	326.84	278.41	12.29	10.47	3.52	3.00	139.50	19.06	24.25	35.43
1989	541.38	79.52	14.69	24.21	15.73	50.02	26.83	4.96	11.95	44.54	410.49	318.66	15.30	11.88	3.75	2.91	145.34	18.46	18.00	40.98
1990	594.55	82.47	13.87	26.31	16.27	51.04	24.77	4.17	12.70	51.27	437.37	346.86	17.66	14.00	3.66	2.90	152.71	16.22	12.75	43.93
1991	586.86	75.10	12.80	27.50	12.20	44.41	16.91	2.88	12.51	73.98	492.72	364.90	29.14	21.58	3.43	2.54	157.05	10.77	11.33	40.33
R1992	601.39	78.17	13.00	29.48	12.01	48.50	19.05	3.17	13.01	68.29	515.75	470.91	27.11	24.37	2.80	2.52	142.46	13.37	8.45	39.36
P1993	605.18	82.94	13.71	29.02	13.25	51.54	22.52	3.72	12.51	55.55	543.94	496.48	24.15	22.05	2.59	2.35	136.08	16.55	N.A.	40.15

Source: Standard & Poor's Analyst's Handbook 1994 (New York: Standard & Poor's Corporation, 1994). Reprinted by permission of Standard & Poor's, a division of The McGraw-Hill Companies.

TABLE 12-5
Electric Companies

Per Share Data—Adjusted to stock price index level. Average of stock price indexes, 1941–1943 = 10

	Oper. Revs.	Depr.	Income Taxes	Net Oper. Income	Oper. Ratio %	Earnings Per Share	Earnings % of Oper. Revs.	Dividends Per Share	Dividends % of Earn.	Prices 1941–43 = 10 High	Prices Low	Price/Earn. Ratio High	Price/Earn. Ratio Low	Div. Yields % High	Div. Yields % Low	Long Term Debt	Equity Per Share	Equity % Return	Capital Expenditures
1963	17.40	1.91	1.93	3.76	78.39	2.45	14.08	1.63	66.53	53.51	48.66	21.84	19.86	3.35	3.05	29.64	—	—	4.51
1964	18.12	1.98	1.97	3.92	78.37	2.65	14.62	1.74	65.66	58.61	52.14	22.12	19.68	3.34	2.97	30.34	—	—	4.99
1965	19.15	2.10	1.96	4.21	78.02	2.90	15.14	1.90	65.52	60.90	57.26	21.00	19.74	3.32	3.12	31.80	—	—	5.82
1966	20.60	2.23	2.05	4.51	78.11	3.09	15.00	2.04	66.02	57.77	45.63	18.70	14.77	4.47	3.53	35.18	—	—	6.97
1967	21.67	2.37	1.99	4.83	77.71	3.28	15.14	2.16	65.85	55.03	46.16	16.78	14.07	4.68	3.93	38.06	—	—	8.23
1968	23.03	2.50	2.15	4.98	78.38	3.25	14.11	2.27	69.85	53.92	49.33	16.59	15.18	4.60	4.21	41.42	—	—	9.50
1969	24.36	2.64	1.99	5.29	78.28	3.38	13.88	2.33	68.93	53.03	41.22	15.69	12.20	5.65	4.39	45.21	—	—	10.98
1970	25.55	2.75	1.44	5.50	78.47	3.40	13.31	2.40	70.59	45.62	35.53	13.42	10.45	6.75	5.26	48.90	—	—	12.56
1971	26.97	2.80	1.30	5.72	78.79	3.45	12.79	2.47	71.59	48.36	40.35	14.02	11.70	6.12	5.11	50.95	—	—	14.09
1972	28.84	2.92	1.33	6.10	78.85	3.69	12.79	2.53	68.56	45.39	38.53	12.30	10.44	6.57	5.57	53.22	—	—	14.54
1973	30.09	3.02	1.33	6.36	78.86	3.72	12.36	2.51	67.47	43.91	30.69	11.80	8.25	8.18	5.72	54.20	—	—	14.92
1974	35.73	3.09	1.24	6.56	81.64	3.47	9.71	2.49	71.76	34.17	20.41	9.85	5.88	12.20	7.29	57.19	—	—	14.58
1975	38.53	3.18	1.77	7.01	81.81	3.73	9.68	2.57	68.90	30.56	24.56	8.19	6.58	10.46	8.41	54.89	—	—	11.77
1976	38.88	3.16	2.22	6.91	82.23	3.85	9.90	2.58	67.01	35.17	29.44	9.14	7.65	8.76	7.34	53.06	—	—	12.48
1977	42.00	3.20	2.59	7.00	83.33	4.08	9.71	2.74	67.16	37.21	33.76	9.12	8.27	8.12	7.36	52.41	37.46	10.89	13.50

(continued)

TABLE 12–5 (concluded)

Per Share Data—Adjusted to stock price index level. Average of stock price indexes, 1941–1943 = 10

	Oper. Revs.	Depr.	Income Taxes	Net Oper. Income	Oper. Ratio %	Earnings Per Share	Earnings % of Oper. Revs.	Dividends Per Share	Dividends % of Earn.	Prices 1941–43 = 10 High	Prices Low	Price/Earn. Ratio High	Price/Earn. Ratio Low	Div. Yields % High	Div. Yields % Low	Long Term Debt	Equity Per Share	Equity % Return	Capital Expenditures
1978	43.05	3.31	2.60	7.00	83.74	4.12	9.57	2.94	71.36	35.52	31.38	8.62	7.62	9.37	8.28	52.45	38.31	10.75	14.53
1979	44.77	3.34	2.29	6.92	84.54	4.16	9.29	3.10	74.52	33.48	27.97	8.05	6.72	11.08	9.26	53.01	38.77	10.73	—
1980	49.07	3.27	2.38	7.27	85.18	4.29	8.74	3.20	74.59	31.09	24.88	7.25	5.80	12.86	10.29	52.37	38.65	11.10	—
1981	52.25	3.32	2.69	7.78	85.11	4.67	8.94	3.42	73.23	31.37	26.28	6.72	5.63	13.01	10.90	52.05	38.95	11.99	—
1982	51.34	3.28	3.40	8.01	84.40	5.14	10.01	3.62	70.43	36.52	29.15	7.11	5.67	12.42	9.91	51.15	40.02	12.84	—
1983	50.40	3.34	4.10	8.33	83.47	5.73	11.37	3.84	67.02	41.20	36.58	7.19	6.38	10.50	9.32	49.97	41.63	13.76	—
1984	52.02	3.50	4.40	8.80	83.08	6.16	11.84	4.06	65.91	42.36	34.02	6.88	5.52	11.93	9.58	52.03	43.64	14.12	—
1985	52.00	3.78	4.33	8.95	82.79	6.26	12.04	4.15	66.29	49.93	41.97	7.98	6.70	9.89	8.31	51.59	44.78	13.98	—
1986	50.45	4.19	4.86	9.59	80.99	6.34	12.57	4.21	66.40	65.24	48.21	10.29	7.60	8.73	6.45	52.22	46.73	13.57	—
1987	49.84	4.62	3.89	9.64	80.66	5.79	11.62	4.34	74.96	64.83	49.71	11.20	8.59	8.73	6.69	54.14	47.73	12.13	—
1988	51.53	5.20	2.81	10.00	80.59	4.95	9.61	4.37	88.28	54.66	48.45	11.04	9.79	9.02	7.99	55.26	48.13	10.28	—
1989	53.08	5.45	3.15	10.44	80.50	5.47	10.31	4.28	78.24	66.55	52.93	12.17	9.68	8.09	6.43	55.64	48.54	11.27	—
1990	54.50	5.64	2.91	9.91	81.82	4.69	8.61	4.45	94.88	66.61	55.88	14.20	11.91	7.96	6.68	56.92	48.55	9.66	—
1991	55.84	5.79	3.37	10.96	80.37	4.98	8.92	4.57	91.77	77.25	61.24	15.51	12.30	7.46	5.92	56.05	48.66	10.23	—
1992	55.52	5.87	3.22	10.52	81.05	5.55	10.00	4.68	84.32	78.02	69.32	14.06	12.49	6.75	6.00	55.01	49.53	11.21	—

Source: Standard & Poor's *Analyst's Handbook 1994* (New York: Standard & Poor's Corporation, 1994). Reprinted by permission of Standard & Poor's, a division of The McGraw Hill Companies.

TABLE 12–6
Financial Statement Tests—Electric Utility Companies

Balance Sheet

1. Current assets should be at least 10 percent of total assets.

2. Current ratio should be close to 1 to 1 and preferably over 1 to 1.

3. Cash and cash items should be close to 4 percent of total assets.

4. Net plant account should be between 82 percent and 90 percent of total assets.

5. Gross plant should not be over 4 times annual operating revenues for steam plants or 6 times for hydroelectric plants.

6. Net plant should not be over 3½ times annual operating revenues.

7. Plant capacity should provide reserves at peak load of at least 15 percent.

8. Long-term debt should not exceed 60 percent of capitalization.

9. Long-term debt plus preferred stock should not exceed 70–75 percent of capitalization.

10. Common stock equity should represent at least 30 percent of capitalization. This would mean that debt should not exceed 55 percent and preferred stock 15 percent of gross plant and 20 percent of net plant.

11. Allowance for accumulated depreciation should be at least 20 percent of gross plant and 25 percent of net plant for steam and for hydroelectric 15 percent of gross plant and 20 percent of net plant.

Income Statement

1. Operating revenues should be well balanced between the various classes of customers.

2. Operating ratio (with operating expenses including all taxes) should not exceed 82 percent for steam plants and 72 percent for hydroelectric plants.

3. Operating income should average at least 18 percent of operating revenues, and at least 7 percent of net plant.

4. Depreciation plus maintenance should not be less than 15 percent of revenues for steam plants and 12 percent for hydroelectric plants.

5. Ratio of fixed charges on long-term debt to operating expenses should be at least 7 percent.

6. Fixed charge coverage for all debt, short term and long term, should be at least 2 times.

7. Coverage on the total of fixed charges plus preferred dividends should be at least 1.90 times.

8. Earnings per share should be more than 10 percent of operating revenues per share.

areas). A multiple regression study by Barry Abramson at Merrill Lynch[4] showed a positive impact on stock price for utilities (electric, gas, and telephone) that so diversified. The findings showed that a company that earned more than 10 percent of net income from diversified activities would add four percentage points in market-to-book value ratio because of a higher return on owners' equity, and an additional two percentage points because of the favor with which the market looked on a more-diversified operating position.

The results of such diversification have proved to be mixed. Companies that diversified into energy-intensive industries such as oil and gas extraction, coal mining, and uranium development aim at taking advantage of potential synergies with the utility. Falling energy prices have hurt the ability of such acquisitions to contribute profitably to the utility. If energy prices rise in the future, however, some of these acquisitions could still prove desirable. Some utilities acquired investment subsidiaries, which have not done well since the stock market crash in October 1987.

ANALYSIS OF THE GAS INDUSTRY

There are three segments of the gas industry: (1) pipelines (intrastate and interstate); (2) distribution companies; and (3) integrated companies performing both functions of pipelines and distribution. Initially, most gas consumed, except in areas contiguous to oil or gas wells, was produced near the area of consumption, but such production today is uncommon. In recent years, most gas consumed is brought by pipelines to the general area of distribution, such as a state, and then distributed by distribution companies. Pipeline companies are classified as intrastate pipelines or interstate pipelines. The interstate pipelines may be subdivided into interstate transmission pipelines and interstate and integrated pipelines, the latter being both pipeline companies and distribution companies. Sales to consumers account for 35 to 40 percent of sales volume, but about 50 percent of revenues.

Demand for Gas

Many analysts feel that the traditional residential, commercial, and industrial markets will post only modest growth in the future. New markets,

---

4 Barry M. Abramson, "Utility Industry, Does Diversification Affect Utility Stock Prices?" (pamphlet) (New York: Merrill Lynch, Securities Research Division, January 20, 1982).

however, are likely to be developed, such as the use of gas for environmental reasons.

The sharp drop in oil prices in the mid-1980s did lead to deteriorating gas company earnings, as customers switched from gas to oil. The price of oil did rebound in 1987, and it seems reasonable to expect stable or rising prices for oil in the future. Moreover, interest rates were low in the mid-1980s, compared to the 1970s, which has benefitted the earnings of gas companies. If interest rates were to drop sharply in the future, however, the allowed rate of return for gas utilities might also drop, hindering earnings growth. Investors should monitor changing demand and interest rate conditions.

The American Gas Association reports that natural gas demand rose 3.3 percent in 1993, with increased natural gas use in the residential market contributing the most to total demand growth. Growth was spurred by colder temperatures in 1993, and natural gas consumption set a new record in January 1994 as frigid weather persisted in much of the eastern United States. The weather is an important factor affecting the demand for gas. Growth in gas demand was expected to rise faster than the historical average in 1995, but may not reach expectations since 1994 was colder than 1995.

The space heating market is likely to remain the largest consumer of gas in the foreseeable future. New housing development is, therefore, also important. By 1993, natural gas commanded a 24 percent share of the United States energy market, and market share is expected to increase through 2010.

Supply of Gas

Proven reserves of natural gas showed a downward trend from 1970–79, then leveled off. Reserves then began rising in the 1980s only to begin falling again after 1983 (see Table 12–8). Additions to reserves were sharply higher in the early 1980s reaching a high ratio of discoveries of 92 percent in 1981 before falling to about 60 percent by 1986 and then dropping further to about 40 percent by 1992. The passage of the Natural Gas Policy Act in late 1978 stimulated exploration by removing the price disparity between interstate and intrastate natural gas and increasing the price of new gas. This stimulus wore off, however, after 1985. Concern with global warming has led President Clinton to propose cutting the growth of greenhouse gases. Part of the plan is for utilities to use more natural gas for power production, but the plan is still voluntary. The proposed plan does contain other directives that could benefit the natural gas industry and possibly stimulate discovery activity.

The United States has been consuming more gas than it discovered since 1968, except for 1970 (when new reserves at Prudhoe Bay were discovered) and 1981. Still, there has been a surplus of deliverable natural gas. Relatively low prices for gas and the oversupply situation were to a great extent caused by producers prior overproduction relative to demand.

Things have changed a bit, leading to a long-term gradual uptrend for gas prices, starting in 1992. Supplemental supplies of natural gas have been required since United States production began falling short of demand in the 1990s. Demand is expected to continue to exceed U.S. production for the foreseeable future, according to Standard & Poor's. The gas surplus seems to have reached a point where it has been eliminated, and the need for supplemental supplies will likely increase. Accordingly, it seems reasonable to expect a continuation of the recent gradual uptrend in gas prices, leading to a more favorable outlook for the gas industry. Rising prices should give producers greater incentive to explore, though increasing competition from Canada and Mexico, stimulated by the North American Free Trade Agreement, could restrict the expected price rises for natural gas.

Order 500 and Order 636

Order 500 was issued by the Federal Energy Regulatory Commission and implemented on January 1, 1988. It eliminates the right of firm-service customers to reduce the amount of gas for which they have contracted. Pipeline customers can fulfill contracted demand by either actually purchasing the gas outright or by having the pipeline transmit an equivalent amount of gas. This order benefits the pipelines.

Order 500 does allow pipelines to exact an inventory charge that reflects the cost of holding gas supplies. It is hoped this will allow pipelines to get their contract and service obligations in line with what customers will actually buy.

Distributors are likely to be the losers, as they will bear increased risks and gain nothing to offset those risks.

Order 636 took effect in 1993 and requires customers to compete for space on the pipeline system. This created concerns regarding the assurability of supply for final users. During the cold winter of early 1994, however, there were no problems. Moreover, experts appear to believe Order 636 helped prevent supply strains and operating problems, since there is a greater flow of information about amounts and locations of gas supplies under this order.

Regulation

Beginning with the federal Natural Gas Act of 1938, regulation of gas flowing in interstate commerce was placed under the jurisdiction of the Federal Power Commission (FPC). With the establishment of the new Department of Energy in the latter part of 1977, functions of many energy-related agencies were redistributed and new agencies established. The intent was to integrate responsibilities of like nature. The Department of Energy Organization Act of August 4, 1977, transferred to a newly formed Federal Energy Regulatory Commission many of the functions of the Federal Power Commission. Among the functions transferred were "the establishment, review, and enforcement of rates and charges for the transportation and sale of natural gas by a producer or gatherer or by a natural gas pipeline or natural gas company under sections 1, 4, 5, and 7 of the Natural Gas Act."[5]

Up until about 1970, the prices established by the Federal Power Commission were not sufficiently encouraging to attract funds for new exploration. As a result, United States reserves of natural gas decreased because of the lack of opportunities for reasonable earnings growth in the interstate area of the business. In the early 1970s, the transportation of gas through interstate lines actually was declining. This tended to cause all gas pipeline securities to become relatively out of favor with investors. This was reflected in sharply decreasing price–earnings ratios through 1974, falling below price–earnings ratios for the general market averages.

In spite of a decline in earnings for interstate pipeline companies, in the 1970s there was a satisfactory earnings growth rate due to the higher rates of return and higher rate bases approved by the Federal Power Commission.

The energy legislation program that was enacted in 1978 has had a major impact on the pricing and other aspects of pipeline regulation, and has improved the outlook for gas companies.

Key Financial Data

Per share data based on Standard & Poor's group stock price indexes for the natural gas industry are shown in Table 12–7, and selected analytical ratios in Table 12–8. Distributors and pipelines showed strong operating revenue growth (a 15.97 percent compound annual rate since 1979), but revenues and earnings fell sharply in 1986 and have not recovered much

---

[5] *Department of Energy Organization Act*, 91 Stat. 565, Public Law 95–91, 95th Cong. August 4, 1977, Section 402.

TABLE 12-7
Producing Wells and Exploratory Activity

Year	Total Producing Gas Wells	New Well Completions				Exploratory Wells Drilled			
		Total	Oil	Gas	% Dry	Total	Oil	Gas	% Dry
1993	286,168	23,959	8,078	9,042	28.5	3,114	375	389	75.5
1992	280,899	23,201	8,675	7,948	28.4	3,383	456	356	69.5
R1991	273,299	28,868	11,908	9,130	27.1	4,311	544	464	59.6
1990	267,891	31,243	11,985	10,122	26.6	4,978	617	579	66.4
1989	261,225	27,913	10,140	8,927	29.3	5,233	580	652	72.3
1988	256,004	32,380	13,240	8,227	30.8	6,221	792	663	64.3
1987	253,856	35,195	15,759	7,603	31.1	6,711	859	673	71.0
1986	250,510	38,809	18,196	7,815	31.1	7,232	988	733	71.6
1985	245,765	71,108	35,882	12,600	29.5	12,606	1,879	1,282	43.7
1984	226,325	86,000	43,824	14,818	29.2	15,416	2,335	1,599	61.3

R—Revised.

Source: American Petroleum Institute, as reported in *World Oil*.

(continued)

TABLE 12–7 (concluded)
U.S. Natural Gas Production and Reserves (in Trillions of Cubic Feet)

Year	Production	Year-End Reserves	New Discoveries	Revisions, Corrections, and Adjustments	Ratios	
					Discoveries to Production	Reserves to Production
1992	17.4	165.0	7.0	2.2	0.4	9.5
1991	17.2	167.1	7.5	3.0	0.4	9.7
1990	17.2	169.3	12.4	1.6	0.7	9.8
1989	17.0	167.1	10.0	3.0	0.6	9.8
1988	16.7	168.0	10.4	2.2	0.6	10.1
1987	16.1	187.2	7.2	1.3	0.4	11.6
1986	15.6	191.6	8.9	1.3	0.6	12.3
1985	16.0	193.4	11.1	-1.7	0.7	12.1
1984	17.2	197.5	13.5	-2.2	0.8	11.5
1983	15.8	200.2	11.4	3.1	0.7	12.7

Source: U.S. Department of Energy

Reproduced from Standard & Poor's *Industrial Surveys, Utility—Gas*, May 26, 1994, page 491. Reprinted by permission of Standard & Poor's, a division of The McGraw-Hill Companies.

TABLE 12–8
Natural Gas

Per Share Data—Adjusted to stock price index level. Average of stock price indexes, 1941–1943 = 10

	Oper. Revs.	Depr.	Income Taxes	Net Oper. Income	Oper. Ratio %	Earnings Per Share	Earnings % of Oper Revs.	Dividends Per Share	Dividends % of Earn.	Prices 1941-43=10 High	Prices Low	Price/Earn. Ratio High	Price/Earn. Ratio Low	Div. Yields % High	Div. Yields % Low	Long Term Debt	Equity Per Share	Equity % Return	Capital Expenditures
1963	58.22	6.04	3.55	8.43	85.52	4.73	8.12	3.25	68.71	84.27	74.19	17.82	15.68	4.38	3.86	69.31	—	—	9.06
1964	61.58	6.45	3.57	8.28	86.55	5.21	8.46	3.41	65.45	91.08	78.53	17.48	15.07	4.34	3.74	73.38	—	—	9.54
1965	63.86	6.71	3.48	8.75	86.30	5.64	8.83	3.60	63.83	94.84	86.11	16.82	15.27	4.18	3.80	76.58	—	—	13.22
1966	76.05	8.55	4.03	11.03	85.50	6.79	8.93	4.12	60.68	94.66	74.43	13.94	10.96	5.54	4.35	91.98	—	—	19.33
1967	82.49	8.82	2.57	11.93	85.54	7.08	8.58	4.32	61.02	98.99	85.26	13.98	12.04	5.07	4.36	104.22	—	—	19.74
1968	99.53	10.04	2.85	13.64	86.30	7.48	7.52	4.55	60.83	118.94	91.30	15.90	12.21	4.98	3.83	116.95	—	—	24.08
1969	107.04	10.67	2.89	15.26	85.74	7.94	7.42	4.68	58.94	119.27	85.25	15.02	10.74	5.49	3.92	124.56	—	—	25.35
1970	115.22	11.36	3.71	16.41	85.76	8.51	7.39	4.51	53.00	115.51	84.92	13.57	9.98	5.31	3.90	131.75	—	—	23.51
1971	121.03	11.35	5.78	17.75	85.33	9.18	7.58	4.62	50.33	121.33	96.43	13.22	10.50	4.79	3.81	129.12	—	—	19.72
1972	129.34	12.17	6.79	19.08	85.25	10.02	7.75	4.85	48.40	133.63	103.36	13.34	10.32	4.69	3.63	127.85	—	—	19.74
1973	131.37	12.32	8.00	18.99	85.54	10.86	8.27	4.96	45.67	132.71	89.01	12.22	8.20	5.57	3.74	118.28	—	—	24.16
1974	176.99	15.68	11.93	21.41	87.90	15.22	8.60	5.43	35.68	112.55	68.79	7.39	4.52	7.89	4.82	137.23			26.19
1975	200.60	16.76	13.30	21.80	89.13	15.81	7.88	5.72	36.18	112.41	89.74	7.11	5.68	6.37	5.09	147.31			39.38
1976	207.40	17.20	14.55	21.86	89.46	16.81	8.11	6.12	36.41	138.62	104.44	8.25	6.21	5.86	4.41	147.02			33.42
1977	254.30	17.69	15.90	27.14	89.33	18.01	7.08	6.87	38.15	147.67	128.70	8.20	7.15	5.34	4.65	134.78	122.14	14.75	37.97

(continued)

TABLE 12–8 *(concluded)*

Per Share Data—Adjusted to stock price index level. Average of stock price indexes, 1941–1943 = 10

	Oper. Revs.	Depr.	Income Taxes	Net Oper. Income	Oper. Ratio %	Earnings Per Share	Earnings % of Oper Revs.	Dividends Per Share	Dividends % of Earn.	Prices 1941-43 = 10 High	Prices Low	Price/Earn. Ratio High	Price/Earn. Ratio Low	Div. Yields % High	Div. Yields % Low	Long Term Debt	Equity Per Share	Equity % Return	Capital Expend-itures
1978	286.50	19.91	15.17	27.87	90.27	19.77	6.90	7.67	38.80	146.83	118.69	7.43	6.00	6.46	5.22	126.61	128.87	15.34	43.62
1979	399.71	22.81	20.08	29.39	92.65	24.46	6.12	8.78	35.90	202.25	121.50	8.27	4.97	7.23	4.34	132.36	143.14	17.09	57.72
1980	502.49	25.31	22.99	33.04	93.42	27.64	5.50	10.23	37.01	287.90	178.58	10.42	6.46	5.73	3.55	141.93	148.20	18.65	64.25
1981	587.73	28.50	24.71	39.11	93.35	33.47	5.69	11.56	34.54	249.07	195.82	7.44	5.85	5.90	4.64	161.53	172.80	19.37	—
1982	660.40	34.01	15.16	39.77	93.98	27.47	4.16	13.17	47.94	207.72	140.65	7.56	5.12	9.36	6.34	193.16	188.39	14.58	—
1983	628.87	32.95	23.45	40.13	93.62	27.66	4.40	12.53	45.30	243.91	164.82	8.82	5.96	7.60	5.14	172.10	187.01	14.79	67.73
1984	677.89	37.84	26.16	41.16	93.93	30.16	4.45	14.67	48.64	261.34	219.83	8.67	7.29	6.67	5.61	170.86	227.59	13.25	53.93
1985	972.56	52.67	17.17	50.99	94.75	13.21	1.36	19.42	—	334.18	240.25	25.30	18.19	8.08	5.81	314.71	264.65	4.99	—
1986	785.12	45.48	d1.03	32.61	95.85	d5.41	def	19.71	def	342.61	298.71	def	def	6.60	5.75	328.96	226.24	def	—
1987	701.45	42.04	17.38	48.75	93.05	19.84	2.83	19.40	97.78	439.23	305.07	22.14	15.38	6.36	4.42	311.47	236.99	8.37	—
1988	694.75	43.63	8.87	41.31	94.05	17.64	2.54	18.06	—	332.46	317.01	18.85	17.97	5.70	5.43	309.26	234.34	7.53	52.89
1989	773.09	40.48	11.94	49.06	93.65	23.01	2.98	19.43	84.44	489.13	332.51	21.26	14.45	5.84	3.97	303.57	244.33	9.42	—
1990	742.13	23.48	24.14	22.89	96.92	14.91	2.01	22.61	—	482.83	404.06	32.38	27.10	5.60	4.68	308.41	234.41	6.36	—
1991	802.39	44.34	d0.11	27.45	96.58	d3.54	def	17.47	def	413.12	326.62	def	def	5.35	4.23	311.37	222.65	def	—
1992	608.22	42.58	8.38	45.62	92.50	14.90	2.45	12.95	86.91	380.07	292.09	25.51	19.60	4.43	3.41	291.21	213.58	6.98	48.73
1993	608.29	39.32	14.37	43.08	7.08	22.14	3.64	12.60	56.91	487.87	351.33	22.04	15.87	3.59	2.58	251.02	228.98	9.67	58.85

Source: Standard & Poor's *Analyst's Handbook 1994* (New York: Standard & Poor's Corporation, 1994). Reprinted by permission of Standard & Poor's, a division of The McGraw-Hill Companies.

TABLE 12–9
Selected Composite Analytical Ratios of the Investor-Owned Gas Utility Industry

Analytical ratios	Total Industry					Transmission Companies		Integrated Companies		Distribution Companies	
	1980	1985	1990	R1991	1992	R1991	1992	R1991	1992	R1991	1992
Earnings											
Utility operating income as % of total plant	6.7	7.0	5.2	4.0	4.9	4.3	4.7	NA	4.2	5.9	5.9
Utility operating income as % of net plant	10.9	12.0	9.6	7.1	8.3	10.8	12.1	NA	7.4	8.7	8.9
Operating revenues as % of total pant	128.1	120.1	58.7	53.4	51.3	40.9	37.5	57.8	60.0	62.2	62.4
Common dividend payout ratio (%)	58.2	108.2	71.2	241.4	106.2	154.1	33.1	NA	85.5	85.0	69.4
Return on common equity (%)	15.2	9.3	10.1	4.2	7.9	4.6	6.8	NA	6.1	10.2	11.4
Expenses											
Operating expenses as % of operating revenues	95.2	94.6	90.8	92.6	90.4	90.1	88.1	100.6	93.0	90.7	90.6
Maint. exp. as % of total plant	1.8	1.9	1.7	1.7	1.6	1.3	1.2	1.8	1.9	1.9	1.8
Deprec. exp. as % of total plant	3.6	3.7	3.1	3.2	3.0	2.7	2.0	3.7	4.2	3.4	3.6
Deprec. exp. as % of deprec. plant	4.1	3.7	3.3	3.3	3.3	2.8	2.1	3.8	4.3	3.6	3.7
Total taxes as % of total plant	7.2	7.6	4.4	3.7	4.7	2.4	3.3	1.9	5.2	5.7	5.9
Total taxes as % of net plant	11.8	13.1	7.8	6.6	7.9	5.4	7.5	3.2	9.1	8.5	9.0
Total taxes as % of net income plus total taxes	53.6	63.5	52.9	70.1	62.1	54.5	53.7	NA	72.9	63.0	61.7
*Current federal income tax as % of net income, plus current federal income tax	27.4	40.0	22.9	45.9	31.8	45.4	36.0	NA	36.8	28.3	25.4

(continued)

TABLE 12-9 *(concluded)*

Analytical ratios	Total Industry					Transmission Companies		Integrated Companies		Distribution Companies	
	1980	1985	1990	R1991	1992	R1991	1992	R1991	1992	R1991	1992
Plant											
Total plant per $ of total operating revenues	0.8	0.8	1.7	1.9	2.0	2.4	2.7	1.7	1.7	1.6	1.6
Net plant per $ of total operating revenues	0.5	0.5	1.0	1.1	1.2	1.1	1.2	1.1	1.0	1.1	1.1
Deprec. reserve as % of total plant	39.0	42.0	43.9	43.7	44.1	56.7	55.3	40.5	43.0	32.8	34.1
Deprec. reserve as % of deprec. plant	44.0	43.1	45.6	44.3	46.2	59.2	57.9	41.1	43.9	34.0	35.3
Total plant per employee ($000)	328.1	423.2	552.4	590.6	621.5	1278.8	1184.1	473.5	489.6	454.9	482.2
Capitalization											
Long-term debt as % of net plant	53.9	52.4	49.1	47.5	45.7	50.7	57.5	52.1	45.6	41.1	40.0
% total capitalization represented by:											
Long-term debt	42.9	40.0	41.6	42.4	42.9	34.3	38.1	51.9	49.0	45.1	49.6
Preferred stock	7.1	5.2	2.8	2.9	2.6	0.6	0.4	3.2	2.8	3.3	2.9
Common equity	50.0	54.8	55.6	54.6	54.5	65.1	61.5	48.2	44.9	51.6	52.8

*Includes: "Provision for Deferred Federal Income Taxes" and "Portion of Current Federal Income Taxes Provided for in Prior Years." R—Revised. NA—Not available.

Source: American Gas Association.

Reproduced from Standard & Poor's *Industry Surveys, Utilities—Gas,* May 26, 1994, page U97. Reprinted by permission of Standard & Poor's, a division of The McGraw-Hill Companies.

since. Gas company earnings were adversely affected in 1986 by a falling price for oil, which caused industrial customers to switch to the less-expensive fuel. The price of oil rebounded, however, in 1987 and the gas companies recovered the sales lost in 1986, leading to some earnings growth. This earnings growth was not distributed evenly among gas companies. Pipelines with gas exploration and production operations suffered from falling gas prices in 1987. Order 500 also hurt many producers.

We do anticipate earnings improvement in the future, based on an expected increase in gas demand, benefits accruing from restructuring of operations, somewhat lower interest rates, and colder winters. Investors should monitor developments carefully in these areas.

Balance Sheet Analysis

Analysts often use the following rules of thumb, based on experience, when analyzing gas industry balance sheets:

1. Net plant should not exceed two times annual operating revenues, and gross plant should not exceed three times annual operating revenues.
2. Total debt should not exceed 60 percent of total capitalization or about the same percentage of net plant.
3. Long-term debt plus preferred stock should not exceed 70 percent of total capitalization; and if it is 70 percent, long-term debt should not exceed 55 percent of total capitalization, leaving 15 percent for the preferred stock.
4. Common stock equity should represent at least 30 percent of total capitalization.

Income Statement Analysis

The following rules of thumb are suggested as standards when analyzing gas industry income statements:

1. Total operating expenses including taxes and depreciation should not exceed 92 percent of total operating revenues, or 74 percent exclusive of depreciation and maintenance. The average has exceeded this level since 1979.
2. Depreciation plus maintenance should equal at least 10 percent of operating revenues.

3. The average rate of return on common equity should be at least 15 percent.

4. The rate of return on total capitalization should be at least 8 percent.

5. Coverage of fixed charges should be at least 2.75 times.

6. Coverage of fixed charges plus preferred dividends should be at least two times and should not exceed 7 percent of operating revenues.

7. The balance available for the common stock dividends should be at least 7 percent of operating revenues.

THE TELEPHONE INDUSTRY

The United States telecommunications industry is undergoing rapid changes. Competition is strong in the long-distance market, and is threatening the local service market. Demand is expected to grow rapidly and is attracting new players. Companies will be able to deliver hundreds of channels of voice, data, and video services, and even home movies. This has led to merger and acquisition activity as well as new entrants. U.S. companies are looking at the international market, as well as the domestic, for growth opportunities.

Increasing demand will require additional investment. The industry is focusing on cost control and workforce realignment to leverage revenue gains into profit growth. There are risks as well as potentially large rewards. Deregulation and competition have emerged as the primary forces affecting the industry.

The local telephone companies are entering new markets, and want to compete in the long-distance service market. Competition can be expected to increase in their markets. Revenue growth should continue on an upward trend through the year 2000, and cash flow from operations should remain strong. Increasing investment needs, however, may slow down dividend growth. Telephone stocks have outperformed other utility stocks since 1988, and offer interesting growth possibilities for the future.

Regulation

Regulatory developments have affected the long-term profit outlook of the telecommunications industry. There has been a philosophical shift toward fewer regulatory constraints. The FCC contends rate-of-return regulation is a disincentive to cost-cutting and innovation. They wish to mandate lower price caps, but allow telephone companies to profit from cost-cutting.

Rate cap legislation as proposed by the FCC is expected to hurt industry profitability in the short run, and the effect on longer-term profits is uncertain. Carriers will have to generate productivity gains 3 percent in excess of the overall economy to benefit from the legislation.[6]

Specifics of Analysis of Telephone Company Securities

For the small, and sometimes even tiny, individual telephone company, the following requirements should be considerably stricter than for larger companies because of the risks inherent in their very small size.

Balance Sheet Analysis

1. The current ratio should be above the one-to-one level.
2. Long-term debt should not exceed 45 percent of total capitalization, and debt plus preferred stock, 60 percent.
3. The turnover of net fixed assets (after depreciation) should be at least 2.8 times, i.e., annual revenue should be at least equal to 36 percent of the value of net plant.
4. The account for accumulated depreciation should be equal to approximately 25 percent of the gross plant account.

Income Statement Analysis

1. The operating ratio should not exceed 85 percent (operating expenses including income taxes). If income taxes are excluded from operating expenses, the operating ratio should not exceed 72 percent.
2. The ratio of maintenance plus depreciation to total gross revenue should not exceed 33 to 35 percent.
3. The rate of return on the capital structure (before deduction of fixed charges), i.e., amount available for fixed charges, should be at least 7 to 7.5 percent.
4. The amount available for fixed charges before taxes should show a coverage of at least 3.8 times.

---

6 Standard & Poor's *Industry Surveys, Telecommunications*, op. cit., pp. 1–2.

WATER COMPANIES

Most water companies are owned by the municipalities they serve. Some of these have issued revenue bonds that are held by private investors. There are still, however, many privately owned water companies, but the ownership is often closely, even family, held. Some larger privately owned municipal companies are located in Birmingham, Alabama; Indianapolis, Indiana; New Haven, Connecticut; New Rochelle, New York; and San Jose, California. One large privately owned water company, American Water Works, controls about 75 companies operating in 15 states.

The gross revenues of water companies usually are stable, and in most areas exhibit consistent growth in revenues and earnings. In fast-growing areas the rate of growth reflects this environment. As with other utilities, fixed assets constitute the bulk of total assets, and the turnover of capital invested in these assets is relatively slow. The operations of water companies are relatively simple, resulting in a relatively low operating ratio.

Financial Analysis

The following proportions should be present:

1. Gross fixed assets should not be greater than 5½ to 6½ times annual revenues.

2. The depreciation should be equal to at least 16 percent of gross plant.

3. Long-term debt should not be greater than two-thirds the value of net assets (gross assets less depreciation), and long-term debt plus preferred stock should not exceed three-quarters of total capitalization.

4. The common equity should represent at least one-quarter of the total capitalization.

5. The operating ratio should not exceed 70 percent.

6. The rate of return on the capital structure should at least be in the 5 to 6 percent range.

7. The fixed charge coverage should be at least 2½ times earnings.

8. Total interest plus preferred dividends should be covered at least 1¾ times.

9. The amount of gross revenues carried down to the common equity should be at least 10 percent.

SUMMARY

There are two broad categories of regulated industries: utilities and transportation companies. In general, regulated industries sell services that are affected with the public interest and in many instances, such as electric and gas utilities and telephone companies, enjoy a monopoly position, and must be regulated to protect the public from excessive prices and poor service.

In analyzing regulated industries, the first and most important step is to determine the regulatory climate—essentially the attitude of the regulatory commission or agency as to rates and service requirements. The question is, is the utility permitted to earn a fair rate of return, fair in the judgment of investors, as expressed in the market yield of its securities compared to similar companies? If it is determined that the regulatory climate is satisfactory from the investor's viewpoint, then the investor can proceed to analyze specific companies in that jurisdiction.

The financial analysis centers on the major financial statements, as is the case with other companies. But each industry has its own special characteristics, and this fact must be given serious consideration in analyzing trends and ratios.

Closely correlated to the financial analysis is the analysis of related statistics that are available to the investor. Most of the larger utility companies furnish financial analysts with statistical booklets to supplement financial statements and other information appearing in annual reports.

Chapter Thirteen

Regulated Industries: Transportation

Two major components of the transportation industry will be discussed in this chapter: the railroad industry and the trucking industry. In a broad legal context, these regulated industries are public utilities. The most vital areas of control cover rates of return, mergers, consolidations, and abandonments, with rate of return being the most significant.

In the late 1970s, the federal government was acting to decontrol the trucking and air transport industries, but the industries themselves and the unions were opposing decontrol, saying they feared cutthroat competition would develop. Air freight rates were decontrolled in 1978. Merger activity was accelerated in the early 1980s by changes in the regulatory environment.

THE RAILROADS

Passenger traffic of the railroads has been shifted to agencies of the federal government—Amtrak for long-haul traffic and Conrail for commuter traffic. Passenger business has been a deficit operation for the railroads. Moreover, it has interfered seriously with freight traffic movements.

The share of railroads in total interstate freight fell from 75 percent in 1929 to a low of 36.7 percent in 1975, before rising to 37.2 percent in 1985 (see Table 13–1). Trucks and oil pipelines gained sharply at the expense of railroads until 1960. Railroads have managed to stabilize the situation since 1970, but have shown little growth in market share since then. Generally, transportation experts assume that the railroads are most efficient for hauls of 400 miles or more, while trucks have the advantage for hauls of 400 miles or less. This is the major reason why the Eastern roads suffered most severely from truck competition on their relatively short hauls, and accounts for the poor record of the Eastern roads relative to the Southern and Western roads.

We would not expect the railroads to ever again carry 74.9 percent of intercity freight and passenger traffic, as they did in the 1920's (see Table 13–1). Still, they have recovered sharply in recent years, benefiting from the 1980 Staggers Act, a coal boom, and a positive economic climate. Mergers, other restructuring moves, increased automation, and new technology have led to record profits and cash flow in 1993 and 1994, and Standard & Poor's expect these records to be broken in 1995[1]. While railroads are still not earning a return equal to their cost of capital, they are headed in the right direction. Costs appear to be under control and traffic volume is growing.

No major Class I railroad had generated a return on net investment that at least equaled their cost of capital prior to 1988, according to ICC statistics. The Illinois Central (14.3 percent ROI) and Kansas City Southern Railway (13.1 percent ROI) did exceed cost of capital in 1993. The industry as a whole, however, generated only a 6.4 percent return on investment (ROI) in 1993.[2]

Labor Costs

The railroad industry has made progress over the past decade in cutting labor costs and boosting productivity of its workers. Still, manpower levels do appear to be somewhat inflated, and the loss of traffic to trucks does reflect excessive labor costs and work rules that impair attaining efficient operations. Investors in railroads should watch labor costs and wage settlements.

New Prosperity?

Railroad ton-miles climbed to a record of 1.175 trillion in 1994 (see Figure 13–1). The compound annual growth rate in rail traffic over the eight years ending in 1994 of 3.8 percent exceeded the 2.6 percent growth rate for industrial production. The industry has been showing strong growth, and lowered labor costs and improved service have led to growing market share relative to trucks and barge operators.

---

[1] Standard & Poor's *Industry Surveys, Railroads and Trucking,* December 8, 1994, p. R28.

[2] Op. cit., p. R29.

TABLE 13–1
Volume of U.S. Intercity Freight and Passenger Traffic—Millions of Revenue Freight Ton-Miles and Percentage of Total

Year	Railroads[a]	%	Trucks	%	Great Lakes	%	Rivers and Canals	%	Oil Pipelines	%	Air	%	Total
1929	454,800	74.9	19,689	3.3	97,322	16.0	8,661	1.4	26,900	4.4	3	—	607,375
1939	338,850	62.4	52,821	9.7	76,312	14.0	19,937	3.7	55,602	10.2	12	—	543,534
1944	746,912	68.6	58,264	5.4	118,769	10.9	31,386	2.9	132,864	12.2	71	—	1,088,266
1950	569,940	56.2	172,860	16.3	111,687	10.5	51,657	4.9	129,175	12.1	318	—	1,062,637
1960	579,130	44.1	285,483	21.7	99,468	7.6	120,785	9.2	228,626	17.4	778	—	1,314,270
1970	771,168	39.8	412,000	21.3	114,475	5.9	204,085	10.5	431,000	22.3	3,295	0.2	1,936,023
1980	932,000	37.5	555,000	22.3	96,000	3.9	311,000	12.5	588,000	23.6	4,840	0.2	2,486,840
1984	935,000	37.5	605,000	24.2	76,000	3.0	306,000	12.3	568,000	22.7	6,600	0.3	2,496,600
1985	895,000	36.4	610,000	24.8	76,000	3.1	306,000	12.5	564,000	22.9	6,710	0.3	2,457,710
1986[p]	896,000	35.8	627,700	25.1	72,000	2.9	321,000	12.8	579,000	23.1	7,340	0.3	2,502,340

(continued)

TABLE 13–1 (concluded)

Millions of Revenue Passenger-Miles and Percentage of Total (Except Private)

Year	Railroads[a]	%	Buses	%	Air Carriers	%	Inland Waterways	%	Total (except private)	Private Automobiles	Private Airplanes	Total (including private)
1929	33,965	77.1	6,800	15.4	—	—	3,300	7.5	44,065	175,000	—	219,065
1939	23,669	67.7	9,100	26.0	683	2.0	1,486	4.3	34,938	275,000	—	309,938
1944	97,705	75.7	26,920	20.9	2,177	1.7	2,187	1.7	128,989	181,000	1	309,990
1950	32,481	47.2	26,436	38.4	8,773	12.7	1,190	1.7	68,880	438,293	1,299	508,472
1960	21,574	28.6	19,327	25.7	31,730	42.1	2,688	3.6	75,319	706,079	2,228	783,626
1970	10,903	5.7	25,300	14.3	109,499	77.7	4,000	2.3	149,702	1,026,000	9,101	1,189,803
1980	11,000	4.5	27,400	11.3	204,400	84.2	NA	—	242,800	1,300,400	14,700	1,557,900
1984	11,500	4.0	27,100	9.4	250,700	86.6	NA	—	289,300	1,436,800	12,500	1,738,600
1985	11,400	3.6	23,800	7.6	277,800	88.8	NA	—	313,000	1,418,300	13,000	1,744,300
1986[P]	11,900	3.5	23,700	6.9	307,600	89.6	NA	—	343,200	1,459,700	12,100	1,815,000

[a]Railroads of all classes, including electric railways, Amtrack, and Auto-train.

[P]These are preliminary estimates and are subject to frequent subsequent adjustments.

Note: Air carrier data from reports of CAB and TAA: Great Lakes and rivers and canals from Corps of Engineers and TAA: All 1980, 1984 through 1986 figures are from Transportation Policy Associations, except rail freight traffic is by the AAR.

Source: *Railroad Facts* (Washington, D.C.: Association of American Railroads, 1987), p. 32.

FIGURE 13–1
Railroad Ton-Miles—Class I Railroads

(in billions)

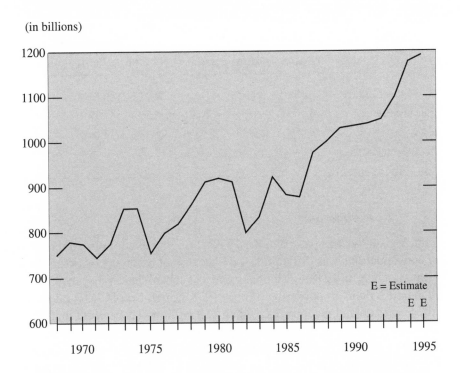

Source: Association of American Railroads; estimates by S&P. Industry Surveys, December 1994, p. R18. Reprinted by permission of Standard & Poor's, a division of The McGraw-Hill Companies.

Investment Favorites

The railroads reviewed in Table 13–2 are considered to be representative of somewhat higher quality than the industry overall, and have interested the investment public. Notice that these railroads are concentrated in the South and the Far West, where long hauls are prevalent. Some regional rails are also looked upon favorably, such as the Chicago, Central & Pacific Railroad, which is reported to have slashed labor costs from 75 percent to 50 percent of operating costs. Finally, the Illinois Central and Kansas City Southern Railway, as previously noted, are the only Class I railroads that have generated a return on net investment that equalled or exceeded their cost of capital in recent years.

TABLE 13–2
Growth in Revenues and Earnings Per Share for Selected Railroads

	Compound Annual Growth Rate					
	Revenues Per Share			Earnings Per Share		
	1993–94	*1989–94*	*1984–94*	*1993–94*	*1989–94*	*1984–94*
Burlington Northern	5.78%	Neg	Neg	29.97%	6.55%	Neg
Santa Fe Pacific	–3.06%	Neg	Neg	5.56%	13.70%	Neg
CSX Corp.	6.88%	2.96%	5.63%	28.70%	11.06%	6.35%
Norfolk Southern	6.86%	5.20%	6.31%	14.75%	7.08%	6.75%

Consolidations

Until legislation was passed in the 1950s, bringing about railroad mergers or consolidations was difficult, largely because of union opposition. However, after helpful 1958 legislation, a series of consolidations began in 1959. Standard & Poor's reported that, "Since 1978 the number of Class I railroads (those with annual revenues exceeding $80 million) has been cut in half as a result of mergers, liquidations, and bankruptcies."[3] The top five rail systems generated 68 percent of industry freight revenues in 1985, and the top ten rail systems accounted for 86 percent of industry freight revenues. Rails have increased their specialization in long-haul freight with a growing dependence on bulk commodities and piggyback hauls.

Merger activity was stimulated in the early 1980s by changes in the regulatory environment. The Railroad Revitalization and Regulatory Reform Act of 1976 directed the ICC to facilitate mergers and streamline our railroad systems into healthier, more efficient carriers. The ICC, however, rejected a proposed combination of the Southern Pacific and Santa Fe railroads in July 1986, signalling an unfavorable shift in the regulatory climate for railroads. This created doubt about the rapid approval of future merger proposals.

3 Standard & Poor's *Industry Surveys*, op. cit., p. R23.

While a number of consolidations (or mergers) have worked out profitably, the massive Penn-Central bankruptcy shows that consolidation is not always the answer to problems, and does not always work out to the advantage of security holders. One must assess the likely impact on revenue generation, cost economies, and profitability when considering whether a pending merger will or will not benefit investors.

A current wave of rail mergers began in June 1994 with Burlington Northern announcing plans to acquire Atchison, Topeka, and Santa Fe Railway. In July 1994, Illinois Central and Kansas City Southern agreed to merge. Other merger discussions were undertaken but not brought to successful conclusion, though some of these may be resurrected in the future. Current mergers have been primarily aimed at building freight volume. Mergers in the past few decades have aimed at building long-haul corridors and opening new markets (often through cutting freight rates). Rate cuts can be offset through economies gained in longer-haul corridors and other cost savings.

Cyclical Traffic

Since a substantial portion of railroad traffic is in the area of heavy durable goods, the railroads are particularly subject to contractions in business cycles. High debt/capitalization ratios create high financial leverage. The combination of the cyclical nature of their business and the high financial leverage of most railroads causes their earnings records to be quite volatile over the business cycle.

Financial Analysis of Railroads

Table 13–3 shows the major items in the railroad income statement for selected years from 1929 to 1993. The distribution of operating revenues for 1986 is shown in Table 13–4. Operating revenues stayed in a relatively narrow range from 1950 to 1969, at $10 to $11 billion. During that period, however, operating expenses rose sharply and profits tended to fall. Net income did not recover to the peak 1929 level until 1980. Net income then fell back sharply during the 1982 recession, again proving the railroads' susceptibility to the business cycle. Operating income and net income reached new highs in 1984, but profits slid about 31 percent in 1985 and dropped a stunning 71 percent in 1986 before recovering sharply in 1987 and maintaining that recovery in 1992 and 1993. Income has not yet gotten back to the level reached in 1984.

TABLE 13–3
Condensed Income Statement—Class I Railroads

Operating Revenue

In 1993 freight revenue accounted for 97.1 percent of total operating revenue. The remaining 2.9 percent of operating revenue was derived from switching, demurrage and incidental charges, including passenger revenue. Operating revenue rose 1.7 percent from 1992 to 1993; freight revenue rose 1.8 percent. (Amounts shown in thousands.)

Year	United States	East	West
1929	$ 6,279,521	$ 3,886,879	$ 2,392,642
1939	3,995,004	2,480,208	1,514,796
1944	9,436,790	5,416,089	4,020,701
1947	8,684,918	5,137,930	3,546,988
1955	10,106,330	5,815,997	4,290,333
1960	9,514,294	5,291,650	4,222,644
1965	10,207,850	5,651,838	4,556,012
1970	11,991,658	6,544,073	5,447,585
1975	16,401,860	8,535,831	7,866,029
1980	28,257,548	13,588,703	14,668,845
1984	29,453,446	13,566,348	15,887,098
1985	27,586,441	12,918,574	14,667,867
1986	26,204,122	12,235,170	13,968,952
1987	26,622,482	12,302,246	14,320,236
1988	27,934,285	12,490,320	15,443,965
1989	27,955,959	12,380,419	15,575,540
1990	28,369,803	12,511,463	15,858,340
1991	27,845,206	12,085,270	15,759,936
1992	28,348,895	12,229,550	16,119,345
1993	28,824,852	12,339,875	16,484,977

Freight Revenue

Freight revenue of the Class I railroads totaled $25.3 billion in 1986, 5.0 percent below 1985. (Amounts shown in thousands.)

	United States	Eastern District	Western District
1929	$ 4,825,622	$ 2,948,430	$ 1,877,192
1939	3,251,096	2,000,183	1,250,913

(continued)

TABLE 13–3 *(continued)*

	United States	Eastern District	Western District
1944	$ 6,998,615	$ 3,991,866	$ 3,006,748
1947	7,041,185	4,114,802	2,926,383
1951	8,634,101	4,983,440	3,650,661
1955	8,538,286	4,828,871	3,709,415
1978	20,236,065	9,531,536	10,704,529
1979	23,447,418	11,199,011	12,248,407
1980	26,200,348	12,036,953	14,163,395
1981	28,925,436	13,414,570	15,510,866
1982	25,627,354	11,943,959	13,683,395
1983	25,835,519	11,743,928	14,091,591
1984	28,471,789	13,032,248	15,439,541
1985	26,687,652	12,444,633	14,243,019
1986	25,343,911	11,803,793	13,540,118
1987	25,797,022	11,909,336	13,887,686
1988	27,095,508	12,199,467	14,972,041
1989	27,058,765	11,997,588	15,061,177
1990	27,470,520	12,132,224	15,338,296
1991	26,949,280	11,701,307	15,247,973
1992	27,507,607	11,882,595	15,625,022
1993	27,990,562	11,986,218	16,004,344

Operating Expenses

Operating expenses totaled $24.9 billion in 1986, down 1.3 percent from 1985. Data for the past four years are not comparable to prior years because of the industry's conversion in 1983 to a standard Depreciation Accounting System which, on paper only, has the effect of decreasing annual costs. Operating expenses for 1985 were increased by $784 million and for 1986 by $1.8 billion due to the inclusion of special charges. (Amounts shown in thousands.)

	United States	Eastern District	Western District
1929	$ 5,109,118	$ 3,178,515	$ 1,930,604
1939	3,511,310	2,146,729	1,364,519
1944	7,179,655	4,274,939	2,904,715
1947	7,725,423	4,690,309	3,035,115
1951	8,991,365	5,318,127	3,673,238
1955	8,621,255	4,989,033	3,632,224

(continued)

TABLE 13–3 *(continued)*

	United States	*Eastern District*	*Western District*
1975	$15,935,542	$ 8,517,851	$ 7,417,691
1978	21,043,143	10,744,912	10,298,231
1979	23,994,154	12,136,793	11,857,361
1980	26,249,920	12,760,818	13,489,102
1981	28,586,890	13,740,751	14,846,139
1982	26,490,278	12,962,260	13,528,018
1983	24,106,254	11,017,643	13,088,611
1984	25,800,454	11,695,740	14,104,714
1985	25,225,295	11,947,595	13,277,700
1986	24,896,015	10,996,766	13,899,249
1987	23,878,116	11,208,727	12,669,389
1988	24,811,138	11,134,887	13,676,251
1989	25,037,666	10,760,634	14,277,032
1990	24,651,542	10,609,981	14,041,561
1991	28,061,187	12,161,307	15,899,886
1992	25,324,506	10,785,690	14,538,816
1993	24,516,966	10,141,410	14,375,556

Principal Categories of Expense
(Amounts shown in thousands.)

	Transportation	*Equipment*	*Way and Structures*	*General and Administrative*
1929	$ 2,079,954	$1,202,912	$ 855,355	$ 970,897
1939	1,417,794	765,935	466,831	860,750
1944	2,973,910	1,587,485	1,263,292	1,354,968
1947	3,476,433	1,558,011	1,212,096	1,478,883
1955	3,769,856	1,787,739	1,387,494	1,676,166
1960	3,832,882	1,759,828	1,191,690	780,936
1965	4,020,161	1,774,878	1,235,801	819,001
1970	4,873,299	2,165,254	1,612,585	1,008,844
1975	6,735,741	2,856,203	2,408,980	3,934,618
1980	12,704,116	6,412,433	4,940,091	2,291,966
1984	12,281,567	6,572,696	4,250,275	2,695,931
1985	11,721,539	6,349,579	4,332,663	2,821,529
1986	10,196,636	6,573,065	4,779,691	3,346,623
1987	10,380,722	6,093,534	4,338,334	3,065,526
1988	10,827,267	6,109,116	4,397,528	3,477,227

(continued)

TABLE 13–3 *(continued)*

	Transportation	Equipment	Way and Structures	General and Administrative
1989	$11,169,208	$6,178,666	$4,431,101	$3,258,691
1990	11,276,732	6,349,784	4,278,075	2,746,951
1991	10,997,671	6,300,006	5,215,582	5,547,928
1992	10,532,994	6,314,426	4,373,006	4,104,080
1993	10,582,252	6,459,363	4,353,206	3,122,145

Ordinary Income

Ordinary income (after income from outside sources and payment of fixed rentals, interest and other charges) amounted to $747 million in 1986, down 58.2 percent from 1985. Ordinary income for 1985 and 1986 were reduced due to the inclusion of special charges. (Amounts shown in thousands.)

	United States	Eastern District	Western District
1929	$ 896,807	$ 560,037	$ 336,769
1939	93,182	122,073	(28,892)
1944	667,188	363,459	303,729
1947	478,875	216,370	262,505
1955	927,122	503,093	424,029
1975	144,362	(156,013)	300,375
1978	306,786	(228,417)	535,203
1979	938,254	286,442	651,812
1980	1,129,392	400,670	728,722
1981	2,041,265	978,245	1,063,020
1982	1,151,548	669,390	482,158
1983	1,777,916	897,755	880,161
1984	2,653,814	1,488,704	1,165,110
1985	1,788,151	779,626	1,008,525
1986	746,965	977,011	(230,046)
1987	1,965,475	810,116	1,155,359
1988	2,286,003	914,448	1,371,555
1989	2,009,094	1,127,238	881,856
1990	1,961,127	1,262,792	698,335
1991	(90,849)	(37,064)	(53,785)
1992	2,055,055	859,916	1,198,139
1993	2,258,037	1,136,526	1,121,511

(continued)

TABLE 13–3 *(concluded)*

Net Railway Operating Income

Net railway operating income (NROI) for 1986 was $507 million, 71.0 percent lower than the previous year. Data for 1983–1986 are not comparable with prior years due to conversion to a Depreciation Accounting System.

Net railway operating income is the remainder of operating revenues after deducting operating expenses, current and deferred taxes, and rents for equipment and joint facilities, but before recording non-operating income and deducting fixed charges. "NROI" is the figure used to determine rate of return on investment. NROI for 1985 and 1986 were reduced due to the inclusion of special charges. (Amounts shown in thousands.)

	United States	*Eastern District*	*Western District*
1929	$1,251,698	$ 767,277	$ 484,422
1939	588,829	410,714	178,116
1944	1,106,327	618,568	487,759
1947	780,694	407,125	373,570
1955	1,127,997	678,557	449,440
1975	350,682	(8,748)	359,429
1978	427,451	(200,893)	628,344
1979	837,232	159,553	677,679
1980	1,312,400	397,891	914,509
1981	1,360,611	622,966	737,645
1982	742,231	262,544	479,687
1983	1,837,854	870,047	967,807
1984	2,536,673	1,318,599	1,218,074
1985	1,746,386	760,143	986,243
1986	506,591	739,971	(233,380)
1987	1,756,460	NA	NA
1988	1,979,719	NA	NA
1989	1,894,315	NA	NA
1990	2,648,258	NA	NA
1991	(37,455)	NA	NA
1992	1,954,835	NA	NA
1993	2,517,138	NA	NA

Source: *Railroad Facts* (Washington, D.C.: Association of American Railroads, 1987) pp. 12, 13, 14, 15, 17, and 20.

Standard & Poor's did report that 1985 and 1986 results were penalized by nonrecurring items, and that operating revenues were expected to inch forward in 1986.[4]

An examination of Table 13–3 shows the overall poor record of the Eastern railroads, and the favorable results recorded by the Western district until the 1980s. The importance of labor costs (about 44 percent of total operating revenues) is clear when reviewing Table 13–4. Substantial progress has been made in cutting labor costs in recent years, aided by mergers and the introduction of new technology. Coupled with the growth in freight volume, there is future promise for long-haul railroads.

Railroad Income Statement Analysis

"Revenues" in railroad accounting terminology, means gross revenues (income) before deducting expenses. "Income" in railroad statements is synonymous with "net income" as used in industrial accounting. Also, while federal income taxes are deductible from net income on industrial company statements, they are included in the same categories as property and excise taxes in railroad accounting. Federal income taxes, therefore, reduce reported net railway operating income, whereas they would not affect net operating income of an industrial company.

Operating Revenues.   The major source of railroad revenues is freight income. The bases for analysis of revenues are therefore: (1) specific sources of revenues (commodity classifications) and trends of major components (the analyst has available, in annual reports, ICC publications, and statistical services complete breakdowns of freight revenues and tonnage by commodity classification and areas); (2) gross revenue carloadings and tonnage analysis and trends; (3) strategic position of traffic, i.e., traffic originated, terminated, and otherwise controlled; (4) trends of traffic between competing systems; (5) trends of traffic density-volume of ton-miles carried; (6) ton-miles carried per dollar of debt; (7) length of average haul; (8) stability of traffic through the last two business cycles; and (9) review of trends of revenues over past cycles and estimates for the next five to six years of annual normal revenues by major commodity classification.

---

4 Standard & Poor's *Industry Surveys*, op. cit., p. R15.

TABLE 13–4
Distribution of Operating Revenues (Dollar Amounts in Millions)

	1986
Total Operating Revenues	$26,204
Wages Charged to Expenses	8,675
Health and Welfare and Pensions	769
Payroll Taxes	2,183
Total Labor Costs	11,627
Income Taxes on Ordinary Income[1]	490
Provision for Deferred Taxes	(327)
Fuel and Power—Locomotives	1,486
Loss and Damage, Injuries, and Insurance	1,024
Depreciation	3,302
All Other Expenses[2]	8,365
Total Expenses and Taxes	25,697
Net Railway Operating Income	507

The Revenue Dollar—1986

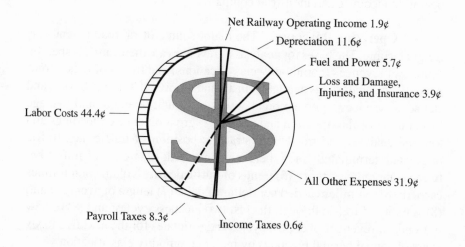

Net Railway Operating Income 1.9¢
Depreciation 11.6¢
Fuel and Power 5.7¢
Loss and Damage, Injuries, and Insurance 3.9¢
Labor Costs 44.4¢
All Other Expenses 31.9¢
Payroll Taxes 8.3¢
Income Taxes 0.6¢

[1]Includes state income taxes

[2]Includes other materials and supplies, miscellaneous equipment, and joint facility rents, current taxes (other than payroll taxes and income taxes), and retirement charges and rent for income from leased roads and equipment.

Source: *Railroad Facts*, op. cit., p. 11.

Analysis of Operating Revenues and Expenses

The profitability of the railroad will depend on its freight traffic, the composition of the freight, the length of the haul, the traffic density, and the strategic position of the railroad in regard to its freight business. The analyst should study the territory served by the railroad to determine the source and the trends of actual and potential freight tonnage and revenues. Important factors are the natural resources in the area studied, the agricultural situation, the type and trend of industry and commerce in the area, the volume of traffic developed, population trends, and per capita income trends. A study of the major items carried by the railroad will give insight into its earning power, since those carrying higher-freight-rate commodities often will be in the most advantageous position. However, certain low-rate commodities such as coal, which can be handled with low labor costs, may also be profitable.

Trend of revenues. The trend of revenues over a period of years should be studied in relationship to the trend of the railroad industry as a whole, the trend of the region, competing roads within the region, competing modes of transportation such as motor carriers and barge lines, and GNP trends.

Tonnage analysis. Figures for a qualitative as well as quantitative analysis are provided in "Freight Commodity Loading Statistics," a report published by the ICC. Railway freight tonnage figures for each railroad are segregated in these reports into approximately 160 classes of commodities.

Strategic position of traffic. In general, the greater the density of traffic, the greater the net profit. In this connection, fairly diversified traffic is desirable, and it should be determined that the major source of traffic is stable and growing. Freight traffic density is measured by the net revenue ton-miles per mile of road.

Ton-miles per dollar of debt. The ton-miles per dollar of mortgage debt is an important ratio for the section of a railroad covered by a specific mortgage. The ratio generally should be at least 40.

Length of average haul. Other things being equal, the longer the average haul for freight carried, the less expensive (on an average per-mile basis) it is to move and the more profitable it is to the railroad. Terminal expenses are major expenses because of high wage costs and the amount of labor costs involved; therefore, the longer the haul, the more these expenses can be allocated on a per-mile basis. The railroads are at a distinct cost disadvantage, in competition with motor carriers, for hauls of less than 400 miles.

Operating expenses. The major operating expenses of the railroads are maintenance, depreciation, transportation expenses, and traffic expenses. Labor costs are the largest individual expense item.

Maintenance. Maintenance is a heavy factor in railroad expenses. In general, a railroad should spend at least 13 to 15 percent of gross revenue for maintenance of ways and structures, 17 to 19 percent for maintenance of equipment, and 38 to 40 percent for transportation expense.

Depreciation. This item has in recent years averaged around 5 percent of gross revenues, or about the same as the amount available for the common stock. Because it is a tax-deductible expense, the effect on net income available for the common stock is apparent.

Labor factors. While railroad management has increased productivity of labor since World War II, reducing the number of workers by half since 1945 while carrying more freight volume, labor costs still represented 44 percent of total revenue in 1986. Average earnings of employees have approximately quadrupled. The benefits of capital expenditures and higher labor productivity have often been absorbed by employee wages, with little or no benefit for security holders.

In 1929, the number of railroad employees was 1,660,850; in 1944, 1,413,672; and in 1947, 1,351,961. However, productivity so increased that the number of employees was reduced to 780,494 by 1960; to 566,282 in 1970; to 458,994 in 1980; and to 275,811 by the end of 1986. While total compensation was $4.35 billion in 1947 for 1,351,961 employees, it rose to $11.3 billion in 1980 for only 458,994 employees, or from $3,218 annually per employee to $24,672 in 1980 and $35,894 by year-end 1986. Labor costs were 44 percent of total operating revenues in 1947, 47 percent of total operating revenues in 1980, and 44 percent in 1986. Therefore, labor costs relative to revenues were about the same in 1986 as in 1947 in spite of the great increase in labor productivity evidenced by the sharp decrease in the number of employees handling a large volume of freight.

TABLE 13–5
Average Operating Expense Ratios* for U.S. Railroads—
Selected Years, 1929–1986

1929	81.36%
1939	87.89
1944	76.08
1955	85.30
1972	93.43
1975	97.16
1980	93.41
1981	92.52
1982	96.32
1983	90.19
1984	87.60
1985	91.44
1986	95.01
1987	89.69
1988	88.82
1989	89.56
1990	86.89
1991	100.78
1992	89.33
1993	85.05

*Calculated by dividing operating expenses by operating revenues.

Source: Calculated on the basis of data provided in *Railroad Facts* (Washington, D.C.: Association of American Railroads, various issues).

Operating ratio. The operating ratio is the ratio of operating expenses to operating revenue and consists largely of transportation expenses plus maintenance expenses. It is by far the most important ratio used in railroad analysis. But taken by itself as an indication of operating efficiency, the operating ratio may give a misleading picture, especially if maintenance is being skimped. Lease rentals, together with maintenance policy, may cause wide differences in operating ratios.

The average operating ratios for Class I railroads are shown in Table 13–5. The operating ratio for all Class I railroads rose to an historic high of 100.78 in 1991, but this appears to be an aberration, since the average operating ratio has remained below 90 percent in other years of the 1990s. The improvement in the operating ratio in the 1990s is encouraging and is reflected in improved profits.

Other income.   Most railroads have some income other than that from their normal railroad operations, and for some railroads this other income is significant. Many investors consider that substantial income from natural resource reserves is a favorable factor if normal railway operations consistently are profitable. Investors considering such railroads should not purchase securities on this basis unless railway operations have been and are expected to be profitable.

Available for fixed charges.   Railroad fixed charges are regular annual fixed expenses such as interest on debt and rentals on leased properties. The amount available for fixed charges consists of (1) net railway operating income plus (2) other income less other deductions. This is the amount available for all security holders, and it provides the numerator in calculating the number of times fixed charges are earned as published in ICC statistics.

For all Class I railroads, the amount available for fixed charges in recent years has averaged about 8 percent of gross operating revenues. The range was from actual deficits to highs of 21 percent, 24 percent, and 36 percent for certain roads.

Times fixed charges earned.   The primary test for bonds is the number of times fixed charges are earned. This figure is calculated by dividing the amount available for fixed charges by the fixed charges. There is a wide range for various railroads for the number of times fixed charges are earned. The industry average in years of good business is around 3×. As with other bonds, the test is also the number of times fixed charges have been earned in recession years.

The amount of debt that a railroad can bear is determined by the traffic and the level of earnings, and is measured in terms of the times fixed charges are earned and the adequacy of cash flow to meet debt amortization requirements.

Preferred dividends.   Some railroads have preferred stock out-standing, and from the standpoint of the common stock, preferred dividends are a fixed charge. Therefore, the investor should calculate the coverage on an overall basis, (i.e., the number of times fixed charges plus preferred dividends are earned).

Earnings available for the common stock.   This is the percent-age of gross income after taxes and all prior charges including preferred dividends, available for common stock. In good years it has averaged about 8 percent of operating revenues for all Class I railroads. This is an important figure for the common stock because it indicates the margin of safety—how much all expenses and prior charges could increase before there would be nothing left for the common stock from the gross revenues.

Earnings available per share of common stock.   As with all corporations, this figure is the most important item for common shareholders. The investor must analyze the record and trend over a period of years and make projections for five to six years into the future. The amount and ratio of other income to gross and net income frequently is significant.

Earnings available to common stock are divided by shareholders' equity to determine the rate of return earned on stockholders' equity. The return on stockholders' equity reached a high of 10.54 percent for Class I railroads in 1981, but fell to a dismal 2.1 percent in 1986 (see Table 13–6). While returns earned in the 1980s and 1990 compare favorably to the 1.4 percent earned during the years 1975–78, they still compare unfavorably to that earned in many other industries. Class I railroads have earned (on average) between 8 and 9½ percent since 1987, though some individual railroads have earned more than 20 percent in a given year (Southern Pacific and Chicago & North Western Transportation).

Railroad Balance Sheet Analysis

A review of the fluctuations and trends of revenues, costs, and profits (especially the number of times fixed charges are earned, the earnings per share, and the dividends received) as discussed in reference to railroad income statement analysis ordinarily provides a good indication of the prospective quality of a railroad security. However, balance sheet analysis also will provide necessary and useful information.

Working capital.   Railroads have modest working capital requirements because receivables are short term and inventories are not a factor. Working capital for all Class I railroads in the 1980s averaged 6 to 7 percent of gross revenues, but the company-to-company range has been broad. Fixed charges must be paid out of working capital. In recent years, working capital for Class I roads has averaged 1.6 to 2× fixed charges for Class I railroads, but again a wide range is present among different roads (see Table 13–7). Net working capital (current assets – current liabilities – inventories) declined sharply until 1975, and again declined sharply in

TABLE 13–6
Rate of Return on Shareholders' Equity

The rate of return on shareholders' equity (ROE) for Class I railroads in 1986 was 2.1 percent. Due to conversion to a Depreciation Accounting System, the figures for 1983–1986 are not comparable with prior years.

ROE represents the relationship of net income (after income from outside sources, payment of fixed charges and adjustment for extraordinary items) to shareholders' equity (the sum of capital stock, capital surplus and retained income). (Dollar amounts in thousands.)

Year	Net Income	Shareholders' Equity*	Rate of Return on Equity*
1967	$ 321,542	$18,083,434	1.78%
1968	564,505	17,978,627	3.14
1969	463,565	17,876,294	2.59
1970	76,179	17,546,055	0.43
1972	228,173	16,338,931	1.40
1973	409,223	16,224,367	2.52
1974	767,065	15,641,679	4.90
1975	278,819	14,943,468	1.87
1976	414,351	15,086,007	2.75
1977	338,580	15,478,492	2.19
1978	202,075	15,295,935	1.32
1979	913,450	16,718,846	5.46
1980	1,129,392	18,777,051	6.01
1981	2,140,905	20,320,268	10.54
1982	1,151,548	21,199,739	5.43
1983	1,797,483	24,775,112	7.26
1984	2,701,064	27,171,974	9.94
1985	1,881,522	27,528,127	6.83
1986	544,407	25,968,536	2.10
1987	2,055,221	25,528,850	8.05
1988	2,381,782	26,156,259	9.11
1989	2,202,808	26,110,281	8.44
1990	1,977,411	24,170,700	8.18
1991	(281,334)	23,132,753	NM
1992	1,800,364	22,690,595	7.93
1993	2,239,638	23,886,642	9.38

NM = Not meaningful (Negative value)

*Average beginning and end of year.

Note: Net income for 1985 and 1986 were reduced due to the inclusion of special charges.

Source: *Railroad Facts*, op. cit.

TABLE 13–7
Net Working Capital

Net working capital is calculated by deducting current liabilities, including debt due within one year, from current assets, which includes the materials and supplies accounts. (Amounts shown in millions.)

Year	Current Assets	Current Liabilities	Net Working Capital
1929	$1,718	$1,201	$ 517
1939	1,293	2,556	(1,263)
1944	4,488	2,844	1,644
1947	3,576	1,943	1,633
1955	3,738	2,138	1,600
1960	2,909	2,231	678
1965	3,183	2,526	657
1970	3,583	3,524	59
1975	4,641	4,573	68
1980	8,678	7,756	922
1984	9,821	7,977	1,844
1985	9,350	8,267	1,084
1986	9,132	8,390	743
1987	8,216	8,182	34
1988	8,403	8,593	(190)
1989	6,735	8,854	(2,119)
1990	5,699	9,204	(3,505)
1991	5,508	9,496	(3,988)
1992	5,156	9,527	(4,372)
1993	5,885	9,180	(3,295)

Source: *Railroad Facts Book*, 1994, op. cit.

1986. Net working capital (on average) has been negative since 1988, which cannot continue indefinitely. This area should be watched. Current ratios fell below 1:1 for several railroads, and investors should be confident working capital is adequate before investing.

Property accounts. The major items on the asset side of a railroad balance sheet are investments in roadways and equipment. These items should be analyzed to determine the new equipment added annually, as well as the depreciation charged. There has been phenomenal modernization and

improvement for the railroad industry as a whole since the end of World
War II. The bulk of new capital funds in the railroad industry has gone into
equipment, at times stimulated by the investment credit.

Some analysts question whether railroads can maintain the present
volume of capital expenditures, which is needed to exploit and accelerate
traffic gains registered in recent years.

Capital structure proportions.   Railroad debt has been declining since the 1930s. Generally, debt for an individual railroad should not
exceed 40 percent of total capitalization, and the remaining 60 percent
should consist of preferred stock, common stock, and surplus. All additional
debt issued to obtain funds since the 1930s has been in the form of
equipment obligations.

The amount of debt that a railroad can bear is determined by the traffic
and the level of earnings. The debt also is measured in terms of the times
fixed charges are earned and the adequacy of cash flow to meet debt
amortization requirements.

THE TRUCKING INDUSTRY[5]

The trucking industry (motor freight carrier industry) has two major divisions: private and for hire. The private division comprises all those businesses that provide their own transportation through owned or leased lines.
The for-hire division is subdivided into interstate, intrastate, and local.
Interstate truckers subdivide further into contract and common carriers,
with the former operating under continuing contracts with specific shippers.
Both common and contract truckers are subject to ICC regulations.

For investment purposes, we are concerned with publicly owned interstate (intercity) common carriers. ICC regulations cover rates, routes,
classes of commodities carried, accounting practices, finances, mergers,
and acquisitions. ICC requires certificates of necessity that designate the
specific routes for each carrier. In 1978, the Carter administration sought
to decontrol the carriers, but the carriers objected strenuously, fearing
ruinous competition. The Teamsters Union also voiced strong opposition
to deregulation. The Motor Carrier Act of 1980, however, deregulated the

---

[5]The basic source material for this section on trucking is Standard & Poor's *Basic Analysis,
Trucking.*

trucking industry, throwing it open to fresh competition, and this led to a host of new entrants. The industry did lose a measure of stability that regulation had provided, but gained the possibility of better control of labor costs. Many smaller carriers have gone out of business. Only the most efficient carriers will survive.

The trucking industry is not yet fully deregulated. Restrictions exist on the kinds of freight that can be hauled, and companies can not hire workers under 21 years of age (though younger drivers are permitted on intrastate trucking and bus routes). Companies have boosted their private fleets, but inefficient private fleet operators can still lose out to for-hire carriers. Industry experts expect that as much as 10 percent of private-market annual revenues could convert to for-hire over the next five to ten years.

The cyclical nature of the trucking industry and its heavy financial leverage are demonstrated in the recovery year of 1976 and can be observed by reviewing sales at earnings per share data in Table 13–8 (gross freight revenues rose about 15 percent, from $22.0 billion to $25.3 billion, but net income doubled from $400 million to $795 million). These data for 1975 and 1976 compares with gross freight revenues for railroads of $15.4 billion in 1975 and $17.4 billion in 1976, and net income of $144.4 million in 1975 and $272.5 million in 1976. In 1976, the motor carriers accounted for 54 percent of total revenues of all regulated carriers of freight, versus 39 percent for the railroads. In 1960, the motor carriers accounted for 39 percent and the railroads 50 percent. The biggest carriers continue to grow larger through expansion of route systems and acquisitions. Bankruptcies have been on the rise, but excess capacity still remains to be wrung out.

Competition

In competition with the railroads, the truckers have taken the type of freight they desire (such as the less-than-carload business) from the railroads, leaving the latter with the heavy freight that truckers cannot carry economically or the long-haul traffic. Therefore, the only real competition with the rails remaining is the piggyback freight handled by the railroads. The deregulation of the industry has led to fierce rate discounting, thereby limiting revenue growth.

Competition therefore is largely intraindustry, but as truck freight rates have risen steadily, competition is being felt in the form of freight forwarders using rail piggyback facilities.

While air freight competition is small, it is growing fast and takes the cream of the traffic—the high-value, high-rate traffic.

Growth and Consolidation

The number of for-hire truckers, stimulated by deregulation, tripled from 17,721 firms in 1980 to 53,510 in 1993, resulting in overcapacity for the industry, an unprofitable rate structure, and slow growth. Entry barriers are low in the trucking industry. Standard & Poor's expects a shakeout in the truckload market, and that the large carriers will gain a growing market share.[6] Industry concentration will rise, and mergers and acquisitions will take place.

The Income Statement of Truck Carriers

As with the railroads, the largest expense items for the truckers are labor costs. Labor costs absorb 60 to 65 percent of total revenues for major unionized Less-than-truckload (LTL) carriers. Labor costs absorb about 25 to 40 percent of revenues in the truckload segment of the market, where unionization is not as strong.

The operating ratio for truck carriers generally ranges from 94 to 97 percent for the largest firms, the Class I truckers. Three items—transportation expenses, terminal costs, and maintenance of equipment—absorb about 73 to 75 percent of total revenue. The balance of revenue is absorbed as follows:

Operating taxes and licenses	6–6½%
Depreciation	3–4
Traffic	3–3½
Insurance and safety	4–4½
General and administration	6–6½
Totals	22–24

Margins have eroded in recent years because of rate discounting aimed at achieving higher freight density (see earnings as a percent of sales data in Table 13–8). Profits in 1993 were 44 percent below 1980 levels, and if adjustment is made for inflation profits in 1993 were 84 percent below those of 1978. The Trucking Industry Regulatory Reform Act of 1994 offers the possibility of curbing discounting, but if this is not accomplished, profit performance will continue to be poor for many truckers. Great care in selection is necessary, and this industry is not really attractive currently. Figure 13–2 clearly shows the depressing performance. Revenues increased in the 1990s, but profits continued to fall.

---

6 Standard & Poor's *Industry Surveys, Railroads & Trucking,* December 8, 1994, p. R33.

FIGURE 13–2
Revenues and Profits—Class I Motor Carriers
(Adjusted for invlation, 1973 = 100)

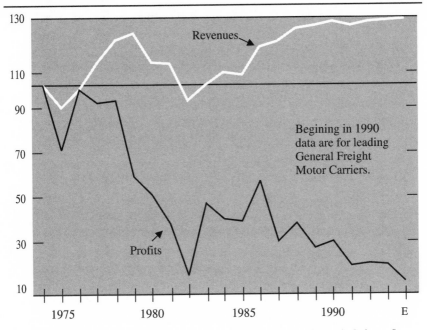

Source: American Trucking Association; estimates by S&P. Standard & Poor's *Industry Surveys, Railroads and Trucking*, 1994, p. R39. Reprinted by permission of Standard & Poor's, a division of the McGraw-Hill Companies.

The Balance Sheet of Truck Carriers

As with other regulated industries, the current ratio for the trucking industry is at 1.00–1.15 to 1 because there are no inventories (except tires and spare parts), and receivables are generally current, as most traffic is on a cash basis. The amount of working capital to cover cash operating expense is considered a more significant ratio than the current ratio.

As a measure of the quality of the funded debt, analysts calculate the ratio of all funded debt to total annual cash flow, i.e., how much of the funded debt could be paid off if all annual cash flow was used for that purpose.

Historically, carriers have attempted to purchase new equipment from annual cash flow, but in recent years they have used revolving credit agreements. The general capital markets are not tapped too frequently for the sale of stocks or bonds; neither are private placements used normally.

TABLE 13-8
Truckers

Per Share Data—Adjusted to stock price index level. Average stock price indexes, 1955 = 10

	Sales	Depr.	Income Taxes	Earnings Per Share	% of Sales	Dividends Per Share	% of Earn.	Prices 1955 = 10 High	Low	Price/Earn. Ratio High	Low	Div. Yields % High	Low	Book Value Per Share	% Return	Work-ing Capital	Capital Expend-itures
1973	—	—	—	4.11	—	1.24	30.17	102.92	70.76	25.04	17.22	1.75	1.20	—	—	—	—
1974	—	—	—	6.57	—	1.37	20.85	101.63	61.78	15.47	9.40	2.22	1.35	—	—	—	—
1975	—	—	—	6.10	—	1.54	25.25	113.14	62.81	18.55	10.30	2.45	1.36	—	—	—	—
1976	—	—	—	8.57	—	1.74	20.30	134.72	108.23	15.72	12.63	1.61	1.29	—	—	—	—
1977	193.27	6.84	8.52	9.91	5.13	2.02	20.38	125.55	87.69	12.67	8.85	2.30	1.61	42.77	23.17	8.30	17.14
1978	232.89	8.44	9.07	10.99	4.72	2.47	22.47	116.31	68.75	10.58	6.26	3.59	2.12	50.81	21.63	8.91	19.99
1979	276.06	10.12	6.81	9.10	3.30	2.93	32.20	86.10	68.96	9.46	7.58	4.25	3.40	56.87	16.00	12.22	24.10
1980	280.89	11.04	5.92	8.67	3.09	3.28	37.83	92.11	62.37	10.62	7.19	5.26	3.56	61.85	14.02	15.23	14.50
1981	246.11	10.20	6.64	9.60	3.90	3.80	39.58	123.61	84.02	12.88	8.75	4.52	3.07	75.81	12.66	30.00	12.14
1982	218.49	9.74	6.35	9.02	4.13	4.01	44.46	153.22	84.89	16.99	9.41	4.72	2.62	79.21	11.39	33.71	15.88
1983	245.06	9.79	10.80	14.77	6.03	4.62	31.28	207.24	142.04	14.03	9.62	3.25	2.23	89.52	16.50	43.17	12.34
1984	308.67	12.51	11.39	15.39	4.99	5.30	34.44	197.41	130.01	12.83	8.45	4.08	2.68	97.08	15.85	24.80	36.38
1985	337.41	16.23	11.07	8.29	2.46	5.70	68.76	236.67	158.73	28.55	19.15	3.59	2.41	106.37	7.79	23.09	36.36
1986	450.19	22.74	13.62	17.76	3.95	6.89	38.80	319.79	229.94	18.01	12.95	3.00	2.15	134.50	13.20	29.26	36.24
1987	488.03	25.72	7.83	13.48	2.76	7.78	57.72	353.92	209.03	26.26	15.51	3.72	2.20	139.38	9.67	30.35	39.58
1988	566.37	28.47	11.23	21.43	3.78	8.12	37.89	283.16	228.34	13.21	10.66	3.56	2.87	142.16	15.07	12.17	51.55
1989	730.09	34.66	6.62	9.47	1.30	8.52	89.97	306.14	252.80	32.33	26.69	3.37	2.78	108.77	8.71	9.93	54.68

(continued)

TABLE 13–8 (continued)

Per Share Data—Adjusted to stock price index level. Average stock price indexes, 1955 = 10

	Sales	Depr.	Income Taxes	Earnings Per Share	Earnings % of Sales	Dividends Per Share	Dividends % of Earn.	Prices 1955 = 10 High	Prices 1955 = 10 Low	Price/Earn. Ratio High	Price/Earn. Ratio Low	Div. Yields % High	Div. Yields % Low	Book Value Per Share	Book Value % Return	Working Capital	Capital Expenditures
1990	813.30	37.46	9.20	12.32	1.51	7.24	58.77	285.88	185.27	23.20	15.04	3.91	2.53	114.96	10.72	7.07	43.92
1991	817.76	36.43	8.22	8.51	1.04	6.10	71.68	317.00	266.10	37.25	26.57	2.70	1.92	121.55	7.00	18.65	34.99
1992	832.86	36.17	10.10	14.11	1.69	6.43	45.57	381.36	286.66	27.03	20.32	2.24	1.69	125.50	11.24	29.65	37.51
1993	944.14	39.53	12.86	14.33	1.52	6.78	47.31	370.16	261.98	25.83	18.28	2.59	1.83	131.51	11.87	13.11	60.18
1994				E5.18				396.89	256.42	66.30	23.60	2.81	1.71				

Source: Standard and Poor's Analyst Handbook, 1994.

Composite Industry Data
*Per share data based on Standard & Poor's group stock price indexes

Truckers
The companies used for this series are: Consolidated Freightways; Overnite Transportation (from 1986); Roadway Express; Yellow Freight Systems. Price: 1955 = 10.

	1986	1987	1988	1989	1990	1991	1992	1993	
	450.19	488.03	566.37	730.09	813.30	817.76	832.86	944.14	Sales
	22.74	25.72	28.47	34.66	37.46	36.43	36.17	39.53	Depreciation

Railroads
The companies used for this series are: Burlington Northern; CNW Corp. (through 1988); Conrail (from 1987); CSX Corp.; Norfolk Southern; Santa Fe Pacific; Union Pacific. Price: 1941–43 = 100.

	1986	1987	1988	1989	1990	1991	1992	1993	
	163.68	172.72	223.85	239.36	273.94	275.80	284.19	290.22	Sales
	13.54	13.42	17.02	18.36	20.93	22.15	23.86	25.05	Depreciation

(continued)

TABLE 13–8 (concluded)

	1986	1987	1988	1989	1990	1991	1992	1993		1986	1987	1988	1989	1990	1991	1992	1993
Taxes	13.62	7.83	11.23	6.62	9.20	8.22	10.10	12.86		0.50	7.20	8.18	8.22	9.50	-1.21	9.47	16.51
Earnings	17.76	13.48	21.43	9.47	12.32	8.51	14.11	14.33		-1.76	9.91	13.77	14.06	17.25	-3.73	17.66	22.25
Dividends	6.89	7.78	8.12	8.52	7.24	6.10	6.43	6.78		4.67	5.00	5.50	6.19	7.27	7.56	8.26	8.74
Earnings as a % of Sales	3.95	2.76	3.78	1.30	1.51	1.04	1.69	1.52		def	5.74	6.15	5.87	6.30	def	6.21	7.67
Dividends as % of Earnings	38.80	57.72	37.89	89.97	58.77	71.68	45.57	47.31		def	50.45	39.94	44.03	42.14	def	46.77	39.28
Price—High	319.79	353.92	283.16	306.14	285.88	317.00	381.36	370.16		158.76	198.61	173.26	223.14	224.40	313.27	349.20	421.15
—Low	229.94	209.03	228.34	252.80	185.27	226.10	286.66	261.98		123.84	129.08	143.47	174.36	169.59	187.82	292.03	346.38
Price-Earnings Ratios—High	18.01	26.26	13.21	32.33	23.20	37.25	27.03	25.83		def	20.04	12.58	15.87	13.01	def	19.77	18.93
—Low	12.95	15.51	10.66	26.69	15.04	26.57	20.32	18.28		def	13.03	10.42	12.40	9.83	def	16.54	15.57
Dividend Yield %—High	3.00	3.72	3.56	3.37	3.91	2.70	2.24	2.59		3.77	3.87	3.83	3.55	4.29	4.03	2.83	2.52
—Low	2.15	2.20	2.87	2.78	2.53	1.92	1.69	1.83		2.94	2.52	3.17	2.77	3.24	2.41	2.37	2.08
Book Value	134.50	139.38	142.16	108.77	114.96	121.55	125.50	131.51		119.46	129.75	136.67	158.62	147.99	133.89	140.40	166.41
Return on Book Value %	13.20	9.67	15.07	8.71	10.72	7.00	11.24	11.87		def	7.64	10.08	8.86	11.66	def	12.58	13.56
†Working Capital	29.26	30.35	2.17	9.93	7.07	18.65	29.65	13.11		3.20	3.95	0.08	-11.88	-16.74	-26.16	-25.67	-18.52
Capital Expenditures	36.24	39.58	51.55	54.68	43.92	34.99	37.51	60.18		21.29	NA	NA	NA	NA	35.22	41.95	39.02

*NOTE: Per Share data are expressed in terms of the S&P Stock Price Index, I.E. stock prices 1984 = 100. Each of the items shown is first computed on a true per share basis for each company. Totals for each company are then reconstructed using the same number of shares outstanding as was used to compute our stock price index as of December 31. This is done because the shares used on reconstructed totals is then related to the base period value used to compute the stock price index. As a double check, we relate the various items to the dividends as these are the most stable series. So, for example, if total sales amount to fifteen times the total dividend payments, then with per share dividends at 3.50 the indicated per share sales will be (15 × 3.50) 52.50 in terms of the S&P Stock Index. For comparability between the various groups, all data are on a calendar year basis, corporate data being posted in the year in which most months fall. Fiscal years ending June 30th are posted in the calendar year in which the fiscal year ends. †Current assets less current liabilities, without allowance for long-term debt. R—Revised, cr—credit, d—deficit. NA—Not available.

Source: Standard & Poor's Analyst's Handbook, 1994. Reprinted by permission of Standard & Poor's, a division of the McGraw-Hill Companies.

TABLE 13–9
Return on Equity—Selected Trucking Companies—Various Years

	1985	1987	1990	1992	1993	1994
Arkansas Best	15.5%	7.7%	2.2%	16.5%	10.4%	8.6%
Builders Transport	18.0	9.9	Neg.	0.6	7.1	9.9
Consolidated Freightways	13.1	10.8	Neg.	0.2	8.1	9.0
J. B. Hunt Transport	21.2	18.5	15.7	12.0	11.7	10.7
M.S. Carriers	31.9	14.3	12.0	14.7	10.3	11.6
Roadway Services	12.4	7.6	15.3	14.4	11.4	1.9
Rollins Truck Leas.	8.0	4.0	13.5	12.9	14.0	15.9
Ryder System	12.9	13.2	5.8	8.0	12.4	13.6
Werner Enterprises	32.3	14.6	14.4	14.4	12.6	13.3
Worldway Corp.	13.7	6.8	1.8	Neg.	Neg.	6.2

Accounting Practices in the Industry

In reporting to stockholders, truckers may report either according to AICPA principles or in accordance with ICC procedures. Under AICPA principles, tax reductions resulting from accelerated tax depreciation and tax credits must be recorded as a deferred federal income tax liability charged to net income. But under ICC procedures this tax liability is not recognized, and tax reduction (savings) flows through to net income. Truckers may expense tires and tubes, as well as other prepaid expenses incurred, or may capitalize them and charge them off during their useful life. The method used will affect the current ratio, which normally is only between 1.0-to-1 and 1.2-to-1. Finally, the reported financial condition of the carrier will reflect the proportion of assets that are owned versus leased.

Rate of Return

The record of the rate of return on equity for selected trucking firms for selected recent years is contained in Table 13–9. Note that the rate of return can vary sharply from year to year and between firms. Also, note that the firms have not returned to the profitable days of 1985.

Summary of Analysis of a Trucking Company

The analyst should determine the economics of the area served, as well as the past and prospective growth trends of the carrier. The analyst also should determine the nature of routes used and the character of restrictions, types of highways, and tax levies. The past financial record then should be analyzed and compared to industry norms and trends in respect to items discussed above. Management's record in respect to the industry norms and management's policies toward mergers and acquisitions should be determined. Finally, the analyst should project revenues and earnings for the next five years, recognizing the cyclical nature of the industry and being especially alert to opportunities in periods of depressed stock markets, discounting general economic recessions.

Chapter Fourteen

Financial Institutions

In this chapter we cover the two largest financial institutions—commercial banks and insurance companies. These institutions are different in their characteristics and regulations, and therefore they are treated separately. Commercial banks are covered in the first part of the chapter and insurance companies in the second part.

COMMERCIAL BANKS

Commercial banks are engaged in a broad range of financial activities, including making both long-term and short-term loans to business firms, installment loans to consumers, mortgage loans to home buyers, offering trust services, and facilitating international transactions. They invest large amounts in U.S. Treasury and agency securities, securities of state and local governments, and money market instruments. Commercial banks are a primary, though not exclusive, provider of checking accounts, and serve individuals through offering a large variety of savings accounts, money market instruments, and certificates of deposit. The nation's commercial banks hold the bulk of the cash assets of individuals, business firms, financial institutions, trust funds, and pension funds, as well as the deposits of federal, state and local governments.

Banking: A Changing Environment

The banking industry has and continues to undergo tremendous change since the 1960s. First, there was the widespread adoption of the one-bank holding company form of organization during the late 1960s and early 1970s. Moreover, bankers realized early in the 1960s that interest-bearing liabilities were likely to become the major source of funds for the support of future asset growth. Banks began to pursue more aggressive asset growth and operating strategies based on their seeming ability to expand liabilities almost at will.

The one-bank holding company form of organization facilitated the underwriting of a growing variety of assets and led banks into business areas not considered traditional areas of bank operations. Such changes offered large potential rewards, but increased risk also was present, as banks have learned to their sorrow. Relatively high dependence on borrowed funds to finance expansion, for example, weakened capital structures and made banks more sensitive to interest rate volatility.

Investors greeted the changes with great enthusiasm during the early 1970s, with bank stocks reaching all-time highs in terms of price–earnings ratios and the relationship of these ratios to the average price–earnings ratio for the stocks included in the Standard and Poor's 500 Stock Price Index (See Table 14–1). Several individual bank stocks sold for even higher price–earnings ratios than recorded by the S&P 500 Index during this period, which was quite unusual since bank stock price–earnings ratios had usually been significantly lower than the average price–earnings ratio for the S&P 500 Index.

The growing favor with which investors looked on bank stocks did not, however, last long. Severe problems facing banks became evident during 1974–75, and price–earnings ratios fell sharply. They began to recover in 1983 and remain relatively strong in the 1990s, as the banking industry now appears strong and has shown growing profits since 1991. There were spectacular failures or near-failures among large bank institutions in the 1970s and 1980s—for example, First Pennsylvania, Continental Bank, and the Texas banks. By 1995, several banks sported price–earnings ratios higher than the average for the Standard and Poor's 500 Index, reflecting the stronger capital position and improved recent profitability record of the banks. Speculation on continued merger activity also stimulated bank stock prices.

A paper presented at a Financial Management Association workshop noted six major developments that have altered the face of United States banking.[1] These factors should be carefully considered when assessing a bank stock. The list is summarized below, with additions and alterations:

1. An increased dependence on purchased money leading to interest expense becoming a large and volatile number, approximating 50

---

[1] *Bank Analysis from External Sources* (New York: Cates, Lyons & Co., Inc., 1979), pp. 3–14.

TABLE 14–1
Major Regional Banks

Per Share Data—Adjusted to stock price index level. Average of stock price indexes, 1941-43 = 10

	Earnings Per Share	Dividends		Prices 1941-43 = 10		Price/Earn. Ratio		Div. Yields %		Equity	
		Per Share	% of Earn.	High	Low	High	Low	High	Low	Per Share	% Return
1963	$ 4.15	$2.11	50.84	$ 78.44	$67.98	18.90	16.38	3.10	2.69	—	—
1964	4.55	2.23	49.01	81.50	74.50	17.91	16.37	2.99	2.74	—	—
1965	4.86	2.32	47.74	75.56	67.90	15.55	13.97	3.42	3.07	—	—
1966	5.49	2.43	44.26	71.81	55.76	13.08	10.16	4.36	3.38	—	—
1967	5.85	2.64	45.13	71.88	63.09	12.29	10.78	4.18	3.67	—	—
1968	6.71	2.75	40.98	101.14	66.87	15.07	9.97	4.11	2.72	—	—
1969	6.96	3.10	44.54	98.78	76.94	14.19	11.05	4.03	3.14	—	—
1970	7.62	3.25	42.65	85.32	64.95	11.20	8.52	5.00	3.81	—	—
1971	7.90	3.42	43.29	94.45	83.26	11.96	10.54	4.11	3.62	—	—
1972	8.48	3.60	42.45	121.84	89.69	14.37	10.58	4.01	2.95	—	—
1973	9.56	3.81	39.85	117.51	95.76	12.29	10.02	3.98	3.24	—	—
1974	10.43	4.13	39.60	111.81	55.87	10.72	5.36	7.39	3.69	—	—
1975	11.49	4.31	37.51	93.02	67.59	8.10	5.88	6.38	4.63	—	—
1976	11.13	4.08	36.66	112.50	84.52	10.11	7.59	4.83	3.63	—	—
1977	12.42	4.21	33.90	108.83	90.85	8.76	7.31	4.63	3.87	$97.30	12.76

(continued)

TABLE 14–1 (continued)

Per Share Data—Adjusted to stock price index level. Average of stock price indexes, 1941-43 = 10

	Earnings Per Share	Dividends Per Share	Dividends % of Earn.	Prices 1941-43 = 10 High	Prices 1941-43 = 10 Low	Price/Earn. Ratio High	Price/Earn. Ratio Low	Div. Yields % High	Div. Yields % Low	Equity Per Share	Equity % Return
1978	$15.44	$4.74	30.70	$116.96	$ 87.95	7.58	5.70	5.39	4.05	$107.30	14.39
1979	17.29	5.58	32.27	119.79	96.06	6.93	5.56	5.81	4.66	118.84	14.55
1980	17.54	6.00	34.21	119.60	86.81	6.82	4.95	6.91	5.02	129.23	13.57
1981	17.57	6.54	37.22	132.29	107.66	7.53	6.13	6.07	4.94	138.40	12.70
1982	15.66	6.77	43.23	118.09	78.92	7.54	5.04	8.58	5.73	141.92	11.03
1983	11.16	6.90	61.83	124.04	97.72	11.12	8.76	7.06	5.56	143.00	7.80
1984	0.45	5.99	—	116.07	77.95	—	—	7.68	5.16	123.12	0.37
1985	6.42	5.46	85.05	110.25	90.80	17.17	14.14	6.01	4.95	121.56	5.28
1986	3.12	3.84	—	126.88	99.20	40.67	31.79	3.87	3.03	120.33	2.59
1987	d9.03	3.98	def	125.78	80.99	def	def	4.91	3.16	84.90	def
1988	1.35	4.38	—	113.11	87.09	83.79	64.51	5.03	3.87	77.46	1.74
1989	10.37	5.09	49.08	138.06	102.65	13.31	9.90	4.96	3.69	85.76	12.09
1990	8.67	5.11	58.94	120.59	63.41	13.91	7.31	8.06	4.24	86.10	10.07
1991	5.26	4.46	84.79	138.02	73.02	26.24	13.88	6.11	3.23	87.08	6.04
1992	10.85	4.50	41.47	171.28	138.36	15.79	12.75	3.25	2.63	96.20	11.28
1993	15.74	5.33	33.86	201.25	163.00	12.79	10.36	3.27	2.65	108.36	14.53

(continued)

TABLE 14–1 (*continued*)
Money Center Banks

Per Share Data—Adjusted to stock price index level. Average of stock price indexes, 1982 = 100

	Earnings	Dividends		Prices 1982 = 100		Price/Earn. Ratio		Div. Yields %		Equity	
	Per Share	Per Share	% of Earn.	High	Low	High	Low	High	Low	Per Share	% Return
1963	$2.15	$1.16	53.95	$39.40	$34.45	18.33	16.02	3.37	2.94	—	—
1964	2.38	1.20	50.42	42.74	36.97	17.96	15.53	3.25	2.81	—	—
1965	2.59	1.30	50.19	41.00	36.86	15.83	14.23	3.53	3.17	—	—
1966	2.80	1.34	47.86	37.73	27.95	13.48	9.98	4.79	3.55	—	—
1967	3.04	1.42	46.71	38.69	34.16	12.73	11.24	4.16	3.67	—	—
1968	3.38	1.55	45.86	53.11	36.20	15.71	10.71	4.28	2.92	—	—
1969	3.29	1.70	51.67	51.71	38.81	15.72	11.80	4.38	3.29	—	—
1970	3.86	1.80	46.63	48.93	37.19	12.68	9.63	4.84	3.68	—	—
1971	4.02	1.92	47.76	51.14	42.26	12.72	10.51	4.54	3.75	—	—
1972	4.20	1.92	45.71	65.08	48.69	15.50	11.59	3.94	2.95	—	—
1973	4.87	1.97	40.45	75.00	56.29	15.40	11.56	3.50	2.63	—	—
1974	5.72	2.13	37.24	69.33	39.30	12.12	6.87	5.42	3.07	—	—
1975	5.86	2.21	37.71	60.91	41.04	10.39	7.00	5.38	3.63	—	—
1976	5.64	2.23	39.54	56.98	46.49	10.10	8.24	4.80	3.91	—	—
1977	5.74	2.34	40.77	54.34	40.31	9.47	7.02	5.81	4.31	$50.82	11.29

(*continued*)

TABLE 14-1 (continued)

Per Share Data—Adjusted to stock price index level. Average of stock price indexes, 1982 = 100

	Earnings	Dividends		Prices 1982 = 100		Price/Earn. Ratio		Div. Yields %		Equity	
	Per Share	Per Share	% of Earn.	High	Low	High	Low	High	Low	Per Share	% Return
1978	$ 7.16	$2.51	35.06	$ 50.91	$ 37.43	7.11	5.23	6.71	4.93	$ 55.35	12.94
1979	8.64	2.76	31.94	49.92	40.92	5.78	4.74	6.74	5.53	61.15	14.13
1980	9.87	3.05	30.90	49.65	37.75	5.03	3.82	8.08	6.14	67.48	14.63
1981	10.55	3.28	31.09	60.60	47.50	5.74	4.50	6.91	5.41	73.74	14.31
1982	11.53	3.68	31.92	70.61	44.45	6.12	3.86	8.28	5.21	80.28	14.36
1983	12.49	3.99	31.95	80.95	59.85	6.48	4.79	6.67	4.93	87.99	14.19
1984	12.45	4.31	34.62	73.35	52.50	5.89	4.22	8.21	5.88	94.86	13.12
1985	14.64	4.59	31.35	100.84	70.87	6.89	4.84	6.48	4.55	104.21	14.05
1986	13.78	4.94	35.85	129.51	95.06	9.40	6.90	5.20	3.81	115.56	11.92
1987	d23.60	5.21	def	134.21	73.07	def	def	7.13	3.88	98.22	def
1988	24.19	5.83	24.10	103.99	75.61	4.30	3.13	7.71	5.61	113.95	21.23
1989	d13.42	6.19	def	137.59	97.55	def	def	6.35	4.50	93.80	def
1990	5.62	6.73	—	115.28	58.25	20.51	10.36	11.55	5.84	94.08	5.97
1991	2.59	4.60	—	102.28	66.44	39.49	25.65	6.92	4.50	92.27	2.81
1992	10.49	3.66	34.89	129.76	97.85	12.37	9.33	3.74	2.82	100.19	10.47
1993	18.04	3.51	19.46	172.47	125.89	9.56	6.98	2.79	2.04	124.89	14.44

(continued)

TABLE 14-1 (*concluded*)
Banks Composite

Per Share Data—Adjusted to stock price index level. Average of stock price indexes, 1982=100

	Earnings	Dividends		Prices 1982=100		Price/Earn. Ratio		Div. Yields %		Equity	
	Per Share	Per Share	% of Earn.	High	Low	High	Low	High	Low	Per Share	% Return
1986	$13.82	$6.49	46.96	$183.75	$138.28	13.30	10.01	4.69	3.53	NA	—
1987	d26.09	6.82	def	187.04	108.40	def	def	6.29	3.65	NA	—
1988	20.75	7.09	34.17	152.78	114.73	7.36	5.53	6.18	4.64	$136.33	15.22
1989	2.18	7.76	355.96	198.10	141.94	90.87	46.23	5.47	3.92	131.84	1.65
1990	10.01	8.17	81.62	167.66	87.83	16.75	8.77	9.30	4.87	131.15	7.63
1991	5.61	6.33	112.83	172.15	100.44	30.69	17.90	6.30	3.68	129.73	4.32
1992	15.65	5.80	37.06	220.26	174.00	14.07	11.12	3.33	2.63	143.64	10.90
1993	23.17	6.51	28.10	258.46	212.15	11.16	9.16	3.07	2.52	165.89	13.97

Source: From Standard & Poor's, *The Analyst's Handbook, 1994.* Reprinted by permission of Standard & Poor's, a division of The McGraw-Hill Companies.

percent or more of total expenses. The resulting leverage offered the potential for greater return, through expansion into new activities with borrowed money, but also increased risk. This becomes serious when the economy that absorbs the loans becomes depressed, as in Texas.

2. A "growth" philosophy, coupled with the need to cover rapidly rising expenses, led to the liberalization of lending policies and a sharp rise in loan losses in the 1970s and 1980s. Critics feel that this liberalization went too far in several cases, and one must consider the quality of bank assets when considering purchase of their stocks. Loan quality improved sharply in the 1990s. The FDIC reported that noncurrent loans and leases totaled $35.9 billion as of June 30, 1994, down 34 percent from $54.2 billion one year earlier. The ratio of noncurrent loans, leases, and other real estate owned to assets declined to 1.27 percent in the second quarter of 1994 from 2.18 percent in the comparable year-earlier-quarter and 1.61 percent at year-end 1993. This has allowed banks to reduce the provision for loan losses, contributing to increased profitability. There was a fear of a serious credit problem for banks in the 1980s, but the threat seems to have been alleviated.

3. The erosion of bank capital. "In the early 1960s bank net worth generally exceeded 10 percent of total assets, with few exceptions. The growth of assets since that Golden Age has so greatly exceeded the growth of capital that this key ratio ranged between 4 percent and 8 percent"[2] in 1979. New risk-adjusted capital guidelines which central banks of 10 nations proposed in 1987 have now been accepted. These requirements are intended to create equitable competition internationally, and provide adequate capital for depositor and stockholder protection. Common and preferred capital has been rising as a percent of total assets during the 1990s (see Table 14–2) and averaged over 9 percent by year-end 1994. This ratio exceeded 8 percent in 1983, for the first time since 1963. Banks have built strong balance sheets in the 1990s.

4. The growth of overhead resulting from the addition of new headquarters buildings, extensive branching networks, and the addition of computer hardware. Staff compensation also has risen sharply. Expense levels are too high at many banks, and they must concentrate on pruning away underperforming businesses and enhancing productivity.

---

2 Ibid, p. 8.

TABLE 14-2
UBPR National Data—All Insured Commercial Banks

	12/31/94	12/31/93	12/31/92	12/31/91	12/31/90
	Summary Ratios				
Earnings and Profitability					
Percent of average assets:					
Interest income (TE)	7.12	7.19	7.96	9.06	9.64
– Interest expense	2.67	2.73	3.49	4.86	5.46
Net interest income (TE)	4.43	4.43	4.45	4.21	4.19
+ Noninterest income	0.72	0.74	0.74	0.72	0.69
Memo: Fee income	0.15	0.15	0.15	0.14	NA
– Non-interest expense	3.30	3.35	3.37	3.34	3.27
– Provision: Loan and lease losses	0.10	0.14	0.23	0.27	0.28
= Pretax operating income (TE)	1.77	1.72	1.62	1.35	1.36
+ Realized gains/losses secs	0.00	0.02	0.03	0.02	0.00
= Pretax net operating inc (TE)	1.75	1.77	1.70	1.40	1.37
Net operating income	1.14	1.16	1.10	0.91	0.89
Adjusted net operating income	1.18	1.20	1.17	0.97	0.96
Adjusted net income	1.18	1.23	1.18	0.98	0.97
Net income	1.14	1.19	1.13	0.93	0.90
Margin Analysis					
Avg earning assets to avg assets	93.09	92.87	92.76	92.79	92.65
Avg. int-bearing funds to avg. ast	77.19	77.86	78.81	79.29	78.77
Int. inc (TE) to avg. earn assets	7.67	7.76	8.61	9.78	10.43
Int. expense to avg. earn assets	2.88	2.94	3.77	5.24	5.91
Net int inc (TE) to avg. earn asset	4.77	4.79	4.82	4.55	4.54
Loan and Lease Analysis					
Net loss to average total LN&LS	0.12	0.18	0.32	0.41	0.41
Earnings coverage of net loss (X)	21.16	16.01	10.72	7.44	7.50
LN&LS allowance to net losses (X)	10.20	7.70	5.16	4.09	3.94
LN&LS allowance to total LN&LS	1.54	1.62	1.66	1.60	1.54
Non-current LN&LS to gross LN&LS	0.68	0.86	1.09	1.39	1.43
Liquidity					
Volatile liability dependence	–3.96	–8.77	–9.66	–8.56	–8.85
Net loans and leases to assets	56.52	53.61	52.29	52.80	52.80
Capitalization					
Tier one leverage capital	9.24	8.94	8.63	8.33	8.24
Cash dividends to net income	35.88	32.49	29.63	35.02	37.26
Retain earns to avg. total equity	6.84	7.47	7.49	5.55	5.07

(continued)

TABLE 14–2 *(continued)*

	12/31/94	12/31/93	12/31/92	12/31/91	12/31/90
Growth Rates					
Assets	3.59	4.05	5.07	4.83	6.50
Tier one capital	7.66	8.63	8.79	6.60	NA
Net loans and leases	9.91	7.34	4.50	3.85	7.20
Temporary investments	−12.24	3.80	5.79	1.44	−1.25
Volatile liabilities	16.40	6.62	−5.84	−3.76	7.29
Total assets ($ millions)	3,970,387	3,699,239	3,490,740	3,417,292	3,376,370
Equity capital ($ millions)	308,299	295,341	262,970	230,557	217,079
Net income ($ millions)	44,196	43,045	31,978	17,838	16,035
Number of banks in nation	10,450	10,958	11,462	11,921	12,341

Overhead, Yield, and Cost Ratios

	12/31/94	12/31/93	12/31/92	12/31/91	12/31/90
Percent of Average Assets					
Personnel expense	1.64	1.63	1.61	1.59	1.59
Occupancy expense	0.42	0.43	0.43	0.43	0.44
Other oper exp (incl. intangibles)	1.19	1.24	1.27	1.26	1.18
Total overhead expense	3.30	3.35	3.37	3.34	3.27
O/H and interest on mort and leases	3.30	3.35	3.37	3.35	3.28
Overhead less noninterest income	2.50	2.51	2.54	2.54	2.50
Other Income and Expense Ratios					
Avg personnel exp per empl ($000)	31.94	30.83	29.81	28.42	27.13
Assets per employee ($ million)	2.04	1.99	1.96	1.89	1.82
Marginal tax rate	35.71	35.11	35.18	35.17	35.28
Yield on or Cost of					
Total loans and leases (TE)	8.98	9.16	9.94	11.07	11.60
Total loans	8.96	9.13	9.91	11.04	11.57
Real estate**	8.70	8.94	9.72	10.73	11.13
Commercial time, demand, oth**	8.74	8.51	9.13	10.57	11.39
Installment**	9.63	10.22	11.12	11.90	12.18
Credit card plans	13.99	14.29	14.76	15.14	15.37
Memo: Agricultural LNS in above	8.63	8.60	9.25	10.75	11.41
Loans in foreign offices	6.35	5.65	6.36	8.42	9.85
Total investment securities (TE)	5.89	6.27	7.38	8.46	8.87
US Treas. agcy and oth debt	5.51	5.92	7.11	8.23	8.61
State and political sub (Book)	5.64	6.05	6.65	7.09	7.37
State and political sub (TE)	8.12	8.72	9.56	10.16	10.53
Equity securities	4.97	4.48	4.56	4.69	4.57

(continued)

TABLE 14–2 *(continued)*

	12/31/94	*12/31/93*	*12/31/92*	*12/31/91*	*12/31/90*
Interest-bearing bank balances	4.51	4.43	5.64	7.42	8.66
Federal funds sold and resales	4.03	2.95	3.44	5.62	8.07
Total interest-bearing deposits	3.44	3.51	4.44	6.14	6.94
Transaction accounts	2.31	2.46	3.18	4.66	5.01
Money market deposit accounts	2.79	2.83	3.54	5.18	5.80
Other savings deposits	2.72	2.87	3.59	4.98	5.20
Large certificates of deposit	4.08	3.93	4.89	6.72	7.89
All other time deposits	4.18	4.25	5.28	6.92	7.82
Deposits in foreign offices	4.28	3.16	3.87	6.10	8.22
Federal funds purchased and repos	4.25	3.03	3.61	5.61	7.68
Other borrowed money	3.63	2.44	2.69	4.33	5.07
Subordinated notes and debentures	7.10	7.15	7.56	8.90	9.22
All interest-bearing funds	3.47	3.51	4.43	6.13	6.94

**Banks under $300 million in total assets report this loan detail (by type) using their own internal categorization systems.

Balance Sheet—Percentage Composition of Assets and Liabilities

Percent of Average Assets

Assets

Total loans	55.99	53.98	53.72	54.23	54.43
Lease financing receivables	0.00	0.00	0.00	0.00	0.00
Less: LN&LS allowance & ATRR	0.87	0.87	0.85	0.83	0.81
Net loans and leases	55.26	53.21	52.94	53.47	53.68
Interest-bearing bank balances	0.21	0.31	0.49	0.76	0.93
Federal funds sold and resales	2.85	4.01	4.30	4.67	5.08
Trading account assets	0.00	0.00	0.00	0.00	0.00
Held-to-maturity securities	18.41	31.99	31.20	29.35	27.89
Available-for-sale securities	10.27	NA	NA	NA	NA
Total earning assets	92.08	91.98	91.70	91.55	91.40
Nonint cash and due from banks	4.19	4.28	4.36	4.35	4.50
Premises, fix assets, and cap leases	1.46	1.43	1.42	1.43	
Other real estate owned	0.10	0.19	0.26	0.28	0.25
Acceptances and other assets	1.64	1.55	1.63	1.76	1.77
Subtotal	7.91	8.02	8.30	8.45	8.60
Total assets	100.00	100.00	100.00	100.00	100.00
Standby letters of credit	0.20	0.19	0.18	0.18	0.19

(continued)

TABLE 14–2 *(continued)*

	12/31/94	*12/31/93*	*12/31/92*	*12/31/91*	*12/31/90*
Liabilities					
Demand deposits	12.23	11.76	11.17	10.92	11.42
All NOW & ATS accounts	13.16	13.07	12.25	11.01	10.48
Money market deposit accounts	9.59	10.11	10.09	9.28	9.12
Other savings deposits	10.00	9.82	8.56	7.05	6.76
Time dep. under $100M	30.52	31.74	34.66	37.69	37.33
Core deposits	80.43	81.37	81.21	80.00	79.15
Time dep. over $100M	6.51	6.39	7.10	8.51	9.35
Deposits in foreign offices	5.78	3.89	3.76	3.94	3.93
Total deposits	88.03	88.71	89.19	89.36	89.35
Federal funds purch and repos	0.57	0.29	0.23	0.20	0.15
Other borrowings incl mat < 1 yr	0.08	0.07	0.04	0.04	0.04
Volatile liabilities	8.95	8.40	8.78	10.08	10.87
Other borrowings mat > 1 yr	0.00	NA	NA	NA	NA
Acceptances and other liabilities	0.65	0.69	0.80	0.94	1.03
Total liabilities (incl mortg)	90.88	91.03	91.39	91.61	91.64
Subordinated notes and debentures	0.00	0.00	0.00	0.00	0.00
All common and preferred capital	9.09	8.93	8.58	8.36	8.33
Total liabilities and capital	100.00	100.00	100.00	100.00	100.00
Memo: All brokered deposits	0.00	0.00	0.00	0.00	0.00
Insured brokered dep.	0.00	0.00	0.00	0.00	NA

Off-Balance-Sheet Items

Percent of Total Assets					
Unused commitments					
Home equity (1–4 Family)	0.18	0.17	0.15	0.12	0.10
Credit card	0.13	0.10	0.09	0.06	0.04
Commercial RE secured by RE	0.57	0.47	0.35	0.28	0.30
Commercl RE not secured by RE	0.00	0.00	0.00	0.00	NA
All other	3.45	3.01	2.62	2.31	1.99
Total LN&LS commitments	6.01	5.36	4.73	4.23	3.91
Securities underwriting	0.00	0.00	0.00	0.00	0.00
Standby letters of credit	0.19	0.18	0.17	0.16	0.16
Amount conveyed to others	0.00	0.00	0.00	0.00	0.00

(continued)

TABLE 14–2 *(continued)*

	12/31/94	12/31/93	12/31/92	12/31/91	12/31/90
Commercial letters of credit	0.00	0.00	0.00	0.00	0.00
Interest rate contracts					
Notional val of int rate swaps	0.00	0.00	0.00	0.00	0.00
Futures and forward contracts	0.00	0.00	0.00	0.00	0.00
Option contracts	0.00	0.00	0.00	0.00	0.00
Foreign exchange rate contracts					
Notional val of exchange swaps	0.00	0.00	0.00	0.00	0.00
Commitments to pur foreign cur	0.00	0.00	0.00	0.00	0.00
Option contracts	0.00	0.00	0.00	0.00	0.00
Principal balance of mtg pools	0.00	0.00	0.00	0.00	0.00
Amount of recourse exposure	0.00	0.00	0.00	0.00	0.00
All oth off-balance-sheet items	0.00	0.00	0.00	0.00	0.00
Gross off-balance-sheet items	6.63	6.04	5.33	4.86	4.53

Capital Analysis

Capital Analysis Ratios

Percent of total equity:					
Net loans & leases (X)	6.29	5.95	6.06	6.34	6.57
Subord notes & debentures	0.00	0.00	0.00	0.00	0.00
Long term debt	0.00	0.00	0.00	0.00	0.00
Com RE & related ventures	101.46	94.47	96.23	99.49	NA
Percent of average total equity:					
Net income	12.21	12.93	12.61	10.60	10.27
Dividends	4.12	3.90	3.42	3.29	3.40
Retained earnings	6.84	7.47	7.49	5.55	5.07
Other capital ratios:					
Dividends to net oper income	35.94	33.36	29.90	35.37	37.70
Equity capital to assets	9.01	9.01	8.62	8.33	8.19
Def tax assets to T1 cap	2.38	0.80	NA	NA	NA
Intang assets % total equity					
Mortgage servicing rights	0.00	0.00	0.00	0.00	0.00
Goodwill	0.00	0.00	0.00	0.00	0.00
Purch credit card relation	0.00	0.00	0.00	NA	NA
All other intangibles	0.00	0.00	0.00	0.00	0.00
Total intangibles	0.01	0.00	0.00	0.00	0.00

(continued)

TABLE 14–2 *(concluded)*

	12/31/94	*12/31/93*	*12/31/92*	*12/31/91*	*12/31/90*
Growth rates:					
Total equity capital	4.01	8.91	8.65	6.58	5.95
Equity growth less asst. growth	−0.11	4.64	3.28	1.18	−1.15
Risk-based capital:*					
Tier one RBC to risk-wgt assets	15.37	15.40	15.01	14.25	13.91
Total RBC to risk-weight assets	16.56	16.60	16.21	15.43	15.09
Tier one leverage capital	9.24	8.94	8.63	8.33	8.24

*All risk-based capital calculations reflect the December 31, 1992 Final Implementation Rules. Peer group data includes estimates for those banks that did not report schedule RC-R data as well as actual reported figures.

Source: "Uniform Bank Peformance Report" (Washington, D.C.: Federal Financial Institutions Examination Council, December 31, 1994).

5. Competition has intensified, both from other banks and from other financial institutions.

6. While too early to make definitive judgments, many questions are being raised about mergers of the last several years. The expected efficiencies and synergies appear to be inadequate to support the high price paid in several instances. Merger activity has expanded sharply in 1994–95.

7. The regulatory climate continues to change, but new powers granted the banks often are in thinner-margined products that will not lead to immediate substantial gains.

8. Bank profitability trended downward in the 1980s, and loan quality problems mounted. The banking industry, however, posted record profits in 1993 and 1994. Profitability was aided by industry-wide efforts to lower expenses by eliminating nonstrategic assets and marginal business lines and by streamlining back-office operations. Standard and Poor's notes that while a "60 percent efficiency ratio (noninterest expense divided by net revenues) was once considered an ambitious target, banks now shoot for efficiency ratios of 55 percent or less."[3] Industry consolidation through mergers and acquisitions has also helped lower costs.

---

3 Stephen Biggar, Standard and Poor's *Industry Surveys, Banking,* November 3, 1994, p. B15.

9. Security markets are providing the most significant competition to giant banks. Borrowers increasingly tap the money markets directly—for example, through the issue of commercial paper. Loans to large corporations actually are made at a loss at times to retain other profitable services sold to these corporations.

10. Deposit growth has been sluggish in the 1990s, reflecting a consumer exodus from low-yielding bank deposits into higher-yielding alternatives (such as money market funds and mutual funds). Bank efforts to compete with these higher-yielding alternatives could cause margins to fall. Banks have increased their participation in the mutual fund business to maintain their customer base. It is not yet clear as to whether the drive into mutual funds will pay off.

11. Improved credit quality, stabilizing margins, cost containment efforts, and stock performance painted a strong picture for banks by mid-1995. Several factors briefly discussed below raise questions about the continuation of this strong performance and should be watched closely:

    a. Loan demand has increased, but fierce competition, both among banks and with other financial institutions, has generated pricing pressures and could compromise credit quality as banks fight for market share.

    b. Banks have experienced favorable interest rate conditions in the early 1990s, but interest rates could begin to rise, especially the rates banks have to pay to attract needed funds.

    c. Banks have been very cost conscious during the 1990s, but they must not let costs begin to rise relative to revenues.

    d. Banks have earned lucrative fees for participating in the derivatives markets. Derivatives are trading instruments whose value derives from the price of another underlying asset. This derivatives market has grown from less than $1 trillion in contract amounts in 1987 to $35 trillion by 1994. Banks have recently experienced some large losses dealing in this market, and bank activity in this area must be watched closely.

Financial Analysis of Commercial Bank Stocks

As with other industries, an investor is interested in the financial strength and the earning power of a bank. Ratio analysis of bank financial statements is the primary tool used by security analysts, paying attention to both the level and trend of the ratios studied. Any such analysis should be forward looking. The goal of any security analysis is to use past and present performance characteristics as a basis for assessing future prospects.

Earnings: The key variable. Banks must earn competitive rates on their capital if they are to be attractive to investors. The relative importance of various income and expense components for commercial banks is presented in Table 14–2. When analyzing bank operations, one should concentrate on bank earnings—that is, income before security transactions, not net income. One should not lose sight, however, of the fact that net income represents the base from which dividends to stockholders are paid and is the primary source of growth capital generated by bank operations. Salomon Brothers produces a useful publication, entitled "A Review of Bank Performance," that offers average ratios for selected banks that can be used for comparative purposes, as can the data in Table 14–2.

Rate earned on average assets. This is the best indicator of the efficiency of bank operations and earnings performance. It is calculated by dividing net income by total average assets. Return on assets (ROA) for most banks falls within a range of 0.60 to 1.40 percent. The average return on assets for all insured commercial banks rose from 1990 to 1993 (1.19 in 1993) and then fell a bit to 1.14 by year-end 1994. Regional and community banks are likely to have an ROA in the upper range, reflecting lower cost of funds and a higher-yielding loan mix. Large regional and money center banks, on the other hand, may well have an ROA in the lower part of the range because of reliance on more-expensive purchased funds. A stock-holder, remember, is more interested in ROA as a component of return on common equity than in the number itself. One should not lose sight of this fact.

Float can distort the interpretation of this ratio since it is not an indicator of management performance.[4] Also, the portion of earnings derived from non-funds-using sources of income (such as trust services) can vary from bank to bank.

Rate earned on average equity capital. Prior to 1980, the rate of return earned on average equity capital was a bit below the average rate

---

[4] Checks in the process of collection can be a large or small fraction of total assets at any given time, thereby tending to raise or lower return on assets.

earned by manufacturing corporations. This could explain the lower price–earnings ratio typically accorded bank stocks during this period. However, the discount at which bank stocks sold relative to earnings performance seemed excessive.

Interestingly, the rate of return earned on stockholders' equity since 1982 by a selected sample of banks (see Table 14–3), has equaled or exceeded the average return for all manufacturing corporations (see Table 11–2). For example, the average for the composite bank sample in 1982 was 14.18 percent, while the average for all manufacturing corporations was only 9.2 percent. While bank price–earnings ratios were higher relative to the S&P 500 in the 1980s than they were through much of the 1970s, they were still at a discount. This could reflect a belief by the market that banks represent higher-than-average risk or that bank profits are overstated, as we will suggest later.

Banks do employ leverage. Equity is a relatively small fraction of bank assets (approximately 8 percent in 1995), and return on equity is accordingly much higher (10–20 percent) than return on assets. The components determining return on equity and assets, as well as a detailed evaluation of the income statement, should be considered as a whole when evaluating a bank stock.

Leverage and rates of return.   Changes in the level of bank earnings from year to year are determined by the rate earned on total bank assets, the rate of growth of those assets, and leverage factors as shown in Table 14–4. A rising return on assets and increased leverage (measured by dividing average total assets by average shareholders' equity) did result in a higher rate of return being earned on stockholders' equity after 1977 than before. Interestingly, bank price–earnings ratios, on average, still fell to a historic low 54.6 percent of the average P/E ratio for the S&P 500 stocks in the fourth quarter of 1980, before recovery. Bank performance just doesn't seem to explain the disfavor into which their common stocks had fallen by the end of 1980. Selective purchases of bank stocks since 1980 would have led to good results.

Noninterest income and expense.   Noninterest income is generated by a variety of sources, including service charges, trust department income, and profits on currency and bond trading. Noninterest income has been rising in relative importance and constitutes about 30 percent of net revenues at most banks. Larger banks tend to have a greater proportion of noninterest income than smaller banks.

TABLE 14–3

Net Income, and as a Percentage of Average Total Equity, 1982–86 (Dollars in Millions)

	1982		1983		1984		1985		1986		1993	
Bank of New York	$ 73	15.29%	$ 91	14.47%	$ 108	14.78%	$ 130	14.61%	$ 155	15.24%	$ 615	13.0%
Bankers Trust NY	223	16.13	257	15.49	307	15.66	371	16.11	428	15.93	1,205	14.0
Chase Manhattan	307	10.00	430	12.89	406	10.93	565	13.59	585	12.45		
Chemical NY	241	13.61	306	14.37	341	14.16	390	14.59	402	13.63	1,294	12.0
Citicorp	723	15.83	860	15.99	890	14.39	998	14.15	1,058	12.56	3,366	19.0
Irving Bank Corp.	81	11.95	92	11.67	98	11.56	116	12.64	128	12.76		
Manufacturers Hanover	295	13.45	337	13.06	353	11.33	407	11.94	411	11.22		
J.P. Morgan & Co.	394	15.50	460	14.78	538	15.29	705	17.40	873	18.25	1,215	13.0
Marine Midland	87	10.21	101	10.13	91	8.39	125	10.88	145	11.36		
Republic NY Corp.	71	17.90	85	15.42	97	14.04	122	13.93	149	13.94	340	13.0
Bank of Boston Corp.	124	14.70	136	14.44	164	15.04	174	13.32	233	14.88	435	14.0
First Chicago	137	10.19	184	11.07	86	4.51	169	8.44	276	12.38	690	15.0
Money Center Total Composite	$2,756	13.71%	$3,337	14.05%	$3,477	12.76%	$4,273	13.87%	$4,843	13.70%		
Fleet Financial	$ 55	16.94%	$ 71	16.44%	$87	16.80%	$ 106	17.36%	$ 137	19.08%	$ 613	18.0%
Norstar Bancorp	44	16.42	58	14.31	77	14.91	93	14.09	105	14.42		
Midlantic Corp.	76	17.10	81	15.83	106	17.17	142	17.69	148	15.43	272	20.0
CoreStates Financial	61	13.91	91	15.62	116	16.56	115	13.86	148	15.54	245	10.0
Mellon Bank Corp.	134	13.20	184	14.25	159	10.35	202	12.26	183	9.79	433	12.0
PNC Financial Corp.	130	16.20	146	16.37	177	16.80	229	17.61	286	18.71	610	14.0

(continued)

TABLE 14–3 (concluded)

	1982	1983	1984	1985	1986	1993
AmeriTrust Corp.	$ 64 10.54	$ 55 8.57	$ 76 11.16	$ 86 11.80	$ 89 11.10	
Banc One Corp	82 13.92	111 14.93	143 15.25	177 16.05	200 15.83	$1,005 13.0
National City Corp.	44 11.33	48 11.84	66 13.87	108 15.51	135 16.76	429 17.0
NBD Bancorp	82 11.29	82 10.57	95 11.43	118 12.84	146 13.97	532 16.0
First Bank System	115 13.10	130 13.15	131 11.85	167 14.15	203 15.31	420 18.0
Norwest Corp.	89 9.36	125 11.53	70 6.03	108 9.04	122 9.59	800 21.0
NCNB Corp.	88 16.10	106 16.38	133 16.30	164 17.23	199 16.31	
First Wachovia Corp.	91 14.52	133 18.73	156 19.05	188 19.57	194 17.68	
Barnett Banks	49 12.36	81 16.16	106 16.72	134 16.51	162 16.77	488 16.0
SunTrust Banks	119 16.74	155 18.37	194 16.62	216 16.39	245 16.81	523 15.0
RepublicBank Corp.	144 17.08	130 13.82	137 12.81	140 11.91	54 4.40	340 13.0
Valley National	51 12.86	46 10.81	60 13.25	77 15.22	65 11.62	
BankAmerican Corp.	395 9.29	390 7.82	346 6.68	−337 −6.83	−518 −12.16	2,176 12.0
First Interstate	221 13.12	247 13.01	276 12.68	313 13.11	338 12.92	734 21.0
Security Pacific	234 16.85	264 16.12	291 15.65	323 15.30	386 14.62	
Wells Fargo & Co.	139 13.09	155 12.29	169 12.60	190 13.50	274 13.37	841 22.0
U.S. Bancorp	52 11.95	52 11.22	60 11.91	66 12.03	77 12.80	151 9.0
Regional Bank Total Composite	$2,560 12.94%	$2,942 12.74%	$3,232 12.35%	$3,125 10.85%	$3,376 10.56%	
Total Composite	$5,316 13.33%	$6,279 13.40%	$6,708 12.56%	$7,398 12.41%	$8,218 12.21%	

Source: T. Hanley, J. Rosenberg, C. D'Arista and E. Krahmer, *A Review of Bank Performance: 1987 Edition* (New York: Salomon Brothers, Inc., April, 1987), p. 29.

TABLE 14–4
The Interplay of Asset Leverage and Profit Margins on Return on Equity, 1982–86

	1982			1983		
	$Leverage^a$ ×	ROA^b =	ROE^c	$Leverage^a$ ×	ROA^b =	ROE^c
Bank of New York	25.6x	0.60%	15.3%	20.3x	0.71%	14.5%
Bankers Trust NY	28.7	0.60	16.1	23.5	0.67	15.5
Chase Manhattan	26.4	0.40	10.0	24.3	0.54	12.9
Chemical NY	25.9	0.54	13.6	22.6	0.64	14.4
Citicorp	26.7	0.60	15.8	23.9	0.67	16.0
Irving Bank Corp.	28.2	0.42	11.9	24.3	0.48	11.7
Manufacturers Hanover	27.0	0.50	13.4	23.8	0.55	13.1
J. P. Morgan & Co.	22.3	0.69	15.5	18.6	0.79	14.8
Marine Midland	22.8	0.45	10.2	20.9	0.49	10.1
Republic NY Corp.	24.9	0.76	17.9	17.9	0.90	15.4
Bank of Boston Corp.	20.7	0.71	14.7	20.0	0.72	14.4
First Chicago	25.9	0.39	10.2	20.8	0.53	11.1
Money Center Composite	25.7x	0.53%	13.7%	22.4x	0.63%	14.1%
Fleet Financial	16.3x	1.04%	16.9%	14.4x	1.15%	16.4%
Norstar Bancorp	12.8	1.29	16.4	11.3	1.27	14.3
Midlantic Corp.	15.4	1.11	17.1	15.9	0.99	15.8
CoreStates Financial	17.1	0.81	13.9	16.0	0.97	15.6
Mellon Bank Corp.	19.2	0.69	13.2	19.3	0.76	14.2
PNC Financial Corp.	15.7	1.03	16.2	15.5	1.06	16.4
AmeriTrust Corp.	10.0	1.06	10.5	9.6	0.89	8.6
Banc One Corp.	14.6	0.96	13.9	14.3	1.07	14.9
National City Corp.	14.9	0.76	11.3	15.4	0.77	11.8
NBD Bancorp	16.7	0.68	11.3	15.4	0.68	10.6
First Bank System	18.1	0.72	13.1	18.3	0.72	13.1
Norwest Corp.	16.5	0.57	9.4	17.1	0.67	11.5
NCNB Corp.	17.4	0.92	16.1	20.0	0.82	16.4
First Wachovia Corp.	16.5	0.89	14.5	16.8	1.12	18.7
Barnett Banks	18.3	0.68	12.4	19.1	0.85	16.2
SunTrust Banks	16.3	1.03	16.7	16.5	1.11	18.4
Republic Bank Corp.	19.0	0.90	17.1	18.5	0.75	13.8
Valley National	16.6	0.78	12.9	17.0	0.64	10.8
Bank America Corp.	28.2	0.33	9.3	24.6	0.32	7.8
First Interstate	22.6	0.58	13.1	21.4	0.61	13.0
Security Pacific	25.0	0.67	16.8	22.6	0.71	16.1
Wells Fargo & Co.	23.4	0.56	13.1	20.2	0.61	12.3
U.S. Bancorp	12.9	0.93	11.19	12.7	0.88	11.2
Regional Bank Composite	20.4x	0.63%	12.9%	19.2x	0.66%	12.7%
Composite	23.1x	0.58%	13.3%	20.8x	0.64%	13.4%

(continued)

TABLE 14–4 (continued)

	1984			1985		
	Leverage[a]	× ROA[b]	= ROE[c]	Leveragea	× ROA[b]	= ROE[c]
Bank of New York	18.4x	0.80%	14.8%	17.3x	0.84%	14.6%
Bankers Trust NY	22.0	0.71	15.7	20.5	0.79	16.1
Chase Manhattan	23.3	0.48	10.9	20.9	0.65	13.6
Chemical NY	22.5	0.63	14.2	20.8	0.70	14.6
Citicorp	23.2	0.62	14.4	22.9	0.62	14.2
Irving Bank Corp.	24.1	0.48	11.6	23.1	0.55	12.6
Manufacturers Hanover	22.7	0.50	11.3	22.0	0.54	11.9
J. P. Morgan & Co.	17.5	0.87	15.3	16.4	1.06	17.4
Marine Midland	20.0	0.42	8.4	17.9	0.61	10.9
Republic NY Corp.	15.9	0.91	14.0	15.2	0.93	13.9
Bank of Boston Corp.	19.1	0.79	15.0	18.2	0.73	13.3
First Chicago	20.1	0.22	4.5	19.8	0.43	8.4
Money Center Composite	21.5x	0.60%	12.8%	20.3x	0.68%	13.9%
Fleet Financial	13.5x	1.25%	16.8%	13.1x	1.33%	17.4%
Norstar Bancorp	12.3	1.16	14.2	12.6	1.12	14.1
Midlantic Corp.	16.4	1.04	17.2	16.4	1.08	17.7
CoreStates Financial	14.8	1.12	16.6	13.9	1.00	13.9
Mellon Bank Corp.	19.2	0.57	10.4	19.4	0.67	12.3
PNC Financial Corp.	15.0	1.12	16.8	15.5	1.14	17.6
AmeriTrust Corp.	9.4	1.18	11.2	10.1	1.17	11.8
Banc One Corp.	14.0	1.13	15.3	13.5	1.23	16.0
National City Corp.	15.4	0.90	13.9	16.9	0.92	15.5
NBD Bancorp	16.0	0.71	11.4	16.5	0.78	12.8
First Bank System	19.0	0.63	11.9	20.2	0.70	14.1
Norwest Corp.	17.9	0.34	6.0	16.7	0.54	9.0
NCNB Corp.	19.4	0.84	16.3	18.7	0.92	17.2
First Wachovia Corp.	17.1	1.11	19.1	16.6	1.18	19.6
Barnett Banks	19.5	0.86	16.7	18.2	0.91	16.5
SunTrust Banks	16.0	1.04	16.6	16.0	1.03	16.4
Republic Bank Corp.	18.9	0.68	12.8	18.6	0.64	11.9
Valley National	17.7	0.75	13.3	17.6	0.86	15.2
Bank America Corp.	23.2	0.29	6.7	24.1	−0.28	−6.8
First Interstate	19.8	0.64	12.7	19.5	0.67	13.1
Security Pacific	22.0	0.71	15.6	22.2	0.69	15.3
Wells Fargo & Co.	20.3	0.62	12.6	20.3	0.67	13.5
U.S. Bancorp	13.5	0.88	11.9	14.2	0.85	12.0
Regional Bank Composite	18.7x	0.66%	12.4%	18.6x	0.58%	10.8%
Composite	20.1x	0.63%	12.6%	19.5x	0.64%	12.4%

[a]Average total assets divided by average shareholders' equity.

[b]Net income divided by average total assets.

[c]Net income retained after dividends on redeemable preferred stock divided by average shareholders' equity.

(continued)

TABLE 14–4 *(concluded)*

	1986		
	Leverage[a] ×	*ROA*[b] =	*ROE*[c]
Bank of New York	17.9x	0.85%	15.2%
Bankers Trust NY	20.2	0.79	15.9
Chase Manhattan	19.3	0.65	12.5
Chemical NY	19.6	0.70	13.6
Citicorp	21.9	0.58	12.6
Irving Bank Corp.	21.3	0.60	12.8
Manufacturers Hanover	20.8	0.54	11.2
J. P. Morgan & Co.	15.3	1.19	18.3
Marine Midland	17.4	0.65	11.4
Republic NY Corp.	16.6	0.85	13.9
Bank of Boston Corp.	19.0	0.78	14.9
First Chicago	17.4	0.71	12.4
Money Center Composite	19.4x	0.71%	13.7%
Fleet Financial	14.0x	1.37%	19.1%
Norstar Bancorp	13.5	1.07	14.4
Midlantic Corp.	16.3	0.95	15.4
CoreStates Financial	14.4	1.08	15.5
Mellon Bank Corp.	19.1	0.54	9.8
PNC Financial Corp.	15.4	1.22	18.7
AmeriTrust Corp.	10.8	1.03	11.1
Banc One Corp.	13.3	1.23	15.8
National City Corp.	15.4	1.09	16.8
NBD Bancorp	16.8	0.83	14.0
First Bank System	20.0	0.76	15.3
Norwest Corp.	15.4	0.62	9.6
NCNB Corp.	19.5	0.84	16.3
First Wachovia Corp.	15.4	1.15	17.7
Barnett Banks	18.2	0.92	16.8
SunTrust Banks	16.4	1.03	16.8
Republic Bank Corp.	17.8	0.25	4.4
Valley National	17.4	0.67	11.6
Bank America Corp.	26.7	−0.45	−12.2
First Interstate	19.1	0.68	12.9
Security Pacific	20.6	0.71	14.6
Wells Fargo & Co.	18.3	0.73	13.4
U.S. Bancorp	14.2	0.90	12.8
Regional Bank Composite	18.4x	0.58%	10.6%
Composite	18.9x	0.65%	12.2%

Source: T. Hanley, et al., op. cit., pp. 56 and 57.

Noninterest expenses also have been rising relative to total income for many banks, often reflecting higher personnel and computer costs. When the level is rising at a particular bank, it can be an indication of inefficient operations. Rises in noninterest expenses should be carefully investigated to determine if they are justified.

Other key performance ratios. Other ratios useful in analyzing bank performance and financial strength are reviewed as follows:

1. The following four ratios should be reviewed to give an indication of possible asset quality problems resulting from the loan decisions of the bank:

   a. Period-end reserve for loan losses to period-end loans.

   b. Net loan charge-offs to average total loans.

   c. Provision for loan losses to net charge-offs of that period.

   d. Nonperforming assets to loans. This ratio indicates the proportion of total loans that are in default.

2. Financial strength is measured by balance sheet as well as income statement ratios. The following are important ratios to study over time.

   a. Subordinated debt to total capital accounts. Although this ratio is low for all insured commercial banks, it tends to be large for large money center banks. While the subordination reduces risk somewhat for the purchaser of such instruments, it really does not reduce bank risk.

   b. Ratio of capital accounts to assets, deposits, and loans. In the early 1960s, bank capital accounts generally exceeded 10 percent of total assets. Asset growth, financed mainly by adding bank liabilities, has reduced this ratio to 4 to 8 percent today, depending on bank size, location, and management policy. There has been an erosion of bank capital, and the low P/E ratios, already reviewed for bank stocks, make raising new equity capital painful. Bank analysts should and do watch the capital formation rate from internal sources in relation to the rate of asset growth. They also monitor the maturity of debt, as well as the total outstanding.

   c. Ratio of time and savings deposits to total deposits. The higher the proportion of time and savings deposits to total deposits for a bank, the greater the interest cost. Time and savings deposits represented only about 22 percent of total deposits for the average bank in 1945. By December 1980, this ratio was about 64 percent. The increased interest expense resulting from this change in deposit makeup has led banks to reach for higher-yielding loans and asset mixes, no doubt thereby increasing investor risk.

d. Ratio of cash and U.S. government securities to total assets and deposits. This ratio indicates the immediate liquidity of the bank. Analysts expect the ratio to be at least 12 percent of total assets and 15 percent of deposits.

e. Dividends per share divided by earnings per share (the payout ratio).

Bank Merger Movement

Technology and deregulation have stimulated consolidation in the field of banking. At the time of writing this book, we are experiencing one of the most active acquisition environments for banks in 15 years. Changes in regional interstate banking laws have led to the creation of giant banks (Nations Bank Corp., First Union, and Banc One Corp., for example). Bills being introduced into Congress (such as the *Financial Services Competitiveness Act of 1995*) would likely further stimulate merger activity. Moreover, size does not appear to eliminate the possibility of being taken over. There is now only one large bank based in Philadelphia, and CoreStates has just ended merger discussions with the Bank of Boston.

Growth of many banks has been relatively flat for the last few years, and banks want to avoid losing more pieces of their business to nonbank competitors. It is worth noting that all other G-10 nations now permit banking organizations to affiliate with security and insurance firms and other financial entities. Clearly the United States is moving to loosen restrictions on bank acquisitions. It appears that bank holding companies could achieve risk reduction through diversification of their financial services.

The merger movement will offer potential gain to investors, but risk will also be present. The banking world is changing rapidly, and selection on the part of investors will be important. Rumors will affect bank stock performance in the short run, and careful valuation analysis is necessary to avoid being caught up in crowd movement. We would expect the number of banks to shrink, while the size of individual banks will grow. Banks with assets of $10 billion to $70 billion are not too big to be taken over.

The net interest margin.   Banks have depended increasingly on purchased money (the incurrence of liabilities) to finance asset growth since 1961. Steadily rising interest rates throughout the 1970s, coupled with the rapidly increasing debt taken on by banks, has resulted in interest expense becoming a large and volatile number. This has led analysts to stress the concept of "net interest margin." Net interest margin is measured by dividing net interest income by average earning assets. This ratio should be considered in terms of the history of the bank being reviewed and the average ratio for similar-sized banks. A net interest margin below the average suggests inefficient use of assets. On the other hand, a ratio that much exceeds the average for similar banks could suggest a bank that has courted high-risk loans and investments.

A break-even yield also can be computed for a bank by dividing total interest expense by average gross earning assets. The break-even yield indicates the yield required on earning assets merely to cover interest expense. "For a retail-oriented bank, heavy in demand and savings-type deposits, the norm for break-even yield tends to range between 2 and 3 percent, changing little from year to year. For many wholesale banks, which "buy" most of their investible funds, the break-even yield is not only much higher (5 to 7 percent), but fluctuates according to interest rate movements."[5]

Financial reports tend to confuse.[6]

In a recent paper, David Cates identifies five frontiers of confusion that hamper effective analysis of bank financial statements. Each of these is discussed below.

1. Recurring profitability often is masked by the handling of nonrecurring and discretionary accounting events. For example, security gains taken in a rising market "may reflect transient trading opportunities captured by an active manager" that may not be repeated in the future. Another example is the highly discretionary approach taken by various banks toward their loan loss provisions. Also, banks have abused the concept of operating earnings by throwing in office building sales, debt buy-back gains, pension re-accounting, and discretionary

---

5 *Bank Analysis from External Sources*, op. cit., p. 31.

6 This section is based on an unpublished paper by David C. Cates, "The Intelligibility of Banks Has Faded Again" (New York: Cates Consulting Analysts, Inc., Summer 1987).

recognition of gains on all manner of investments. "To illustrate, of the 50 largest bank holding companies reporting in 1986, 24 showed nonrecurring gains and/or net securities gains (all after tax) equal to 15 percent or more of net income, and 14 (excluding Texas banks) reported such items equal to 25 percent or more of net income."[7] This will overstate return on assets in a comparative sense. Investors should attempt to assess recurring earnings when studying bank statements, and reflect this number in return on asset comparisons.

2. Banks are currently permitted to include "equity contract notes" in primary capital. These obligate the bank to sell common stock sufficient to retire the note at or before maturity. This poses possible large dilution to earnings per share, but the amount of dilution is just about impossible to calculate. For a high-quality bank the danger is probably not great, but the damage could be serious for a low-quality bank that has a poor standing in the stock market. Pooling-of-interest accounting also can distort earnings per share comparisons, as we have previously discussed in the book.

3. While assets classified as investment can be restated to market, it is difficult to make similar adjustments for loans. Analysts evaluate loans from signals given by: (a) loan yield; (b) loan mix; (c) demand deposit level; (d) nonperforming loan statistics; (e) net lost interest income; (f) secondary-market bids for LDC debt; and (g) junk bond yields.

4. Large banks have accumulated huge commitments and contingencies represented by off-balance-sheet items. Off-balance-sheet assets may dwarf recorded assets. Income does often include the earnings of these assets, and return on assets is distorted. Analysts need to know much more than is presented in annual reports to properly evaluate the contribution of these activities to the bank and the risk involved.

5. Accounting statements "create fictional capital whose reality must be tested by the market value of assets and by the market value of capital itself."[8] The adequacy of capital must be judged in relation to the risk profile of the bank. Regulators focus on depositor safety, and their measures are not likely to represent stockholders' best interests, which should be the focal point of a stock analysis.

---

7 Ibid, p. 11.

8 Ibid, p. 19.

INSURANCE COMPANY STOCKS

Insurance companies can be divided into two major groups: (1) property and casualty companies, and (2) life insurance companies. The characteristics of these two groups are different so they will be dealt with separately. One difference is that contracts for property and liability companies are relatively short, usually one, two, or three years, while contracts issued by life insurance companies usually run for many years. Some companies are writing multiline life insurance, health and accident policies, and fire and casualty policies. Insurance companies are also classified as either (1) mutual companies, or (2) stock companies. Stock companies are the only ones in which investors can invest.

Insurance Accounting: Regulatory versus GAAP Accounting

Statutory insurance accounting rules that govern the preparation of statutory statements were developed to facilitate the achievement of the objectives of regulation of insurance in the public interest. Statutory statements are basically aimed at helping regulators monitor the solvency of insurers, while working toward assuring fairness, equity, and reasonableness in insurance markets. Conservative valuation rules are, accordingly, applied to both assets and liabilities. Assets are undervalued in terms of GAAP rules and liabilities are overvalued.

In reporting to stockholders, fortunately, insurers typically prepare financial statements based on GAAP rather than statutory rules, as GAAP rules are believed to produce statements that are more meaningful to investors. GAAP rules emphasize the income statement and proper matching of income and expenses, rather than the balance sheet as is emphasized under statutory rules.

Some major ways in which statutory accounting principles differ from GAAP are:[9]

1. GAAP makes no distinction between admitted and nonadmitted assets, as are made under statutory rules. Admitted assets are those recognized as sound assets by appropriate state regulatory authorities

---

[9] This summary is based on Terrie E. Troxel and George E. Bouchie, *Property-Liability Insurance Accounting and Finance* (Bryn Mawr, PA, American Institute for Property and Liability Underwriters, Inc., 1990).

and must be readily convertible to cash at their balance sheet values. Nonadmitted assets are excluded from the balance sheet because they are not readily convertible into cash for an amount approximating their realistic value as operating assets. This reflects the regulators emphasis on solvency of insurance companies to protect policyholders. For example, agents' balances outstanding beyond 90 days and furniture and fixtures would be excluded from the statutory balance sheet, but be included in the balance sheet under GAAP rules.

2. Unauthorized reinsurance is reinsurance that has been placed with an insurer that is not licensed to transact insurance business in a given state. Such reinsurance is not recognized under statutory rules unless the ceding company retains funds adequate to pay potential claims arising under such contracts. GAAP rules eliminate the ceding company's liability for unauthorized reinsurance.

3. Statutory formulas establish minimum estimated liabilities for loss and loss adjustment expense reserves, regardless of the adequacy of case reserves. GAAP adds current increases in these special reserves (excess loss reserves) back to policyholder surplus.

4. The cost of acquiring new insurance business is treated under statutory accounting rules as periodic expenses when costs are incurred, rather than being amortized over the life of the contract, as GAAP rules would suggest. The corresponding premium revenue, on the other hand, is realized as income over the contractual period. Accordingly, statutory statements could show a large underwriting loss in the period when new business was acquired, followed by large underwriting profits in the remaining years of the policy's life.

   GAAP capitalizes acquisition expenses, creating a prepaid expense account in the year of acquisition, which is amortized over the period during which revenues are realized. GAAP rules will, therefore, show a more consistent profit over the life of the policy.

5. No adjustment appears in statutory financial statements for federal income tax charges or credits that arise out of differences between pretax statutory income and taxable income as reported to the IRS. If statutory statements were adjusted to be consistent with GAAP, a deferred federal income taxes account would be recognized.

The analyst should be sure as to whether the statements being analyzed are prepared under statutory or GAAP rules. As a result of reports and requirements issued by the AICPA, and also SEC requirements and pressures from the Financial Analysts Federation, most companies whose securities are traded publicly now submit supplementary schedules in addition to statutory reporting. These are necessary for statutory accounting to be reconciled to conform with GAAP accounting. Therefore, analysts operating outside the company are given the reconciliations or can make them with data supplied.[10] Statutory statements could be of interest to an analyst, as well as GAAP statements, when assessing risk.

The Property and Casualty Industry

Approximately 3,600 companies operated in the highly competitive environment called the property-casualty industry. About 900 of those firms account for most of the business, but no one company controls more than 10 percent of the market.

Property insurance is designed to protect individuals and businesses from the impact of financial risks associated with the ownership and operation of property. Casualty insurance is designed to insure against potential liabilities arising from harm caused to others.

Analysis of Property and Casualty Insurance Companies

The income of insurance companies consists of underwriting premiums collected plus investment income. The expenses consist of underwriting expenses, losses and expenses associated with covered policy losses, and proportionate general and administrative overhead.

While the demand for property and casualty insurance is fairly stable (reflecting basically real growth of the economy and inflation), the supply curve is volatile. As interest rates rise, the willingness of companies to offer such insurance increases because each premium dollar generates more investment income. Property and casualty companies often have shown little or no underwriting profits, depending on successful investment results to earn adequate returns for the owners (see Table 14–5).

---

10 See (a) *Audits of Fire and Casualty Insurance Companies*, an AICPA Industry Audit Guide, prepared by the Committee on Insurance Accounting and Auditing of the American Institute of CPAs (New York: 1966). See also annual editions of *Financial Reporting Trends—Fire and Casualty Insurance*, Ernst and Ernst (New York).

(b) *Audits of Stock Life Insurance Companies*, an Industry Audit Guide prepared by the Committee of Insurance Accounting and Auditing of the American Institute of CPAs (New York: 1972).

(c) See also annual editions of *Financial Reporting Trends—Life Insurance*, Ernst and Ernst (New York).

TABLE 14–5
Property/Casualty Operating Results, 1983–86 (Dollar Figures in Millions)

	1983	1984	1985	1986
Net Premiums Written	107,803	117,744	143,882	176,993
Percent Change from Previous Year	4.6	9.2	22.2	23.0
Net Premiums Earned	105,787	114,257	132,651	166,381
Percent Change from Previous Year	4.6	8.0	16.1	25.4
Pure Losses	76,623	87,917	102,243	116,852
Loss Adjustment Expense	11,459	12,731	15,631	18,914
Underwriting Expenses	30,796	32,981	37,365	44,587
Total Expenses	116,878	133,628	155,239	180,353
Underwriting Gain/(Loss)	(11,091)	(19,371)	(22,587)	(13,972)
Policy Holder Dividends	2,194	2,084	2,199	2,165
Underwriting Gain/(Loss) After Dividends	(13,285)	(21,455)	(24,788)	(16,137)
Net Investment Income	15,784	17,448	19,375	21,924
Other Income	(308)	46	(113)	476
Pre-tax Operating Income	2,191	(3,961)	(5,525)	5,312

Source: A. M. Best. As reproduced in Standard & Poor's *Industry Surveys, Insurance & Investment* (New York: Standard & Poor's, Inc., 12/31/87), p. I 28.

Revenues and insurance leverage. An insurance company that has a higher percentage of its premium volume derived from liability lines will have greater insurance leverage than a company emphasizing property lines. Liability lines require larger loss reserves, and these loss reserves are a source of funds for the insurer. An insurer that writes predominately property insurance policies will pay out in loss settlements each year a high percentage of its premium dollars. Liability policies, on the other hand, result in claims that may not be settled for many years. The larger an insurer's loss reserves, the greater the extent to which the company is using other peoples' money to invest. Selling a higher percentage of liability insurance relative to property insurance can, accordingly, increase a company's total rate of return, thereby improving investment results.

The reduction in underwriting standards that may be necessary to write a higher proportion of liability insurance, however, could result in underwriting losses that exceed the added investment income. Insurance leverage increases the potential for return, but also increases risk. A. M. Best

TABLE 14–6
Combined Ratio and Its Components—Property/Casualty Insurance, 1980–86
(All figures in percent)

Year	Loss Ratio	Expense Ratio	Dividend Ratio	Combined Ratio
1987	77.9	25.3	1.3	104.6
1986	81.6	25.2	1.3	108.1
1985	88.9	25.9	1.6	116.5
1984	88.2	28.0	1.8	118.1
1983	81.5	28.4	2.1	112.0
1982	79.7	28.0	2.0	109.7
1981	76.8	27.3	1.9	106.0
1980	74.9	26.5	1.7	103.1
1975	79.3	27.3	1.3	107.9
1970	70.8	27.6	1.7	100.1

Source: Best's Aggregates & Averages: Property/Casualty (Oldwick, New Jersey: A. M. Best & Co., 1988), p. 83.

Company, well-regarded insurance rating agency, uses seven leverage tests: (1) changes in net premiums written, (2) net premiums written to policyholders' surplus, (3) net liabilities to policyholders' surplus, (4) net leverage, (5) ceded reinsurance leverage, (6) gross leverage, and (7) surplus to policyholders' surplus.

Underwriting tests of profitability. There are three major tests of underwriting profitability: the loss ratio, the expense ratio, and the combined loss and expense ratio. The historic ratios for the insurance industry are shown in Table 14–6.

Loss ratio. This ratio is generally calculated as the ratio of losses incurred plus loss adjustment expenses to premiums earned times 100 percent (net loss ratio). The loss ratio may be calculated with or without loss adjustment expenses in the numerator, but it is usually considered preferable to include such expenses so that all costs associated with the losses are considered. The net loss ratio should be calculated after adjustments for reinsurance assumed or ceded. Accordingly, any losses under reinsurance assumed are included in losses incurred by the company, and any loss recoveries from reinsurers reduce the numerator of this ratio. Also, premiums earned are increased by premiums earned on reinsurance assumed and reduced by premiums paid on insurance ceded to reinsurers.

Expense ratio. The expense ratio may be calculated on either a trade or financial basis, as shown below:

$$\text{(1)} \quad \frac{\text{Expense ratio}}{\text{(Trade basis)}} = \frac{\text{Expenses incurred}}{\text{Premiums written}} \times 100\%$$

$$\text{(2)} \quad \frac{\text{Expense ratio}}{\text{(Financial basis)}} = \frac{\text{Expenses incurred}}{\text{Premiums earned}} \times 100\%$$

It is useful to study both ratios to help reconcile financial ratios with the statutory underwriting results. Expenses incurred include all underwriting expenses other than losses incurred and loss adjustment expenses incurred that are deducted in determining the net underwriting gain, and are net of reinsurance transactions. These ratios are a test of managements' efficiency in operations.

Combined loss and expense ratio. This ratio is the sum total of the net loss and expense ratio for a company and is usually calculated on the trade basis. When the combined ratio is under 100, it indicates the degree of profitability of underwriting, and when over 100, the degree of unprofitability of underwriting. A combined ratio that includes losses based on premiums earned and expenses based on premiums written (trade basis) is felt to produce a more meaningful measure of underwriting profit when premium volume is increasing or decreasing, because acquisition costs are a function of premiums written.

The combined ratio is useful for comparing operating performance among various lines of insurance, among companies, and over time. Moreover, it gives some indication of the quality of business a company writes and may suggest the adequacy of the company's premium rates. A company may be profitable, of course, even though the combined ratio exceeds 100, since investment profit may more than offset any underwriting loss.

Profit ratios. Profit ratios, typically used by analysts, may be calculated in four different ways: (1) profits related to revenues (premiums earned), (2) profits related to investments, (3) profits related to net worth, and (4) profits related to the number of shares of common stock outstanding.

Underwriting profit ratio. The underwriting profit ratio is calculated by subtracting the combined ratio from one. Investment income and portfolio gains or losses are not recognized in this ratio. The ratio is a useful test of the efficiency of underwriting, but not a measure of overall profitability. Analysts should study trends in this ratio and make comparisons of a given company's ratio with the average for all property and casualty companies and with specific other property and casualty companies. The adjusted combined ratio has typically exceeded one (100 percent), as shown in Tables 14–5 and 14–6, resulting in an underwriting loss after dividends to policyholders. The trend, however, has been favorable since 1984.

Return on invested funds.   The investment earnings ratio is calculated as shown below:

$$\text{Investment earnings ratio} = \frac{\text{Net investment income}}{\text{Average admitted assets}}$$

Investment income includes interest, dividends, and income from real estate investments less investment expenses, before federal income taxes. A broader, and, the writer believes, more useful measure is:

$$\text{Investment profit ratio} = \frac{\text{Total investment profit (loss)}}{\text{Average admitted assets}}$$

Capital gains and losses are included in this ratio. Analysts should compare this ratio to averages for the property and casualty industry and study trends over time.

Net operating gain to total assets.   This ratio is typically calculated on an after-tax basis by dividing net operating gain after taxes by the prior year admitted assets. It is a measure of insurance earnings in relation to the company's total asset base. Past history shows a range for this ratio of .4 to 1.5 percent. A ratio lower than .4 percent is, accordingly, considered below the accepted norm and should be investigated carefully.

Net operating gain before taxes to total revenue.   The usual range for this ratio is 1.5 to 6 percent. A ratio below 1.5 percent is, accordingly, considered below the norm and should be investigated carefully before considering investment in the company. American Travellers Corporation, for example, was below the norm for the industry, even though total revenues and pretax operating earnings grew at a compound annual rate of about 40–70 percent over the years 1984–93. Unfortunately, benefits and expenses also grew at about the same compound annual growth rate, so performance did not significantly improve.

Return on equity.   This ratio is calculated by dividing net profit by policyholders' surplus. Net profits include underwriting gain or loss, investment income, and realized capital gains, and is after tax. A better ratio is adjusted return on net worth, calculated as shown below:

$$\text{Adjusted return on net worth} = \frac{\text{Adjusted net profit}}{\text{Adjusted policyholders' surplus}}$$

This ratio recognizes that unrealized investment gains and losses are included in policyholders' surplus but not in profit. The adjusted ratio includes only capital and adjusted surplus in the denominator, eliminating other resources. In other words, it does not include all investable funds in the denominator, thereby being consistent with the profit figure used in the numerator.

Change in capital and surplus.   Capital and surplus is the amount by which a company's assets exceed its liabilities. The ratio is calculated as shown below:

$$\text{Change in surplus ratio} = \frac{\text{Change in adjusted surplus}}{\text{Adjusted surplus prior year}} \times 100\%$$

An adjustment is made in the current and prior year's surplus for acquisition expenses subject to deferral under GAAP. The industry norm for this test is about 5 to 15 percent.

Recent profit experience.   Insurance Services Office reported that losses and loss adjustment expense accounted for 75 percent of total industry expenses in 1986. Losses and expenses exceeded earned premiums in 1986, resulting in an underwriting loss of $15.9 billion after policyholder dividends of $2.0 billion. While this is a large loss, it represents a 35 percent improvement over the $24.8 billion loss incurred in 1985. Operating results were aided in 1986 by a low level of insured catastrophic losses in 1986, and the improved 1986 results may, therefore, not be an accurate gauge of the future.

The relatively favorable performance recorded by the industry in 1986 reflects rising premium revenues, lower underwriting losses, and increased investment income. The industry earned over $5 billion in 1986 as pretax net operating income, compared to losses of close to $4 billion in 1984 and over $5 billion in 1985. On the other hand, the pace of increase in premium revenues began to slow in 1986, and losses are difficult to predict.

Recurring cycles in fire and casualty business. An examination of past history indicates the cyclical nature of underwriting. The business will experience profitability for a period of years and then, especially in years of inflation, the business will become unprofitable. When it is unprofitable, the companies will seek rate increases. Increases in rates for the industry as a whole have always been granted by state insurance commissioners, and the industry then has returned to a period of profitability, which again is followed by a period of unprofitability. Purchasers of fire and casualty insurance stocks during the unprofitable and out-of-favor phase of the cycle must assume a return to profitability, which to date has always followed, as it did in 1986.

In the period 1956–80, for the stock companies, the lowest combined ratios were 95.4 in 1972 and 95.8 in 1971, and the highest ratio was 107.9 in 1975. The combined ratio (ignoring dividends) reached an all-time high of 118.1 in 1984 before declining to 104.6 in 1987. Investors can expect only slight total profitability when underwriting is unprofitable because the net loss must be absorbed by investment income, which is the source of dividends and the basis for capital gains secured by investors. These ratios represent industry averages. But, of course, certain companies have a better record than the averages and other companies a poorer one.

In general, investors in property and liability insurance companies do not expect much in the way of underwriting profits, only wanting the combined loss and expense ratio to be equal to or somewhat below 100 percent. Their major expectation for income and capital gains centers on investment performance and investment income. Therefore, the investor making an analysis of an insurance company must give major attention to the company's investment portfolio and investment results over a period of years. The comparative investment and underwriting record for selected years over the period 1970–87 is shown in Table 14–7.

Troublesome underwriting losses. The stock property-casualty companies have recorded underwriting losses during the 1980s. Moreover, rising interest rates could erode the value of insurers' bond portfolios.

Analysts feel the industry was suffering from excess capacity brought on by the attraction of relatively high rates of return on equity capital in recent years. High interest rates in the late 1970s encouraged rate cutting to attract funds to invest. Rising inflation rates further exacerbated the problem by causing claim settlements and operating expenses to rise sharply. Price competition again emerged in 1988, and the growth in industry-wide premiums slowed in 1987. Still, operating earnings were expected to

TABLE 14–7
Property and Casualty Stock Insurance Companies—Comparative Investment and Underwriting Record (Dollar Figures in Millions)

	Investment Income		Underwriting Profit or Loss	
Year	Dollars	Percent of Mean Assets	Dollars	Percent of Earned Premiums
1987	18,824	6.03	(5,450)	(4.14)
1986	16,872	6.35	(10,446)	(8.95)
1985	14,957	6.73	(17,879)	(19.40)
1984	13,695	6.91	(15,670)	(19.84)
1983	12,381	6.58	(9,090)	(12.41)
1982	11,846	6.79	(6,475)	(9.17)
1981	10,291	6.37	(3,681)	(5.41)
1980	8,836	6.02	(1,956)	(2.98)
1975	3,143	4.83	(2,880)	(8.34)
1970	1,439	3.57	(154)	(0.72)

Source: Best's Aggregates & Averages: Property/Casualty (Oldwick, New Jersey: A. M. Best & Co., 1988), p. 87.

advance in 1988 and then declined in the 1989–90 period. These trends should be watched closely by investment analysts.

Investment policy requirements. Investment policy is based partly on regulations and partly on management decisions. Regulations governing fire and casualty investments are considerably less restrictive than regulations controlling investments of life insurance companies. For fire and casualty companies, there is no specific limitation on stock investments.

The minimum capital required, which in recent years has averaged about 8 percent of assets, must be invested in cash and U.S. government securities. Unearned premium reserves and required reserves must be invested in cash, government securities, and approved corporate bonds. The balance of funds may be invested in either stocks or bonds as long as the issuers have maintained satisfactory records of interest and dividend payments and are solvent.

Investment policy. Investment income is the principal component of the earnings of property and casualty insurers, and has kept the industry profitable during every year since 1975, except for 1984.

The bulk of investment funds of property and casualty insurers are kept in investments that can be sold readily, including stocks and bonds. The portion invested in bonds increased to 73.38 percent in 1984 from 59.6 percent in 1973.[11] Holdings of common stocks declined to 19.67 percent from 26.32 percent over the same time period.

The dollar growth in municipal securities from 1975 to 1981 was impressive. Special revenue bonds of colleges, universities, and public works programs dominated the fixed-income portfolio at the end of 1984, representing 30 percent of that portfolio. Property and casualty companies find such securities particularly interesting if the combined ratio is below 100 percent, since they are certain to face a federal income tax on investment earnings.

The higher the ratio of capital and surplus to unearned premium reserves for a company, the more justifiable is a large investment in common stocks. Analysts should relate the common stock investment to capital funds and estimate the effect of a given decline in market value of common stocks on capital and surplus of the company.

Investment results.   An insurance company's total earnings consist of the adjusted underwriting gain (or loss) plus net investment income. The underwriting earnings tend to be quite variable, fluctuating considerably over the years, and in numerous years companies experience underwriting losses. The pattern is suggested in Table 14–7. But fortunately, investment income, largely from debt instruments, tends to be stable and rising. This means that dividends are paid generally or entirely from investment income. Earnings per share should be calculated after income taxes and their trend and cyclical nature determined.

While companies experience both capital gains and losses in their investment portfolios, security analysts generally do not include portfolio gains or losses in calculating annual earnings. This is in line with the usual accounting practices of excluding nonrecurring gains from income on an annual basis.

Summary of major factors to consider in analysis of fire and casualty companies.   After analyzing the underwriting record and the investment record of a company, the analyst should determine

---

11 As reported by the Insurance Information Institute.

growth in each of several categories. Growth factors for which the compound annual growth should be determined are:

1. Assets.
2. Capital funds.
3. Total income.
4. Premium income.
5. Other income.
6. Net income from operations after income tax.
7. Earnings per share.
8. Dividends per share.
9. Liquidating value per share (adjusted book value).

Stability of items 3 through 9 also is of interest. The following analytical tests for fire and casualty insurance companies are suggested:

1. Cash and investment-grade bonds (rated in the top four grades) should be at least equal to 90 percent of liabilities, with cash and U.S. government securities at least equal to 20 percent of total assets and 30 percent of liabilities. The higher the ratio, the less concern for market fluctuations in securities, especially common stocks.
2. The ratio of common equity (exclusive of equity in unearned premium reserve) to total assets should be at least 35 percent.
3. The analyst should calculate the effect on capital and surplus if stock prices should decline 50 percent.
4. The loss ratios over both the last 5 and 10 years should not average over 72 percent.
5. The expense ratio over the last 5 and 10 years should not average over 23 percent.
6. The combined loss and expense ratios should not average over 95 percent for the last 5 and 10 years.
7. The rate of return on average assets should have been at least 5 percent over the most recent 5 years.
8. Investment income should rise on the average at least as fast as the growth in assets plus the rate of growth in interest rate on A-rated bonds.
9. There should be a satisfactory record of at least 10 years of growth in assets, net income, earnings per share, and dividends per share.

Life Insurance Companies

The life insurance industry is a major component of the American financial scene. Economic recovery coupled with relatively low interest rates has led to better than 10 percent income growth for life insurers in 1993. The low interest rates have allowed life insurers to keep the rates paid on policies and annuities low, thereby helping margins. Interest rates did begin to rise in 1994, heightening competitive pressures facing life insurers and forcing them to raise credited rates on policies. This squeezed profit margins. Moreover, insurer's portfolios contained many relatively low-yielding bonds. Also, banks have recently been authorized to underwrite annuities, further adding to competitive pressures.

Total life insurance in force grew from $5,500 billion in 1984 to $11,104.7 billion in 1993, for a compound annual growth rate of 8.12 percent. Total assets of United States life insurance companies grew from $723 billion in 1984 to $1,839 billion in 1993, for a compound annual growth rate of 10.93 percent (see Table 14–8).

The life insurance industry has traditionally been dominated by mutual companies, which are both older and larger than the stockholder-owned companies.

Growth of life insurance industry. The life insurance industry is well known for its continuous and considerable growth over long periods, including the growth of investment income. This is in sharp contrast to the erratic underwriting record of fire and casualty insurance companies.

In the post–World War II years, the life insurance industry has shown a fairly steady growth rate, although the rate of growth slowed in the 1955–70 period only to regain the 1945–55 growth rate after 1969. Growth rates for major categories are shown for the period 1983–94 in Table 14–9. The growth rates in the 1990s have been below those for the 1980s.

The evolution into financial services continues in this industry. Life insurance companies, therefore, compete not only among themselves for the consumers' savings dollar, but also against other financial institutions, such as banks and brokerage houses.

Relatively high interest rates and inflation in the late 1970s and the early 1980s, and a low rate of return on the savings feature for consumers' whole life policies (approximately 5 percent), caused many buyers to shift to lower-margined term insurance and invest the difference at higher rates of return. This led to an increase in policy terminations and policy loans, heightening liquidity and profitability problems for the industry. The sharp

TABLE 14-8
Life Insurance in Force and Total Assets for U.S. Companies

Operating data of U.S. life insurance companies

Year	Life insurance in force, in billions of $			Premiums, in millions of $				Reserves (mil. $)	Investment income (mil. $)	Rate of return (%)
	Ordinary	Group	Total*	Life	Annuities	Health	Total			
1993	6,428.4	4,456.3	11,104.7	94,448	156,445	68,658	319,551	1,549,803	124,205	0.00
1992	5,941.8	4,240.9	10,405.8	83,868	132,645	65,545	282,058	1,407,091	121,389	0.00
1991	5,677.8	4,057.6	9,986.3	79,301	123,590	60,900	263,791	1,304,778	188,984	9.09
1990	5,367.0	3,753.5	9,392.6	76,692	129,064	58,254	264,010	1,196,967	111,853	9.31
1989	4,940.0	3,469.5	8,694.0	73,290	114,997	56,079	244,366	1,083,678	103,965	9.47
1988	4,511.6	3,232.1	8,020.2	75,531	103,278	52,306	229,115	968,963	92,042	9.41
1987	4,139.1	3,043.8	7,452.5	76,737	88,677	47,549	212,963	862,133	82,875	9.39
1986	3,658.2	2,801.0	6,720.3	66,213	83,712[1]	44,153	194,078	761,924	75,435	9.64
1985	3,247.3	2,561.6	6,053.1	60,127	53,899	41,837	155,863	665,302	67,952	9.87
1984	2,887.6	2,392.4	5,500.0	51,274	42,859	40,671	134,804	584,193	59,213	9.65

*Includes industrial and credit.

[1] Unusually large increase due to the National Association of Insurance Commissioners' mandated change in statutory reporting methods.

Source: American Council of Life Insurance

TABLE 14–9
Key Life Insurance Statistics

	1983	1992	1993	% Change 1992–91	% Change 1993–92
LIFE INSURANCE IN FORCE IN THE UNITED STATES (000,000 omitted)					
Ordinary	$2,544,275	$ 5,941,810	$ 6,428,434	4.7	8.2
Group	2,219,573	4,240,919	4,456,338	4.5	5.1
Industrial	31,354	20,973	20,451	–6.7	–2.5
Credit	170,659	202,090	199,518	–11.5	–1.3
Total	$4,965,861	$10,405,792	$11,104,741	4.2	6.7
AVERAGE AMOUNTS OF LIFE INSURANCE IN FORCE IN THE UNITED STATES					
Per Household	$56,300	$106,600	$111,600	3.8	4.7
Per Insured Household	$69,500	$136,600	$143,100	5.1	4.8
LIFE INSURANCE PURCHASES IN THE UNITED STATES (000,000 omitted)					
Ordinary	$ 753,444	$1,048,135	$1,101,327	0.6	5.1
Group	271,609	440,143	576,823	–23.3	31.1
Industrial	1,388	222	149	12.1	–32.9
Total	$1,026,441	$1,488,500	$1,678,299	–7.9	12.8
BENEFIT PAYMENTS IN THE UNITED STATES (000,000 omitted)					
Payments to Beneficiaries	$15,660	$27,235	$28,819	7.2	5.8
Payments to Policyholders	22,636	30,258*	30,831	2.4*	1.9
Payments to Annuitants	13,654	37,550	40,325	2.6	7.4
Total	$51,860	$95,043*	$99,975	3.8*	5.2
PREMIUM RECEIPTS OF U.S. LIFE INSURANCE COMPANIES (000,000 omitted)					
Life Insurance	$ 50,265	$ 83,868	$ 94,448	5.8	12.6
Annuity Considerations	30,544	132,645	156,445	7.3	17.9
Health Insurance	38,201	65,545	68,658	7.6	4.7
Total	$119,010	$282,058	$319,551	6.9	13.3
ASSETS OF U.S. LIFE INSURANCE COMPANIES (000,000 omitted)					
Government Securities	$ 76,615	$ 320,109	$ 384,124	18.8	20.0
Corporate Bonds	232,123	670,206	729,729	7.5	8.9
Stocks	64,868	192,403	251,885	17.0	30.9
Mortgages	150,999	246,702	229,061	–7.0	–7.2
Real Estate	22,234	50,595	54,249	8.3	7.2
Policy Loans	54,063	72,058	77,725	8.6	7.9
Other Assets	54,046	112,458	112,354	–2.5	–0.1
Total	$654,948	$1,664,531	$1,839,127	7.3	10.5
NET RATE OF INVESTMENT INCOME OF U.S. LIFE INSURANCE COMPANIES (BEFORE FEDERAL INCOME TAXES)					
Including Separate Accounts	8.96%	8.08%	7.52%	—	—
Excluding Separate Accounts	9.08%	8.58%	8.04%	—	—

*Revised.

Source: American Council of Life Insurance. Taken from Life Insurance Fact Book (Washington, D.C.: American Council of Life Insurance, 1994) p. 5.

TABLE 14–10
Voluntary Termination Rate—Ordinary Policies in Force in the United States

Year	Policies in Force Less Than 2 Years	Policies in Force 2 Years or More	All Policies in Force	Year	Policies in Force Less Than 2 Years	Policies in Force 2 Years or More	All Policies in Force
1951	9.4%	2.2%	3.2%	1978	19.6%	4.6%	6.6%
1955	11.4	2.5	3.8	1979	21.0	5.1	7.2
1960	14.5	3.7	5.2	1980	22.4	5.8	8.1
1965	15.4	3.5	5.1	1981	23.5	6.6	8.9
1966	16.2	3.5	5.2	1982	24.4	7.6	10.0
1967	16.5	3.6	5.2	1983	25.1	8.6	11.0
1968	18.0	3.7	5.5	1984	23.0	9.6	11.9
1969	18.3	3.7	5.6	1985	20.9	10.3	12.3
1970	19.3	3.9	5.9	1986	21.7	9.0	11.1
1971	19.0	3.9	5.8	1987	20.5	8.3	10.2
1972	19.3	3.9	6.0	1988	19.8	7.0	9.3
1973	18.8	4.3	6.3	1989	18.6	6.7	8.8
1974	19.5	4.5	6.5	1990	19.0	6.6	8.7
1975	20.9	4.5	6.7	1991	19.4	6.5	8.6
1976	19.7	4.6	6.6	1992	18.3	6.4	8.3
1977	19.5	4.7	6.6	1993	17.4	5.8	7.6

Note: The rate is the ratio of the number of policies lapsed or surrendered to the mean number of policies in force. American Council of Life Insurance.

Source: Life Insurance Fact Book, op. cit., p. 67.

increase in lapses and surrenders in the 1980s is highlighted in Table 14–10. The factors that spurred these changes abated after 1988, but the lapse ratio is still a bit higher than 1979 and prior years. Investors should watch to see if the slowdown in the rate of lapses and surrenders continues.

Earnings prospects for the industry were questionable at the time of writing this material. The following factors cloud the near-term earnings horizon:

1. Fear of rising interest rates, which could accelerate the trend away from whole life and would have an adverse effect on the value of large bond holdings by the industry.

2. Higher tax rates beginning in 1987.

3. A cyclical decline in group health results and the danger represented by AIDS. Insurers have instituted price hikes in the health area which should help alleviate this problem.

Economic recovery and low interest rates did result in double-digit income growth for life insurers in 1993. Interest rates began rising in 1994, however, heightening competitive pressures life insurers face from banks and security firms. Moreover, many insurer's portfolios contain relatively low-yielding bonds. Finally, banks can now underwrite annuities.

New and discontinuing companies. Each year many new companies are established, and many companies go out of business. Sometimes promoters start companies and accept low-quality risks at low premiums to show a rapid increase in insurance in force, expecting that the price of their stock will rise rapidly, permitting them to sell out at a large profit before the low quality of risks produces poor results. Furthermore, the insurance in force figure may rise rapidly without a significant increase in assets if most new policies are term policies. New companies, therefore, usually are of such high risk as not to fit the objectives of most long-term investors.

Financial statements of life insurance companies. Tables 14–11 and 14–12 offer historical balance sheet information for life insurance companies, which should be understood and used for comparative purposes in analyzing particular companies. Table 14–11 presents the major assets and Table 14–12 the major liabilities, reserves, capital, and surplus items.

Analysis of assets of life insurance companies. Utilizing the data in Table 14–11, we find that debt instruments (government securities, bonds, mortgages, and policy loans) represented 77.3 percent of total assets in 1993 and 80.4 percent in 1980. This breakdown is typical for life insurance companies. State regulations governing the investments of insurance companies generally limit investment in equities to 10 percent of total assets, except for pension fund assets, which are set aside in separate accounts.

Pension fund assets are segregated since such assets may be invested entirely in common stocks if the insurance company wishes to do so. Insurance companies had invested only 49.4 percent of total separate account (pension fund) assets in common stocks at the end of 1980. The rate of return earned is a bit lower when separate accounts are included than when they are excluded, as shown in Table 14–13. This occurs because of the higher proportion of common stocks held in these accounts.

The largest class of securities is corporate securities, representing 53.4 percent of all assets in 1993 (39.7 percent bonds and 13.7 percent equity), and 46.2 percent in 1986. The next-largest class is government securities, representing 20.9 percent of assets in 1993 and 15.4 percent in 1986.

TABLE 14-11
Distribution of Assets of U.S. Life Insurance Companies

Year	Government Securities	Corporate Securities		Mortgages	Real Estate	Policy Loans	Misc. Assets	Total
		Bonds	Stocks					
AMOUNT (000,000 omitted)								
1917	$ 562	$ 1,975	$ 83	$ 2,021	$ 179	$ 810	$ 311	$ 5,941
1920	1,349	1,949	75	2,442	172	859	474	7,320
1925	1,311	3,022	81	4,808	266	1,446	604	11,538
1930	1,502	4,929	519	7,598	548	2,807	977	18,880
1935	4,727	5,314	583	5,357	1,990	3,540	1,705	23,216
1940	8,447	8,645	605	5,972	2,065	3,091	1,977	30,802
1945	22,545	10,060	999	6,636	857	1,962	1,738	44,797
1950	16,118	23,248	2,103	16,102	1,445	2,413	2,591	64,020
1955	11,829	35,912	3,633	29,445	2,581	3,290	3,742	90,432
1960	11,815	46,740	4,981	41,771	3,765	5,231	5,273	119,576
1965	11,908	58,244	9,126	60,013	4,681	7,678	7,234	158,884
1970	11,068	73,098	15,420	74,375	6,320	16,064	10,909	207,254
1975	15,177	105,837	28,061	89,167	9,621	24,467	16,974	289,304
1976	20,260	120,666	34,262	91,552	10,476	25,834	18,502	321,552
1977	23,555	137,889	33,763	96,848	11,060	27,556	21,051	351,722
1978	26,552	156,044	35,518	106,167	11,764	30,146	23,733	389,924
1979	29,719	168,990	39,757	118,421	13,007	34,825	27,563	432,282
1980	33,015	179,603	47,366	131,080	15,033	41,411	31,702	479,210
1981	39,502	193,806	47,670	137,747	18,278	48,706	40,094	525,803
1982	55,516	212,772	55,730	141,989	20,624	52,961	48,571	588,163
1983	76,615	232,123	64,868	150,999	22,234	54,063	54,046	654,948

(continued)

TABLE 14-11 (continued)

Year	Government Securities	Corporate Securities		Mortgages	Real Estate	Policy Loans	Misc. Assets	Total
		Bonds	Stocks					
1984	$ 99,769	$259,128	$ 63,335	$156,699	$25,767	$54,505	$ 63,776	$ 722,979
1985	124,598	296,848	77,496	171,797	28,822	54,369	71,971	825,901
1986	144,616	341,967	90,864	193,842	31,615	54,055	80,592	937,551
1987	151,436	405,674	96,515	213,450	34,172	53,626	89,586	1,044,459
1988	159,781	480,313	104,373	232,863	37,371	54,236*	97,933	1,166,870
1989	178,141	538,063	125,614	254,215	39,908	57,439	106,376	1,299,756
1990	210,846	582,597	128,484	270,109	43,367	62,603	110,202	1,408,208
1991	269,490	623,515	164,515	265,258	46,711	66,364	115,348	1,551,201
1992	320,109	670,206	192,403	246,702	50,595	72,058	112,458	1,664,531
1993	384,124	729,729	251,885	229,061	54,249	77,725	112,354	1,839,127
PERCENT								
1917	9.6%	33.2%	1.4%	34.0%	3.0%	13.6%	5.2%	100.0%
1920	18.4	26.7	1.0	33.4	2.3	11.7	6.5	100.0
1925	11.3	26.2	.7	41.7	2.3	12.5	5.3	100.0
1930	8.0	26.0	2.8	40.2	2.9	14.9	5.2	100.0
1935	20.4	22.9	2.5	23.1	8.6	15.2	7.3	100.0
1940	27.5	28.1	2.0	19.4	6.7	10.0	6.3	100.0
1945	50.3	22.5	2.2	14.8	1.9	4.4	3.9	100.0
1950	25.2	36.3	3.3	25.1	2.2	3.8	4.1	100.0
1955	13.1	39.7	4.0	32.6	2.9	3.6	4.1	100.0
1960	9.9	39.1	4.2	34.9	3.1	4.4	4.4	100.0
1965	7.5	36.7	5.7	37.8	3.0	4.8	4.5	100.0
1970	5.3	35.3	7.4	35.9	3.0	7.8	5.3	100.0

(continued)

TABLE 14-11 (concluded)

Year	Government Securities	Corporate Securities		Mortgages	Real Estate	Policy Loans	Misc. Assets	Total
		Bonds	Stocks					
1975	5.2%	36.6%	9.7%	30.8%	3.3%	8.5%	5.9%	100.0%
1976	6.3	37.5	10.7	28.5	3.3	8.0	5.7	100.0
1977	6.7	39.2	9.6	27.5	3.2	7.8	6.0	100.0
1978	6.8	40.0	9.1	27.2	3.0	7.8	6.1	100.0
1979	6.9	39.1	9.2	27.4	3.0	8.1	6.3	100.0
1980	6.9	37.5	9.9	27.4	3.1	8.6	6.6	100.0
1981	7.5	36.8	9.1	26.2	3.5	9.3	7.6	100.0
1982	9.4	36.2	9.5	24.1	3.5	9.0	8.3	100.0
1983	11.7	35.4	9.9	23.1	3.4	8.3	8.2	100.0
1984	13.8	35.8	8.8	21.7	3.6	7.5	8.8	100.0
1985	15.0	36.0	9.4	20.8	3.5	6.6	8.7	100.0
1986	15.4	36.5	9.7	20.6	3.4	5.8	8.6	100.0
1987	14.5	38.8	9.3	20.4	3.3	5.1	8.6	100.0
1988	13.7	41.2	8.9	20.0	3.2	4.6	8.4	100.0
1989	13.7	41.4	9.7	19.5	3.1	4.4	8.2	100.0
1990	15.0	41.4	9.1	19.2	3.1	4.4	7.8	100.0
1991	17.4	40.2	10.6	17.1	3.0	4.3	7.4	100.0
1992	19.2	40.3	11.5	14.8	3.1	4.3	6.8	100.0
1993	20.9	39.7	13.7	12.5	2.9	4.2	6.1	100.0

*Excludes some $600 million of policy loans securitized during 1988.

Note: Beginning with 1962, these data include the assets of separate accounts.

Spectator Year Book and American Council of Life Insurance.

Source: Life Insurance Fact Book (Washington, DC: American Council of Life Insurance, 1994) p. 84.

TABLE 14-12
Obligations and Surplus Funds—U.S. Life Insurance Companies (000,000 omitted)

Year	Policy Reserves	Policy Dividend Accumu- lations	Funds Set Aside for Policy Dividends	Other Obligations	Mandatory Securities or Asset Valuation Reserve†	Interest Maintenance Reserve	Surplus Funds	Capital (Stock Companies)	Total
1952	$ 62,579	$ 1,675	$ 841	$ 3,024*	NA	—	$ 4,884	$ 372	$ 73,375
1955	75,359	2,239	1,201	3,562	$ 1,063	—	6,475	533	90,432
1960	98,473	3,381	1,780	4,851	1,417	—	8,827	847	119,576
1965	127,620	4,326	2,647	7,295	3,160	—	12,468	1,368	158,884
1970	167,779	6,068	3,540	10,295	2,249	—	15,651	1,672	207,254
1975	237,116	8,814	4,875	16,241	1,695	—	18,635	1,928	289,304
1976	262,775	9,633	5,252	18,395	3,486	—	20,077	1,934	321,552
1977	287,932	10,427	5,839	20,628	3,279	—	21,669	1,948	351,722
1978	318,483	11,319	6,380	23,067	4,428	—	24,285	1,962	389,924
1979	351,637	12,112	7,158	25,995	5,377	—	28,023	1,980	432,282
1980	390,339	12,727	7,659	27,701	6,426	—	32,274	2,084	479,210
1981	428,031	13,261	8,355	33,223	5,511	—	35,211	2,211	525,803
1982	479,360	13,706	8,914	38,001	6,731	—	39,105	2,346	588,163
1983	532,441	13,939	10,078	44,022	8,084	—	43,978	2,406	654,948
1984	584,193	14,395	10,745	55,955	7,344	—	47,800	2,547	722,979
1985	665,302	14,638	11,710	66,932	10,539	—	54,039	2,741	825,901

(continued)

TABLE 14-12 (concluded)

Year	Policy Reserves	Policy Dividend Accumulations	Funds Set Aside for Policy Dividends	Other Obligations	Mandatory Securities or Asset Valuation Reserve[†]	Interest Maintenance Reserve	Surplus Funds	Capital (Stock Companies)	Total
1986	$ 761,924	$15,174	$11,704	$69,270	$15,330	—	$ 61,314	$2,835	$ 937,551
1987	862,133	15,837	12,043	71,063	16,013	—	64,496	2,874	1,044,459
1988	968,963	16,601	12,478	75,939	17,939	—	72,021	2,929	1,166,870
1989	1,083,678	17,278	13,373	82,306	19,438	—	80,613	3,070	1,299,756
1990	1,196,967	18,000	13,921	73,164	14,783	—	88,128	3,245	1,408,208
1991	1,304,778	18,531	13,196	89,804	18,854	—	102,645	3,393	1,551,201
1992	1,407,091	19,189	13,102	85,212	20,801	$ 3,899	111,810	3,427	1,664,531
1993	1,549,803	19,619	13,172	93,205	25,063	10,245	124,501	3,519	1,839,127

NA = Not Available separately.

*Includes Mandatory Securities Valuation Reserve in 1952 only.

†Beginning in 1992, the Asset Valuation Reserve replaced the Mandatory Securities Valuation Reserve.

American Council of Life Insurance.

Source: Life Insurance Fact Book, op. cit., p. 81.

TABLE 14–13
Income of Life Insurance Companies

Life insurance companies receive funds from two main sources: premiums paid by policyholders and earnings on investment. There is a close relationship between these income elements. Part of each premium payment becomes available for investment in the nation's economy. In calculating premiums, the anticipated investment earnings are taken into account, thereby reducing the price of life insurance to policyholders.

Income of U.S. Life Insurance Companies (000,000 omitted)

Year	Premium Receipts				Invest-ment Income**	Other Income†	Total Income
	Life Insurance Premiums	Annuity Consider-ations	Health Insurance Premiums*	Total Premium Receipts			
1911	$ 626	$ 4	—	$ 630	$ 182	$ 24	$ 836
1915	776	6	—	782	241	20	1,043
1920	1,374	7	—	1,381	341	42	1,764
1925	2,340	38	—	2,378	551	89	3,018
1930	3,416	101	—	3,517	891	186	4,594
1935	3,182	491	—	3,673	1,013	386	5,072
1940	3,501	386	—	3,887	1,231	540	5,658
1945	4,589	570	—	5,159	1,445	1,070	7,674
1950	6,249	939	$1,001	8,189	2,075	1,073	11,337
1955	8,903	1,288	2,355	12,546	2,801	1,197	16,544
1960	11,998	1,341	4,026	17,365	4,304	1,338	23,007

(continued)

TABLE 14-13 *(continued)*

	Premium Receipts						
Year	Life Insurance Premiums	Annuity Consider- ations	Health Insurance Premiums*	Total Premium Receipts	Invest- ment Income**	Other Income†	Total Income
1965	$16,083	$ 2,260	$ 6,261	$ 24,604	$ 6,778	$ 1,785	$ 33,167
1970	21,679	3,721	11,367	36,767	10,144	2,143	49,054
1971	22,935	4,910	12,897	40,742	11,031	2,429	54,202
1972	24,678	5,503	14,318	44,499	12,127	2,222	58,848
1973	26,373	6,771	15,524	48,668	13,670	2,415	64,753
1974	27,750	7,737	17,123	52,610	15,144	2,256	70,010
1975	29,336	10,165	19,074	58,575	16,488	2,959	78,022
1976	31,358	13,962	21,059	66,379	18,758	3,421	88,558
1977	33,765	14,974	23,580	72,319	21,713	3,953	97,985
1978	36,592	16,339	25,829	78,760	25,294	4,152	108,206
1979	39,083	17,939	27,894	84,916	29,562	4,661	119,139
1980	40,829	22,429	29,366	92,624	33,928	4,336	130,888
1981	46,246	27,579	31,803	105,628	39,774	6,464	151,866
1982	50,800	34,644	34,960	120,404	45,532	4,108	170,044
1983	50,265	30,544	38,201	119,010	50,862	6,154	176,026
1984	51,274	42,859	40,671	134,804	59,213	12,092	206,109
1985	60,127	53,899	41,837	155,863	67,952	10,212	234,027

(continued)

TABLE 14–13 (concluded)

Year	Premium Receipts				Invest-ment Income**	Other Income†	Total Income
	Life Insurance Premiums	Annuity Consider-ations	Health Insurance Premiums*	Total Premium Receipts			
1986	$66,213	$ 83,712‡	$44,153	$194,078	$ 75,435	$12,744	$282,257
1987	76,737	88,677	47,549	212,963	82,875	18,460	314,298
1988	73,531	103,278	52,306	229,115	92,042	16,983	338,140
1989	73,290	114,997	56,079	244,366	103,965	18,987	367,318
1990	76,692	129,064	58,254	264,010	111,853	26,337	402,200
1991	79,301	123,590	60,900	263,791	118,984	28,247	411,022
1992	83,868	132,645	65,545	282,058	121,389	23,469	426,916
1993	94,448	156,445	68,658	319,551	124,205	22,594	466,350

Note: Consideration for supplementary contracts with and without life contingencies are included under "Other Income." Prior to 1947, the business of health departments was not included in this series.

*Includes some premiums for Workers' Compensation and auto and other liability insurance.

**Beginning with 1951, investment income is net of investment expenses in this series.

†Beginning in 1975, "Other Income" includes commissions and expense allowance on reinsurance ceded. In 1975, this amounted to $382 million. Beginning in 1992, includes amortization of the Interest Maintenance Reserve (IMR), which amounted to $837 million in 1993.

‡Unusually large increase in annuity premiums in 1986 was due to an NAIC-mandated change in statutory reporting methods.

Spectator Year Book and American Council of Life Insurance.

Source: Life Insurance Fact Book, op. cit., p. 68.

The income statement.   A typical income statement of a stock life insurance company is presented in Table 14–14 and historical income data in Table 14–13. Premium income represents about 68 percent of total income, and net investment income about 27 percent. Benefits, related payments, and additions to policy and special reserves absorb about 80 percent of income. Operating expenses absorb another 15 percent, and income taxes about 1.5 percent, leaving 3.5 percent for dividends and additions to surplus.

The actual proportions in the income statement can vary by size of stock company. Smaller companies (those with assets of less than $500 million) could show as much as 78 percent of income derived from premium receipts. Expense proportions also may vary, depending on such factors as types of coverage offered by a given company and its ratio of recently issued insurance to total insurance in force. The figures given are general averages for all stock insurance companies.

Sources of earnings—underwriting.   Normally the investor can take a noninsurance company's sales for a given period and subtract the costs to arrive at the company's profit. In life insurance, the sales unit referred to is a promise by the company to pay $1,000 at a future time. The amount received by the company is usually no more than a year's premium, which is a small fraction of this $1,000. It is the premium payment received each year, and not the contract sale, that provides income for the insurance company.

Fixing premiums.   In fixing premiums, the insurance company will calculate the amount that must be received each year so that, with interest earned, the amounts received will equal the benefits expected to be paid out over the duration of the contracts. This amount per year is called the net level premium and corresponds to the cost of goods sold for an ordinary business. To this net level premium the company then adds an amount that it estimates will cover its costs, including commissions, and give it a small margin of profit. This amount is called the load and is the same as the markup for a seller of goods.

Conservative nature of reported earnings.   In calculating the profit that a life insurance company will make, it must be emphasized that most of the cost factors are estimates and assumptions for long periods of time in the future. The differences between these estimates and the actual costs that occur are the sources of additional possible profit or loss to the

TABLE 14–14

A Typical Condensed Income Statement of a Life Insurance Company

Sources of Funds—Income		
Premiums Receipts	69.8%	
Net Investment Income	26.7	
Other Income	4.5	
		100.0%
Use of Funds or Distribution of Income		
Benefits including surrender benefits	42.5	
Annuities and mutual endowment	7.5	
Miscellaneous deduction	5.5	
Increase in policy and special revenues	24.5	
		80.0
Expenses of Operation		
Agents' commissions	6.0	
General expenses	6.3	
Taxes other than income taxes	2.7	
		15.0
Total of above		95.0
Income Taxes		1.5
Total		96.5
Net Gain After Income Tax, Before Dividends		3.5
Dividends to Policyholders		2.3
Net Gain After Dividends to Policyholders		1.2
Changes to Surplus		
Surplus beginning of fiscal period		xxxx
Add: Net gains after income tax	3.5	
Net gain from sale of investments	.5	
Increase in market value of investments	1.0	
Total increase in surplus		xxxx
Less: Dividends to policyholders	2.3	
Increase in security valuation reserves	1.0	
Surplus at end of fiscal period		xxxx

company. Since the estimates and assumptions used have been conservative (that is, have tended to overstate the costs), these differences have more often been profits than losses.

Determining companies to consider. The quantitative measures discussed in the following paragraphs are useful in assessing the quality and potential return for life insurance stocks.

Measures of efficiency. The tests of management in this area, as in other companies, are such measures as the return on stockholders' equity and the growth of earnings. Also it will be helpful to look at specific indicators, especially in the area of expenses. Renewal expense and investment yield are useful.

1. To calculate renewal expense per $1,000 of old business in force, renewal expense first must be estimated. This is done by subtracting from general insurance expense the identifiable first-year expenses that are contained in this item. The renewal expense per $1,000, particularly when calculated separately for ordinary business, provides a measure that is suitable for comparison between companies or with a general standard.

2. Investment yield is the ratio of net investment income to mean assets. The trend of a company's investment yield should be rising in line with the general trend for the industry.

Growth in earnings. Growth in earnings per share is by far the most important factor to be considered in measuring the growth of a company. The rates of growth of both reported and adjusted earnings should be at a satisfactory level. Any divergence of the two over a period of several years should be investigated.

Quality of business. The investor must attempt to measure the quality of the business. This also indicates the quality of the earnings. The following factors will be of assistance in this effort.

1. Lapse ratio. This is the ratio of voluntary terminations (including both lapses and surrenders) to business in force (average of beginning and ending). The lower the lapse ratio, the longer a company's business is remaining in force on the average and the greater is the profit that can be expected.

2. Composition of business in force. The proportion of most profitable lines, particularly ordinary life (whole life and endowment), and the trends are important. Investors should prefer life insurance companies that have concentrated on ordinary life rather than group business.

TABLE 14–15
Suggested Standards for Ratios for Life Insurance Companies

	Minimum	Maximum
Stockholders' equity ratio	8%	
Maximum decline in earnings in a given year:		
Reported		20%
Adjusted		15%
Years of earnings decline in past 10 years		3
Renewal expense per $1,000		$2.50
Yield on investments	4.5%	
Growth rate of earnings per share	6%	
Lapse ratio		8%
Composition of business in force:		
Ordinary and industrial	50%	
Term		30%
Group		30%
Composition of premium income:		
Ordinary and industrial	50%	
Health insurance		20%
First-year compensation		90%
First-year expense ratio		125%
Return on stockholders' equity	10%	

3. Composition of premium income. As with the composition of business in force, the composition of premium income measure should show a substantial proportion of premium income from ordinary life insurance.

Return on stockholders' equity. This is the most important single measure of benefit to stockholders in any line of business. It shows how well management is using the funds provided by stockholders and is used for comparison with other companies. It should be calculated using both reported and adjusted earnings and stockholders' equity. The adjusted figures may be more accurate, but a satisfactory return should be indicated by both calculations.

Standards for quantitative measures. Table 14–15 presents standards that should be applied in the analysis of a life insurance company stock.

Performance of life insurance stocks. Life insurance stocks enjoyed a period of extreme popularity during the period 1946–56; the S&P Monthly Index of Life Insurance Stocks rose nearly 10 times, from 18.6 to 177.7, while the S&P 500 rose only 2.4 times. Life insurance stocks then moved pretty much horizontally from 1961 to 1981.

Life insurance stocks were one of the popular groups in 1961 and rose strongly from about 180 to about 280 in terms of the S&P Index of Life Insurance. Life insurance stocks then fell before reaching a high of about 365 in 1964. That peak was not surpassed until the 1980s. The index had bear market lows of 190 in 1966, 147 in 1970, and 115 in 1974.

In 1981 the index began rising sharply, reaching a peak of about 823 in 1986 before beginning to fall again. Life insurance stocks have been passed over in recent years by investors who seek stocks with more exciting growth prospects. The primary problem area for life insurance company prospects has been the troubled group health area and the related specter of AIDS.

SUMMARY

The main functions of commercial banks are to receive deposits from other segments of the economy and to make loans and discounts to industry, commerce, agriculture, and individuals and to federal, state, and local governments through purchase of their securities. The nation's commercial banks hold the bulk of the cash assets of individuals, business firms, and financial institutions. This means that, in total, the assets and deposits must grow with the growth of GNP. In fact, the growth rates are interrelated.

While management is important with all corporations, it is of special importance in the case of banks because the quality of assets, especially loans, is the most important factor in the determination of the investment status of a bank.

About 90 percent of a bank's assets consist of cash, security investments (currently about evenly divided between U.S. government and agency securities on the one hand and municipals on the other), and loans and discounts, with the latter representing 50 to 60 percent of total assets. Again, the quality of these loans is the crucial factor, and, as recent experience has proved, it is difficult for the analyst or investor outside the bank to determine accurately the quality of loans.

In addition to aggressively seeking time deposits and certificates of deposits, the large banks have actively entered the capital market for funds by selling debentures, which they are permitted to include in the category "capital accounts." Banks have had strong pressure to increase their equity capital because of the substantial increase in deposits, and substantial increases in debentures and other debt outstanding. However, in many cases the fact that market prices of several bank stocks have been below book values, in addition to the relatively high cost of equity under such conditions, has created difficulty in selling more stock.

As with other industries, the investor is interested in the financial strength and liquidity of the corporation (bank) and then in the growth rate of earnings past and expected. It must be noted that while earnings may grow satisfactorily for a time based on lower-quality loans, this will result in loan losses that will penalize current and retained earnings.

Insurance companies can be divided into two major groups: (1) fire and casualty, and (2) life insurance companies. Historically, insurance companies reported to stockholders in the same form as to regulatory authorities—that is, statutory reporting—and the analyst was forced to attempt to adjust reported earnings to conform with GAAP. However, as a result of pressure from financial analysts, the SEC, stock exchanges, and the accounting profession, insurance companies recently have followed the practice of not only reporting on a statutory basis but also on a GAAP basis. This has reduced the problem of analysis.

For fire and casualty insurance companies, the three most important ratios are: (1) the expense ratio, which measures the operating efficiency of the company; (2) the loss ratio, which measures the quality of the business; and (3) the combined expense and loss ratio, which indicates the operating profit or loss of the business.

Investment policy is based on regulations and on management decisions. The higher the ratio of capital and surplus to unearned premium reserves (liabilities), the more justification for a relatively large investment in common stock.

Debt instruments represent about 90 percent of the assets of life insurance companies, and equity investments only about 10 percent. Therefore, the almost continuous upward trend of interest rates 1946–81 was a favorable factor for the life insurance companies. This was particularly noteworthy in the period after 1966–68 when the level of common stock prices remained in a wider but fairly horizontal channel. Interest rates fell after 1981 and are not expected to rise much in the near future. Problems in the group health area have plagued life insurance companies in recent years, and they remain a drag on earnings. AIDS could be a serious threat to growth in this industry.

A number of quantitative measures for assessing the quality and potential return for life insurance stocks have been presented. As with other corporations, the most significant factors are those that contribute to past and expected growth and stability of earnings. In recent years, P/E ratios, having come down from their peaks of earlier years have contributed to a return of some investment interest in such stocks.

Types of Questions Analysts Ask When Visiting Companies[1]

Sales

1. Percentage gain or loss, year to date versus year before.
2. Estimates for full year:
   a. Units and dollars.
   b. Identical store sales (retailing).
3. Explanation of sales changes, either way.
4. Sales breakdowns (year to date):
   a. By divisions.
   b. By major product groups.
   c. By major consuming markets.
5. Explanation of sales trends above or below the industry average.
6. Demand prospects: near, intermediate, and longer term.
7. Inventory status of company, its distributors, ultimate users.
8. Price levels versus year ago—impact on unit and dollar sales.
9. Outlook for selling price: firm, up, or down. Why?
10. Company's percent of industry sales (i.e., "trade position"?).

1 Joseph M. Galanis, "A Primer for Field Contact Work," *Financial Analysts Journal*, (August 1956).

385

11. Foreign sales aspects:
    a. Percent of export sales.
    b. Percent contributed by foreign branches.
    c. Outlook abroad by countries.
12. Percent of sales derived from government business—type of work.

Selling and Distribution

1. Methods used: direct to users, via wholesalers, retailers, branch warehouses, or combination of these.
2. Percent of selling costs to total sales.
3. Methods of compensation to selling forces: number of salespeople employed.
4. Advertising and promotional efforts, use of TV and other publicity media, with actual costs of this type of expense.
5. Extent of geographic coverage of the nation: plans, if any, to extend marketing areas, add new distributors, etc.
6. Economic radius of distribution from individual points; importance of freight rates.

Competition

1. What concerns are viewed as chief competitors?
2. Few or many competitors?
3. Is competition cutthroat or live-and-let-live type?
4. Are competitors strongly or weakly financed units?
5. In what way do company's products and services have an advantage, if any, over competition?
6. Is new competition entering field?
7. Where does company rank in its field or fields?
8. Importance of brand names, trademarks, patents, or servicing methods.

Patent Aspects

1. Importance re sales and prices.
2. Expiration dates of basic or supplementary patents; expected impact on sales, price structure, profit margins, etc., upon expirations.

Production

1. Rate of operations to date versus year ago; prospective rates of operation over foreseeable future.
2. Basis of operations: 1-2-3 shift, 7–8 hour day, or continuous operations?
3. Overtime premium pay?
4. Number of plants and character of their construction; multistory or single-story (modern).
5. Status of equipment: new, modernized, or obsolete?
6. Does company rate as low-cost, high-cost, or average-cost producer?
7. Steps, if any, being taken to improve production methods and to increase productive efficiency.

Raw Materials

1. Major raw materials used; sources, domestic and foreign. Ample supplies of storage?
2. Price history of raw materials used. Volatility?
3. Extent of integration.
4. If LIFO method of inventory valuation used?

Financial

1. Most recent capitalization and changes.
2. Any current bank loans outstanding? Explanation.
3. Adequacy of working capital in relation to current and anticipated sales, compared with earlier years.
4. Near term maturities? Refundings? Retirements? Comment on ability to meet these obligations.
5. Any new financial in offing? Kind.
6. Insured, replacement, or appraisal value of fixed assets (especially natural resources) versus book value.

Dividend Policies and Prospects

1. Payout policy, percent of earnings, percent of cash flow.
2. Prospect for extras.

3. Prospect for stock dividends.

4. Chances for increase (or decrease) in regular annual rate.

Earnings

1. Trend of labor and materials costs, percent of each to sales.
2. Ability to adjust selling prices to higher costs.
3. Cost savings programs and comments.
4. Profit margins versus year ago.
5. Trend of earnings to date versus year ago.
6. Per share earnings for full year.
7. Nonrecurring items. Explanation.
8. Nonoperating sources of income versus year ago.

Miscellaneous Topics

During the average interview, the analyst will think of spur-of-the-moment questions inducted by information or comments of the contact. In addition, it may prove advisable to request comment on such individual topics as

1. Status of current litigation.
2. Impact of Government Consent Decree.
3. Status of particular long-term sales contracts.
4. Problems arising as result of a current strike or aftermath of one settled.
5. Extent of insurance coverage in connection with floods or other disasters.

Expansion

1. Details of program: plant locations, additional product lines to be added.
2. Capital outlays involved; methods of financing, if any, contemplated.
3. Percent to be added to plant capacity on a square foot basis, or in physical units, or in dollar sales volume.
4. Any certificates of necessity or fast amortization of new facilities involved?
5. Any new acquisitions in mind?

6. Costs of new construction and equipment per unit added production versus one to five years ago.

7. Expected sales per $1 of new plant account investment versus other years.

Research

1. Amounts, or percent, of sales spent annually on research.
2. Number employed and number possessing advanced degrees.
3. Record of recent patents granted as result of research.
4. New products on the fire and their prospects.
5. Percent of current sales from new products traceable to research over the past five to fifteen years. (This is the most important factor in evaluating research.)

Management

1. Does management show continuity or frequent changes?
2. Average age of top management officials.
3. Is the company a one-person outfit?
4. Methods of recruiting and training executives.
5. Is management centralized or decentralized?

Employee Relations

1. Long-term strike record.
2. Percent of employees unionized—which plants?
3. Management policies on labor relations.
4. Chief employee benefits.
5. Labor turnover rates.

Index

About the Author

John C. Ritchie, Jr., is professor of finance at Temple University in Philadelphia. He received his Ph.D. in finance from the University of Pennsylvania in 1963 and, in addition to teaching finance, has been a consultant to
a number of corporations, industry trade associations, pension funds, banks,
and an investment management firm. He has authored numerous articles,
which have appeared in business and financial journals and as chapters in
books on financial and investment topics. Most recently, he authored a
textbook on investments that is widely used.

Thank you for choosing Irwin Professional Publishing for your information needs. If you are part of a corporation, professional association, or government agency, consider our newest option: Custom Publishing. This service helps you create customized books, manuals, and other materials from your organization's resources, selected chapters of our books, or both.

Irwin Professional Publishing books are also excellent resources for training/educational programs, premiums, and incentives. For information on volume discounts or custom publishing, call 1-800-634-3966.

Other books of interest to you from Irwin Professional Publishing . . .

TAKING CONTROL OF YOUR FINANCIAL FUTURE
Making Smart Investment Decisions with Stocks and Mutual Funds
Thomas E. O'Hara and Helen J. McLane
Taking Control of Your Financial Future walks investors through the entire investment process with numerous worksheets, graphs, and checklists. Experienced investors can develop and fine tune their own techniques with the hints and investment insights offered in this book.
ISBN: 0-7863-0139-2

STOCKS FOR THE LONG RUN
A Guide to Selecting Markets for Long-Term Growth
Jeremy J. Siegel
This substantive guide to investing wisely in the stock market includes a detailed description of market performances and an analysis of long-term stock opportunities in foreign markets—a timely topic for today's investors.
ISBN: 1-55623-804-5

THE ULTIMATE STOCK PICKER'S GUIDE
20 Top Experts Pick the Hot Stocks of Tomorrow
Warren Boroson
Truly the "ultimate" book of stock market tips and advice for the average investor. It covers the single best stock to own, the best ten stocks to own, the growth industries of tomorrow, and how to identify a good long-term stock.
ISBN: 1-55738-823-7

AL FRANK'S NEW PRUDENT SPECULATOR
The Master of Value Investing Shows You How to Pick Winning Stocks,
Revised Edition
Al Frank
In this revised edition of his classic book, *The Prudent Speculator,* Frank discusses his investment philosophy and reveals precisely how he goes about picking stocks and managing a portfolio. In addition, he provides advice on an important, but often neglected, subject—the psychological aspects of investing.
ISBN: 1-55738-873-3

Available in fine bookstores and libraries everywhere!